FAIRY TAIL

フェアリーテイル

19

HIRO MASHIMA

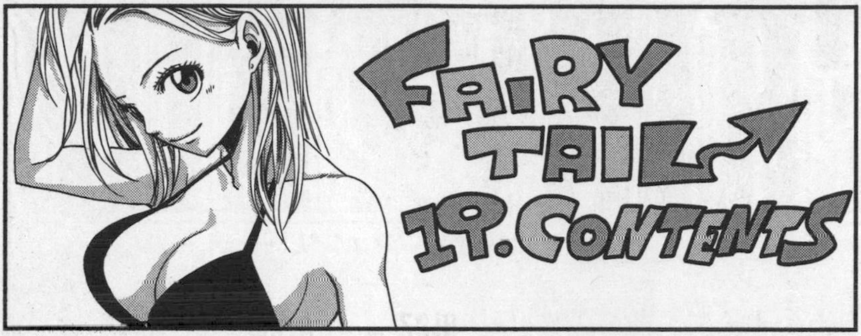
FAIRY TAIL
19. CONTENTS

Published in serial form by Weekly Shônen Magazine 2009 Volumes 44 - 51

FAIRY TAIL

フェアリーテイル

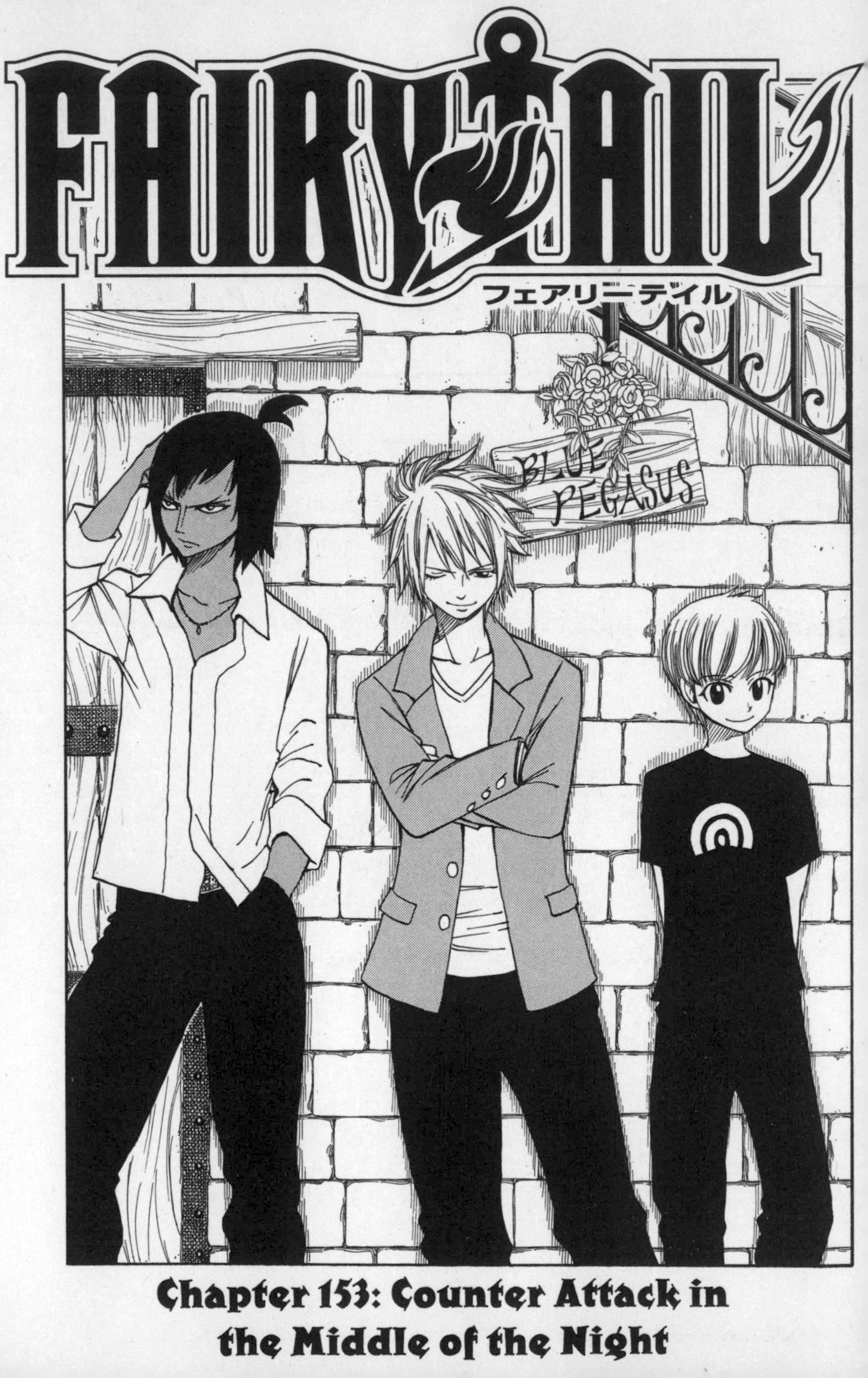
BLUE PEGASUS

Chapter 153: Counter Attack in the Middle of the Night

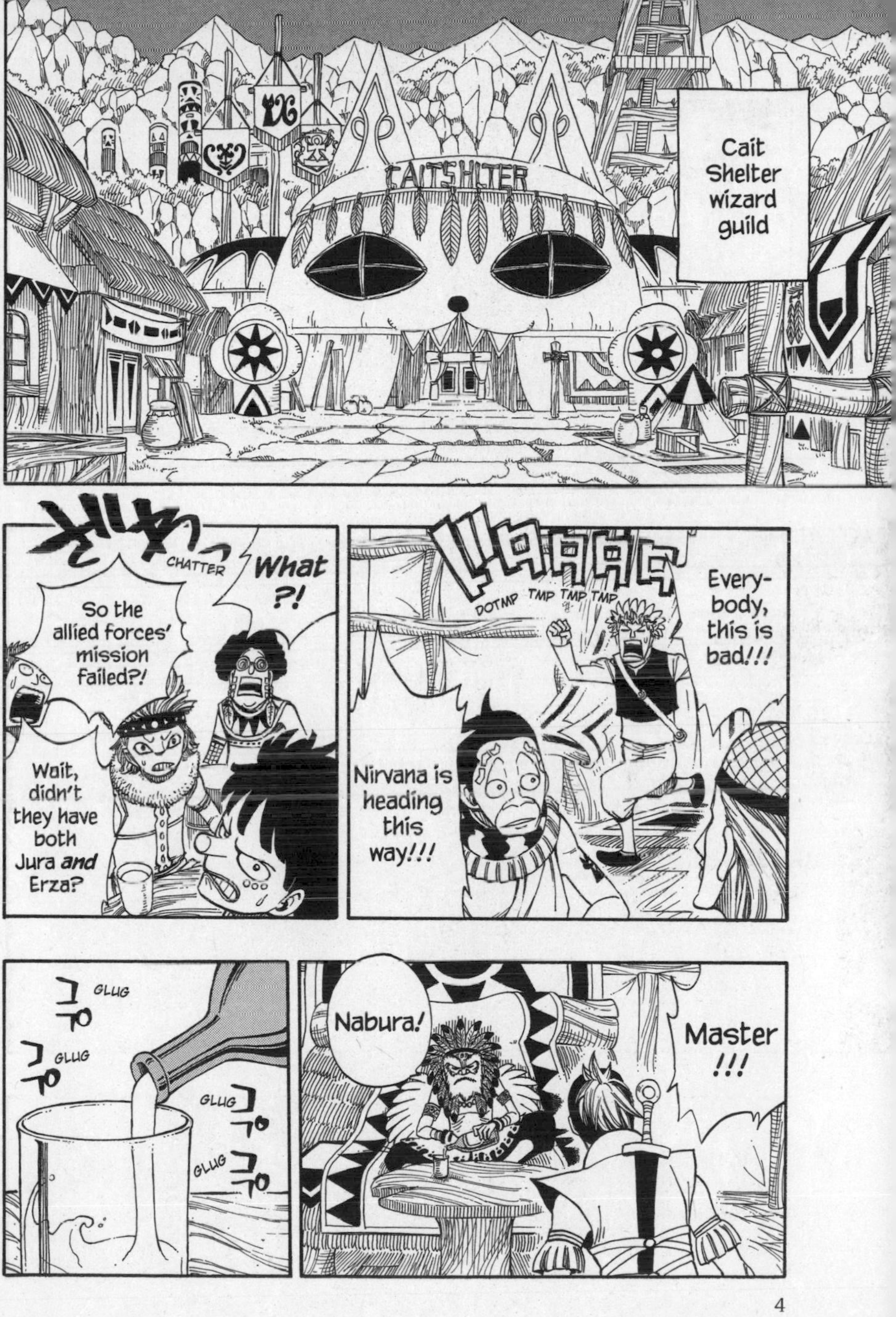
CAITSHLTER
Cait Shelter wizard guild
DOTMP TMP TMP TMP
Everybody, this is bad!!!
Nirvana is heading this way!!!
CHATTER
What?!
So the allied forces' mission failed?!
Wait, didn't they have both Jura *and* Erza?
Master!!!
Nabura!
GLUG
GLUG
GLUG
GLUG

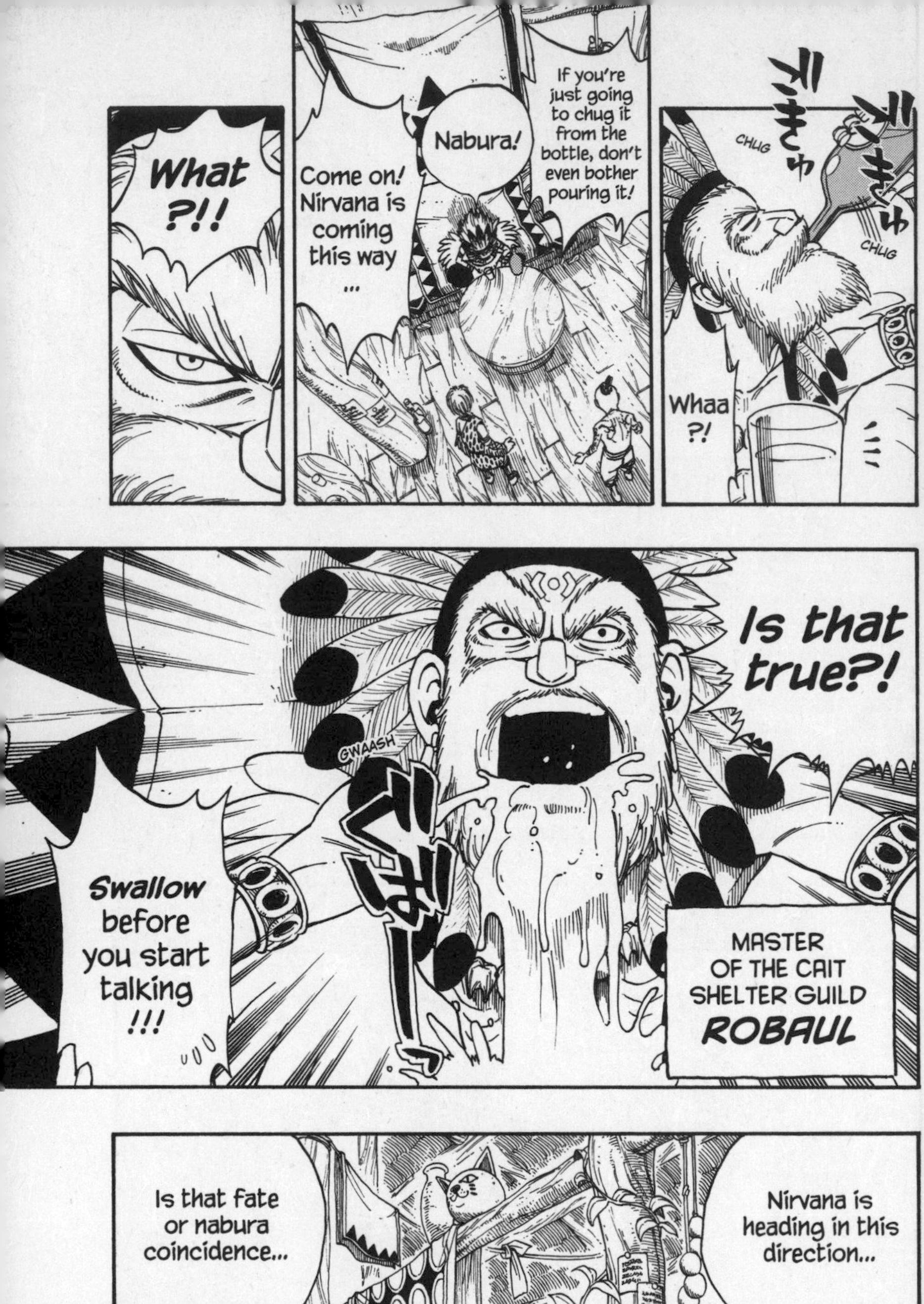
CHUG
CHUG
Whaa ?!
If you're just going to chug it from the bottle, don't even bother pouring it!
Nabura!
Come on! Nirvana is coming this way ...
What ?!!
Is that true?!
MASTER OF THE CAIT SHELTER GUILD ROBAUL
GWAASH
Swallow before you start talking !!!
Nirvana is heading in this direction...
Is that fate or nabura coincidence...

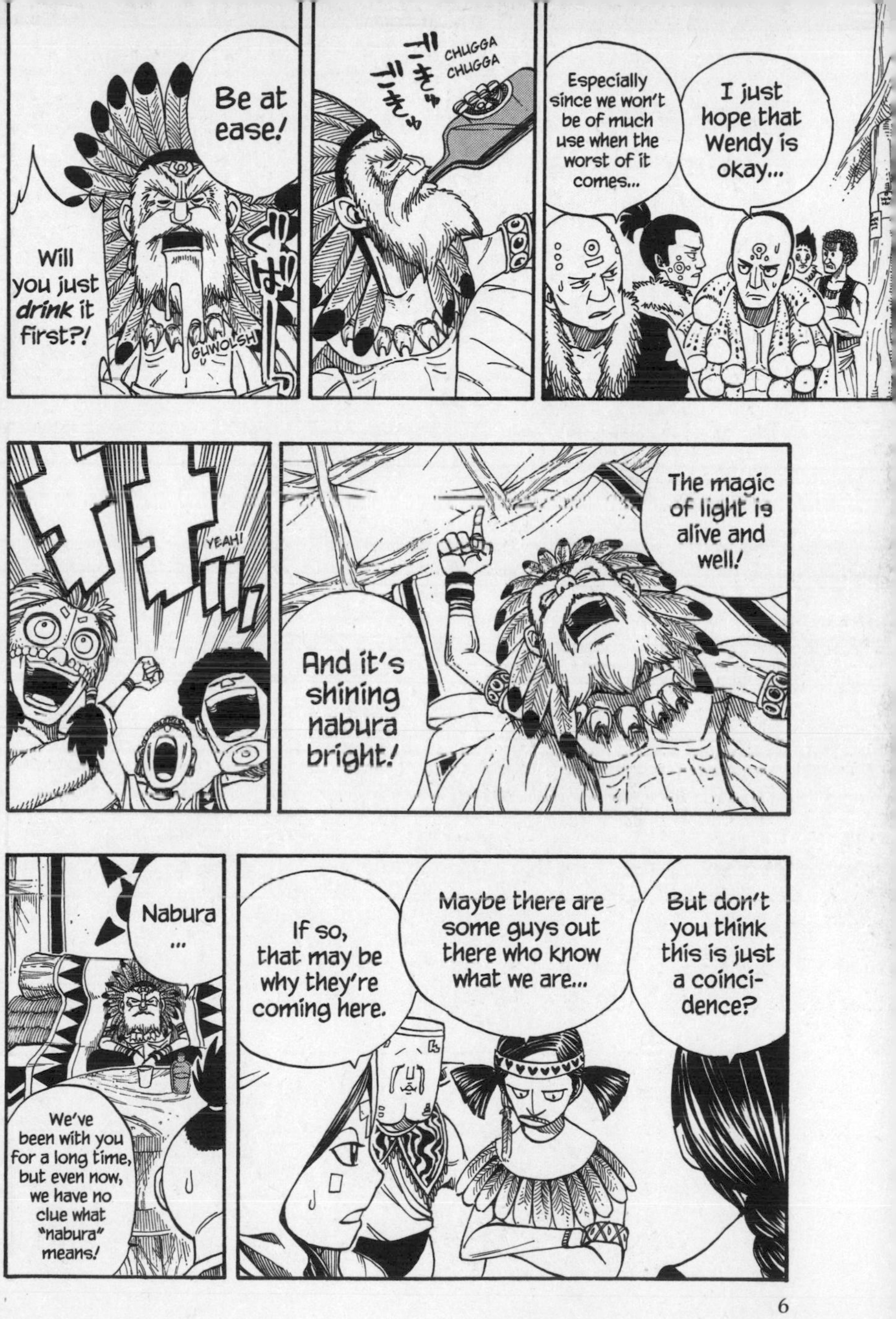
I just hope that Wendy is okay...
Especially since we won't be of much use when the worst of it comes...
ごきゅ ごきゅ
CHUGGA CHUGGA
Be at ease!
ぐばっ
GUWOLSH
Will you just *drink* it first?!
The magic of light is alive and well!
And it's shining nabura bright!
YEAH!
But don't you think this is just a coinci-dence?
Maybe there are some guys out there who know what we are...
If so, that may be why they're coming here.
Nabura ...
We've been with you for a long time, but even now, we have no clue what "nabura" means!

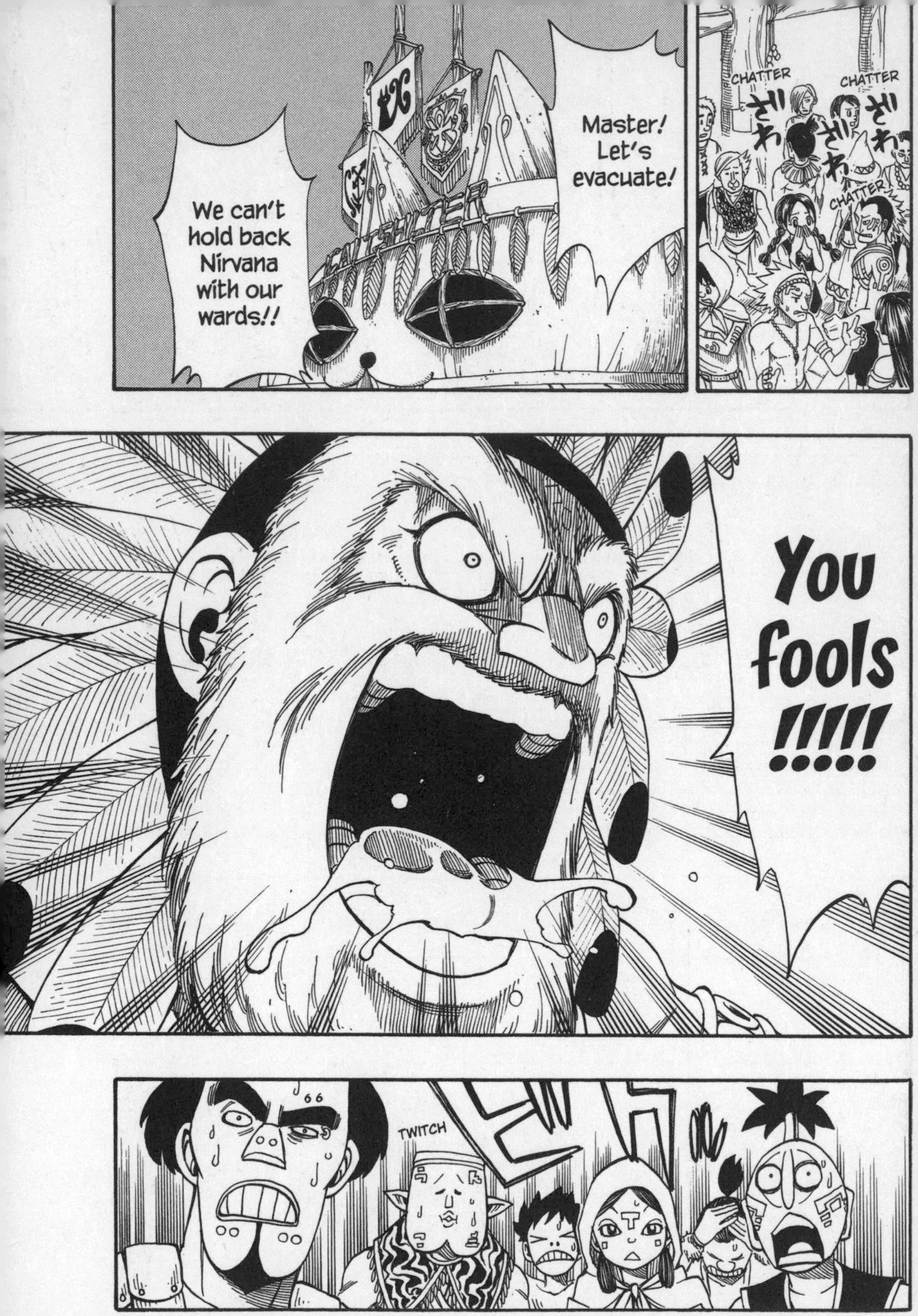
CHATTER
CHATTER
ざわ
ざわ
ざわ
CHATTER
Master! Let's evacuate!
We can't hold back Nirvana with our wards!!
You fools!!!!!
TWITCH

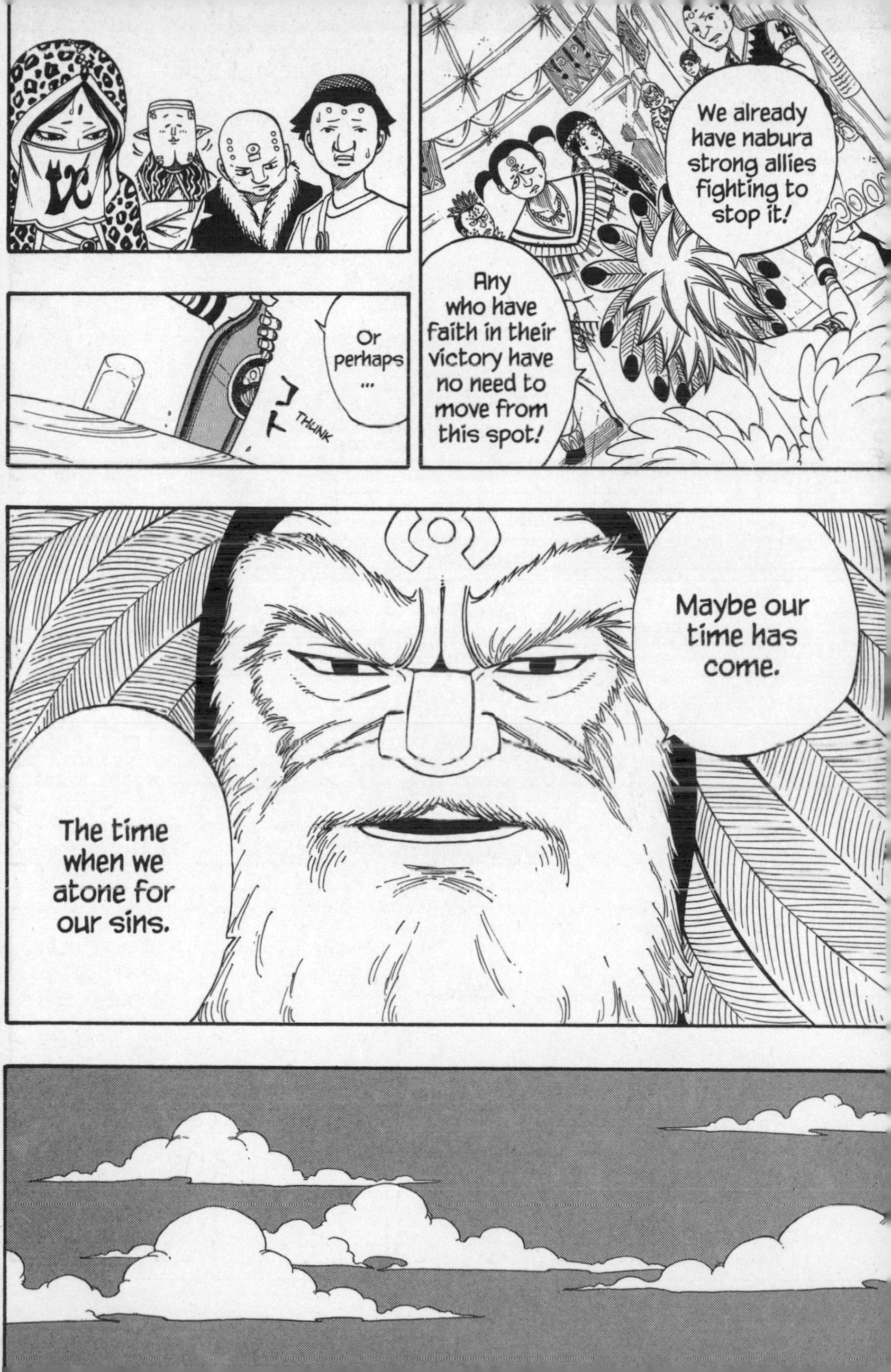

We already have nabura strong allies fighting to stop it!
Any who have faith in their victory have no need to move from this spot!
Or perhaps ...
THUNK
Maybe our time has come.
The time when we atone for our sins.

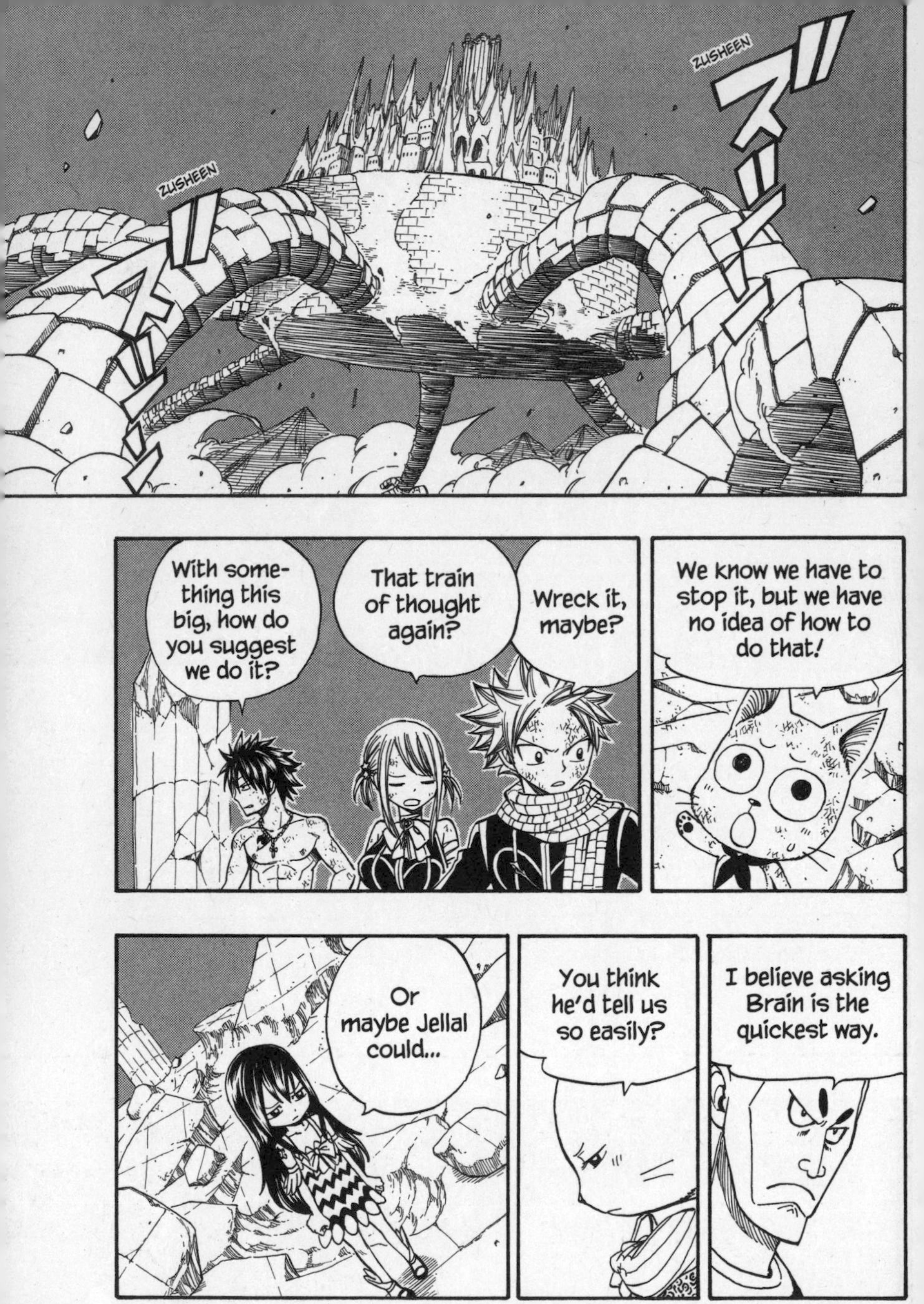
ZUSHEEN
ZUSHEEN
We know we have to stop it, but we have no idea of how to do that!
Wreck it, maybe?
That train of thought again?
With some-thing this big, how do you suggest we do it?
I believe asking Brain is the quickest way.
You think he'd tell us so easily?
Or maybe Jellal could...

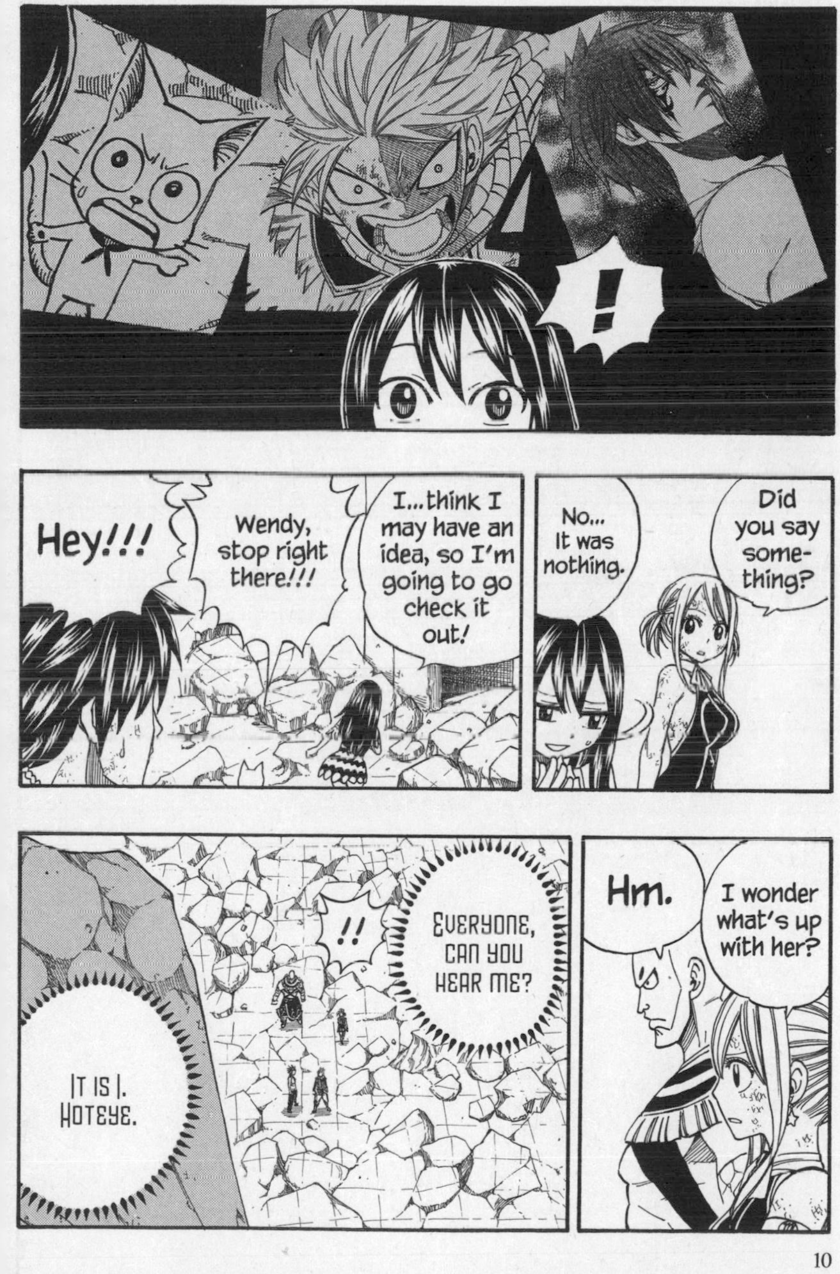
!
Did you say something?
No... It was nothing.
I...think I may have an idea, so I'm going to go check it out!
Wendy, stop right there!!!
Hey!!!
I wonder what's up with her?
Hm.
Everyone, can you hear me?
!!
It is I. Hoteye.

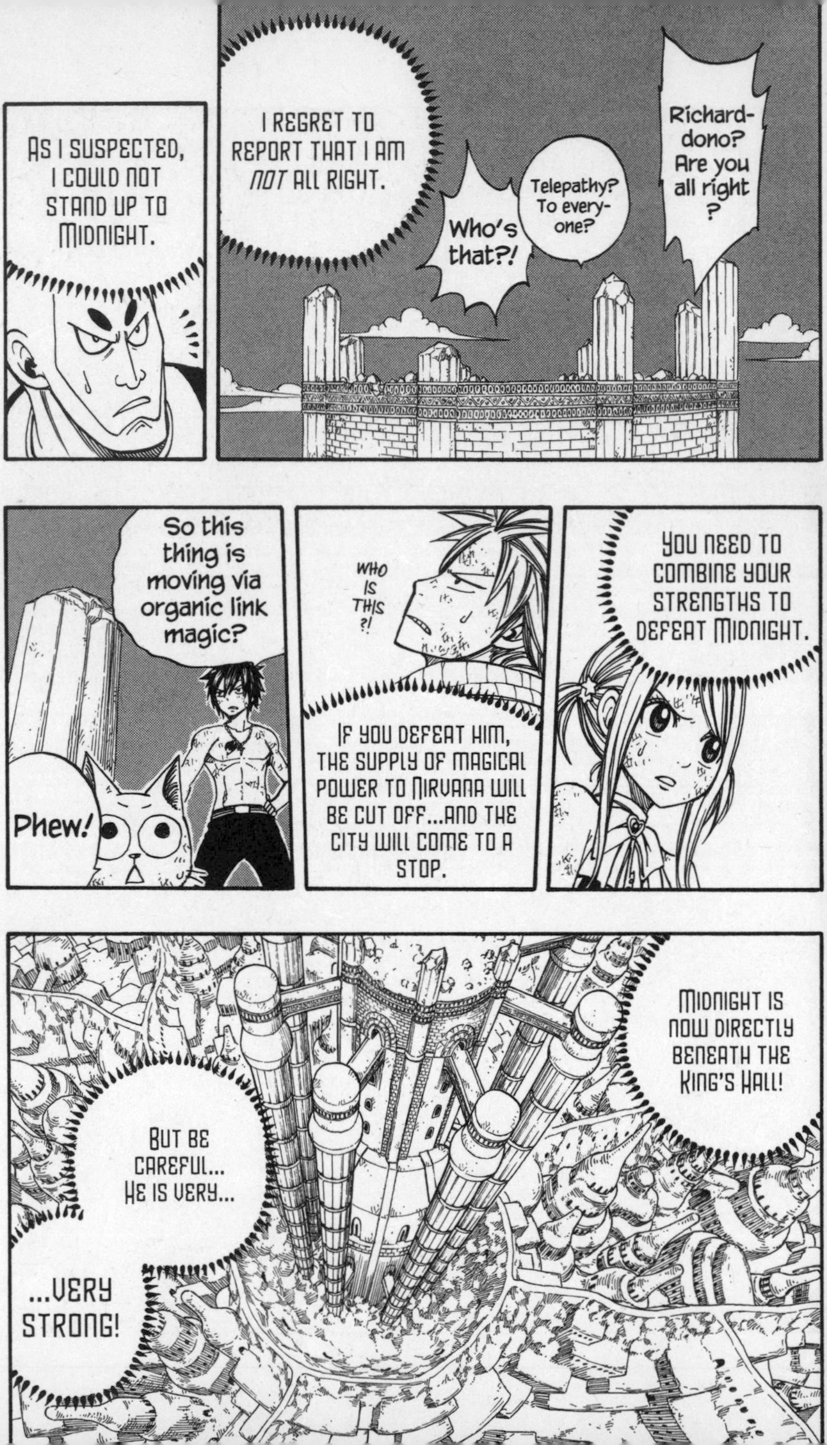
Richard-dono? Are you all right?
Telepathy? To every-one?
Who's that?!
I REGRET TO REPORT THAT I AM *NOT* ALL RIGHT.
AS I SUSPECTED, I COULD NOT STAND UP TO MIDNIGHT.
YOU NEED TO COMBINE YOUR STRENGTHS TO DEFEAT MIDNIGHT.
WHO IS THIS ?!
IF YOU DEFEAT HIM, THE SUPPLY OF MAGICAL POWER TO NIRVANA WILL BE CUT OFF...AND THE CITY WILL COME TO A STOP.
So this thing is moving via organic link magic?
Phew!
MIDNIGHT IS NOW DIRECTLY BENEATH THE KING'S HALL!
BUT BE CAREFUL... HE IS VERY...
...VERY STRONG!

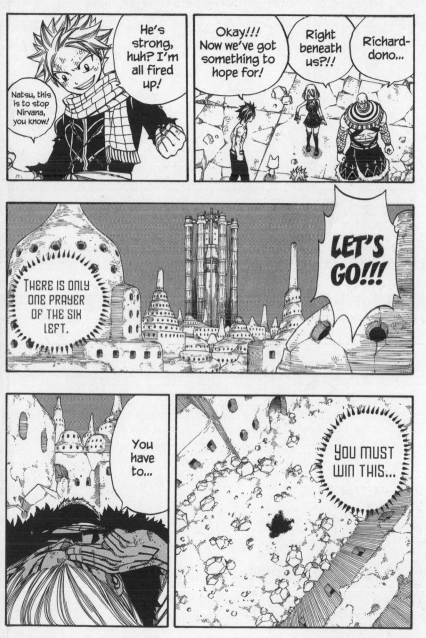

Richard-dono...
Right beneath us?!!
Okay!!! Now we've got something to hope for!
He's strong, huh? I'm all fired up!
Natsu, this is to stop Nirvana, you know!
LET'S GO!!!
THERE IS ONLY ONE PRAYER OF THE SIX LEFT.
YOU MUST WIN THIS...
You have to...

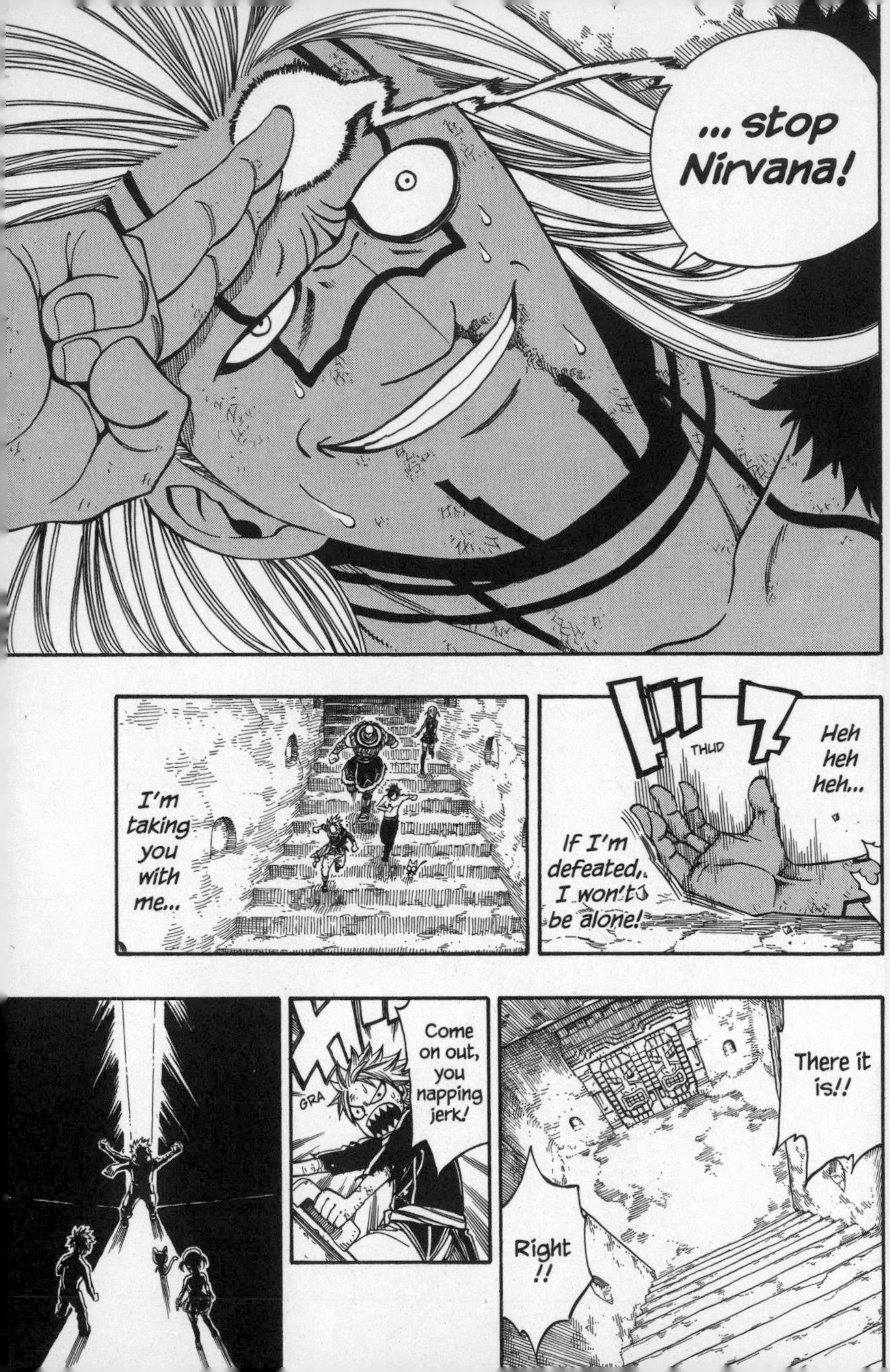

... stop Nirvana!
Heh heh heh...
THUD
If I'm defeated, I won't be alone!
I'm taking you with me...
There it is!!
Right !!
Come on out, you napping jerk!
GRA

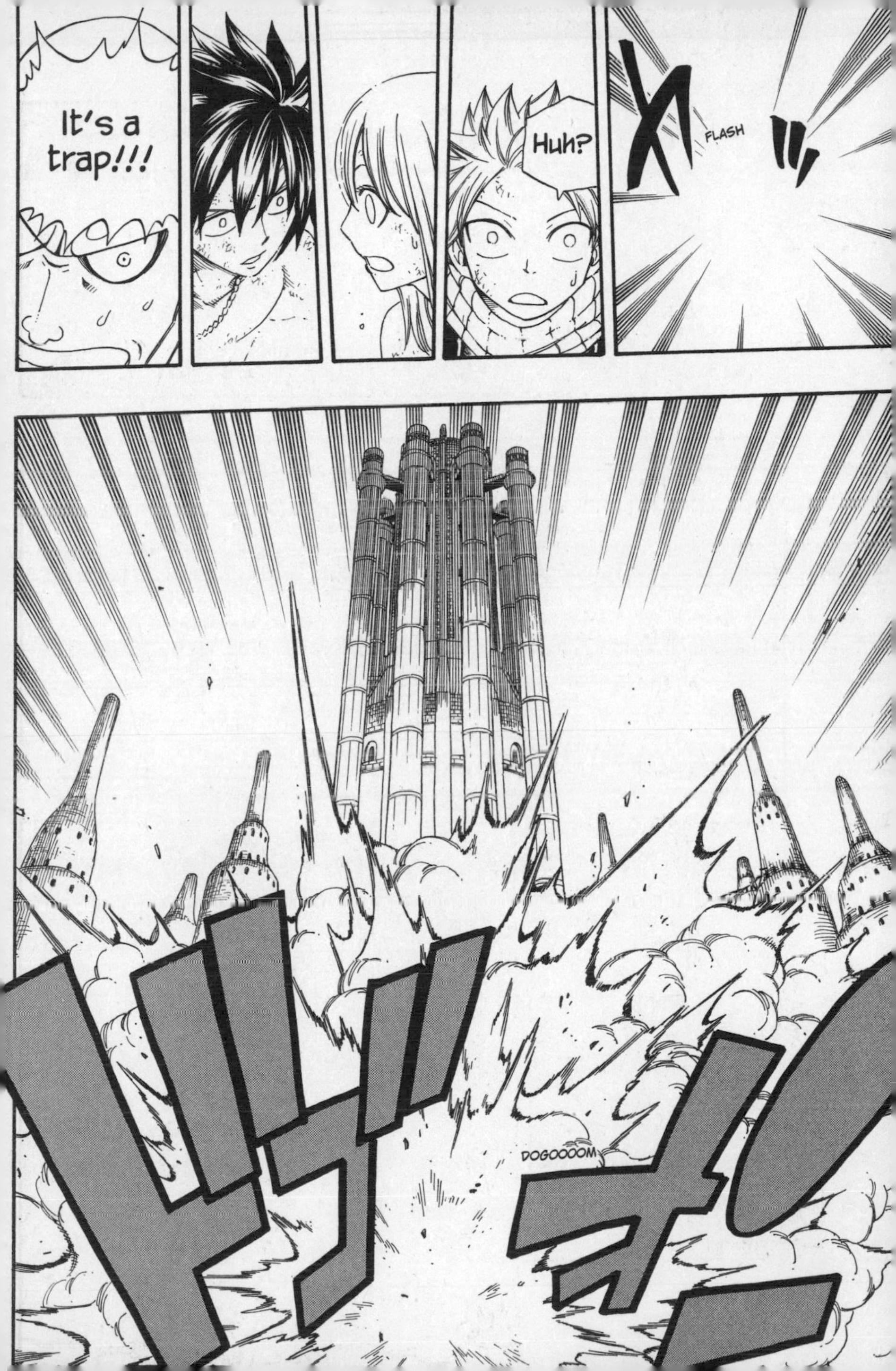
FLASH
Huh?
It's a trap!!!
DOGOOOOM

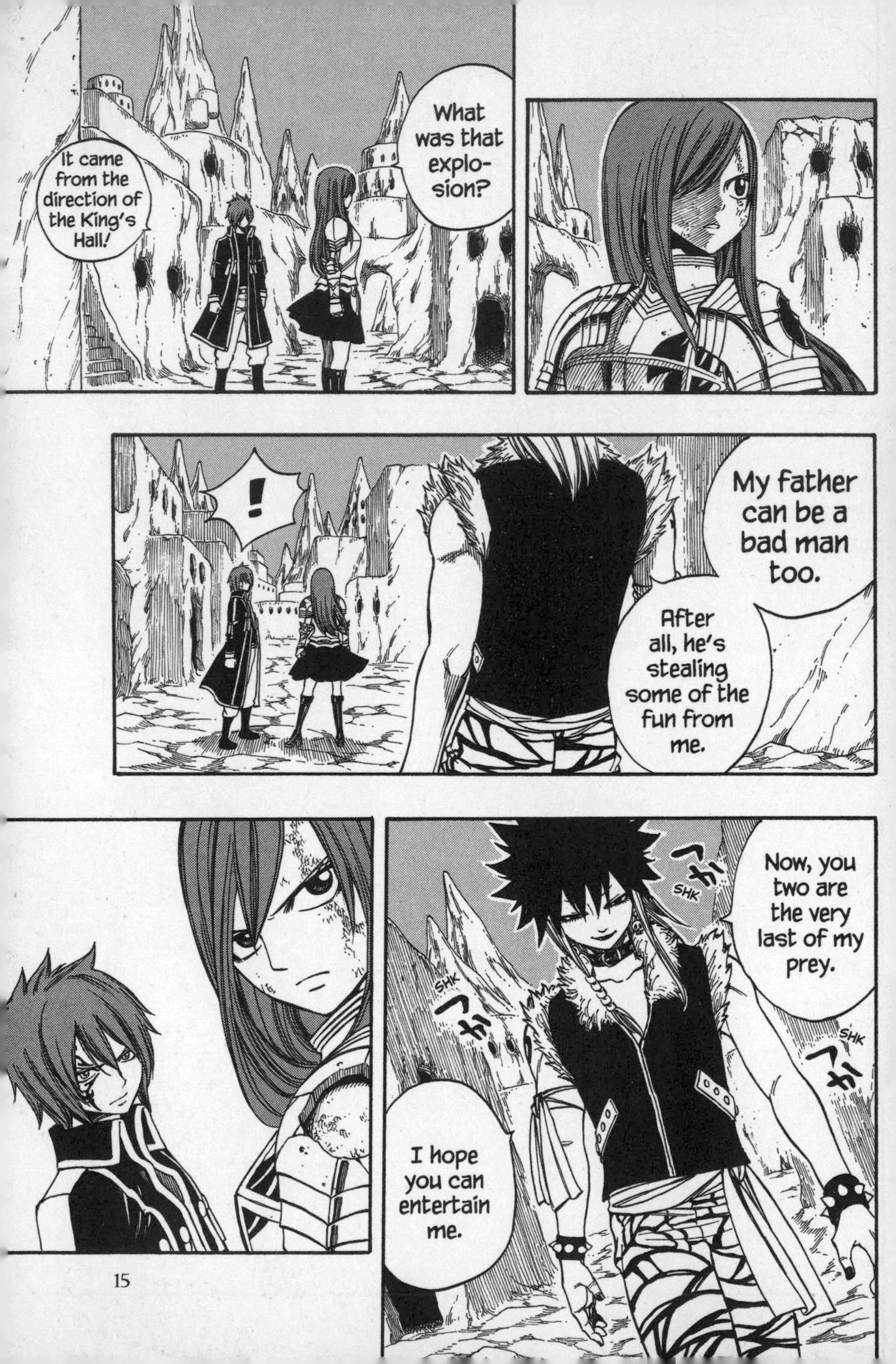
What was that explosion?
It came from the direction of the King's Hall!
My father can be a bad man too.
After all, he's stealing some of the fun from me.
!
Now, you two are the very last of my prey.
SHK
SHK
SHK
I hope you can entertain me.

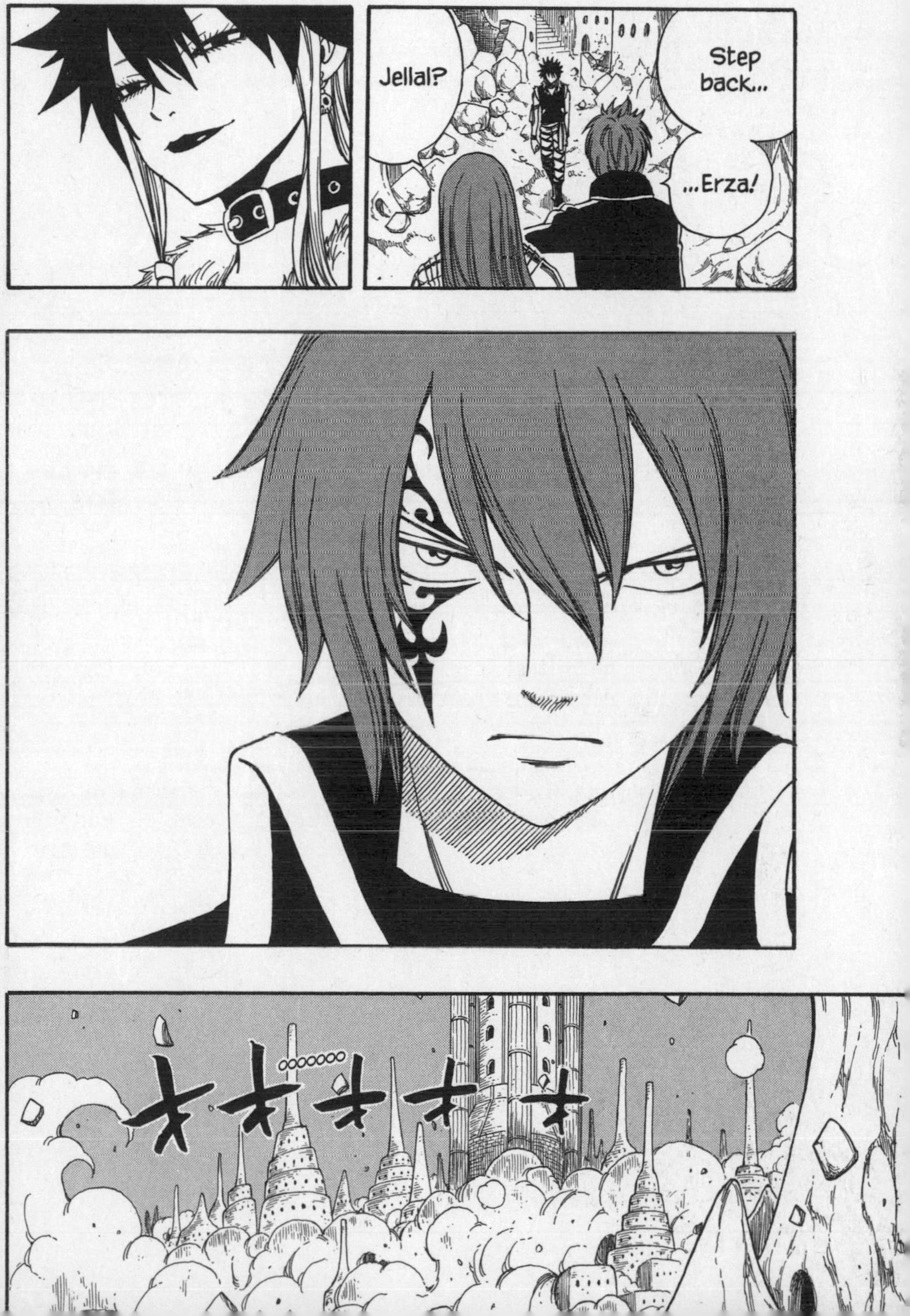
Step back...
...Erza!
Jellal?
ooooooo

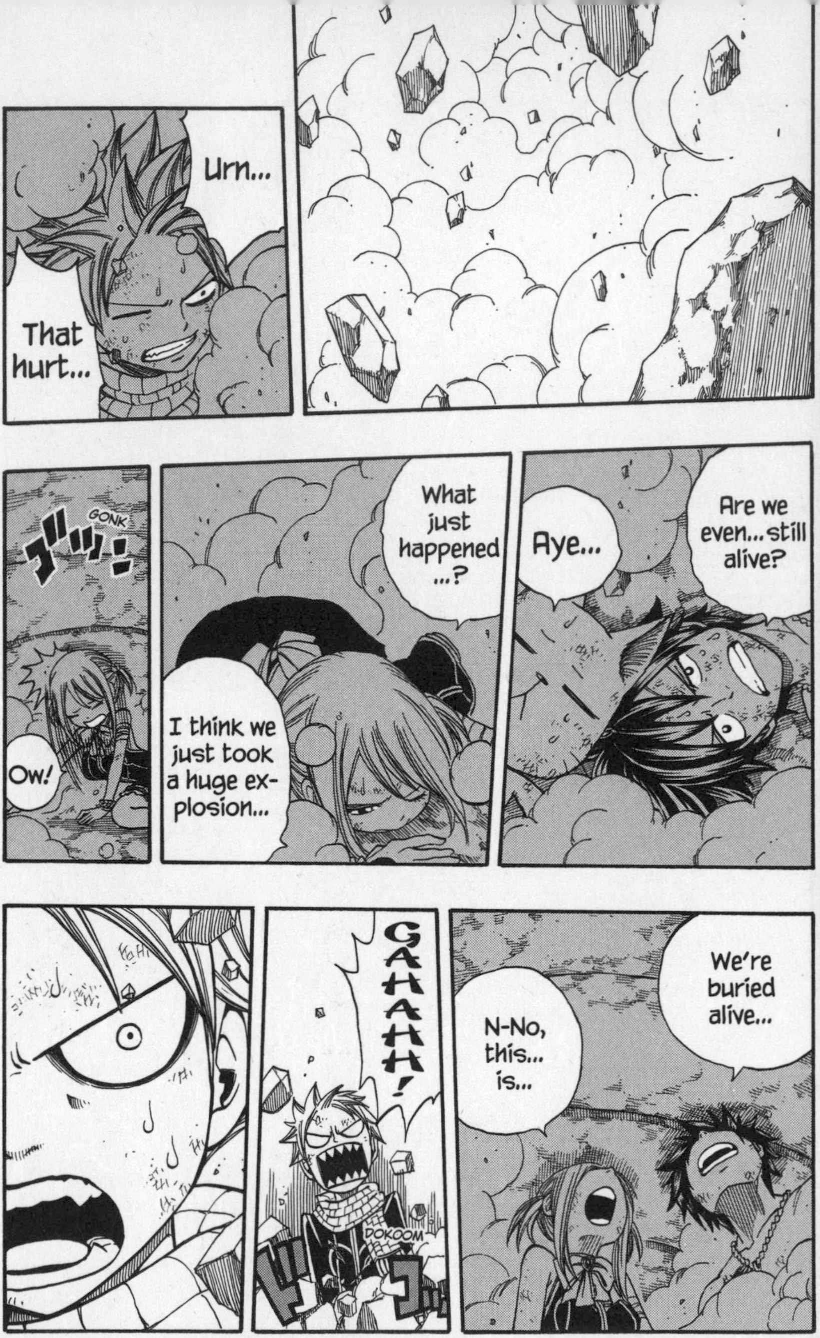
Urn...
That hurt...
Are we even...still alive?
Aye...
What just happened ...?
I think we just took a huge explosion...
GONK
Ow!
We're buried alive...
N-No, this... is...
GAHAHH!
DOKOOM

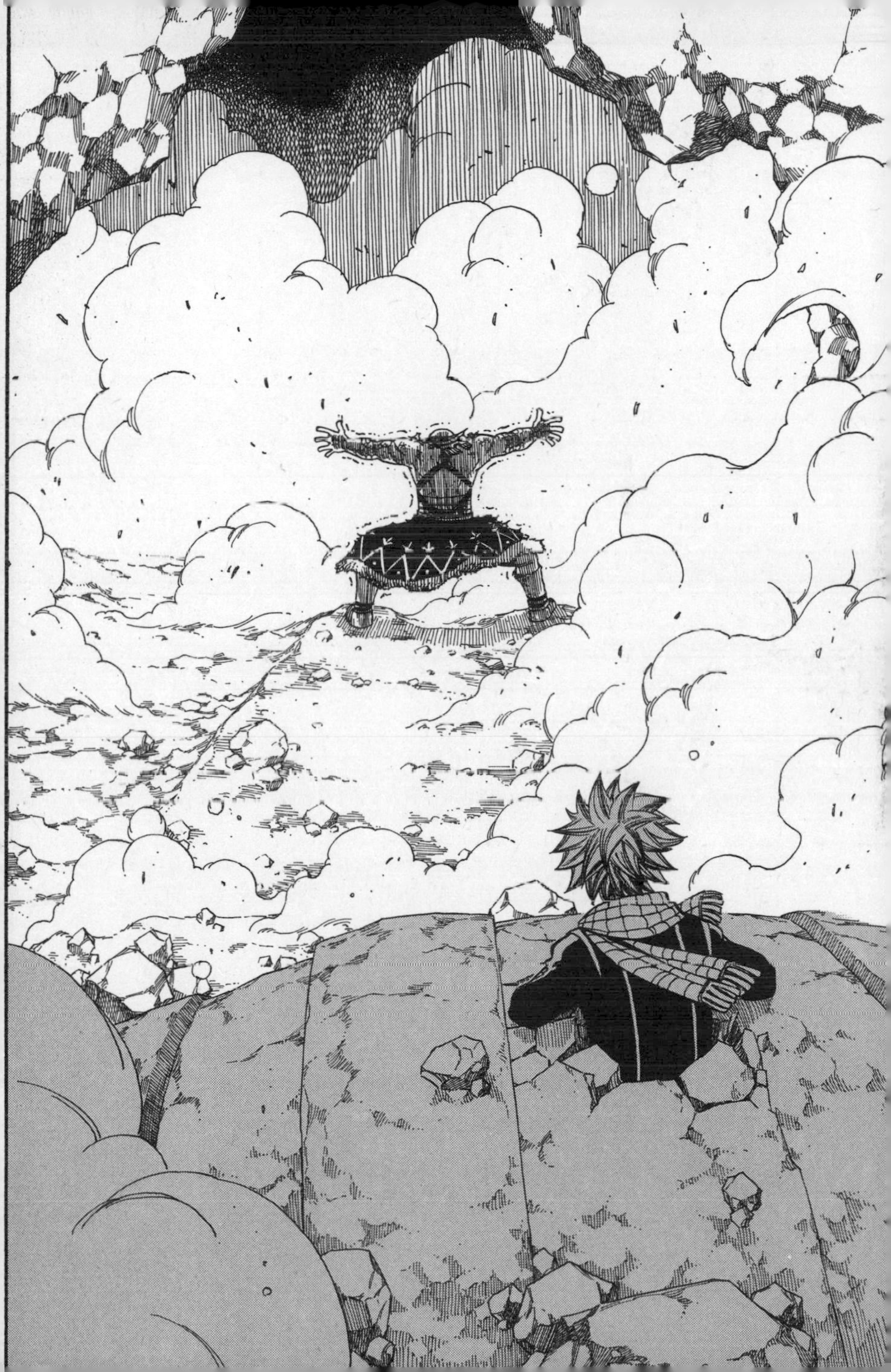

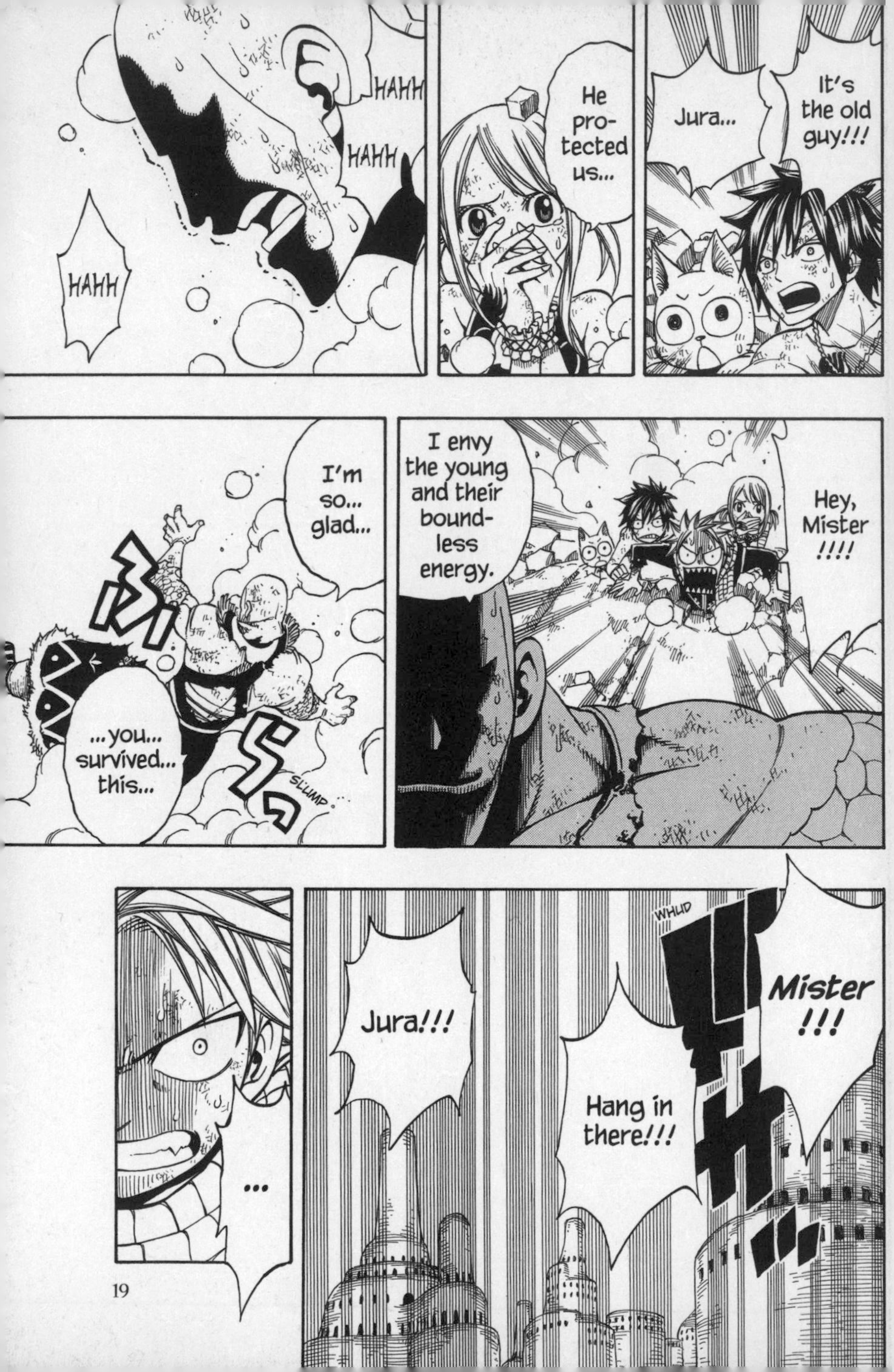
It's the old guy!!!
Jura...
He protected us...
HAHH
HAHH
HAHH
Hey, Mister!!!!
I envy the young and their boundless energy.
I'm so... glad...
...you... survived... this...
SLUMP
WHUD
Mister!!!
Hang in there!!!
Jura!!!
...

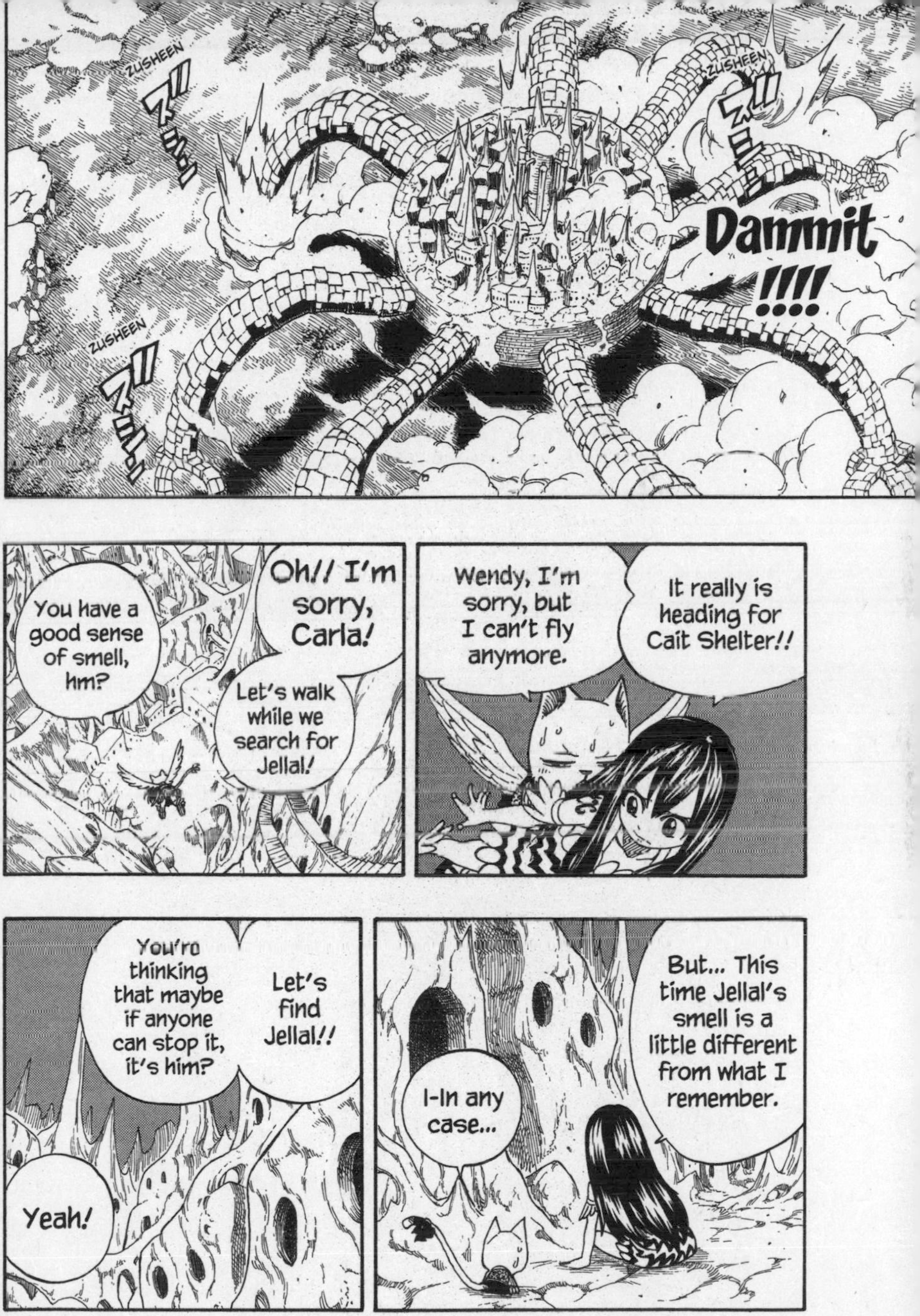

ZUSHEEN
ZUSHEEN
Dammit!!!!
ZUSHEEN
It really is heading for Cait Shelter!!
Wendy, I'm sorry, but I can't fly anymore.
Oh!! I'm sorry, Carla!
Let's walk while we search for Jellal!
You have a good sense of smell, hm?
But... This time Jellal's smell is a little different from what I remember.
I-In any case...
Let's find Jellal!!
You're thinking that maybe if anyone can stop it, it's him?
Yeah!

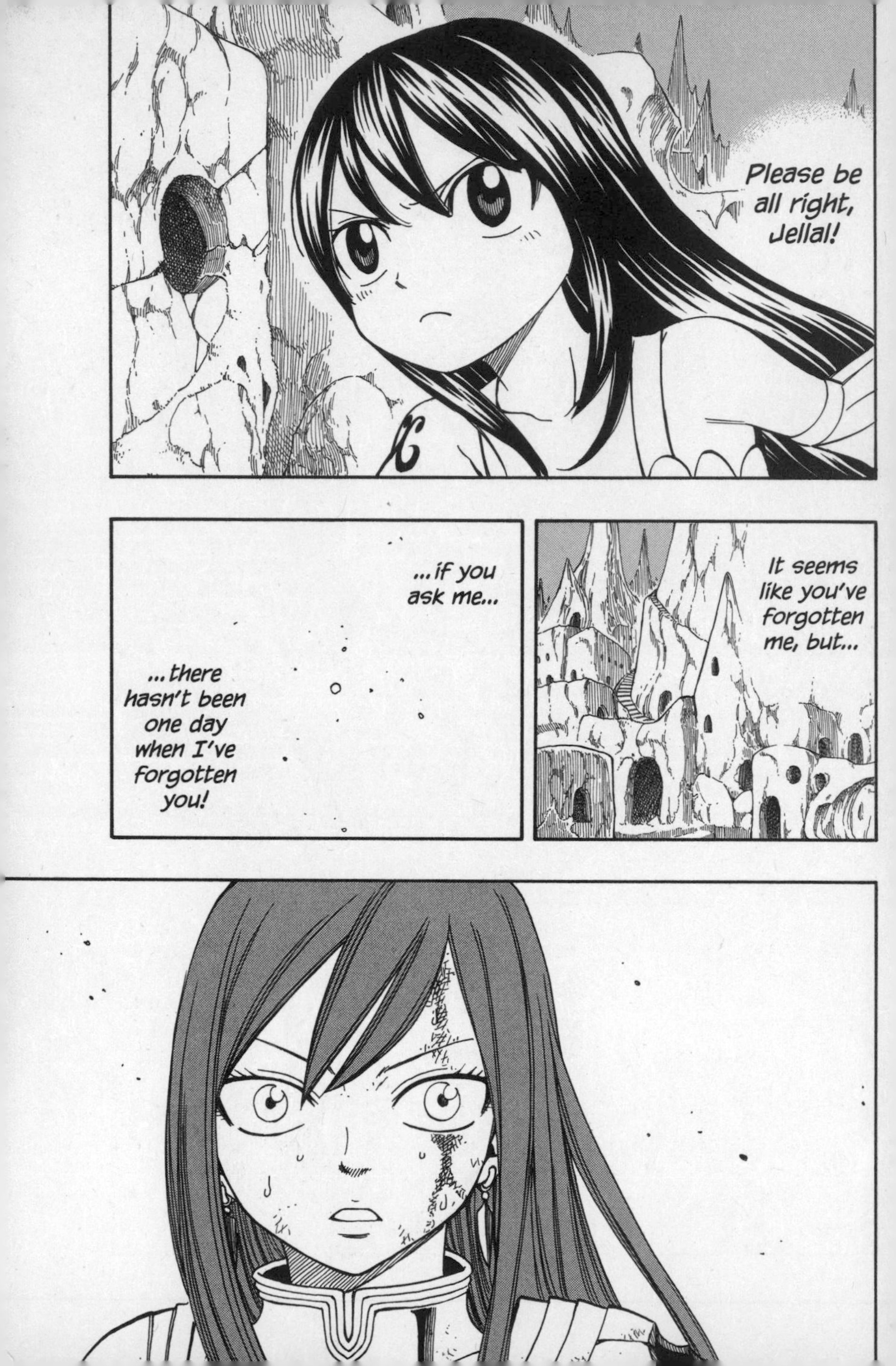
Please be all right, Jellal!
It seems like you've forgotten me, but...
...if you ask me...
...there hasn't been one day when I've forgotten you!

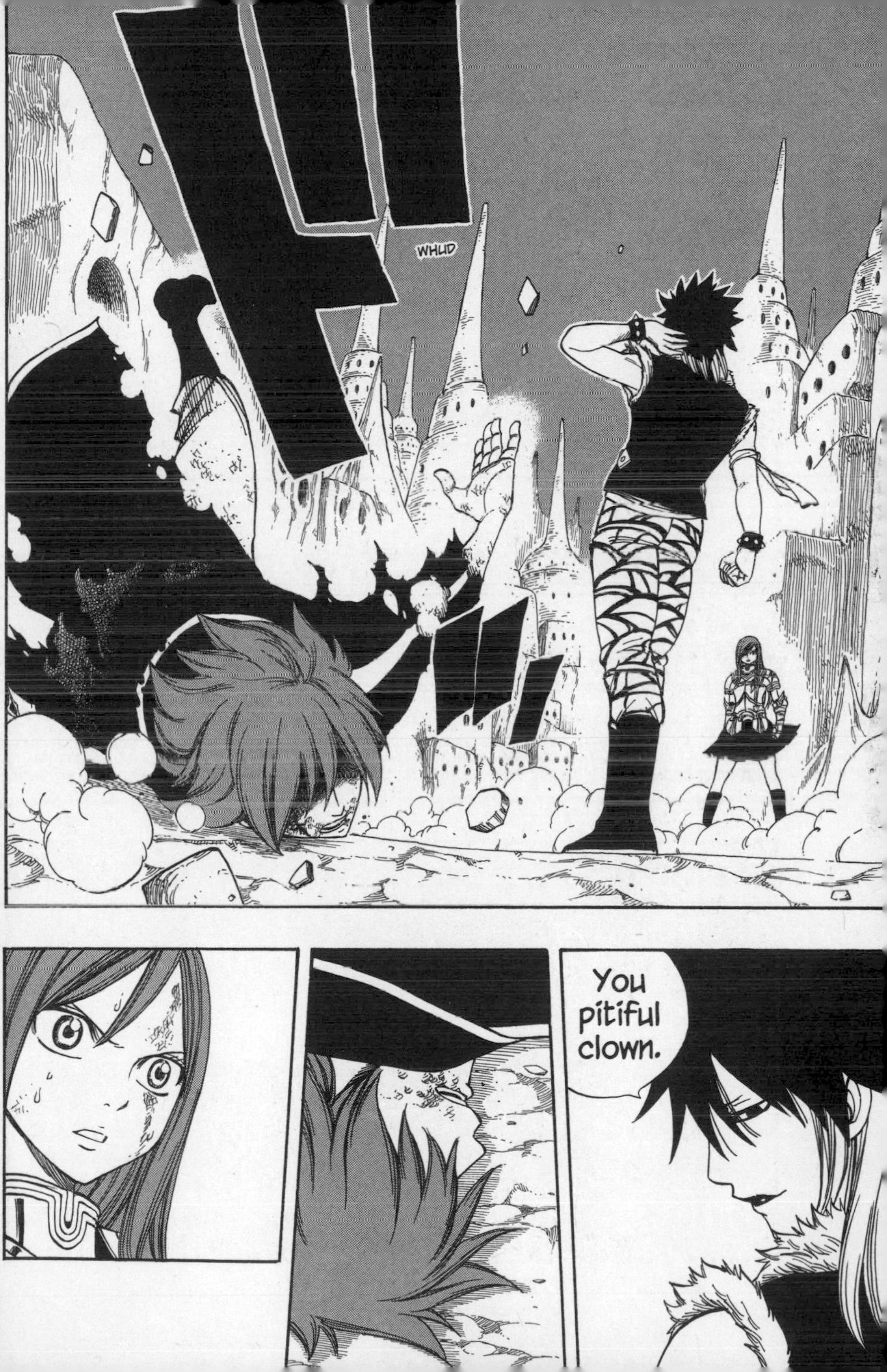
WHUD
You pitiful clown.

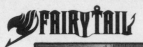

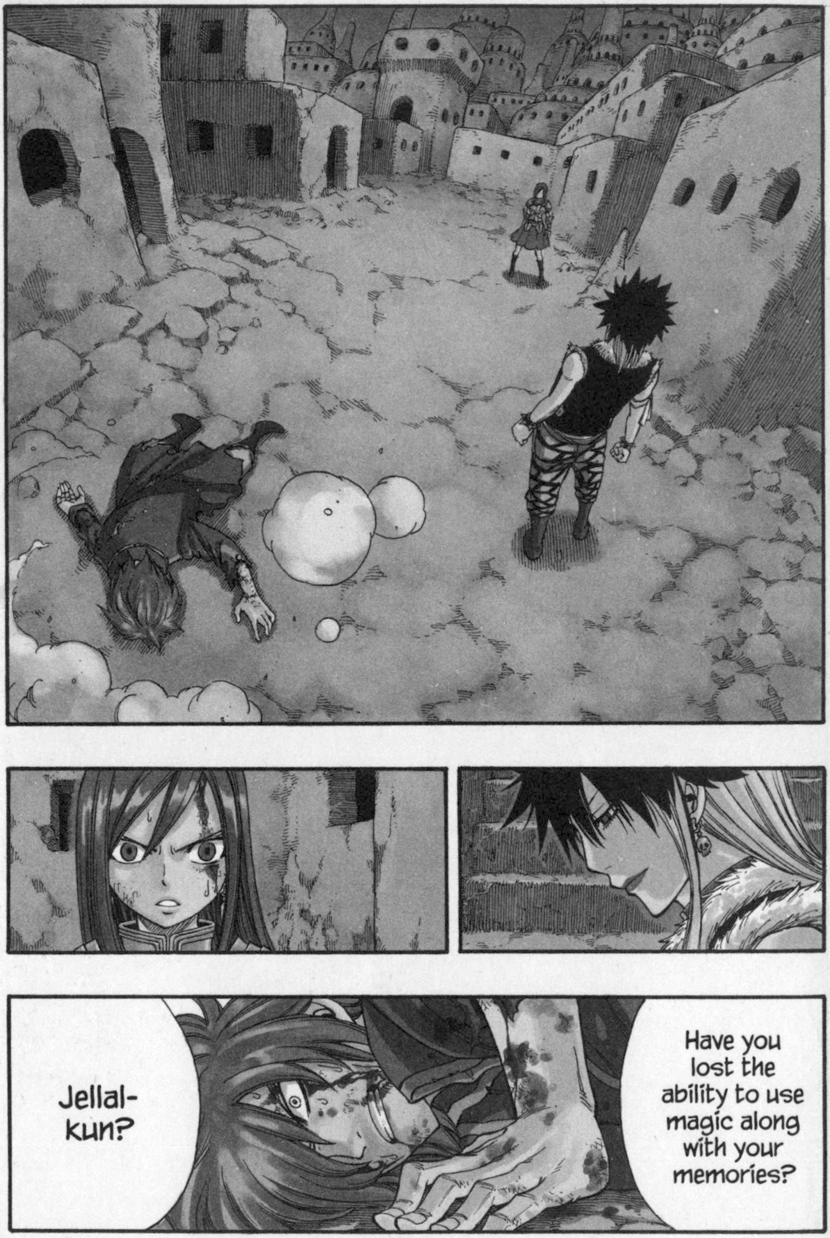
Have you lost the ability to use magic along with your memories?
Jellal-kun?

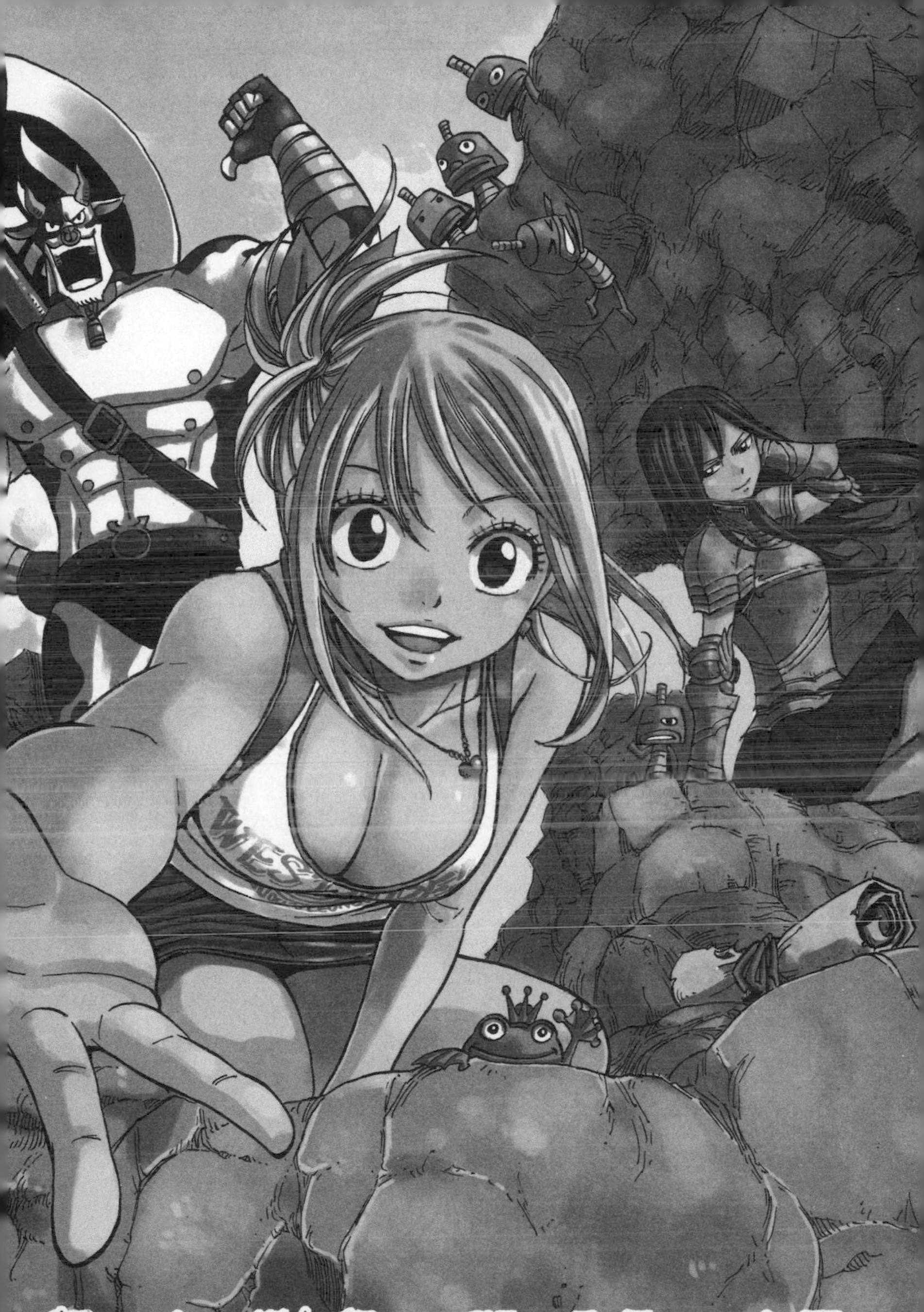

Chapter 154: Your Words Especially

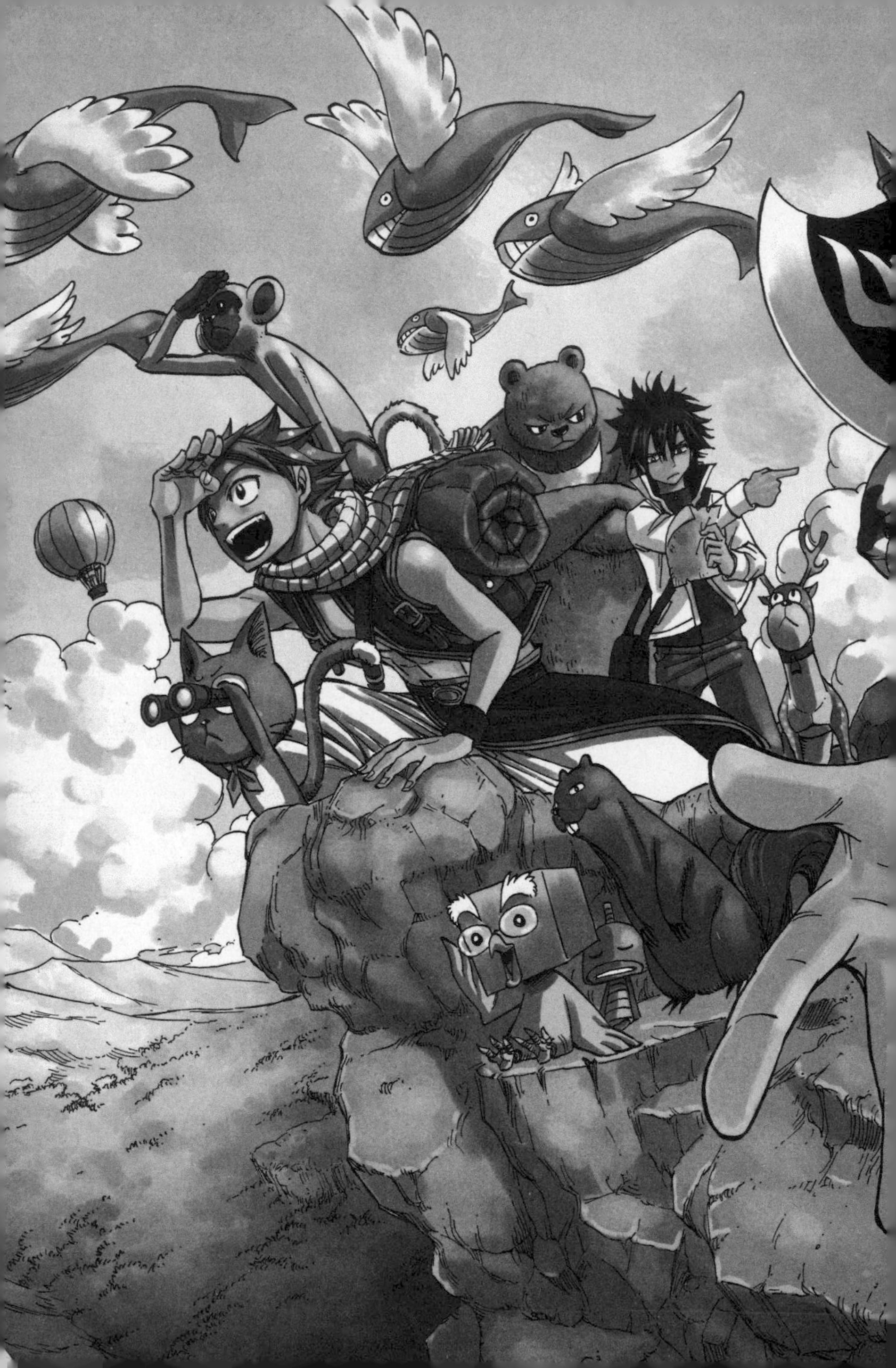

FAIRY TAIL

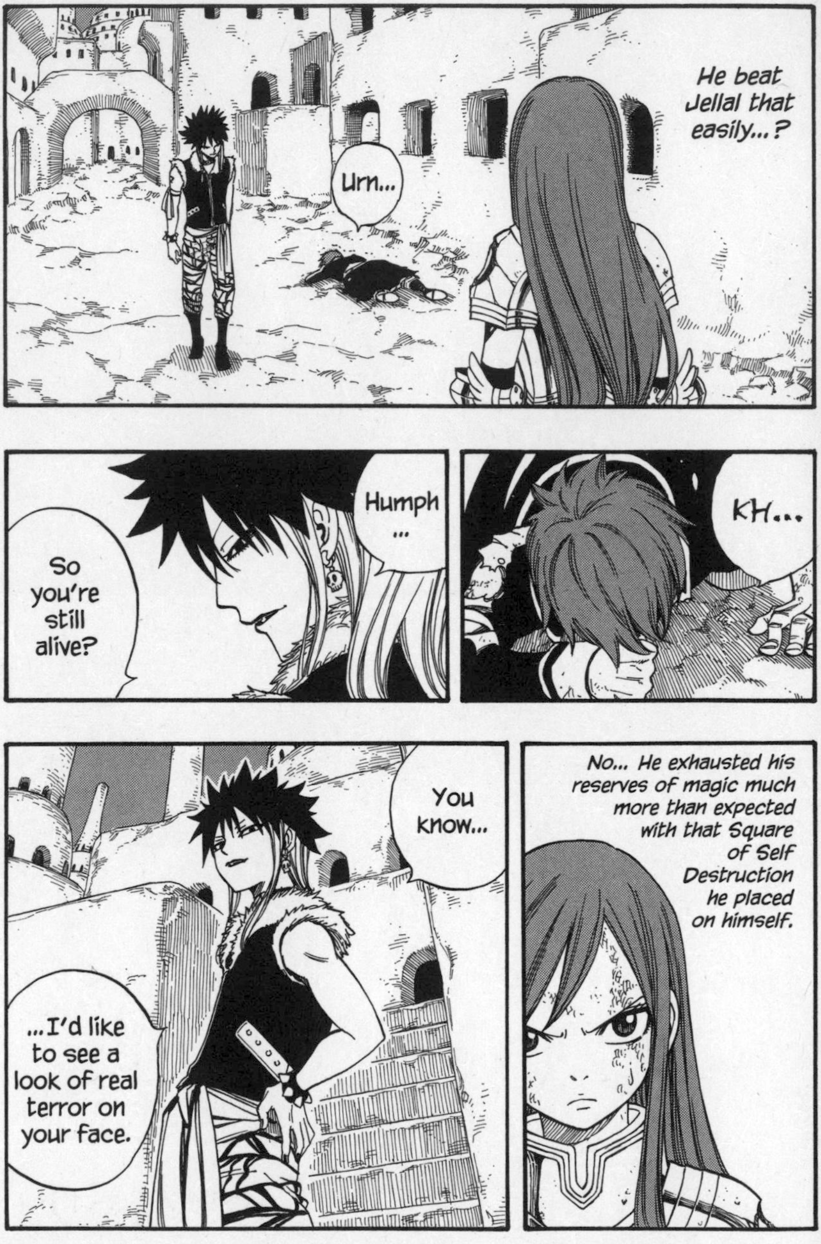
He beat Jellal that easily...?
Urn...
KH...
Humph ...
So you're still alive?
No... He exhausted his reserves of magic much more than expected with that Square of Self Destruction he placed on himself.
You know...
...I'd like to see a look of real terror on your face.

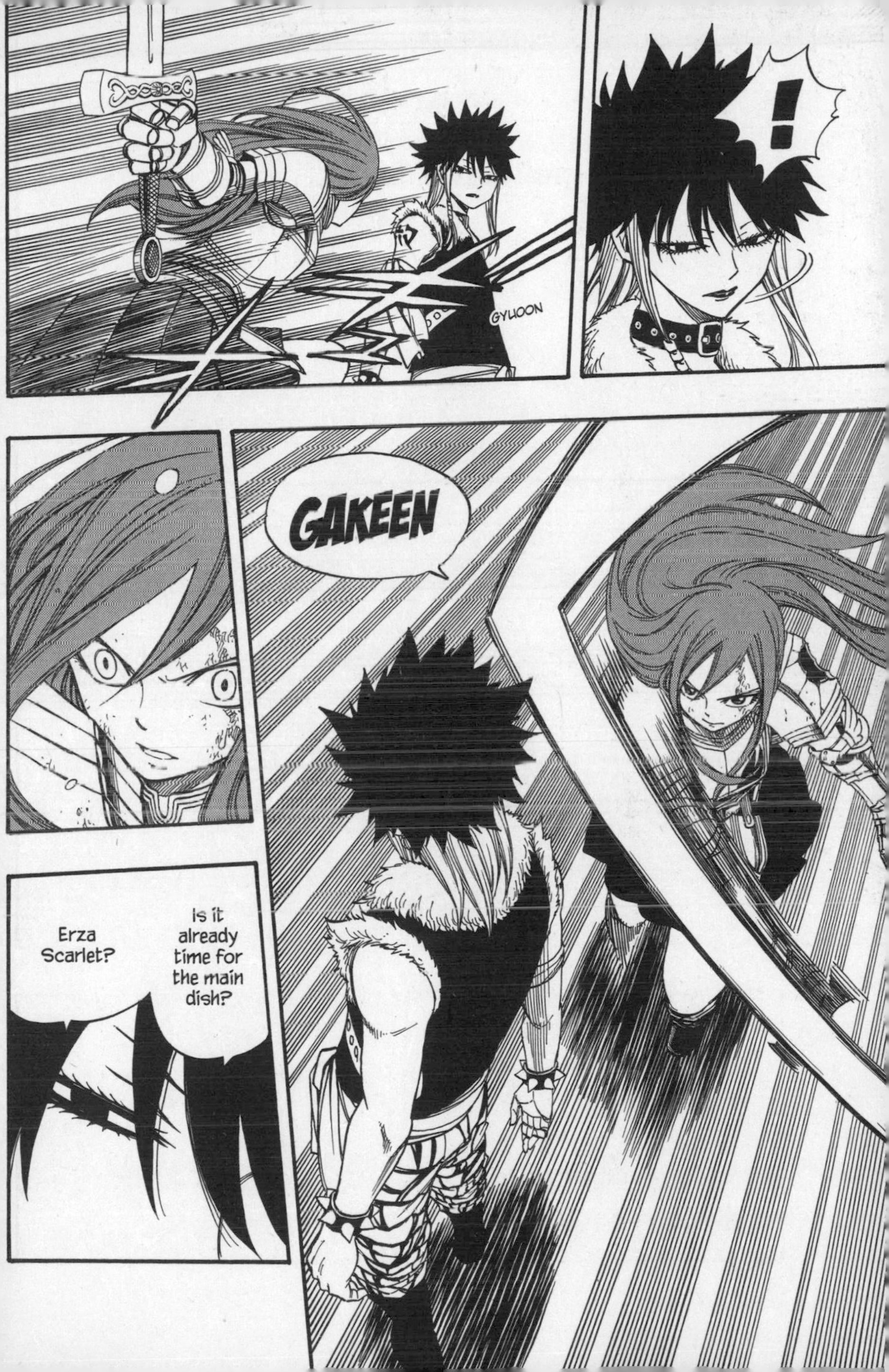
!
GYUOON
GAKEEN
Is it already time for the main dish?
Erza Scarlet?

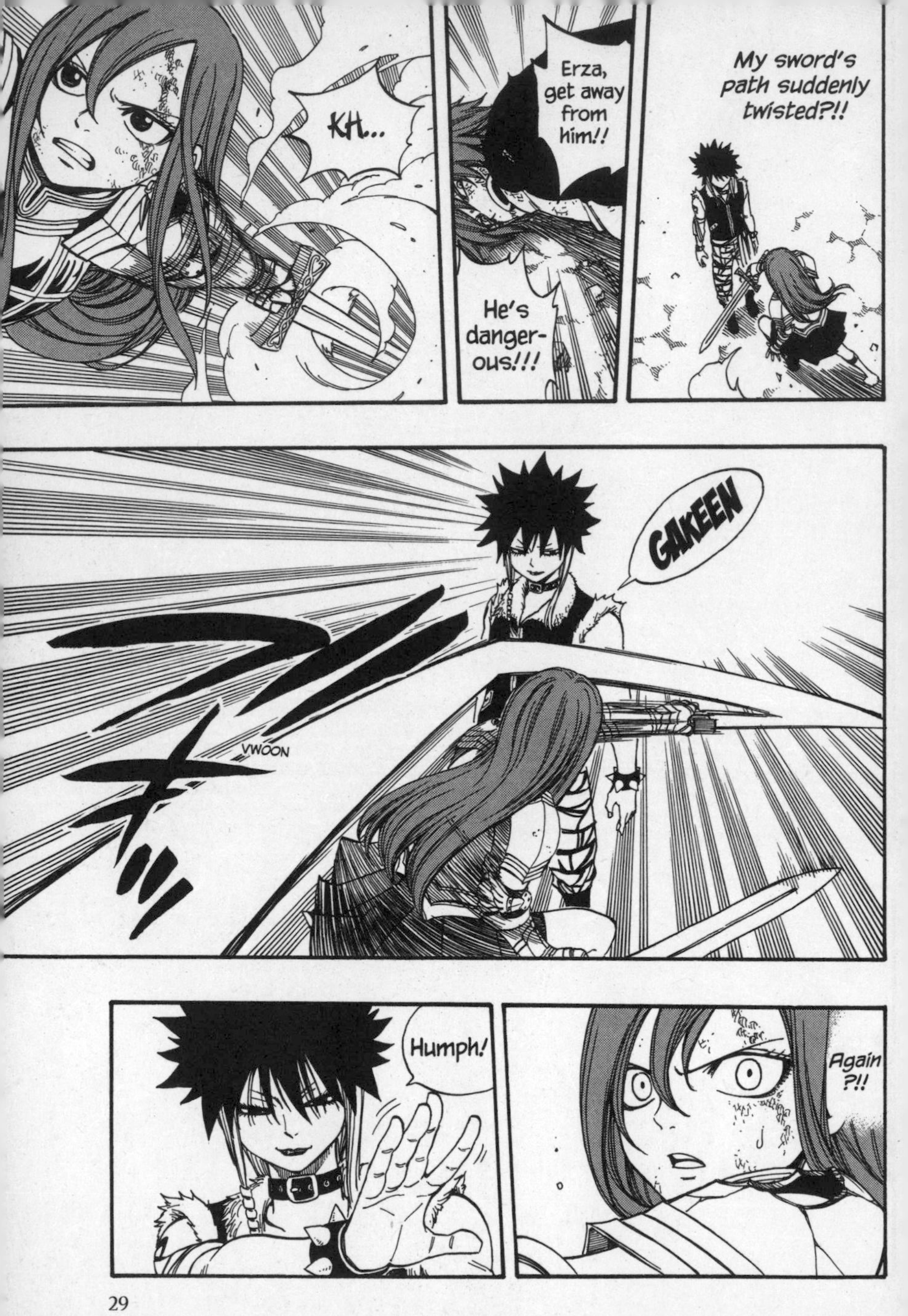
My sword's path suddenly twisted?!!
Erza, get away from him!!
He's danger-ous!!!
Kh...
GAKEEN
VWOON
Again?!!
Humph!

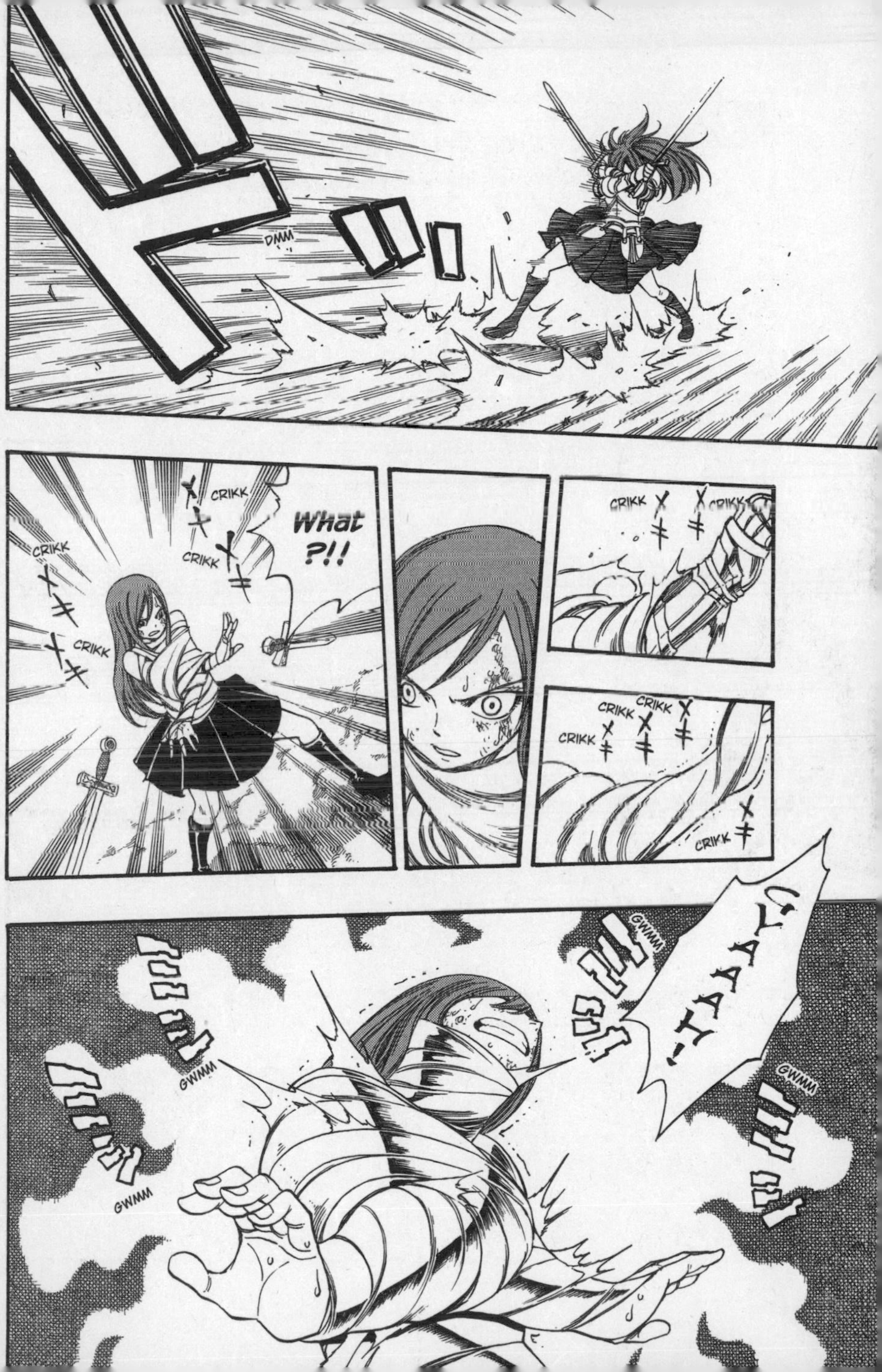
DMM
CRIKK
CRIKK
CRIKK
CRIKK
CRIKK
CRIKK
CRIKK
CRIKK
CRIKK
CRIKK
What ?!!
GYAAAH!
GWMM
GWMM
GWMM
GWMM

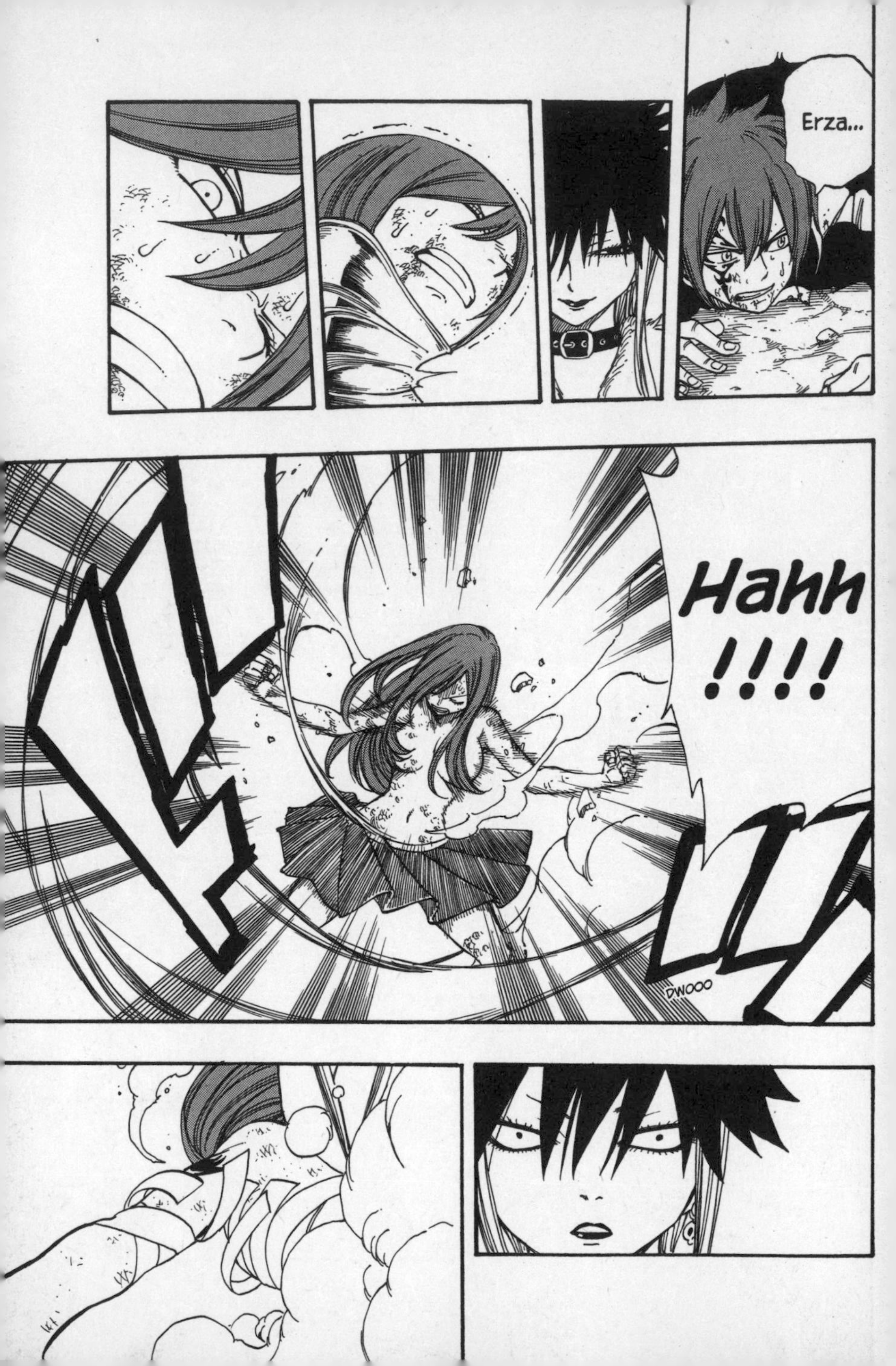
Erza...
Hahh !!!!
DWOOO

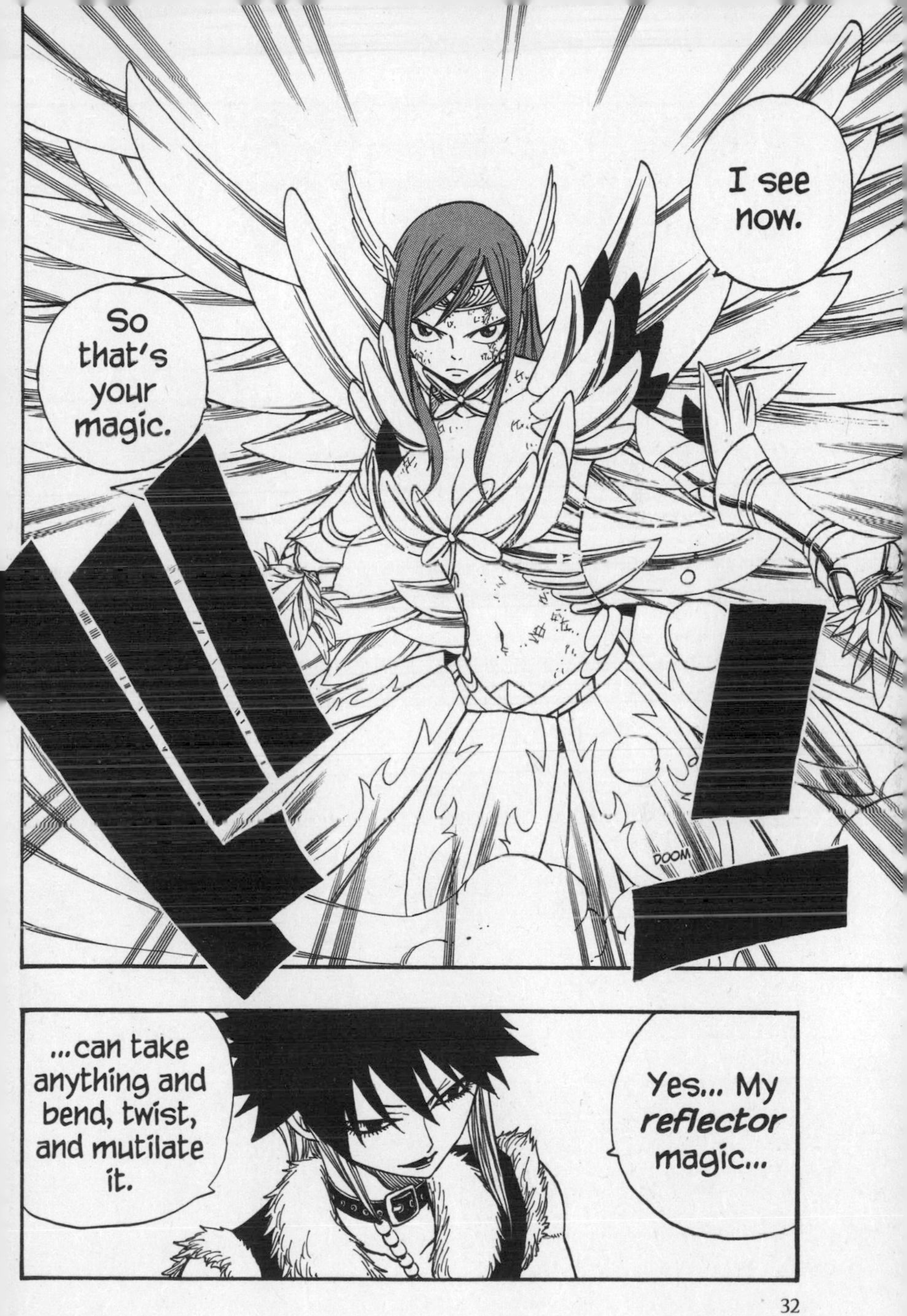
I see now.
So that's your magic.
DOOM
Yes... My *reflector* magic...
...can take anything and bend, twist, and mutilate it.

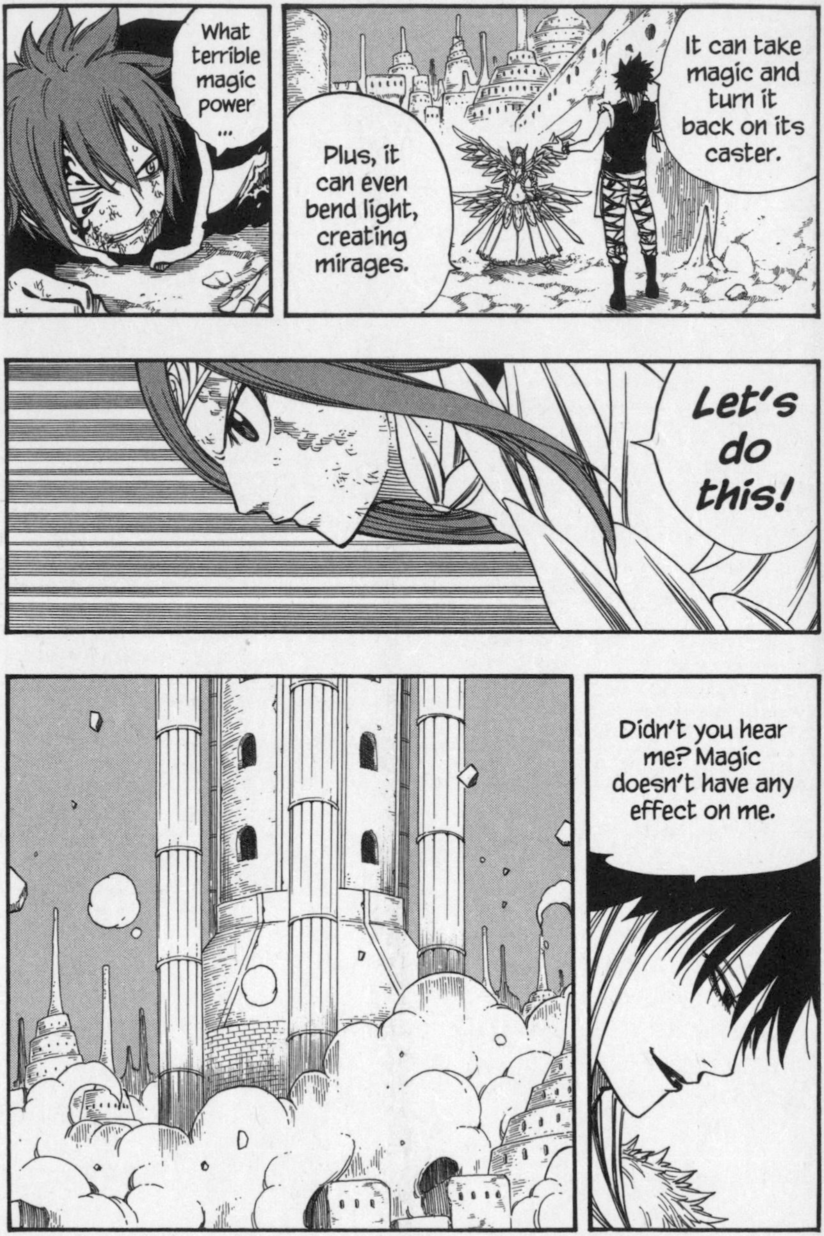
It can take magic and turn it back on its caster.
Plus, it can even bend light, creating mirages.
What terrible magic power ...
Let's do this!
Didn't you hear me? Magic doesn't have any effect on me.

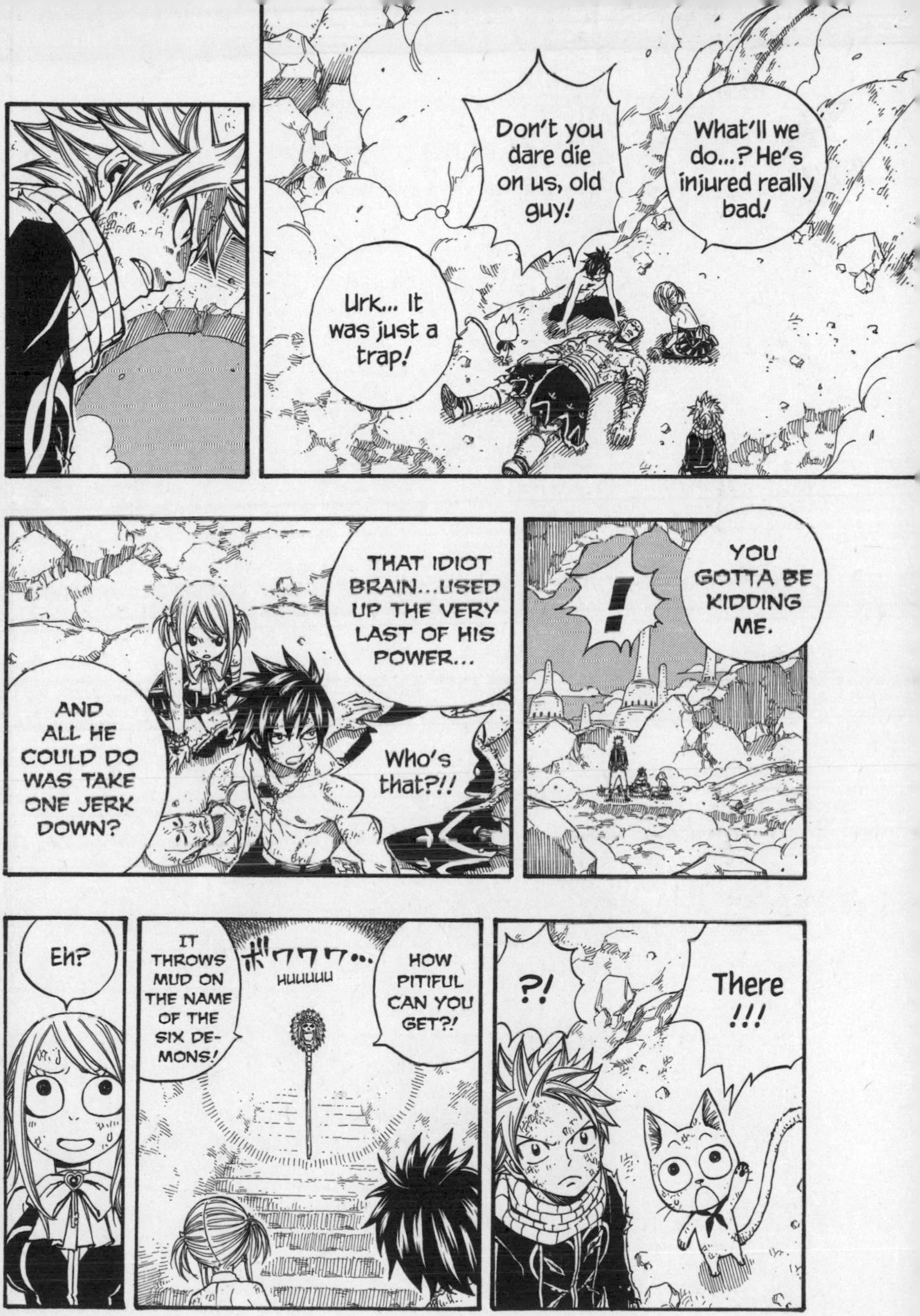
What'll we do...? He's injured really bad!
Don't you dare die on us, old guy!
Urk... It was just a trap!
YOU GOTTA BE KIDDING ME.
!
THAT IDIOT BRAIN...USED UP THE VERY LAST OF HIS POWER...
Who's that?!!
AND ALL HE COULD DO WAS TAKE ONE JERK DOWN?
There !!!
?!
HOW PITIFUL CAN YOU GET?!
ボワワワ…
HUUUUU
IT THROWS MUD ON THE NAME OF THE SIX DE-MONS!
Eh?

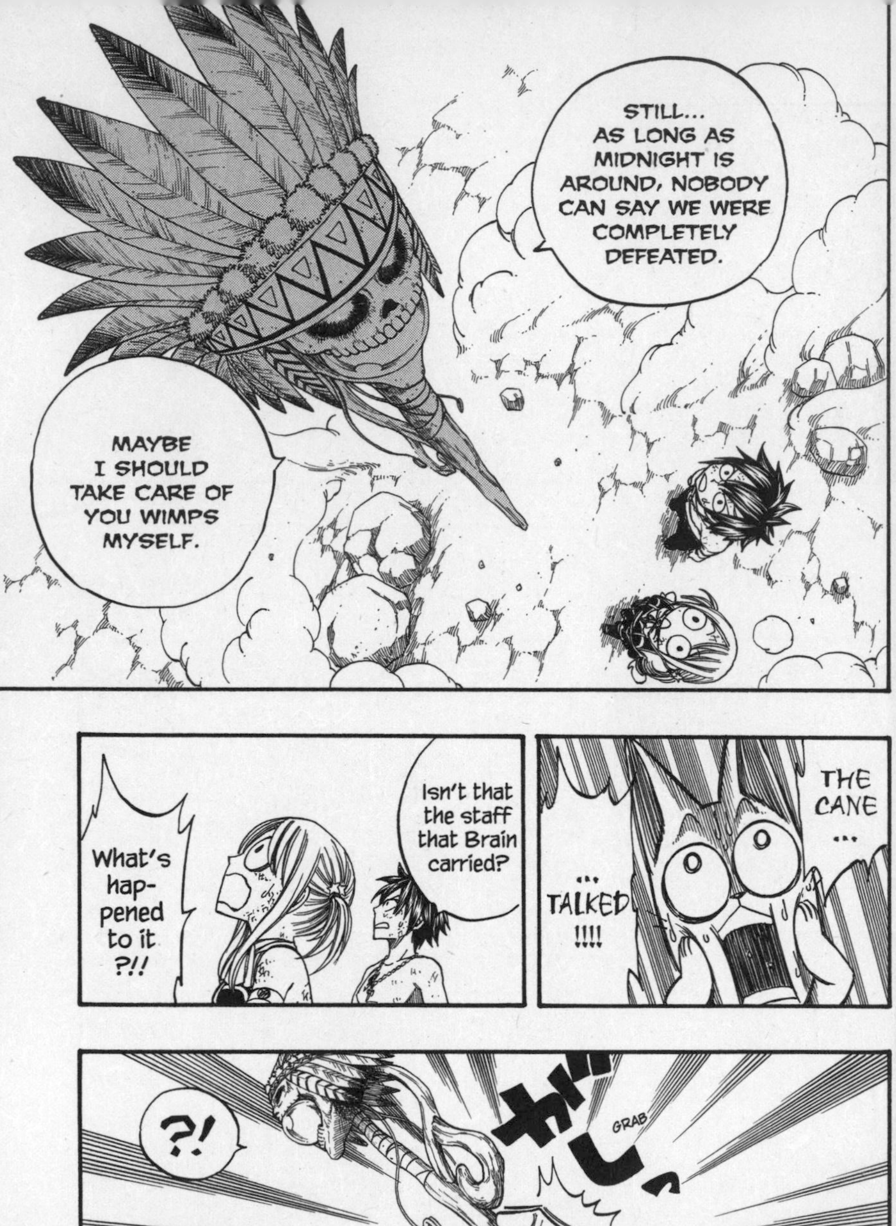
STILL... AS LONG AS MIDNIGHT IS AROUND, NOBODY CAN SAY WE WERE COMPLETELY DEFEATED.
MAYBE I SHOULD TAKE CARE OF YOU WIMPS MYSELF.
THE CANE ...
... TALKED !!!!
Isn't that the staff that Brain carried?
What's happened to it ?!!
GRAB
?!

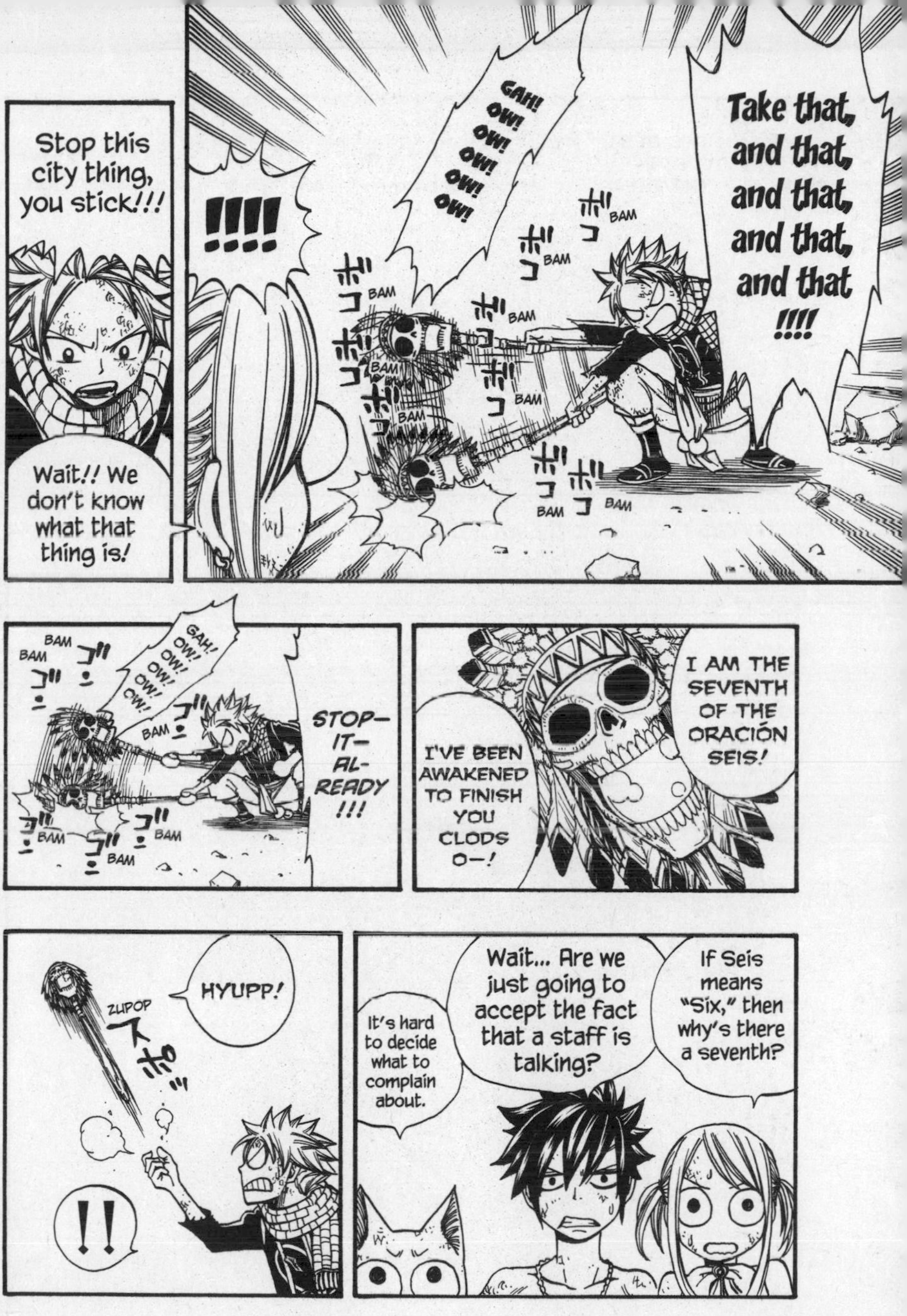
Take that, and that, and that, and that, and that!!!!
BAM
BAM
GAH! OW! OW! OW! OW! OW!
BAM
BAM
BAM
BAM
BAM
BAM
BAM
!!!!!
Stop this city thing, you stick!!!
Wait!! We don't know what that thing is!
I AM THE SEVENTH OF THE ORACIÓN SEIS!
I'VE BEEN AWAKENED TO FINISH YOU CLODS O—!
STOP—IT—AL-READY!!!
BAM
GAH! OW! OW! OW! OW!
BAM
BAM
BAM
BAM
BAM
If Seis means "Six," then why's there a seventh?
Wait... Are we just going to accept the fact that a staff is talking?
It's hard to decide what to complain about.
HYUPP!
ZUPOP
!!

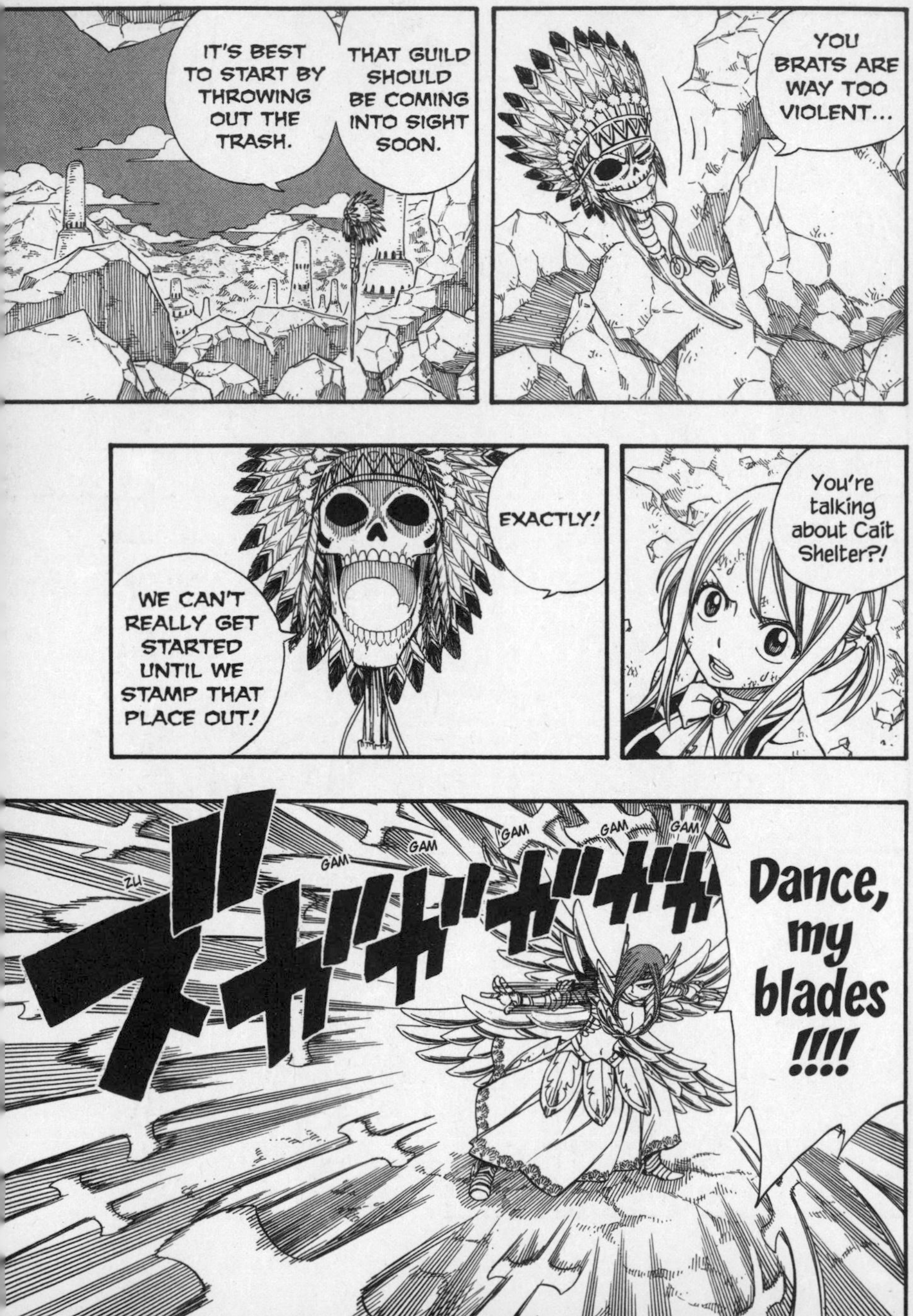
YOU BRATS ARE WAY TOO VIOLENT...
THAT GUILD SHOULD BE COMING INTO SIGHT SOON.
IT'S BEST TO START BY THROWING OUT THE TRASH.
You're talking about Cait Shelter?!
EXACTLY!
WE CAN'T REALLY GET STARTED UNTIL WE STAMP THAT PLACE OUT!
Dance, my blades!!!!
ZU
GAM
GAM
GAM
GAM
GAM

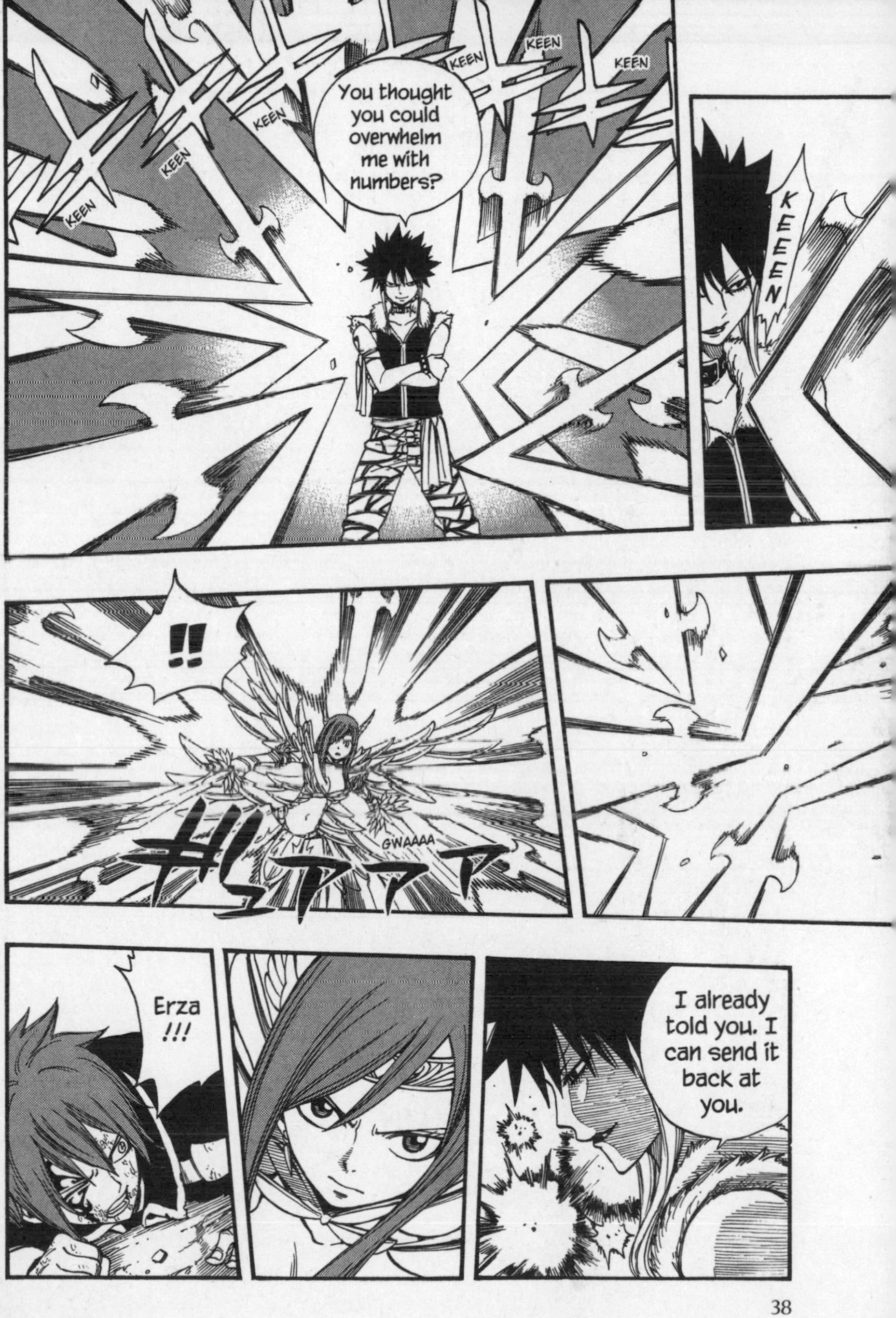
KEEEN
KEEN
KEEN
KEEN
KEEN
KEEN
KEEN
You thought you could overwhelm me with numbers?
!!
GWAAAA
I already told you. I can send it back at you.
Erza !!!

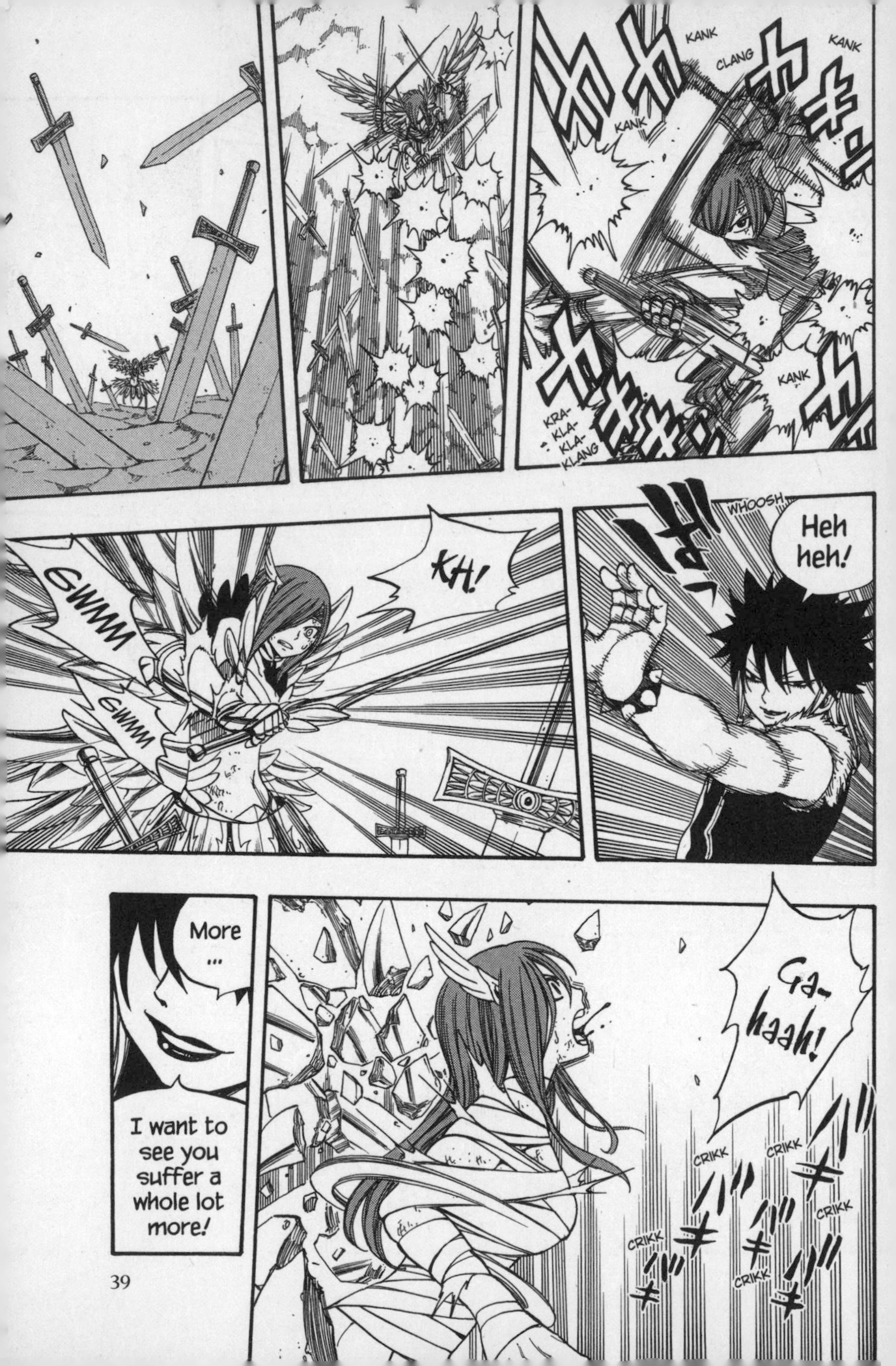

KANK
CLANG
KANK
KANK
KANK
KRA-KLA-KLA-KLANG
WHOOSH
Heh heh!
KH!
GWMM
GWMM
Ga-haaah!
CRIKK
CRIKK
CRIKK
CRIKK
CRIKK
More ...
I want to see you suffer a whole lot more!

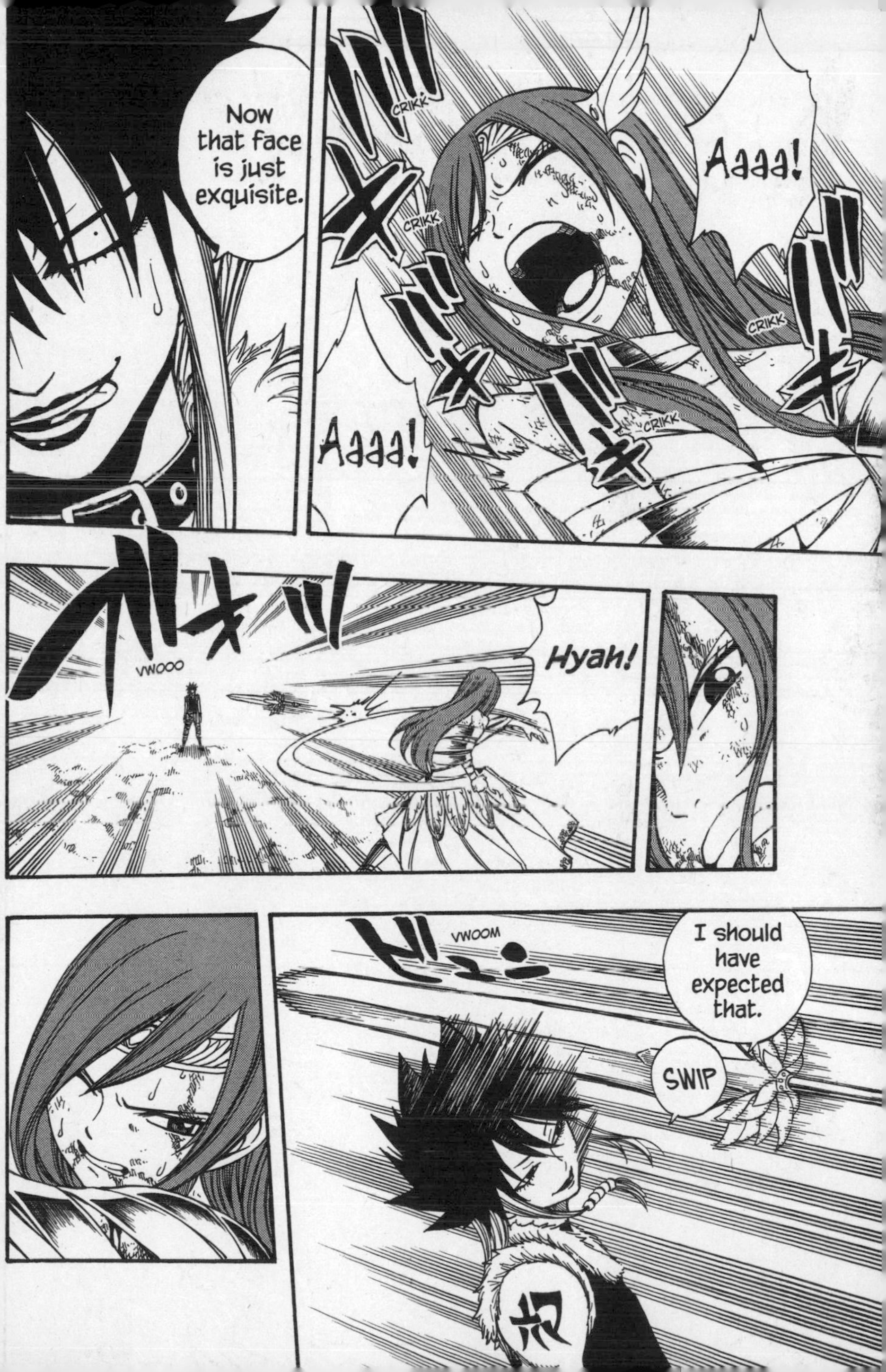
Aaaa!
CRIKK
CRIKK
CRIKK
CRIKK
Aaaa!
Now that face is just exquisite.
Hyah!
VWOOO
I should have expected that.
VWOOM
SWIP

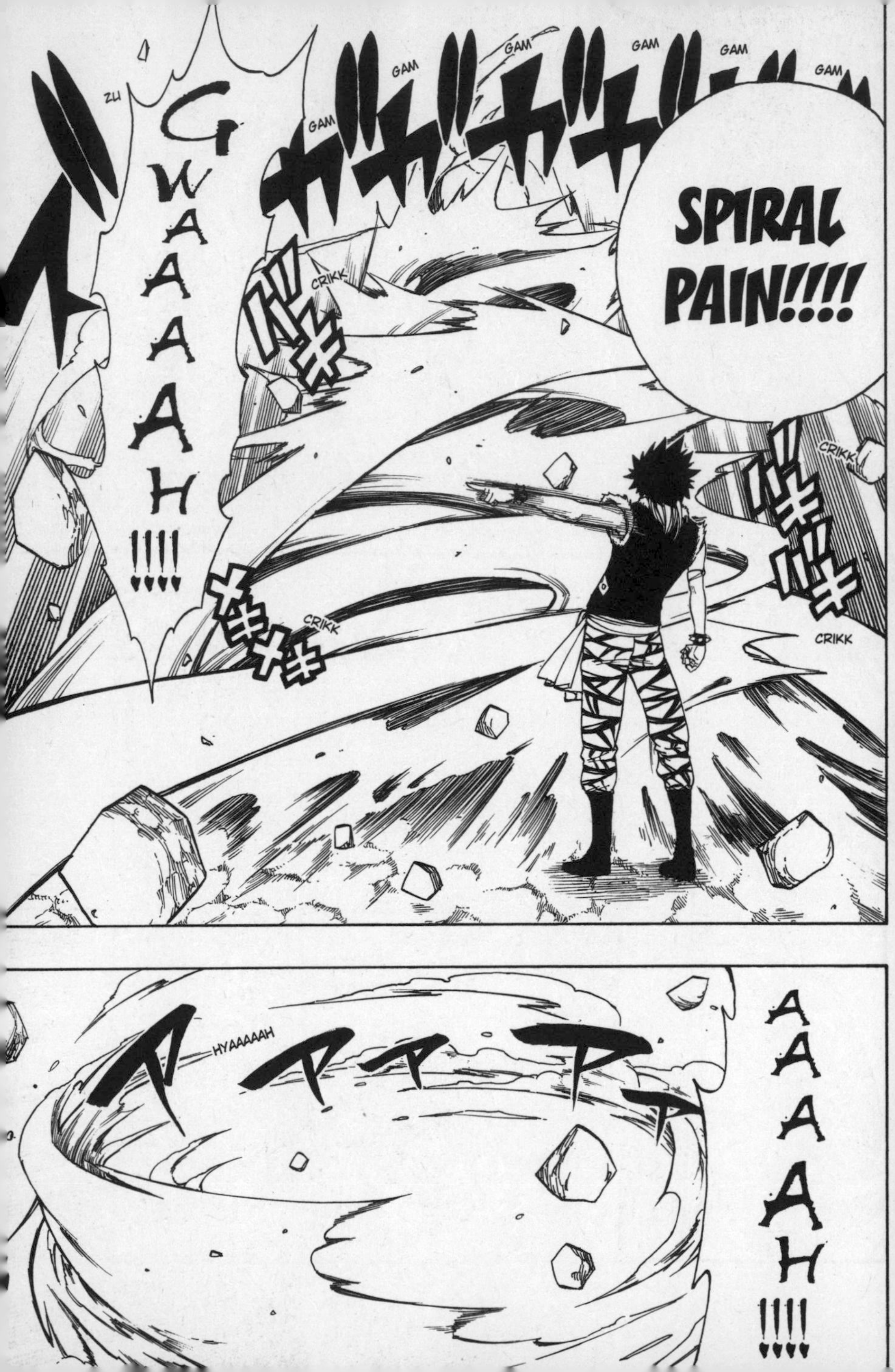
SPIRAL PAIN!!!!
GAM
GAM
GAM
GAM
GAM
GAM
CRIKK
CRIKK
CRIKK
CRIKK
GWAAAAH!!!!
ZU
AAAAH!!!!
HYAAAAAH

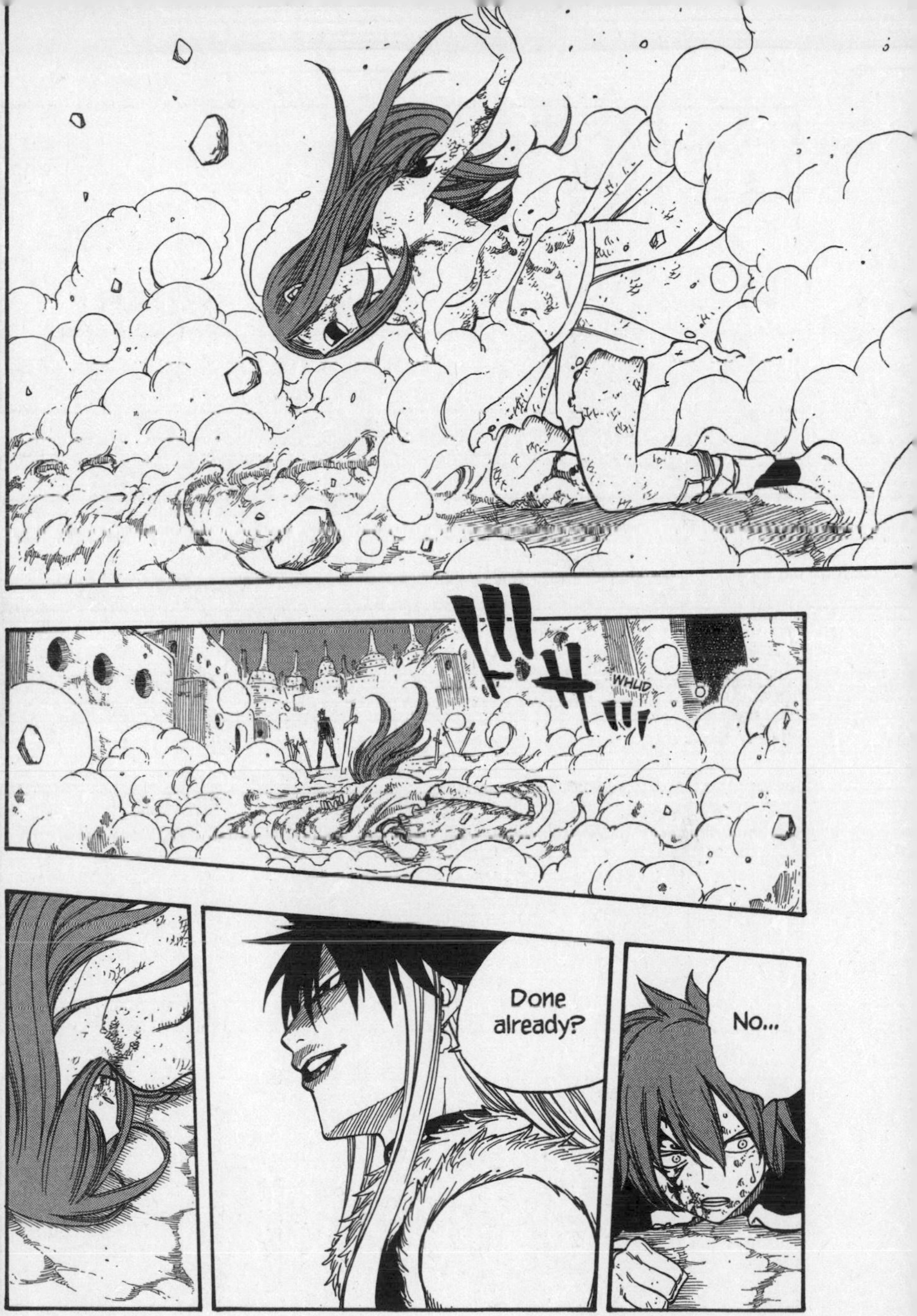
WHUD
No...
Done already?

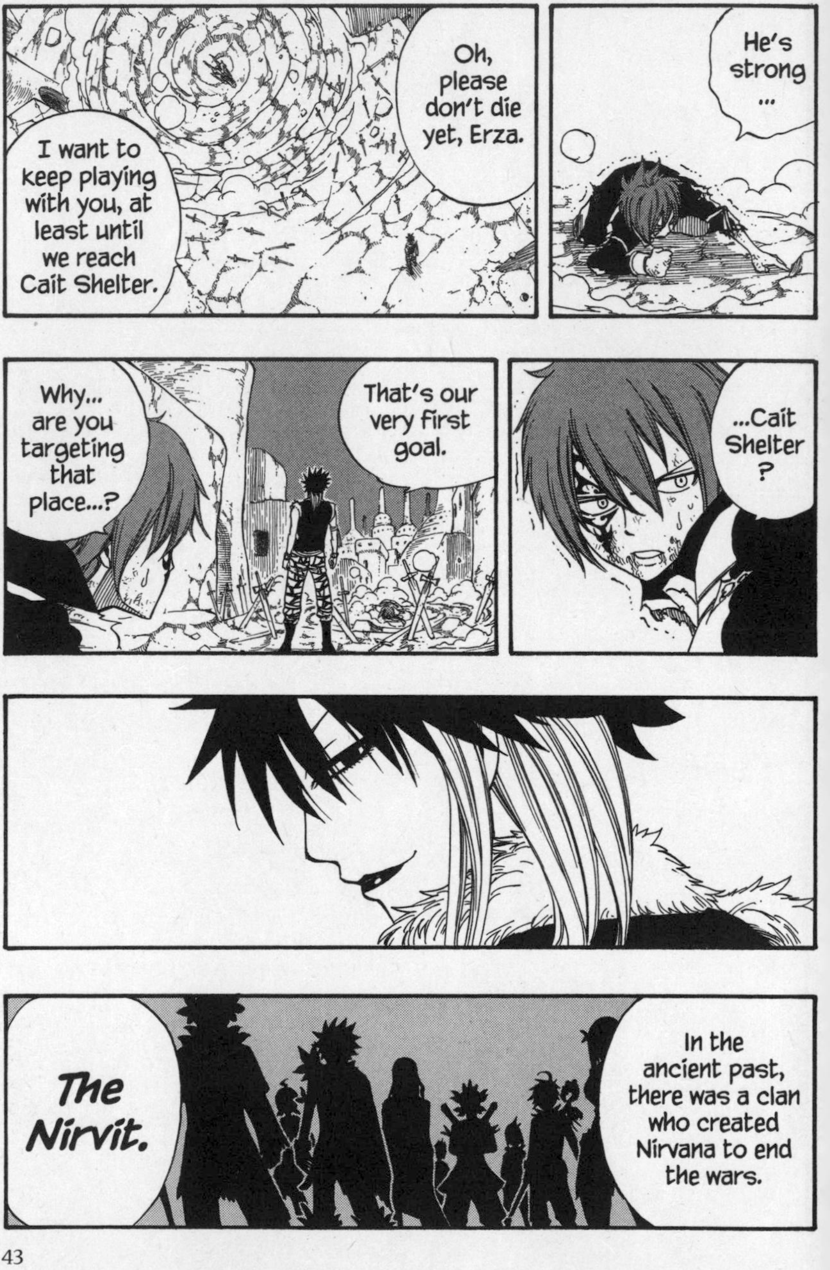

He's strong ...
Oh, please don't die yet, Erza.
I want to keep playing with you, at least until we reach Caít Shelter.
...Caít Shelter?
That's our very first goal.
Why... are you targeting that place...?
In the ancient past, there was a clan who created Nirvana to end the wars.
The Nirvit.

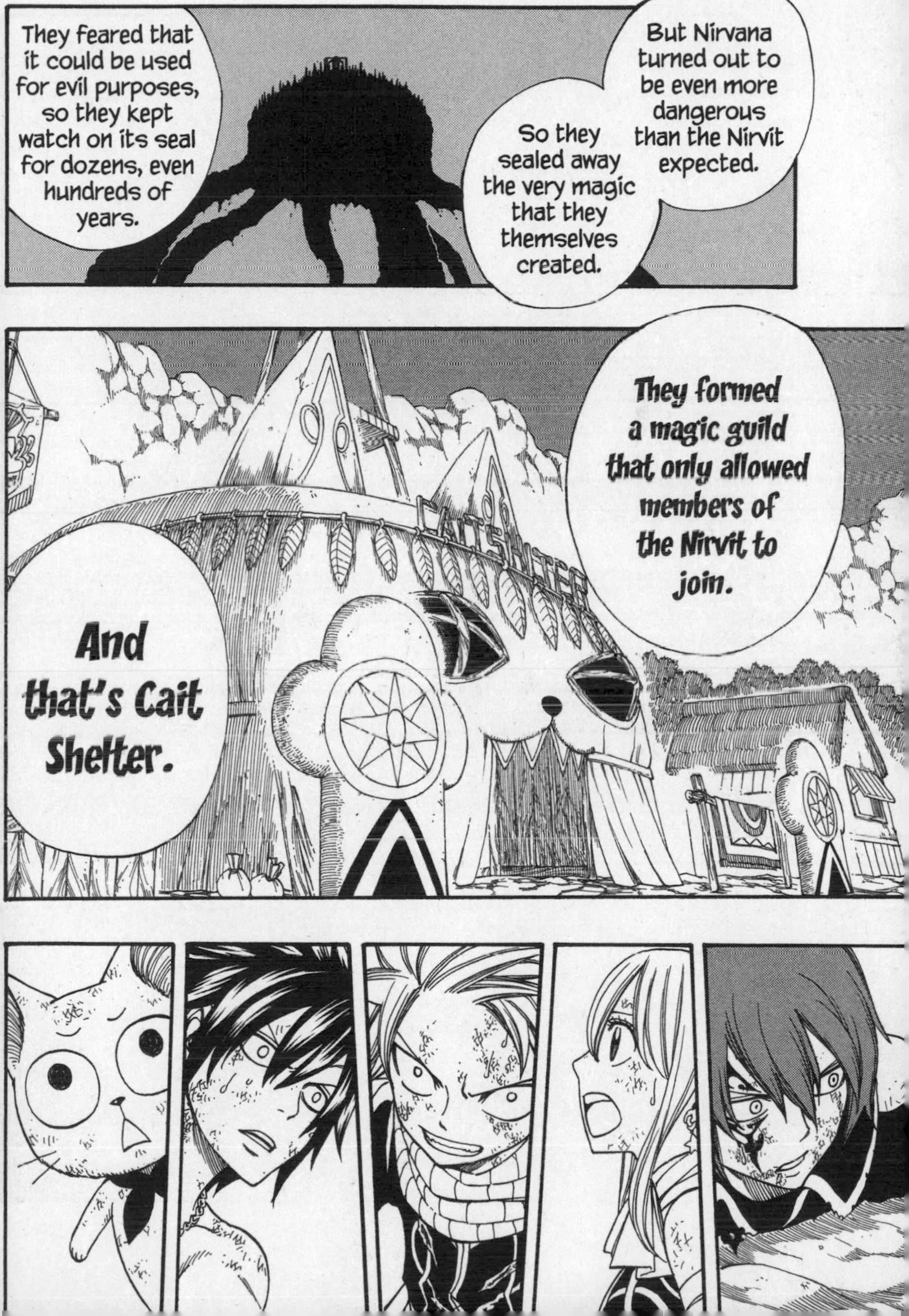
But Nirvana turned out to be even more dangerous than the Nirvit expected.
So they sealed away the very magic that they themselves created.
They feared that it could be used for evil purposes, so they kept watch on its seal for dozens, even hundreds of years.
They formed a magic guild that only allowed members of the Nirvit to join.
And that's Cait Shelter.

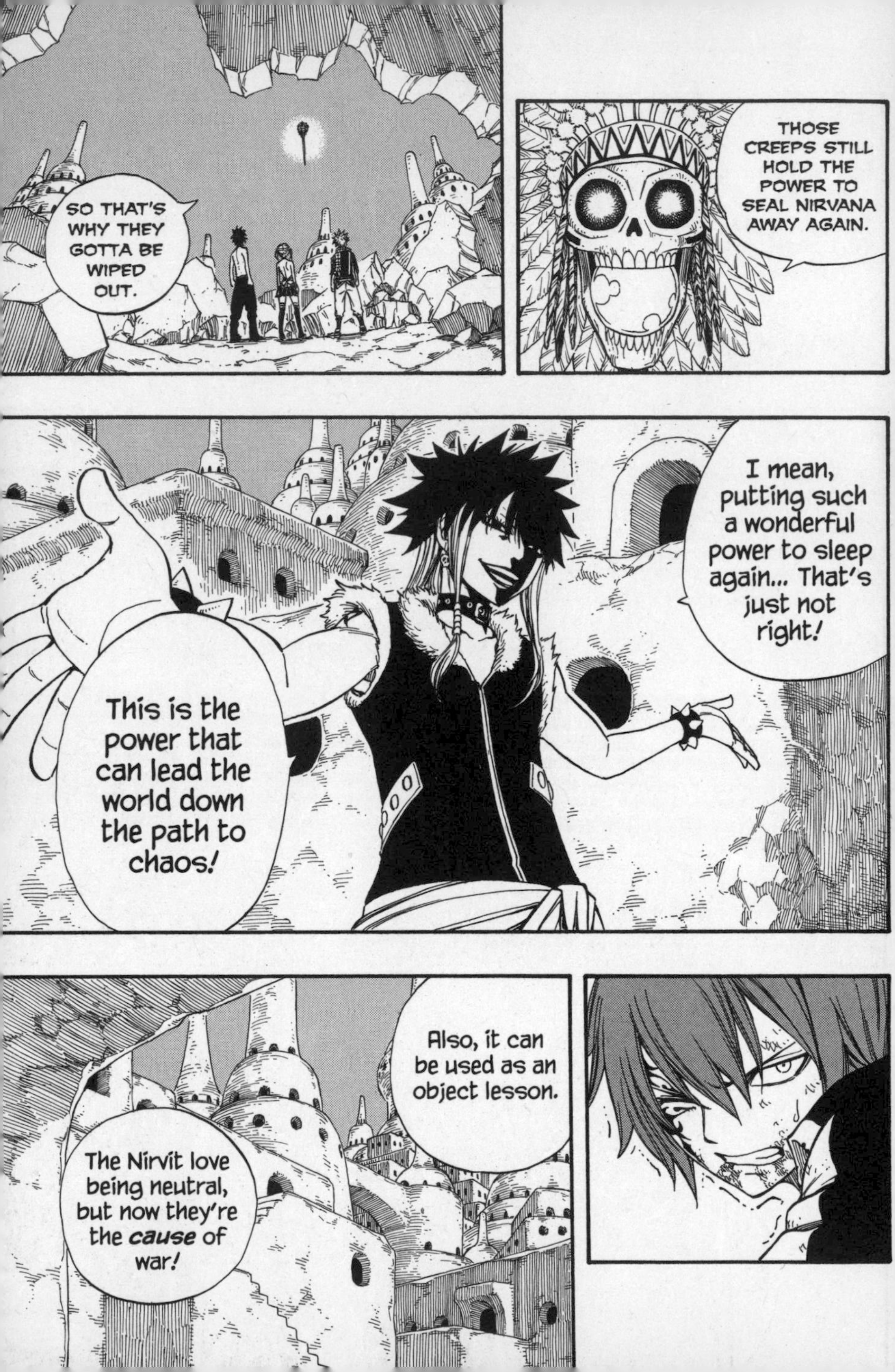
THOSE CREEPS STILL HOLD THE POWER TO SEAL NIRVANA AWAY AGAIN.
SO THAT'S WHY THEY GOTTA BE WIPED OUT.
I mean, putting such a wonderful power to sleep again... That's just not right!
This is the power that can lead the world down the path to chaos!
Also, it can be used as an object lesson.
The Nirvit love being neutral, but now they're the *cause* of war!

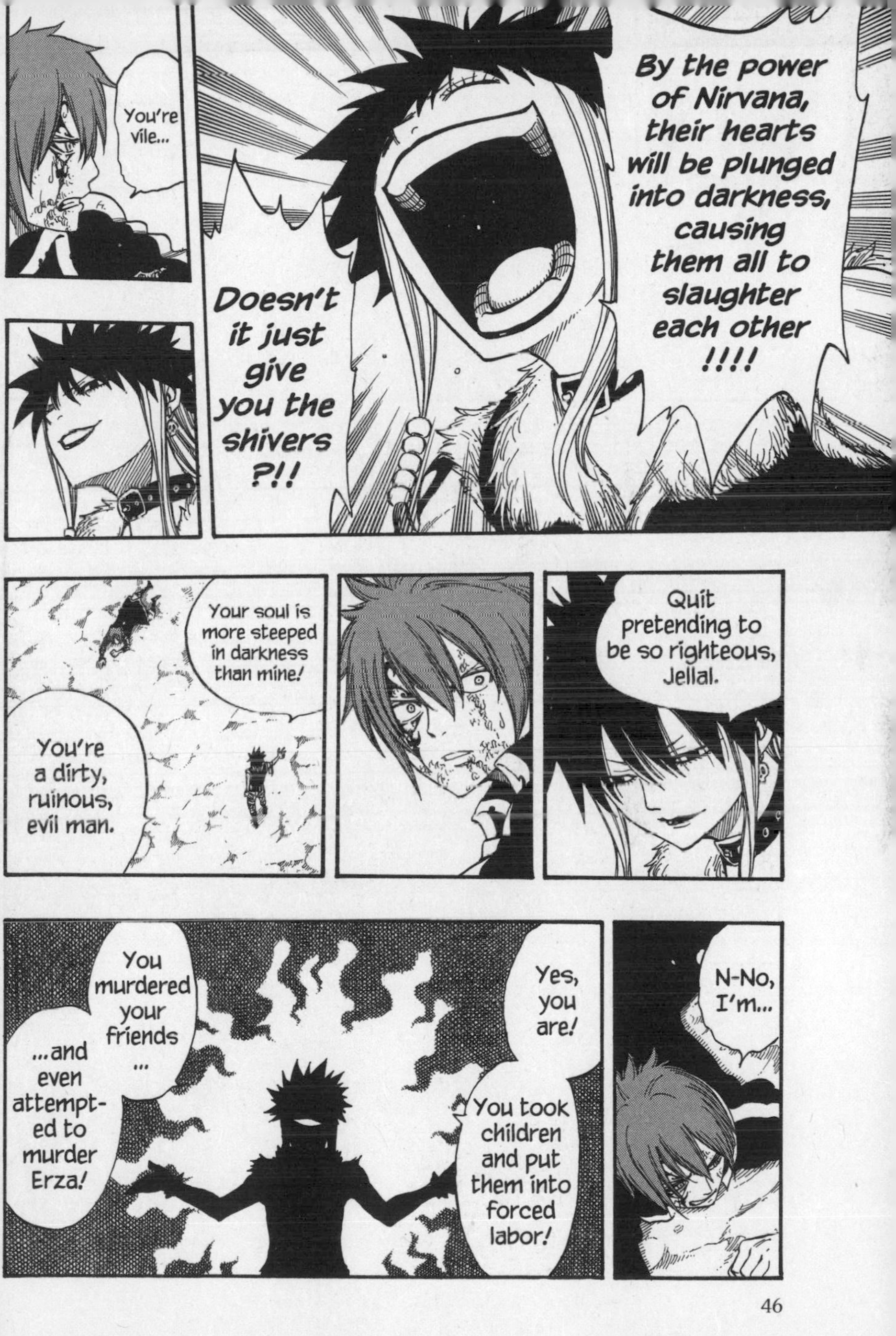
By the power of Nirvana, their hearts will be plunged into darkness, causing them all to slaughter each other!!!!
Doesn't it just give you the shivers?!!
You're vile...
Quit pretending to be so righteous, Jellal.
Your soul is more steeped in darkness than mine!
You're a dirty, ruinous, evil man.
N-No, I'm...
Yes, you are!
You took children and put them into forced labor!
You murdered your friends...
...and even attempted to murder Erza!

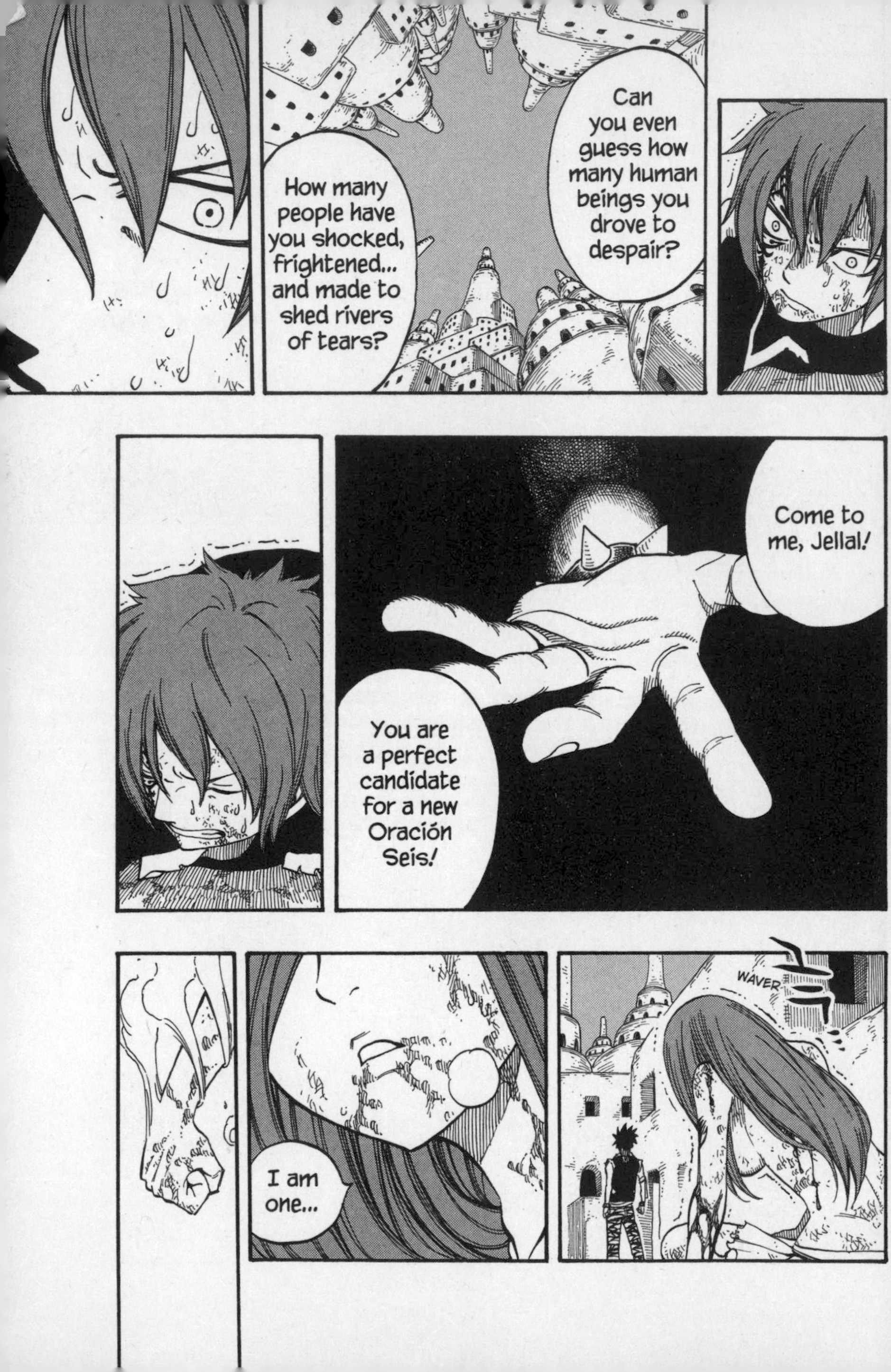
Can you even guess how many human beings you drove to despair?
How many people have you shocked, frightened... and made to shed rivers of tears?
Come to me, Jellal!
You are a perfect candidate for a new Oración Seis!
WAVER
I am one...

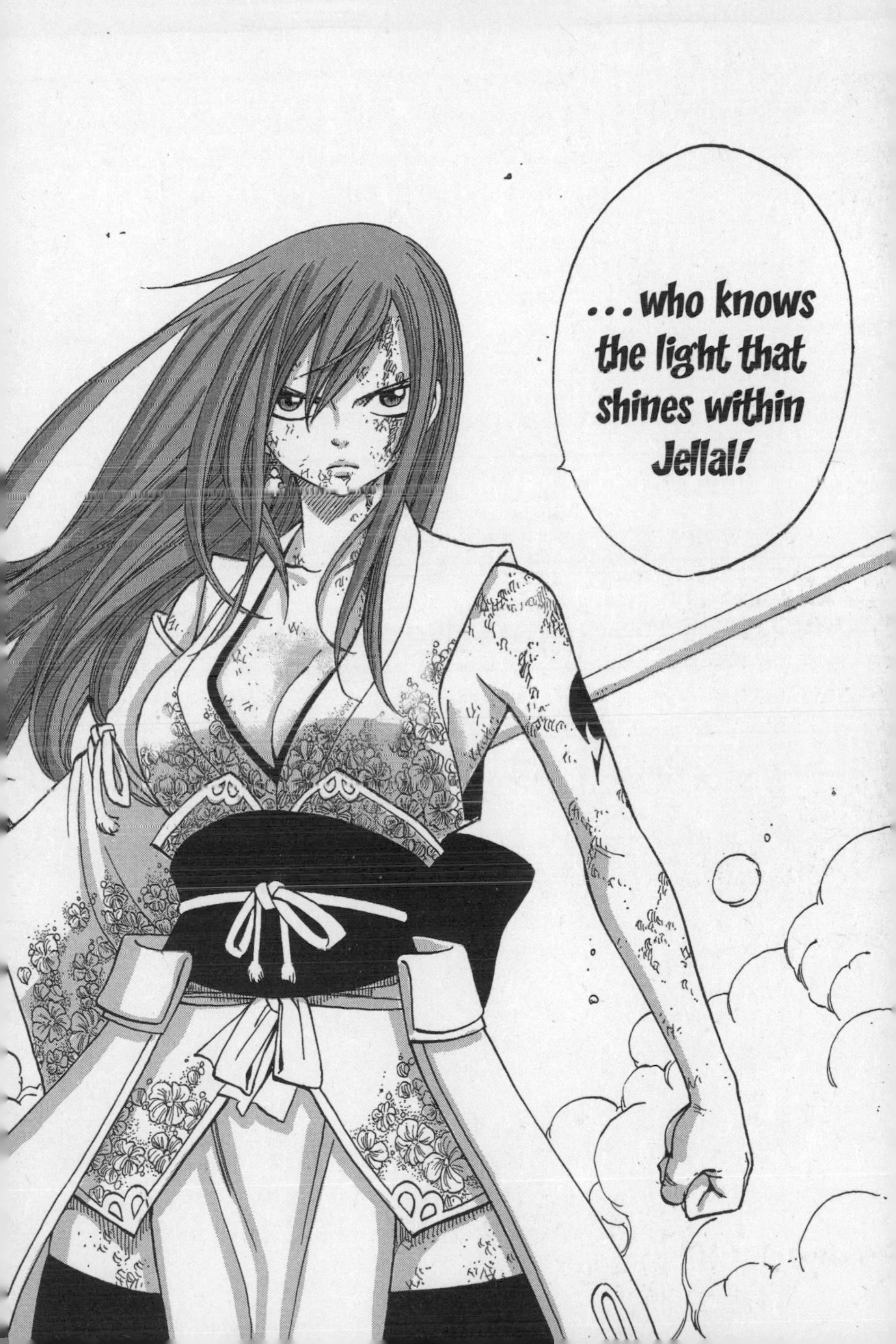
...who knows the light that shines within Jellal!

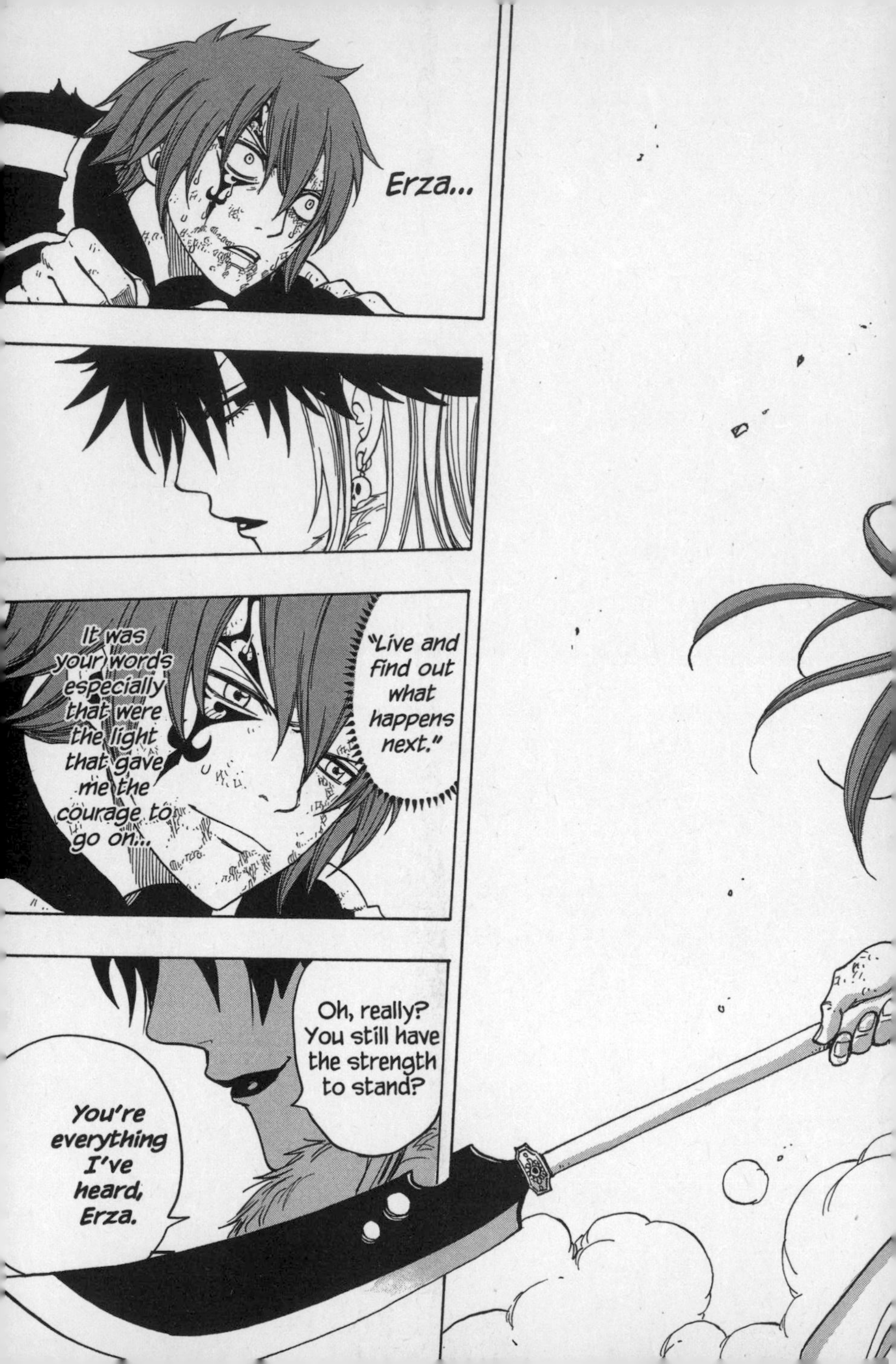
Erza...
"Live and find out what happens next."
It was your words especially that were the light that gave me the courage to go on...
Oh, really? You still have the strength to stand?
You're everything I've heard, Erza.

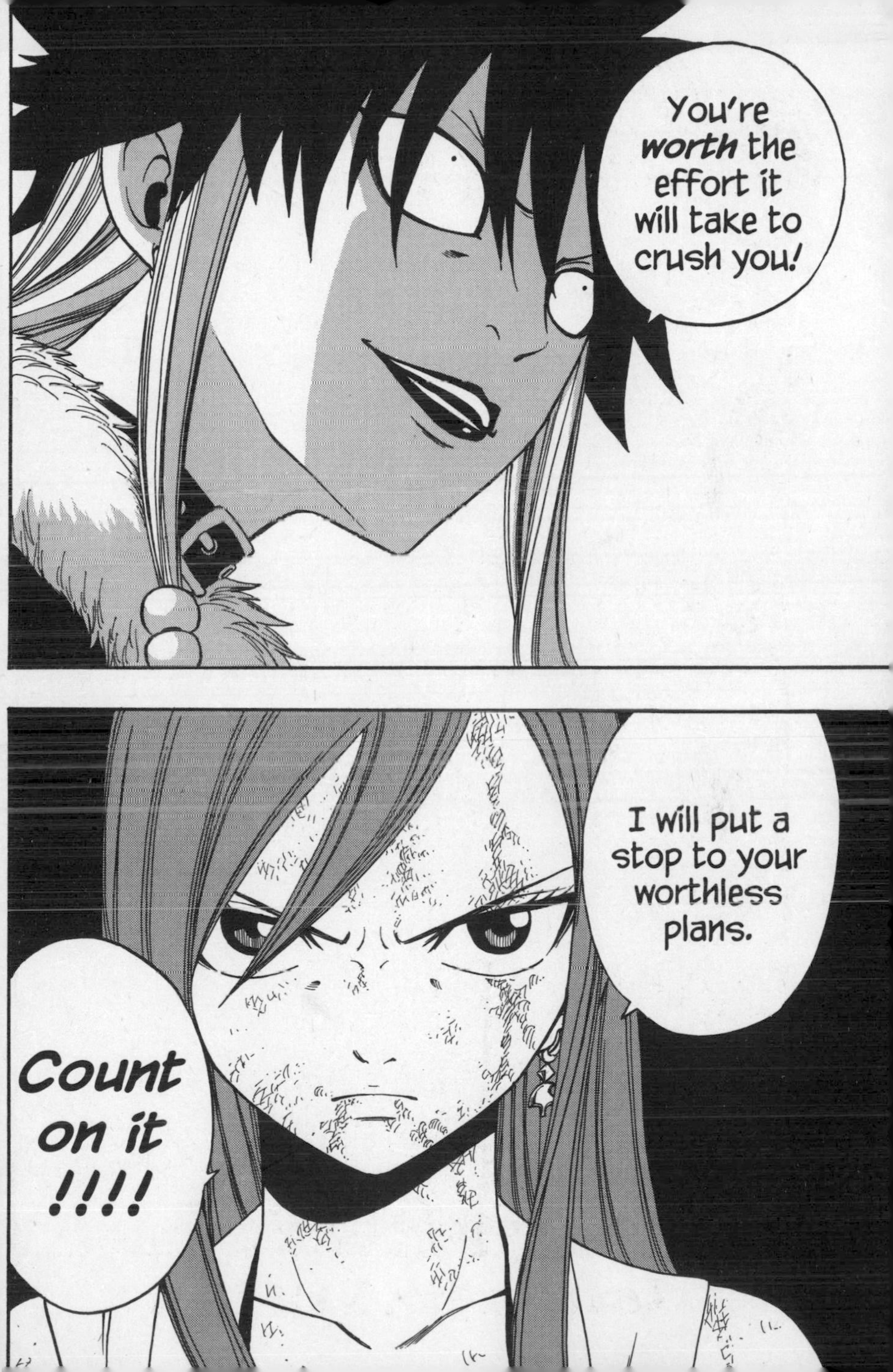
You're *worth* the effort it will take to crush you!
I will put a stop to your worthless plans.
Count on it !!!!

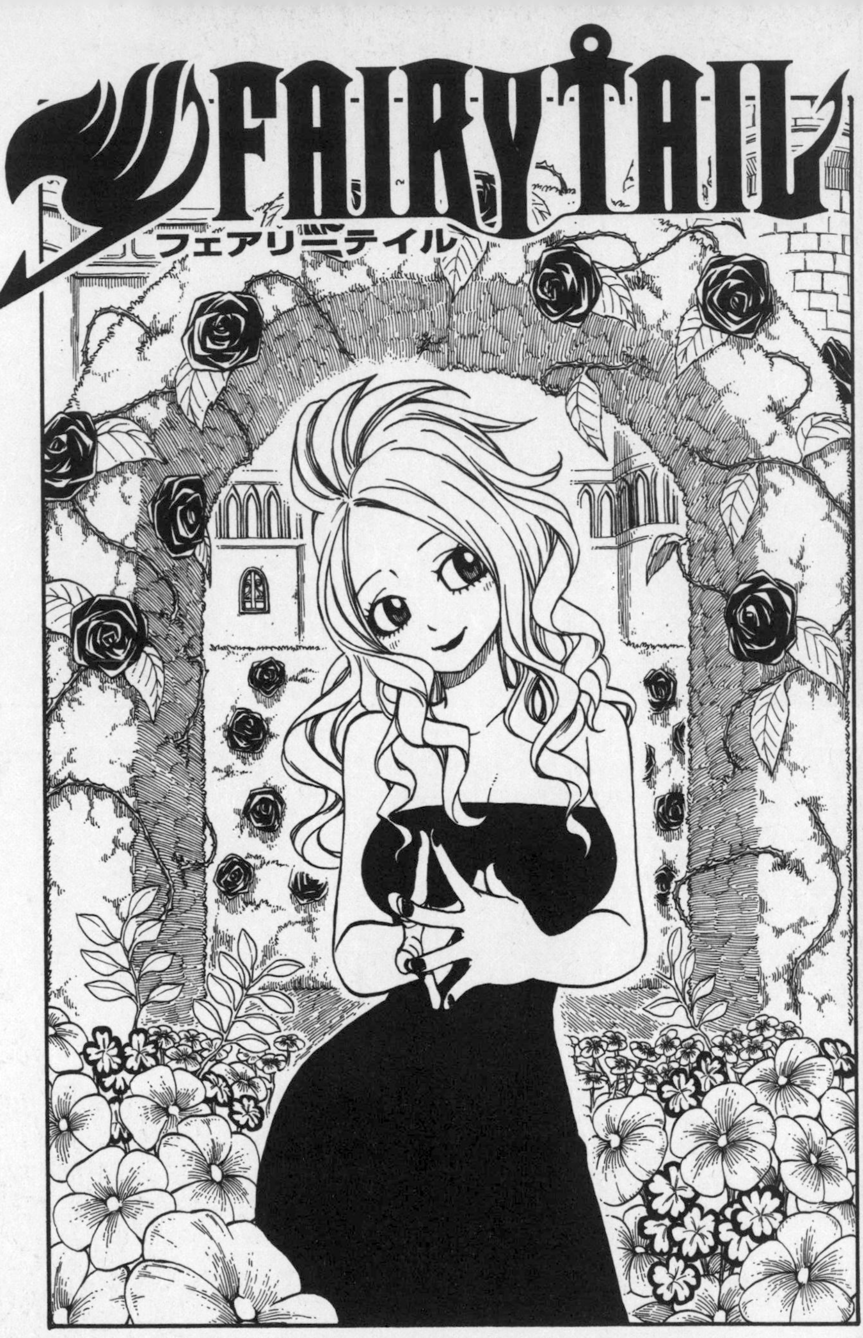
FAIRY TAIL
フェアリーテイル

Chapter 155: Last Man

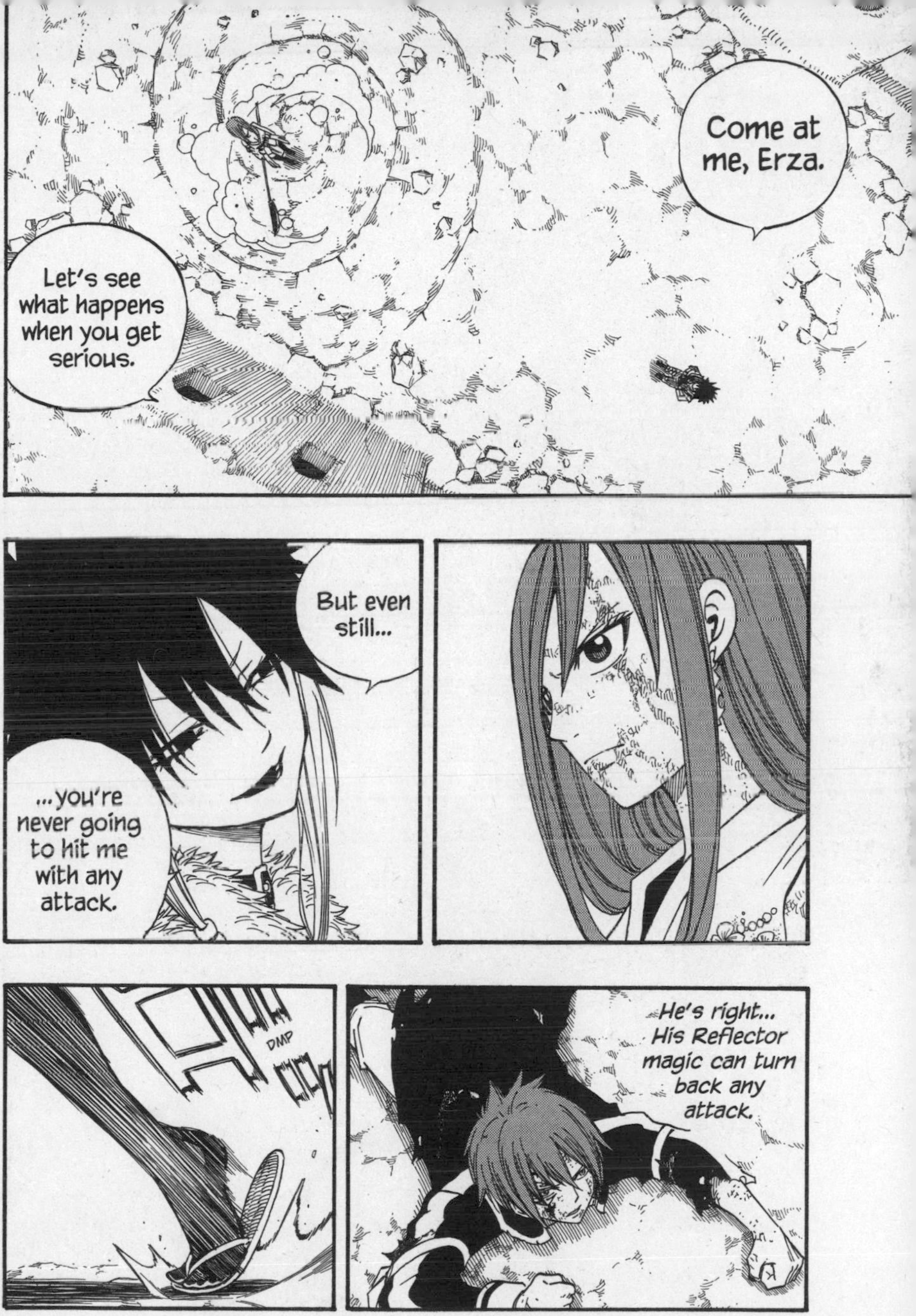
Come at me, Erza.
Let's see what happens when you get serious.
But even still...
...you're never going to hit me with any attack.
He's right... His Reflector magic can turn back any attack.
DMP

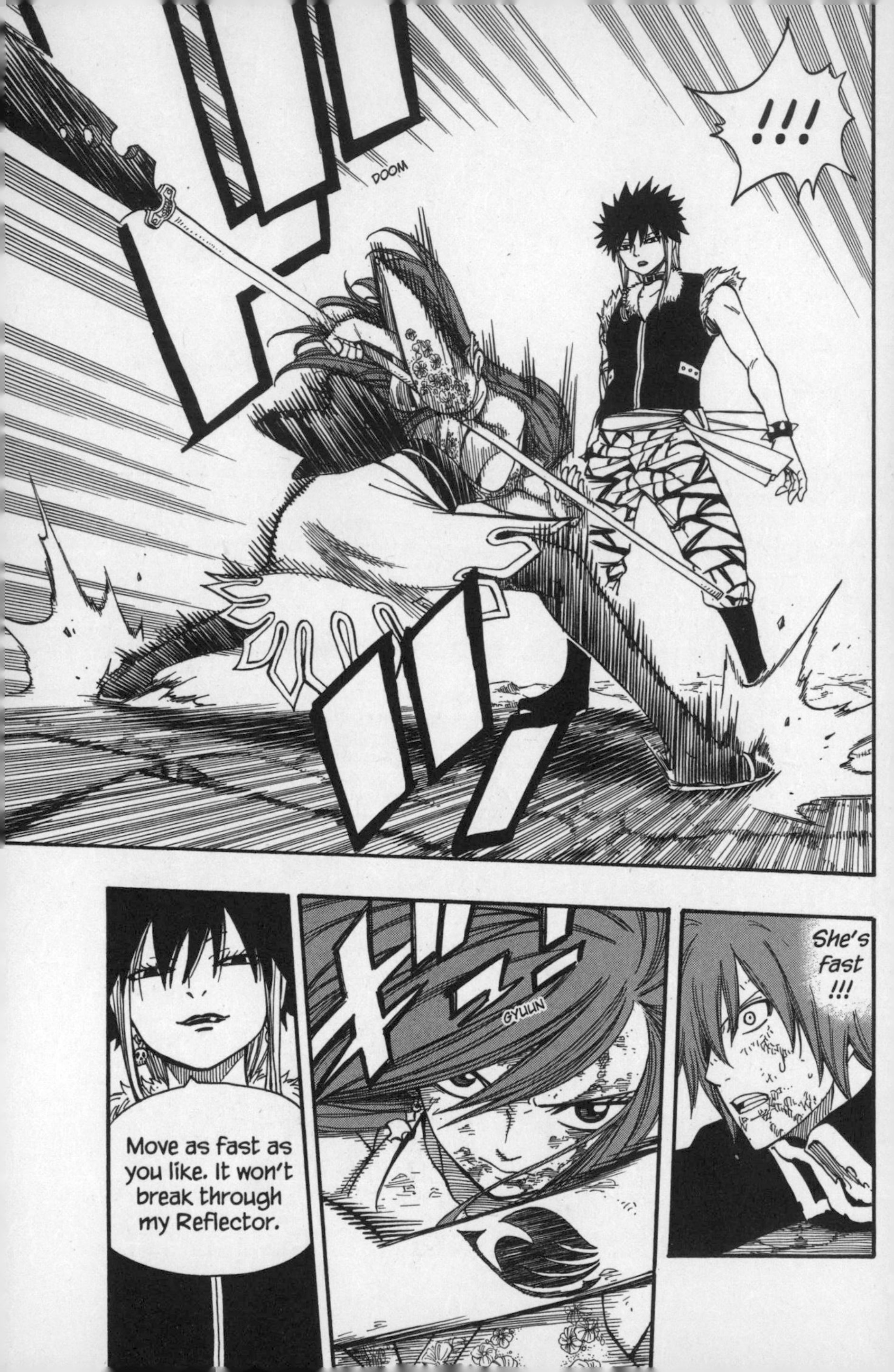
!!!
DOOM
She's fast!!!
GYUUN
Move as fast as you like. It won't break through my Reflector.

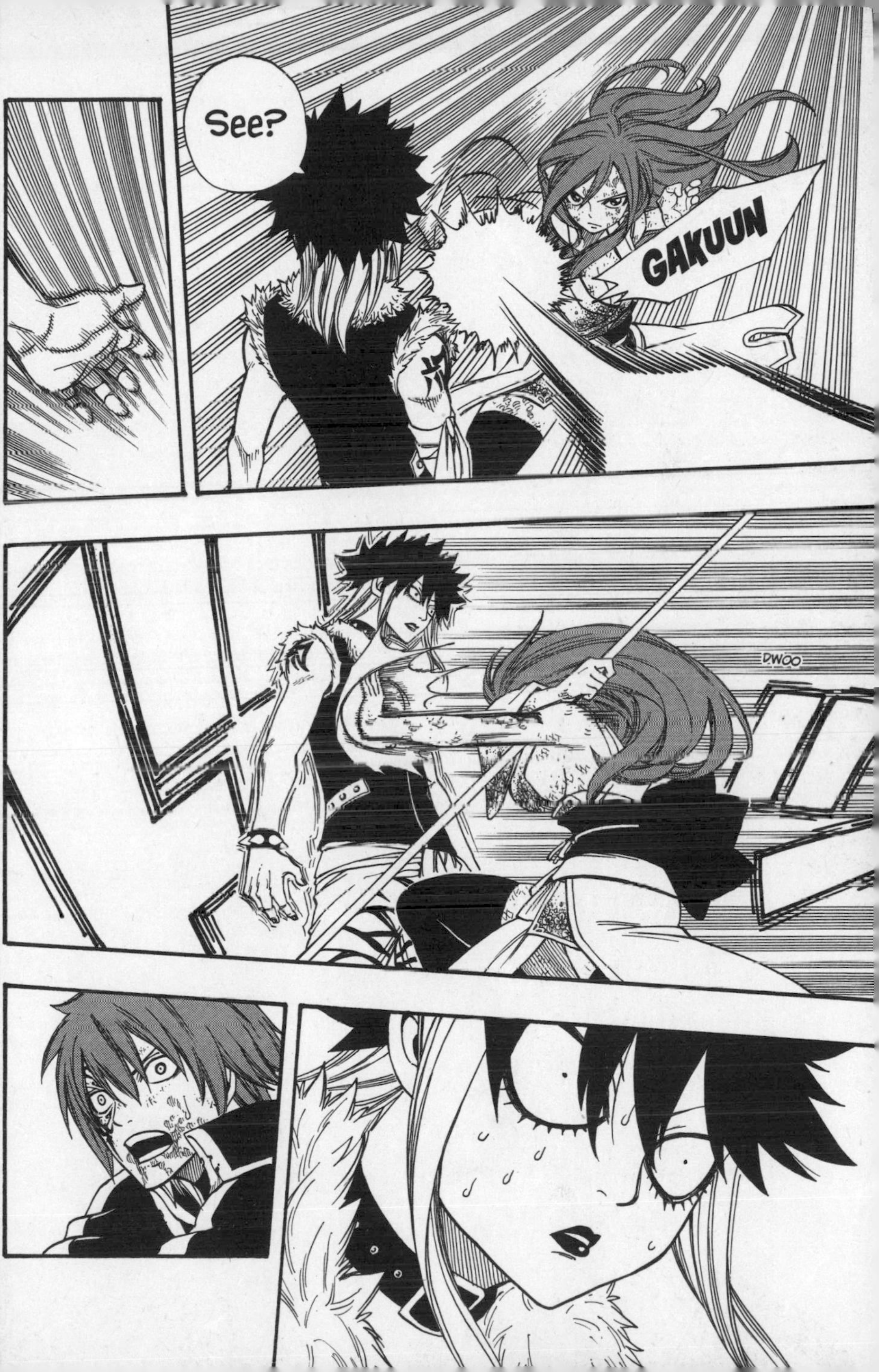
See?
GAKUUN
DWOO

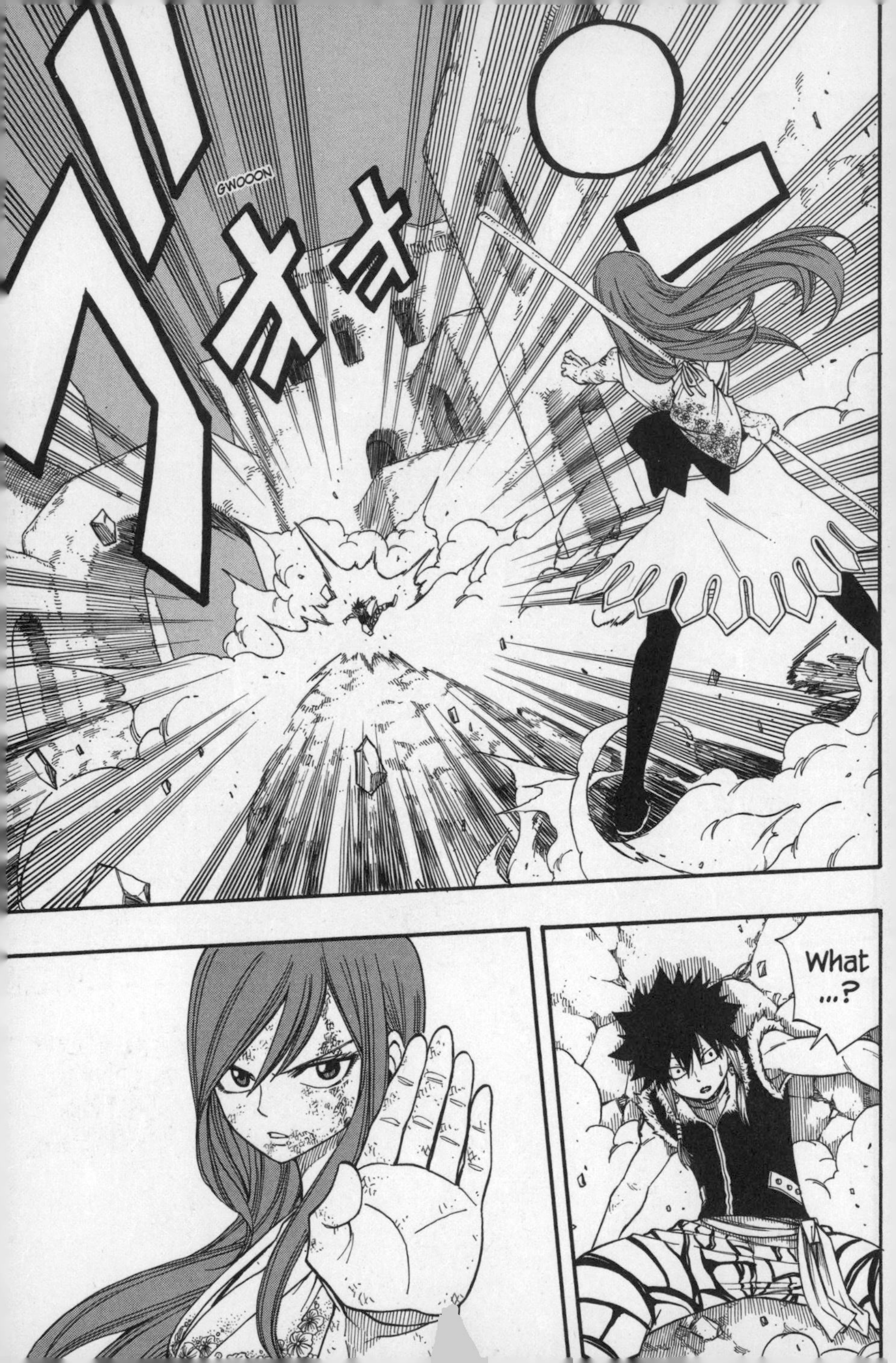
ゴオオン
GWOOON
What ...?

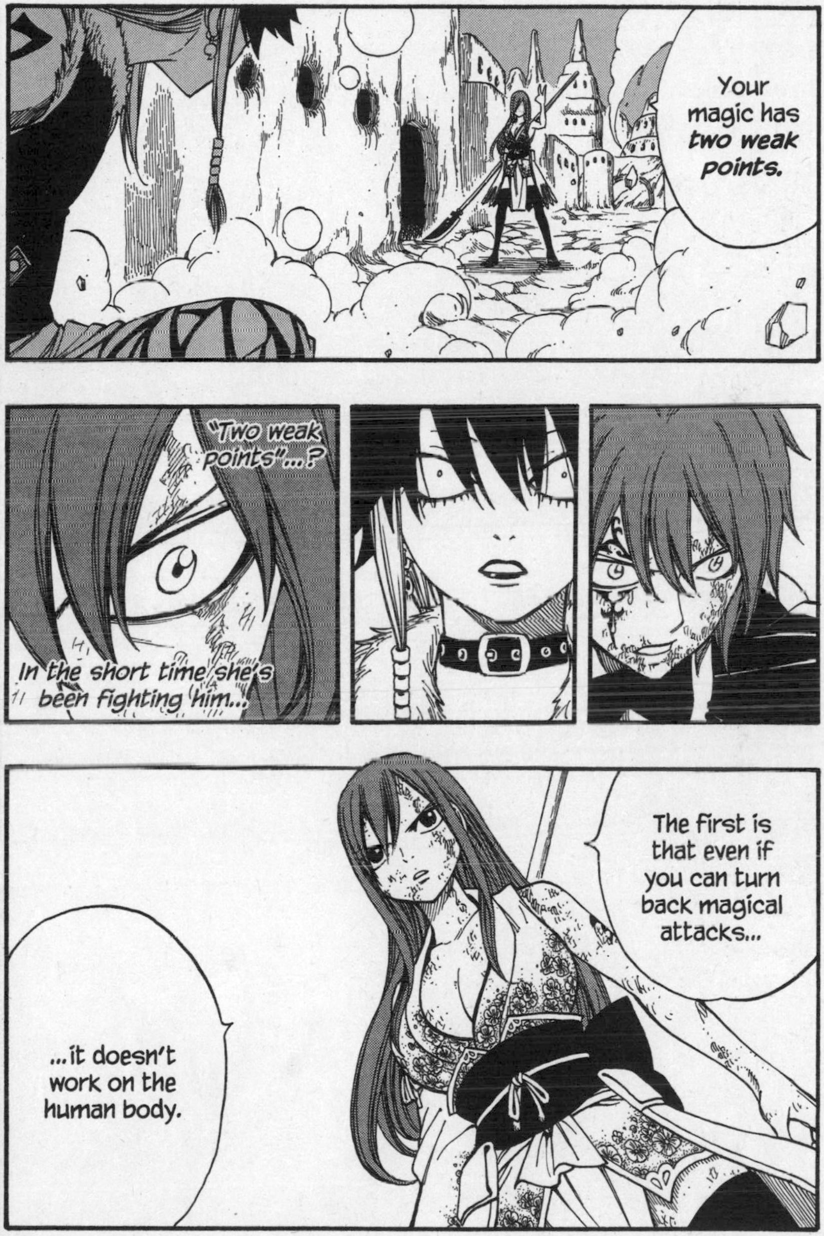
Your magic has *two weak points.*
"Two weak points"...?
In the short time she's been fighting him...
The first is that even if you can turn back magical attacks...
...it doesn't work on the human body.

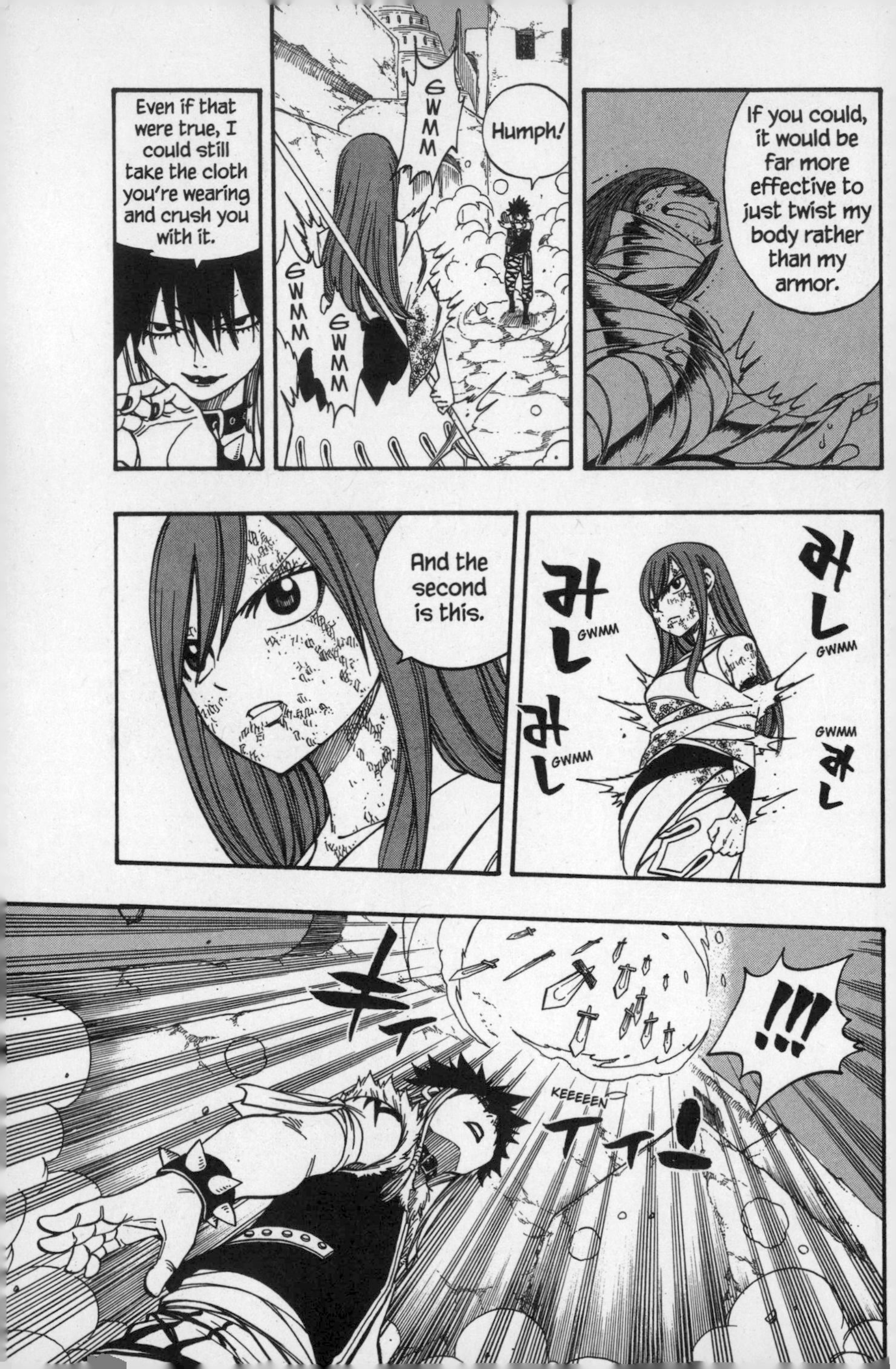
If you could, it would be far more effective to just twist my body rather than my armor.
Humph!
GWMM
GWMM
GWMM
Even if that were true, I could still take the cloth you're wearing and crush you with it.
みし GWMM
GWMM みし
みし GWMM
みし GWMM
And the second is this.
!!!
KEEEEEN

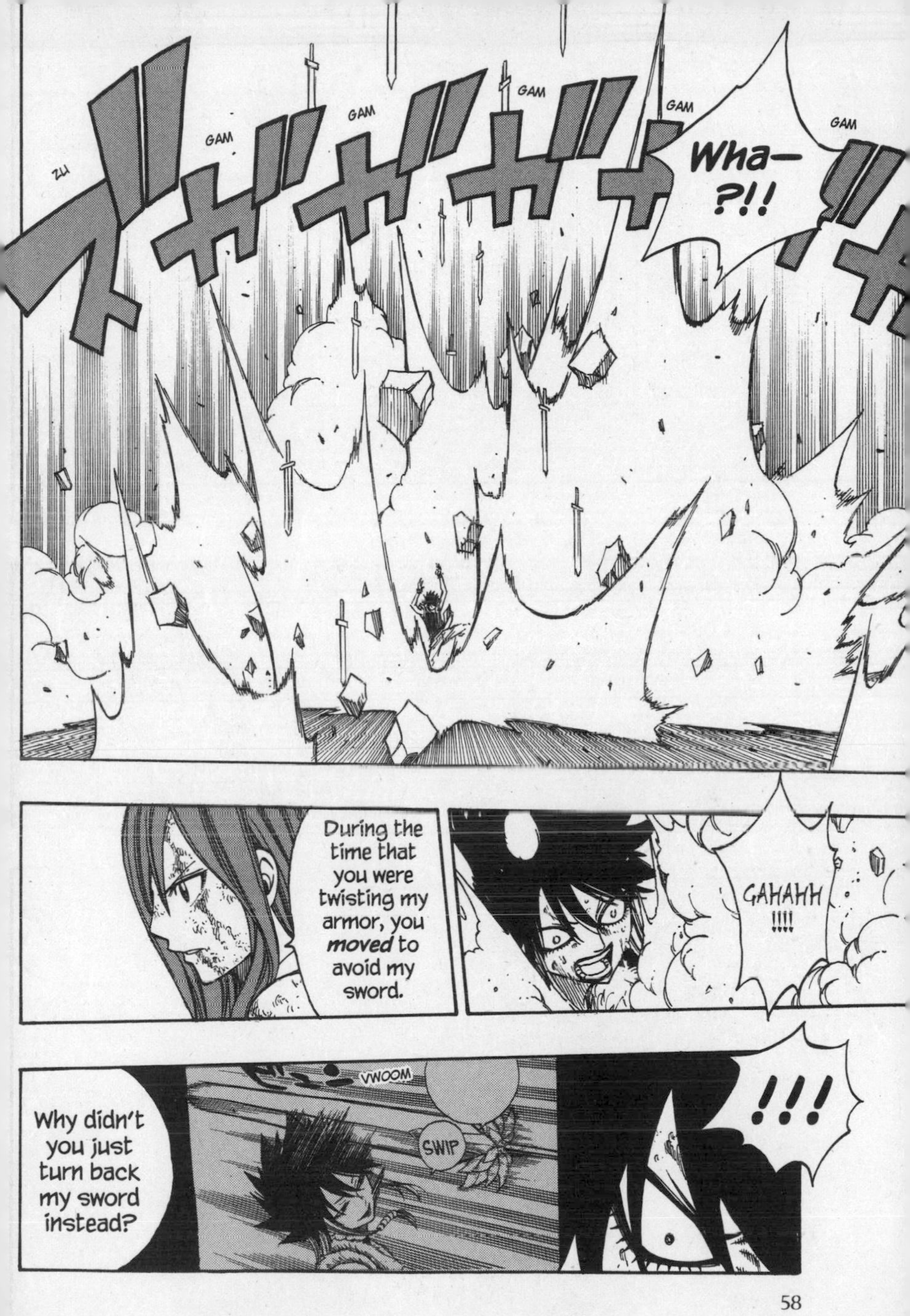
GAM
Wha—?!!
GAM
GAM
GAM
GAM
ZU
GAHAHH !!!!
During the time that you were twisting my armor, you *moved* to avoid my sword.
!!!
VWOOM
SWIP
Why didn't you just turn back my sword instead?

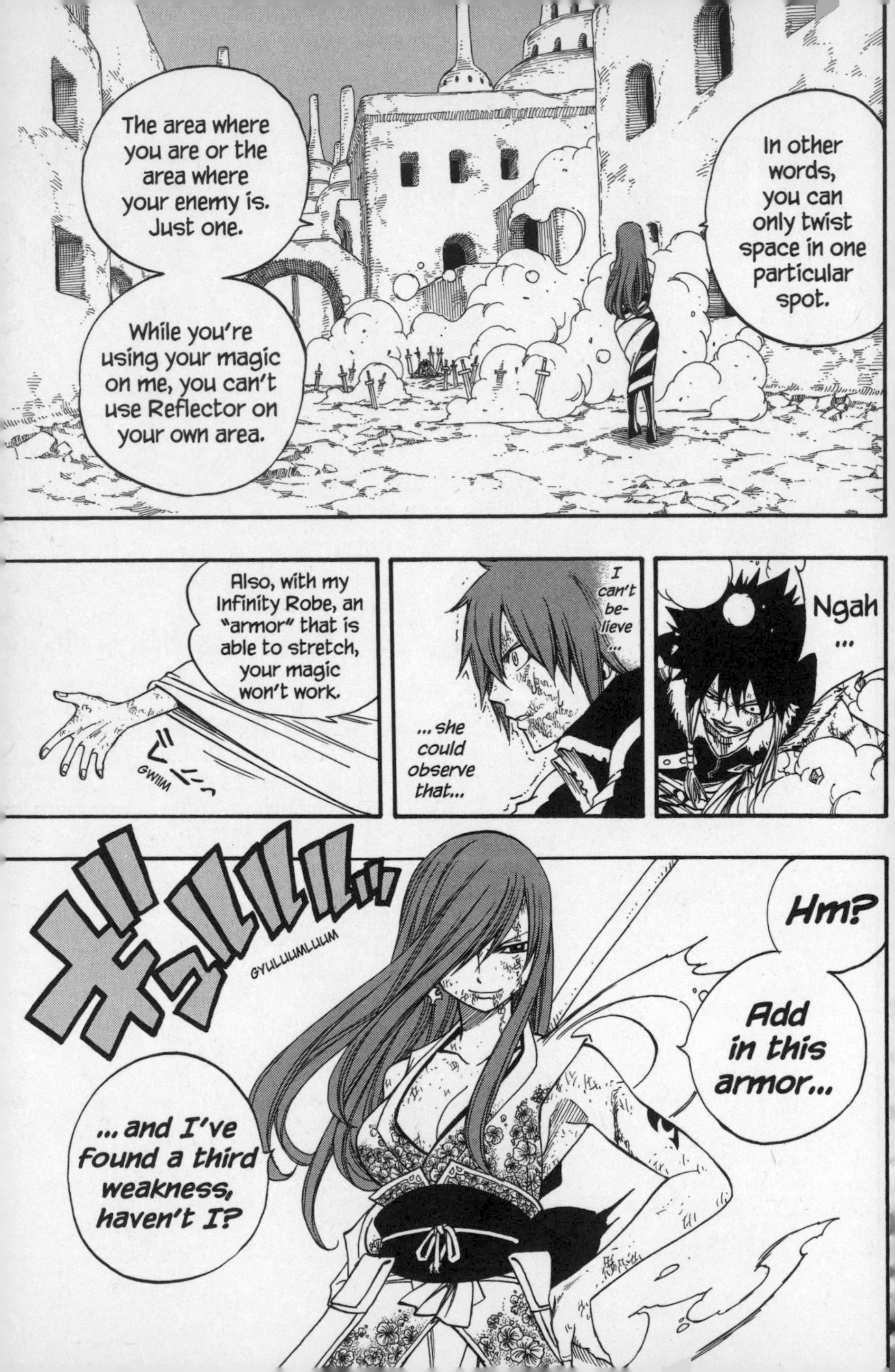
In other words, you can only twist space in one particular spot.
The area where you are or the area where your enemy is. Just one.
While you're using your magic on me, you can't use Reflector on your own area.
Ngah ...
I can't be-lieve ...
... she could observe that...
Also, with my Infinity Robe, an "armor" that is able to stretch, your magic won't work.
GWIM
Hm?
Add in this armor...
... and I've found a third weakness, haven't I?
GYULUUMLUUM

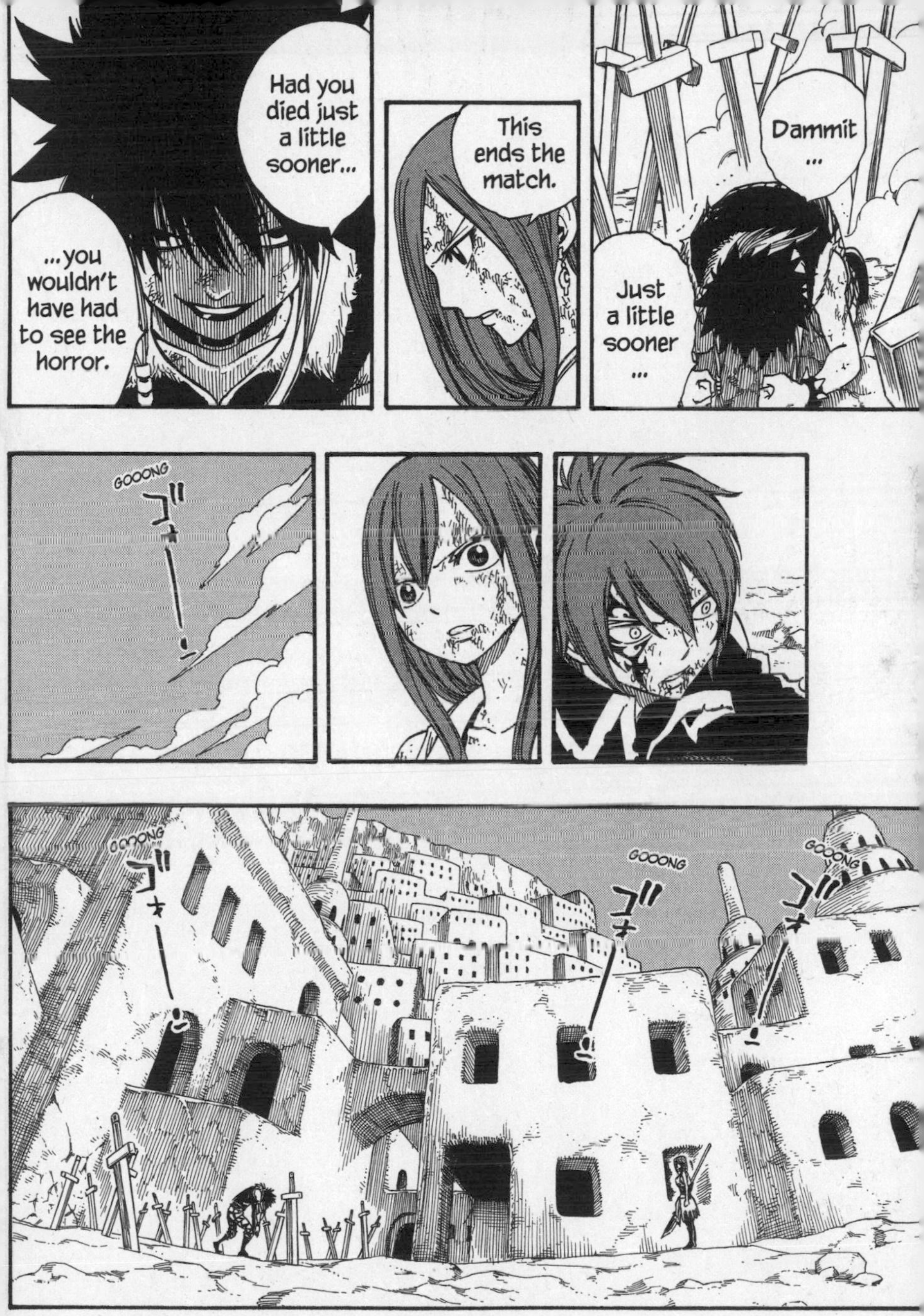
Dammit
...
Just
a little
sooner
...
This
ends the
match.
Had you
died just
a little
sooner...
...you
wouldn't
have had
to see the
horror.
GOOONG
GOOONG
GOOONG
GOOONG

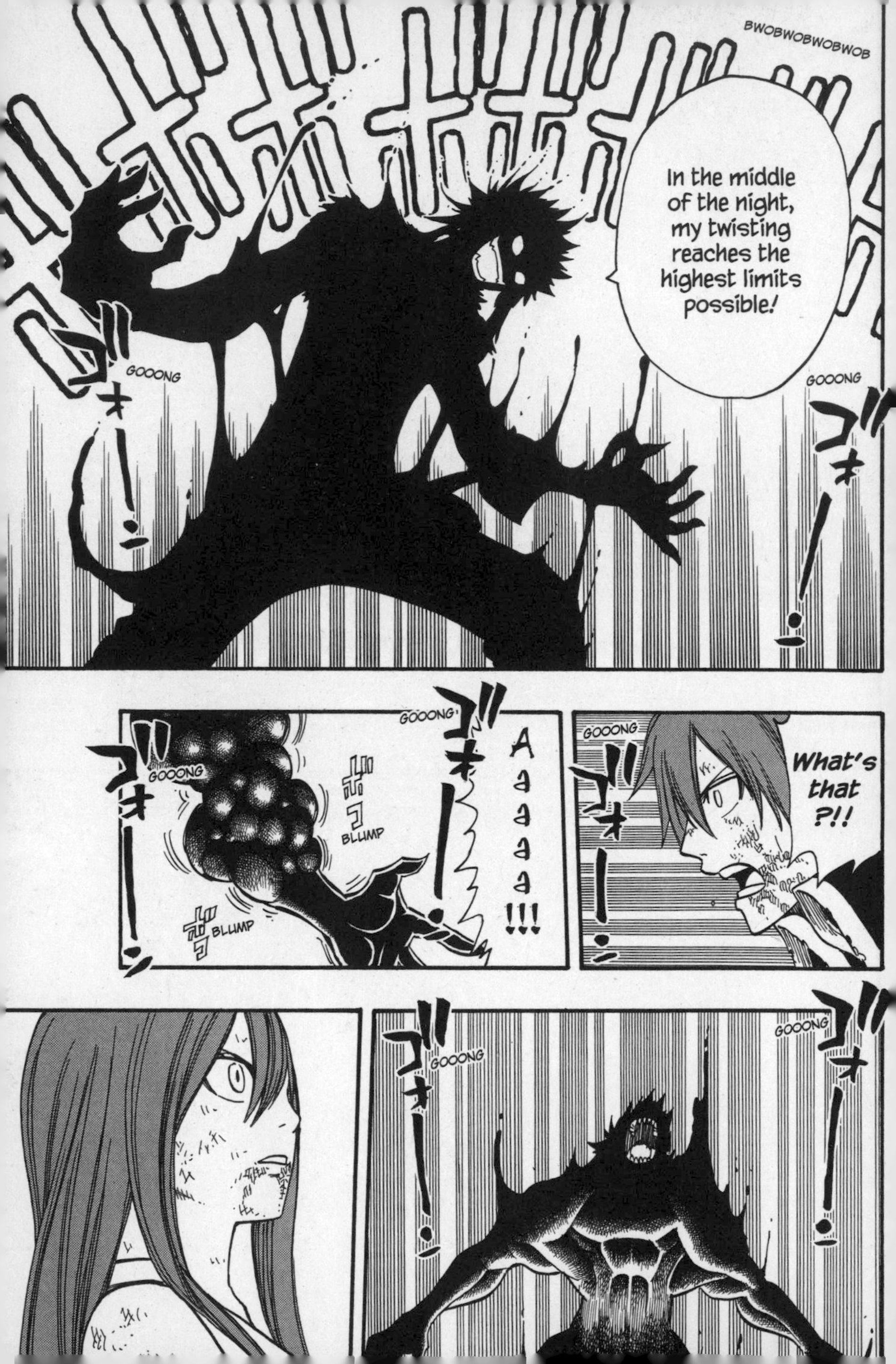
BWOBWOBWOBWOB
In the middle of the night, my twisting reaches the highest limits possible!
GOOONG
GOOONG
GOOONG
What's that ?!!
GOOONG
Aaaaaa!!!
BLUMP
GOOONG
BLUMP
GOOONG
GOOONG

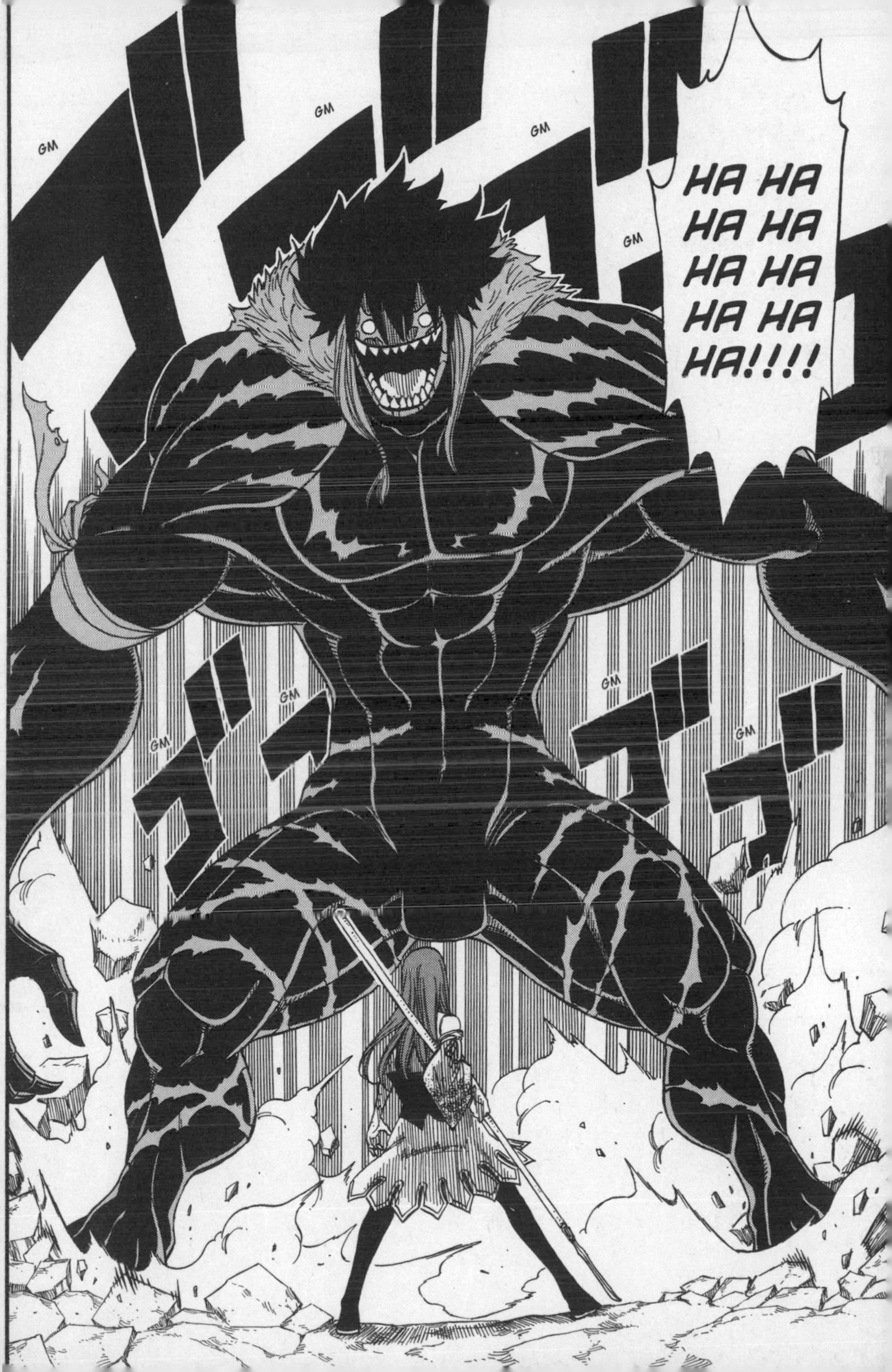
HA HA
HA HA
HA HA
HA HA
HA!!!!
GM
GM
GM
GM
GM
GM
GM
GM

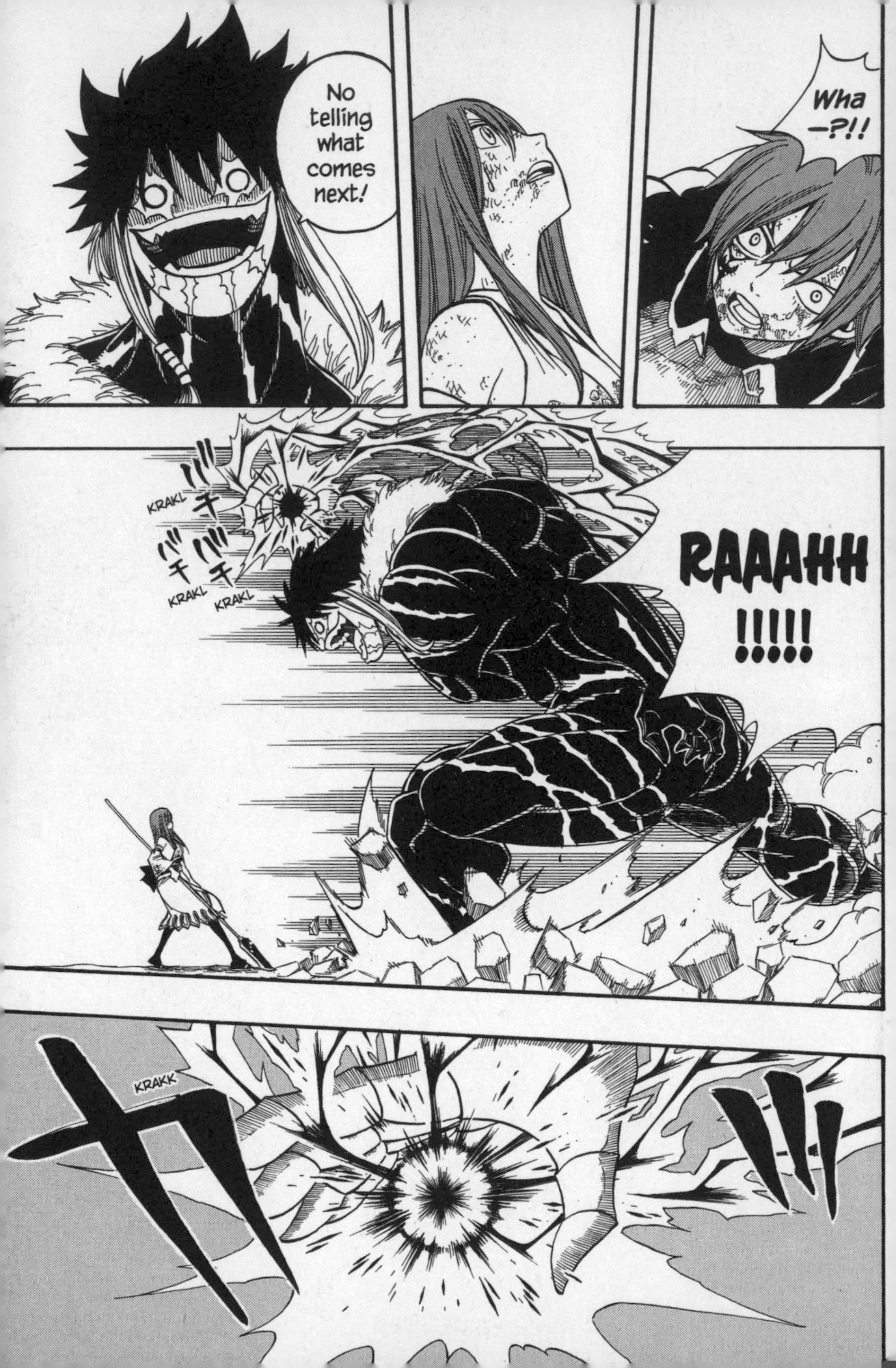
Wha—?!!
No telling what comes next!
RAAAHH!!!!!
バチ
KRAKL
バチ
KRAKL
バチ
KRAKL
KRAKK

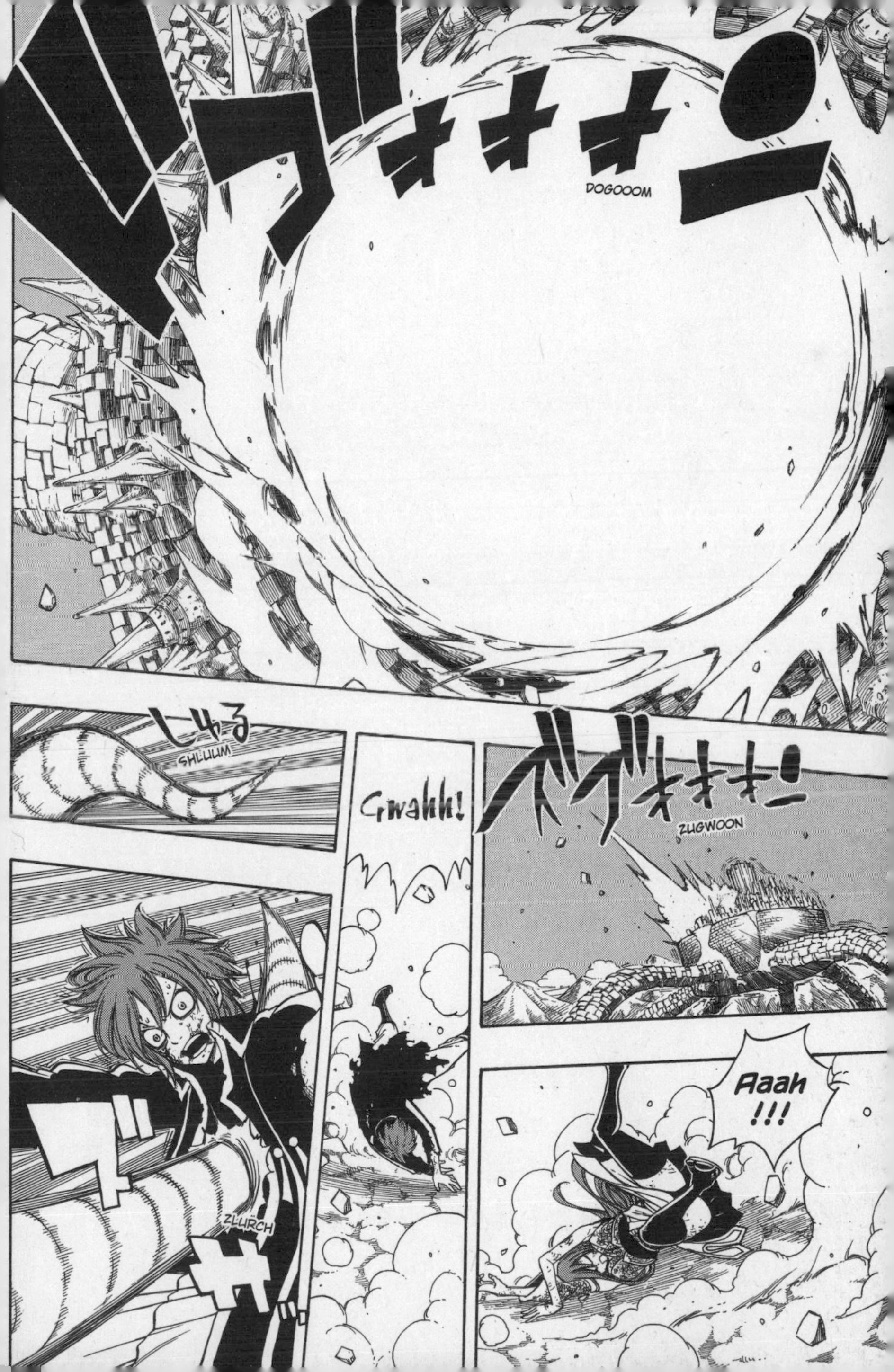
DOGOOOM
ZUGWOON
Aaah !!!
Gwahh!
SHLUUM
ZLURCH

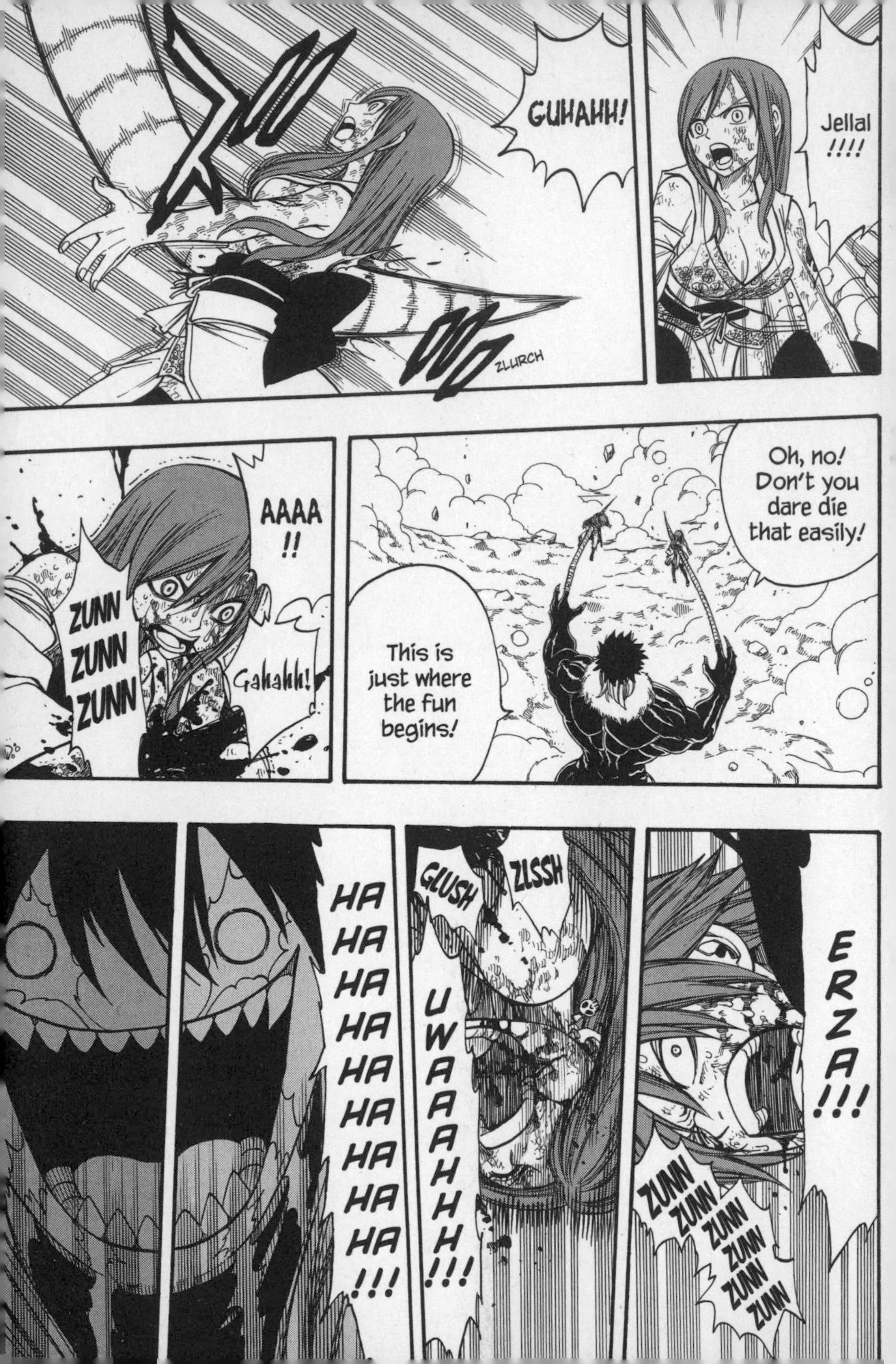

Jellal !!!!
GUHAHH!
ZLURCH
Oh, no! Don't you dare die that easily!
This is just where the fun begins!
AAAA !!
ZUNN ZUNN ZUNN
Gahahh!
ERZA!!!
ZUNN ZUNN ZUNN ZUNN ZUNN ZUNN
ZLSSH
GLUSH
UWAAAHHH!!!
HA HA HA HA HA HA HA HA HA !!!

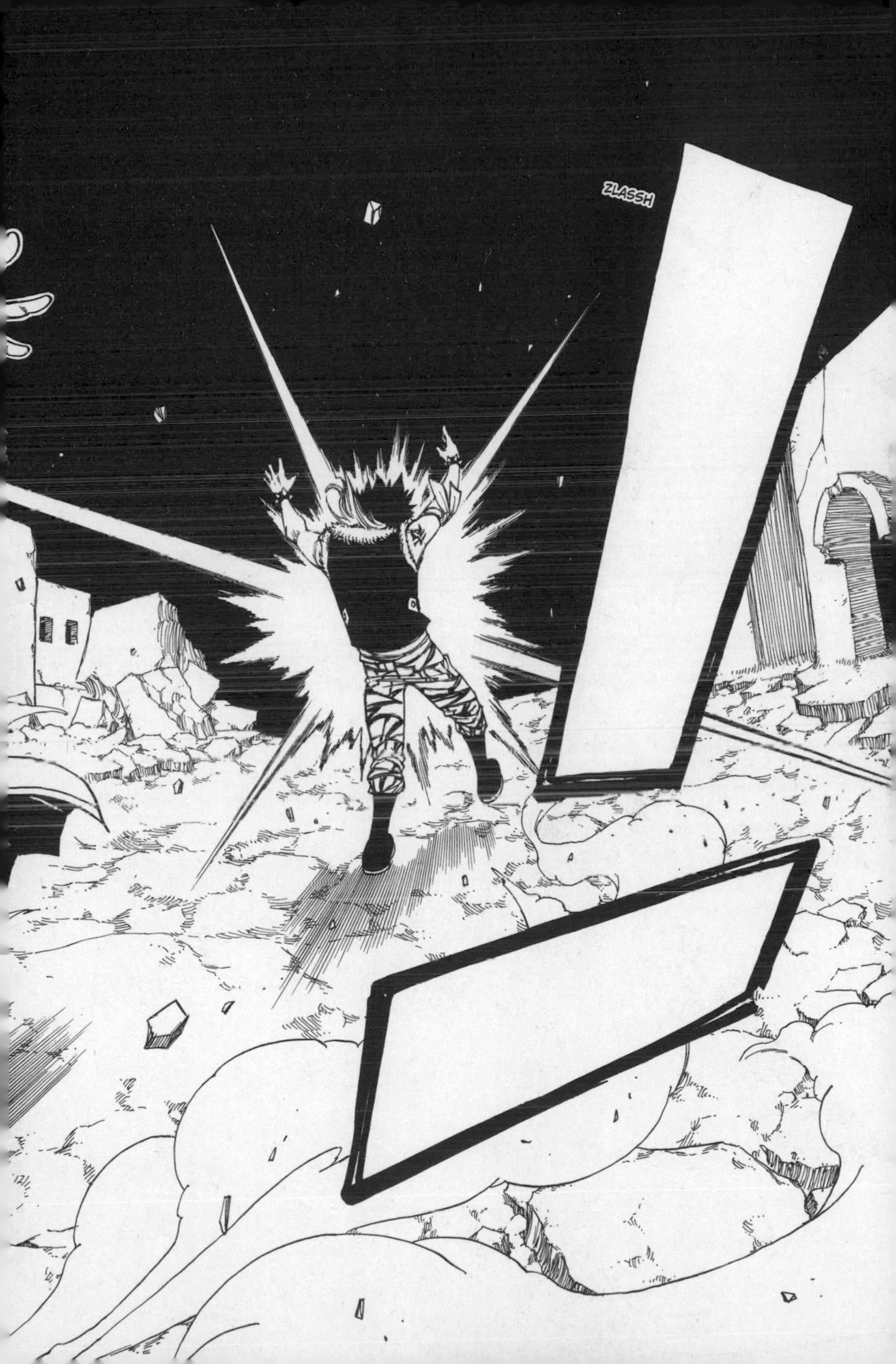
ZLASSH

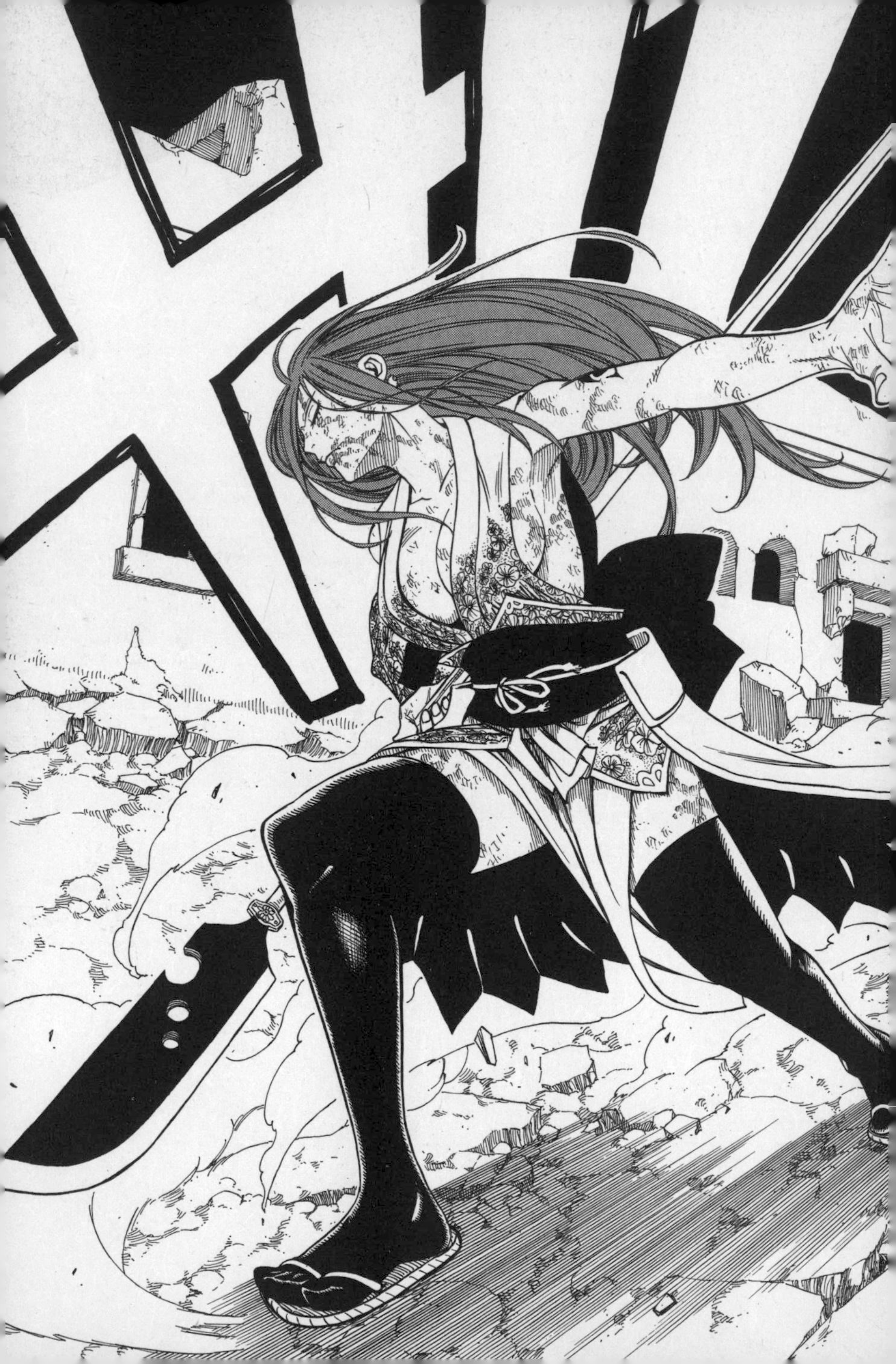

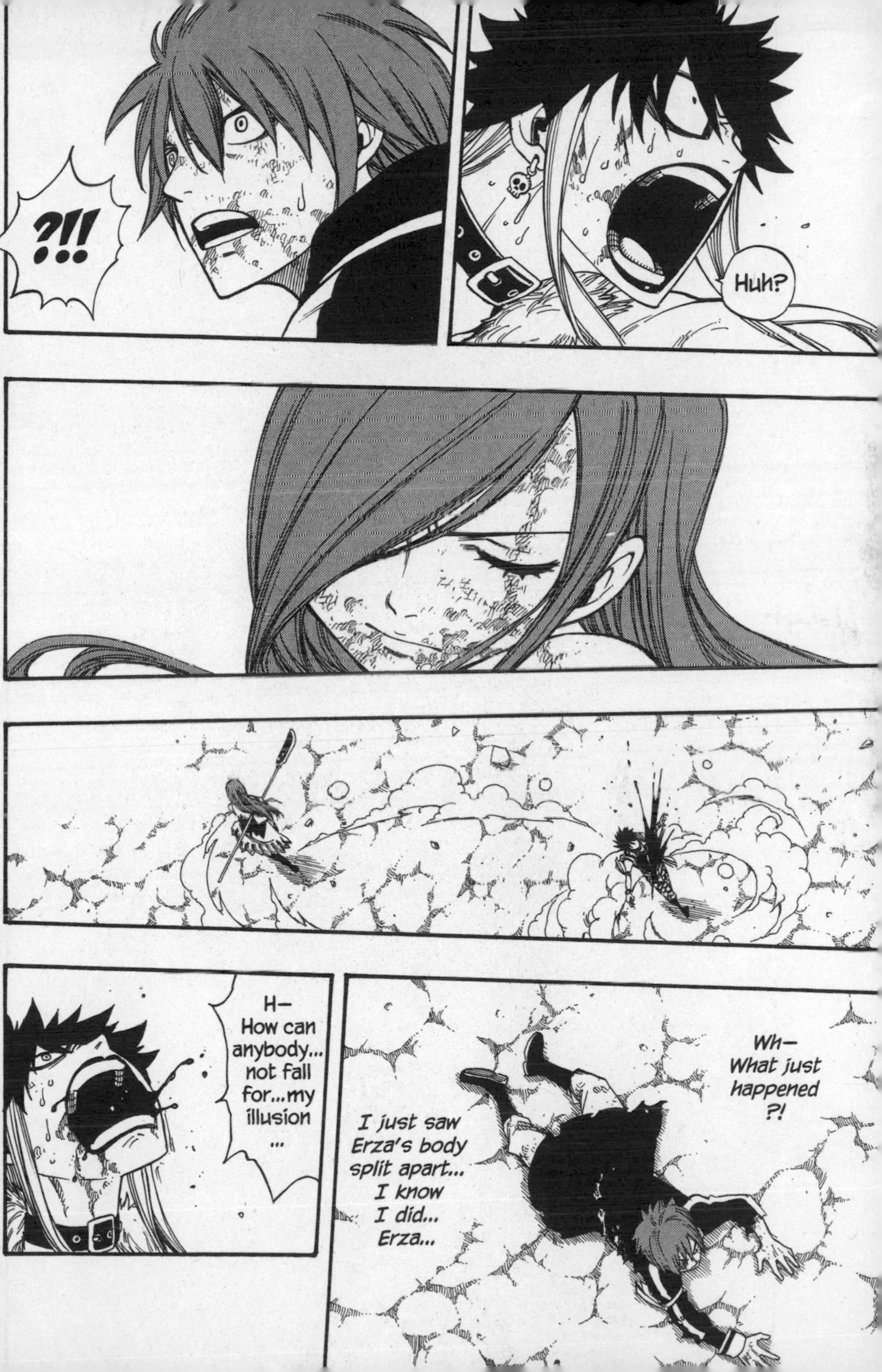
Huh?
?!!
Wh— What just happened ?!
I just saw Erza's body split apart... I know I did... Erza...
H— How can anybody... not fall for...my illusion ...

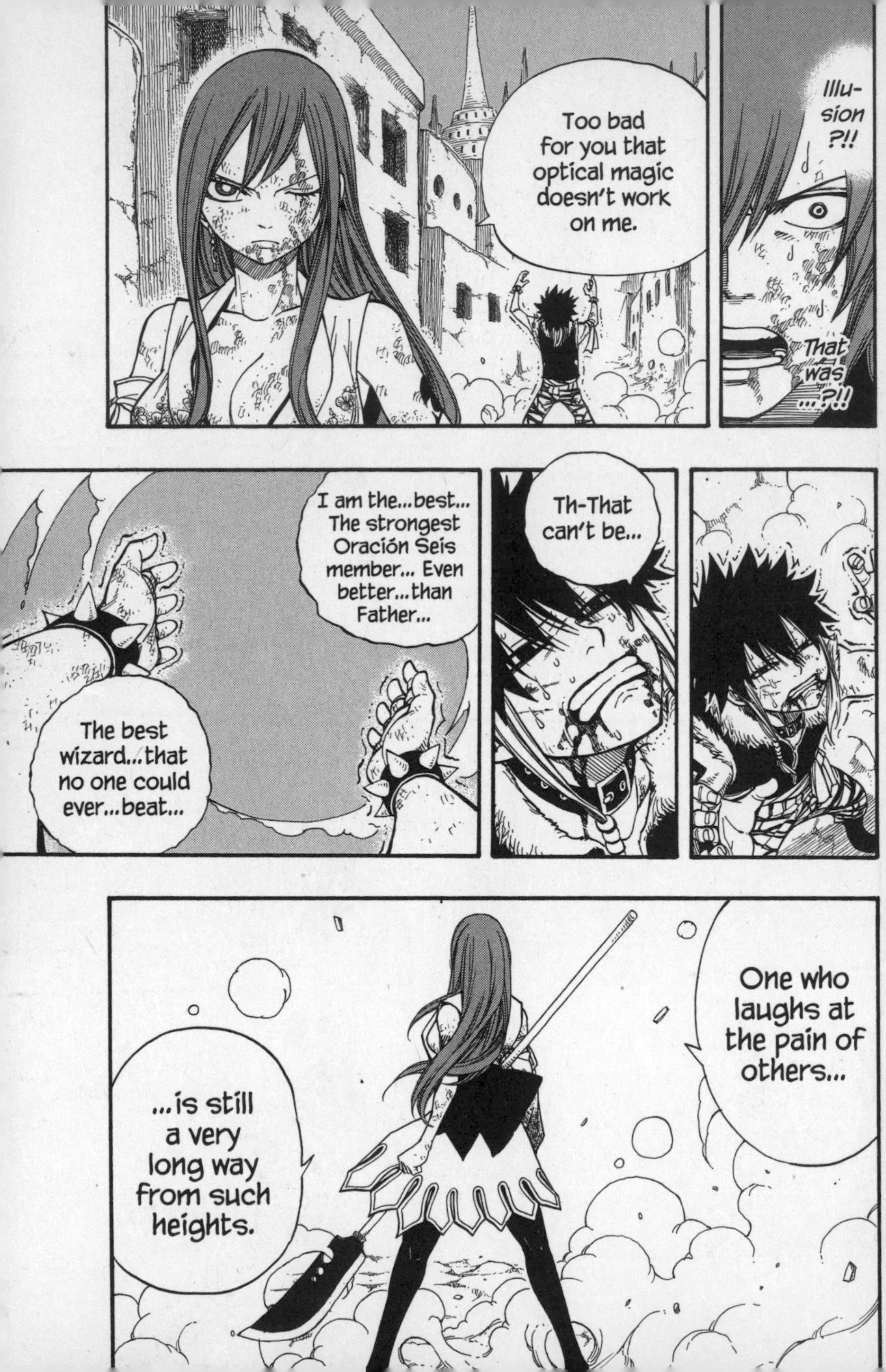
Illu-sion ?!!
That was ...?!!
Too bad for you that optical magic doesn't work on me.
Th-That can't be...
I am the...best... The strongest Oración Seis member... Even better...than Father...
The best wizard...that no one could ever...beat...
One who laughs at the pain of others...
...is still a very long way from such heights.

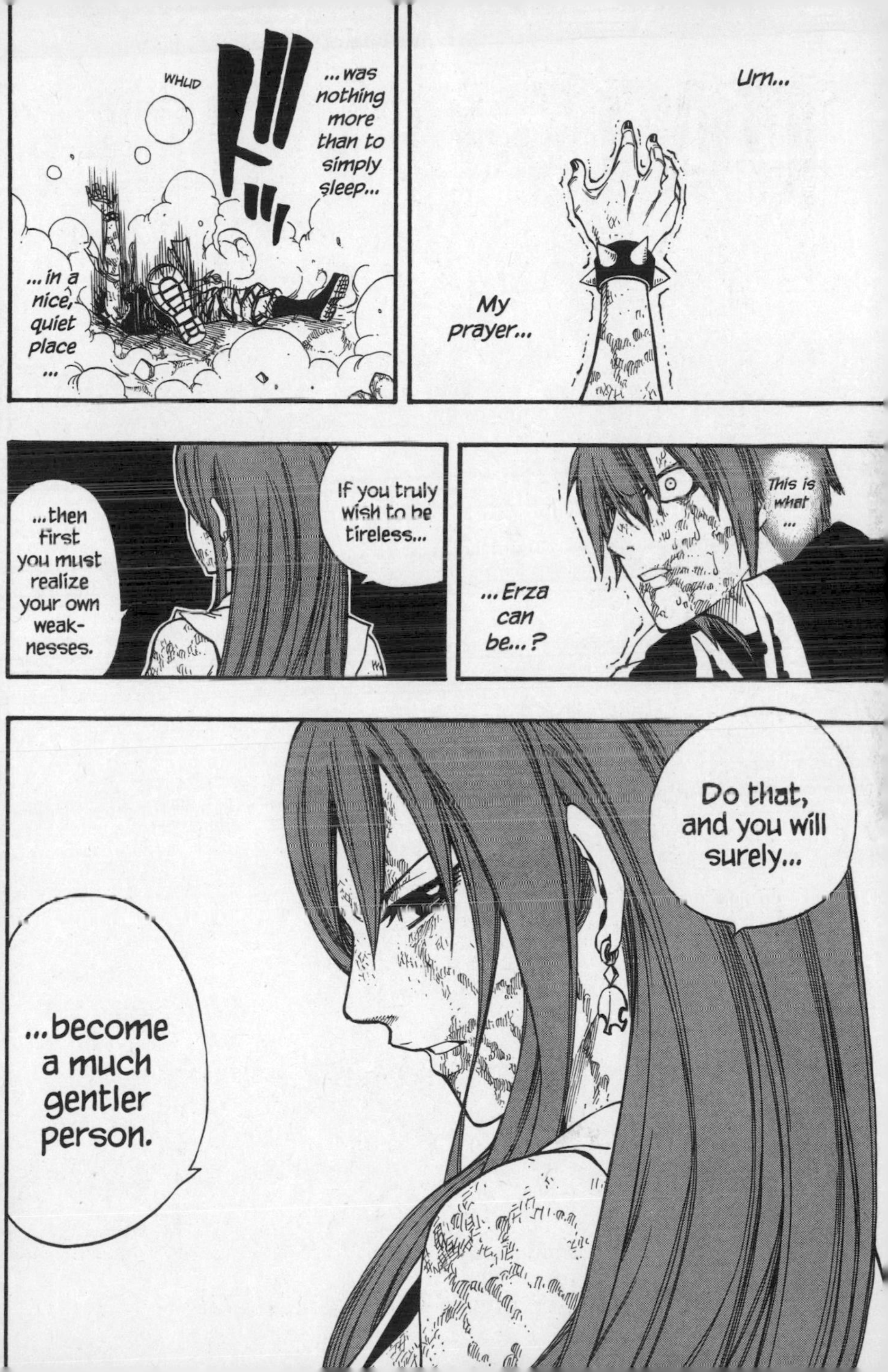
Urn...
My prayer...
...was nothing more than to simply sleep...
WHUD
...in a nice, quiet place...
This is what...
...Erza can be...?
If you truly wish to be tireless...
...then first you must realize your own weak-nesses.
Do that, and you will surely...
...become a much gentler person.

FAIRY TAIL

フェアリーテイル

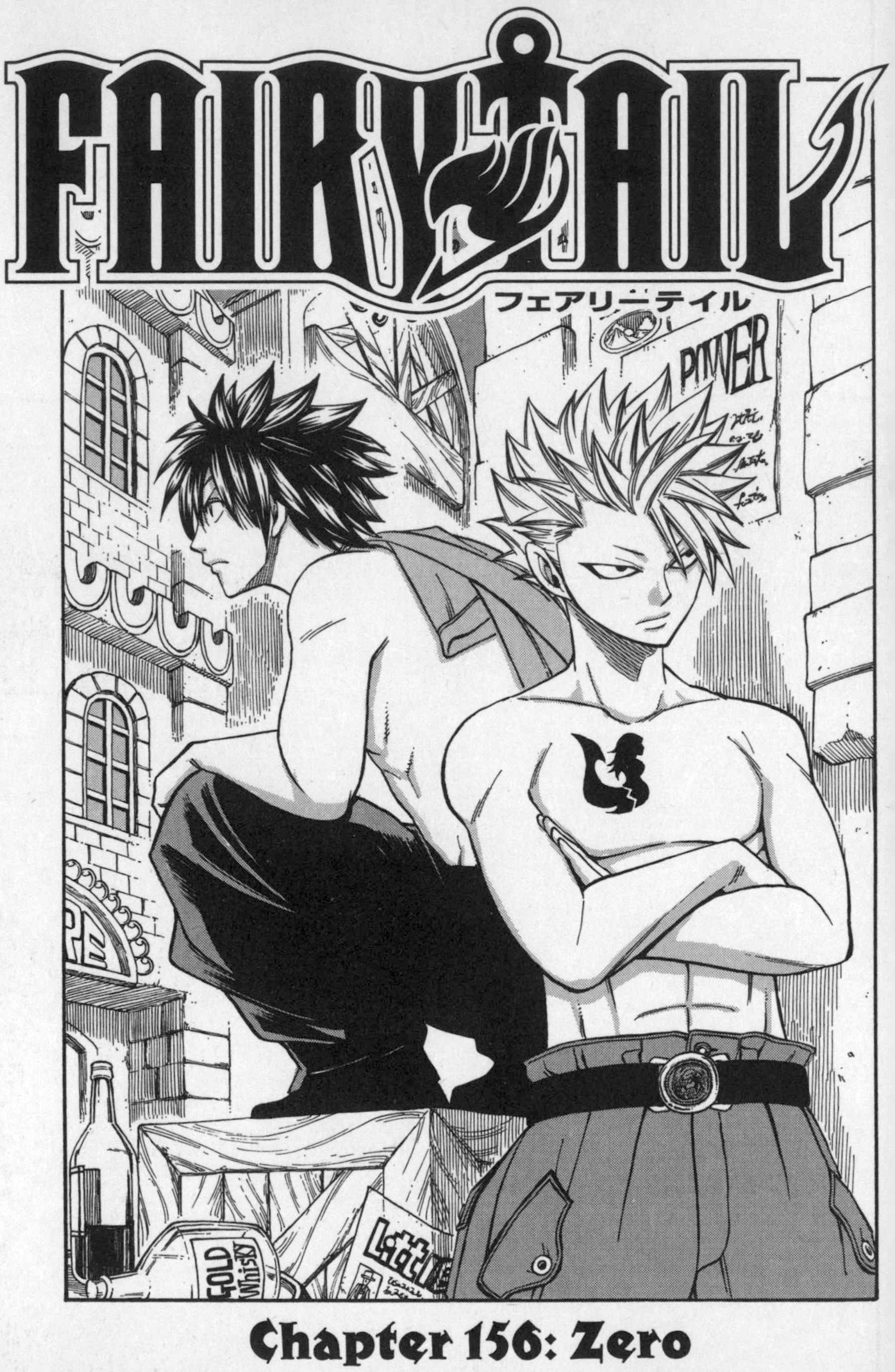
GOLD
Whisky

Chapter 156: Zero

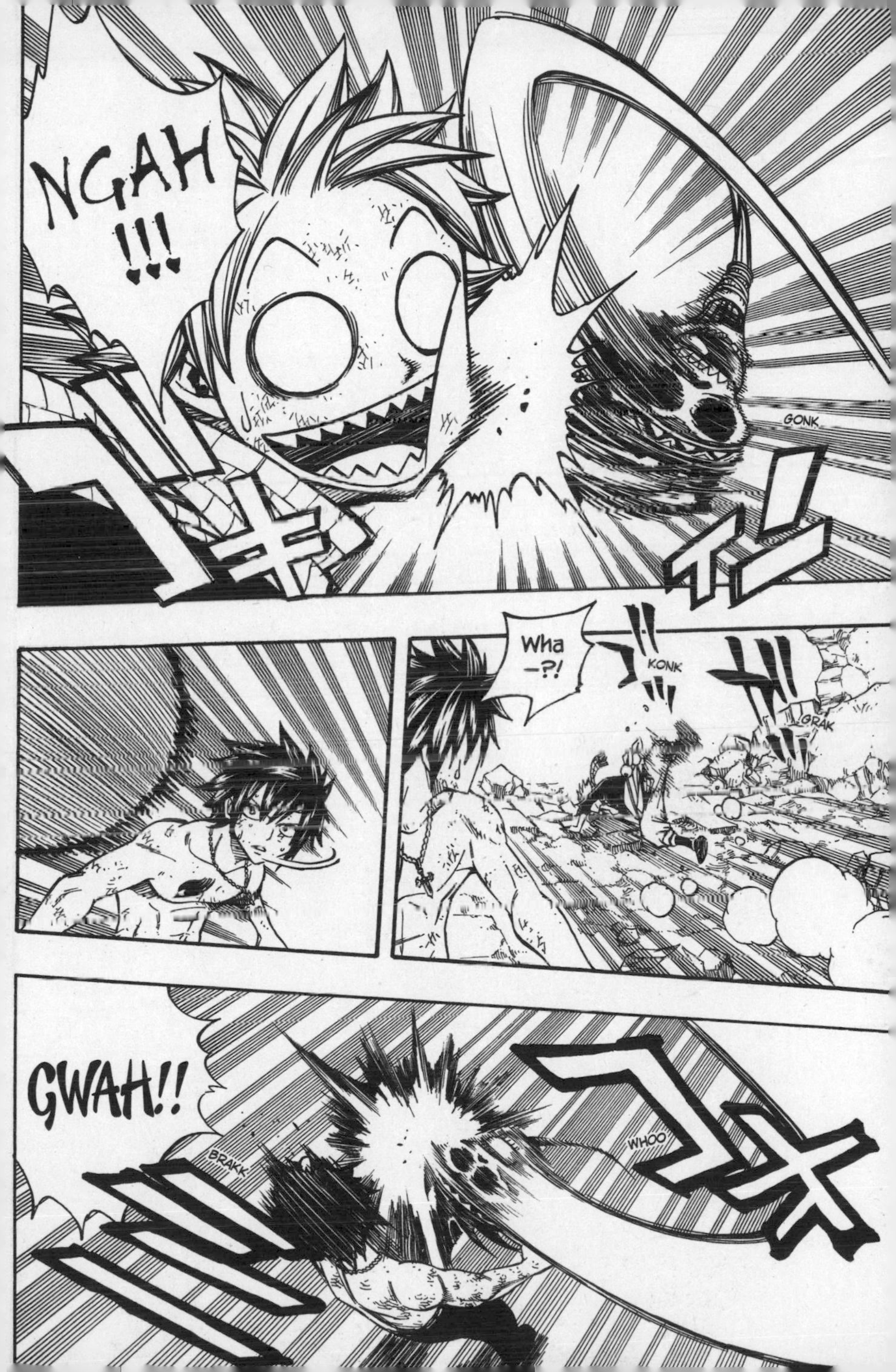

GONK
NGAH !!!
Wha —?!
KONK
GRAK
WHOO
GWAH!!
BRAKK

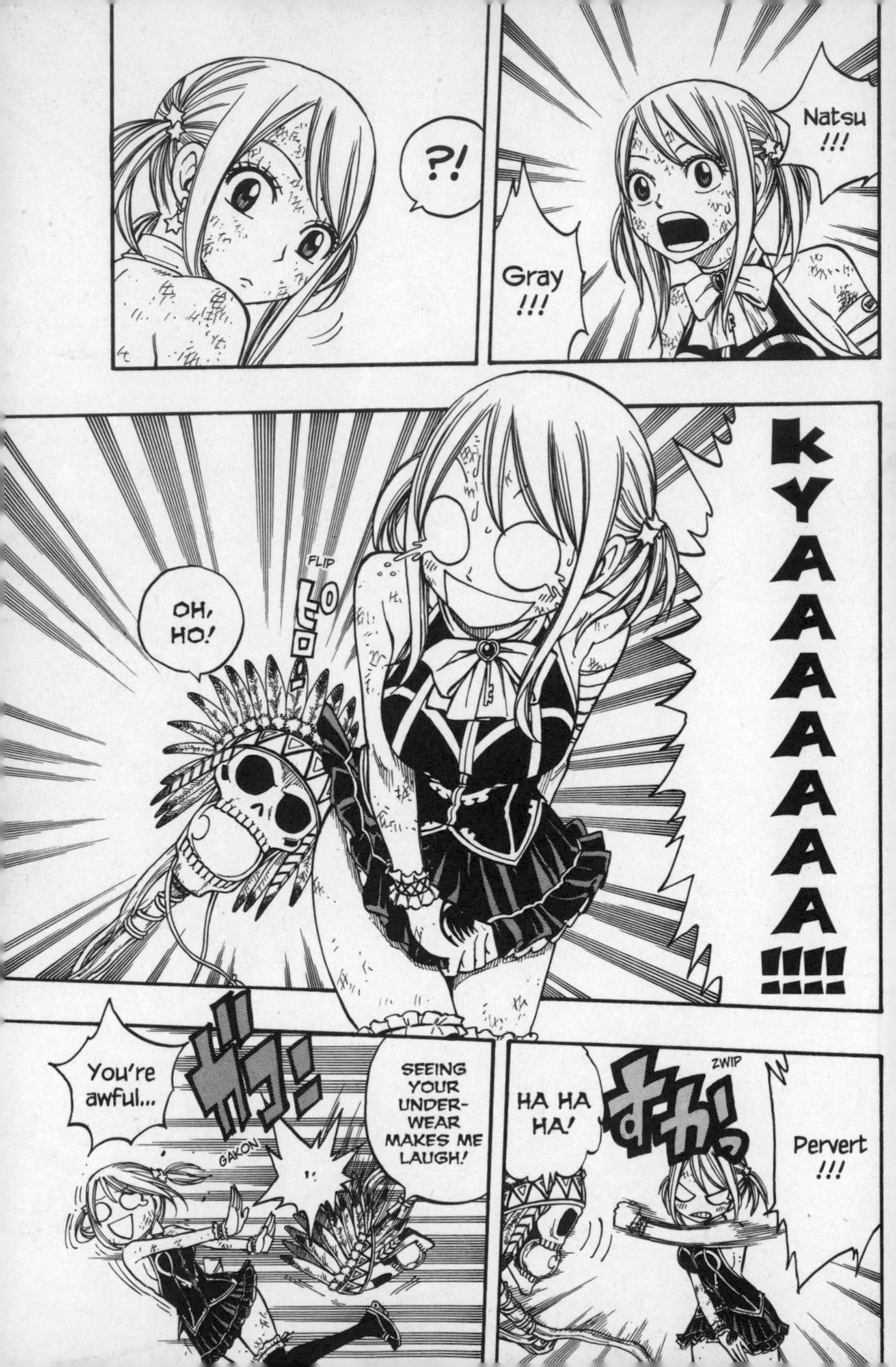
Natsu !!!
Gray !!!
?!
KYAAAAAAA !!!!
FLIP
OH, HO!
Pervert !!!
ZWIP
HA HA HA!
SEEING YOUR UNDER-WEAR MAKES ME LAUGH!
You're awful...
GAKON

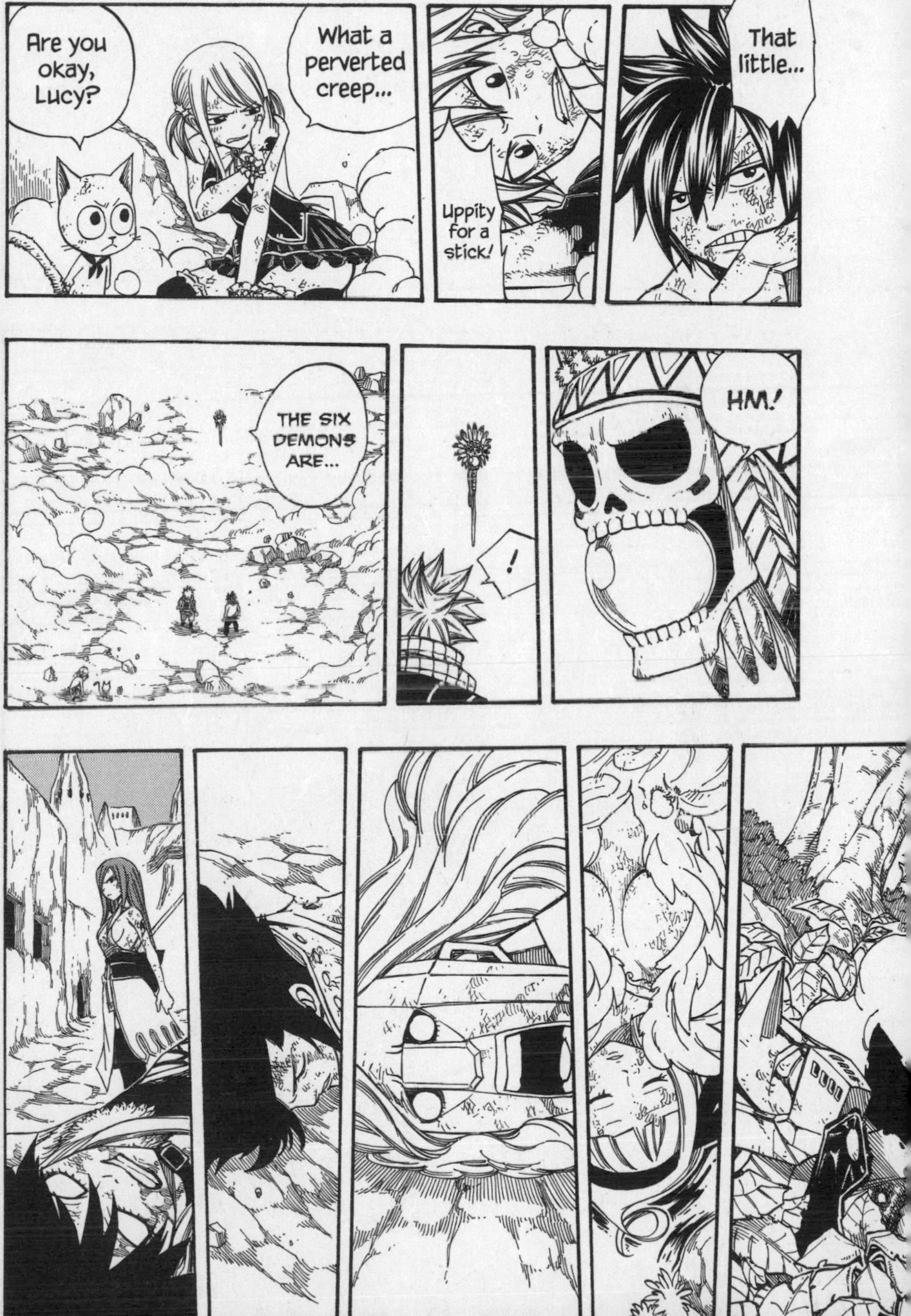

That little...
Uppity for a stick!
What a perverted creep...
Are you okay, Lucy?
HM!
!
THE SIX DEMONS ARE...

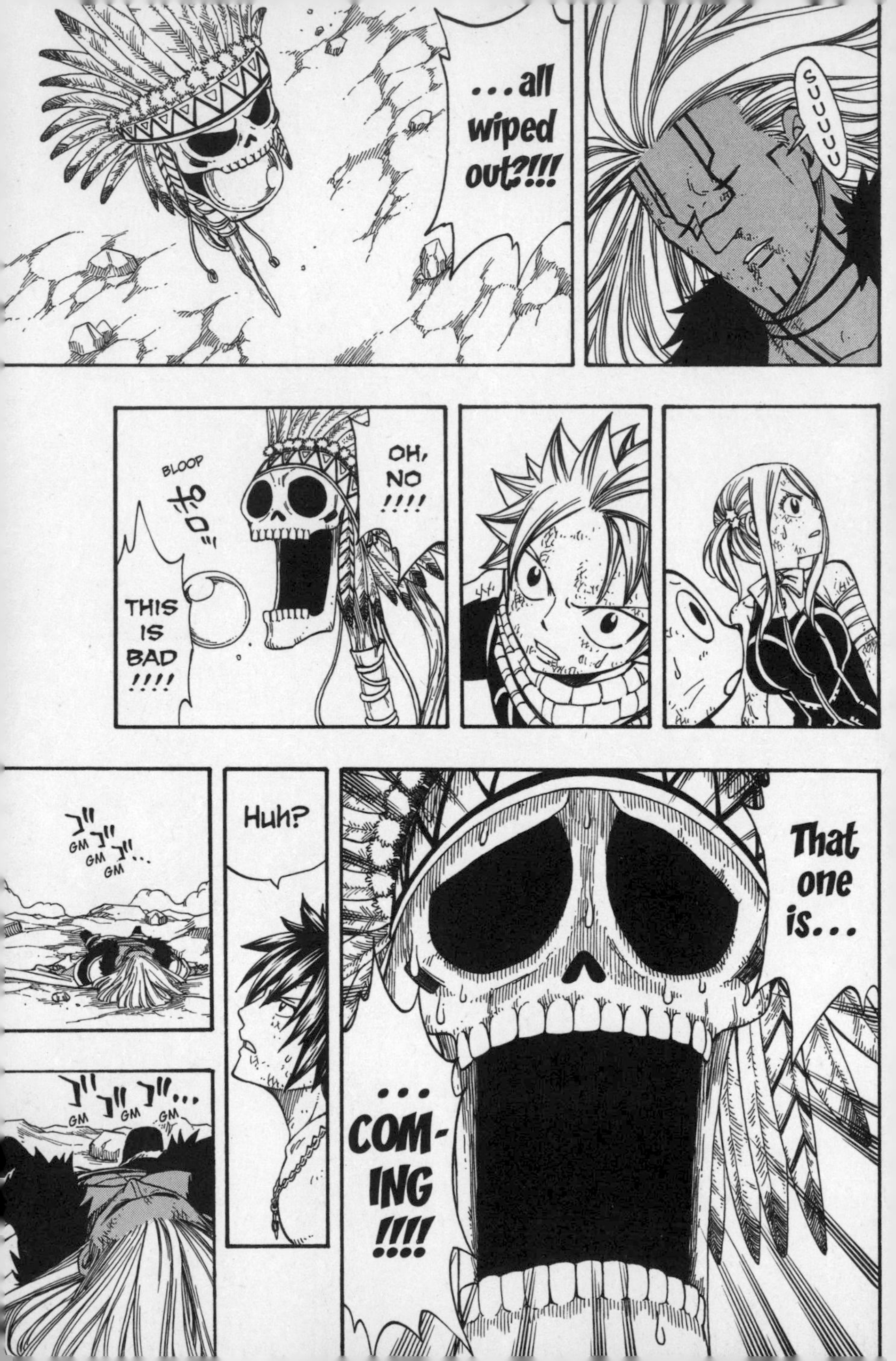
SUUUUU
...all wiped out?!!!
OH, NO!!!!
BLOOP
THIS IS BAD!!!!
That one is...
...COMING!!!!
Huh?
GM GM GM...
GM GM GM...

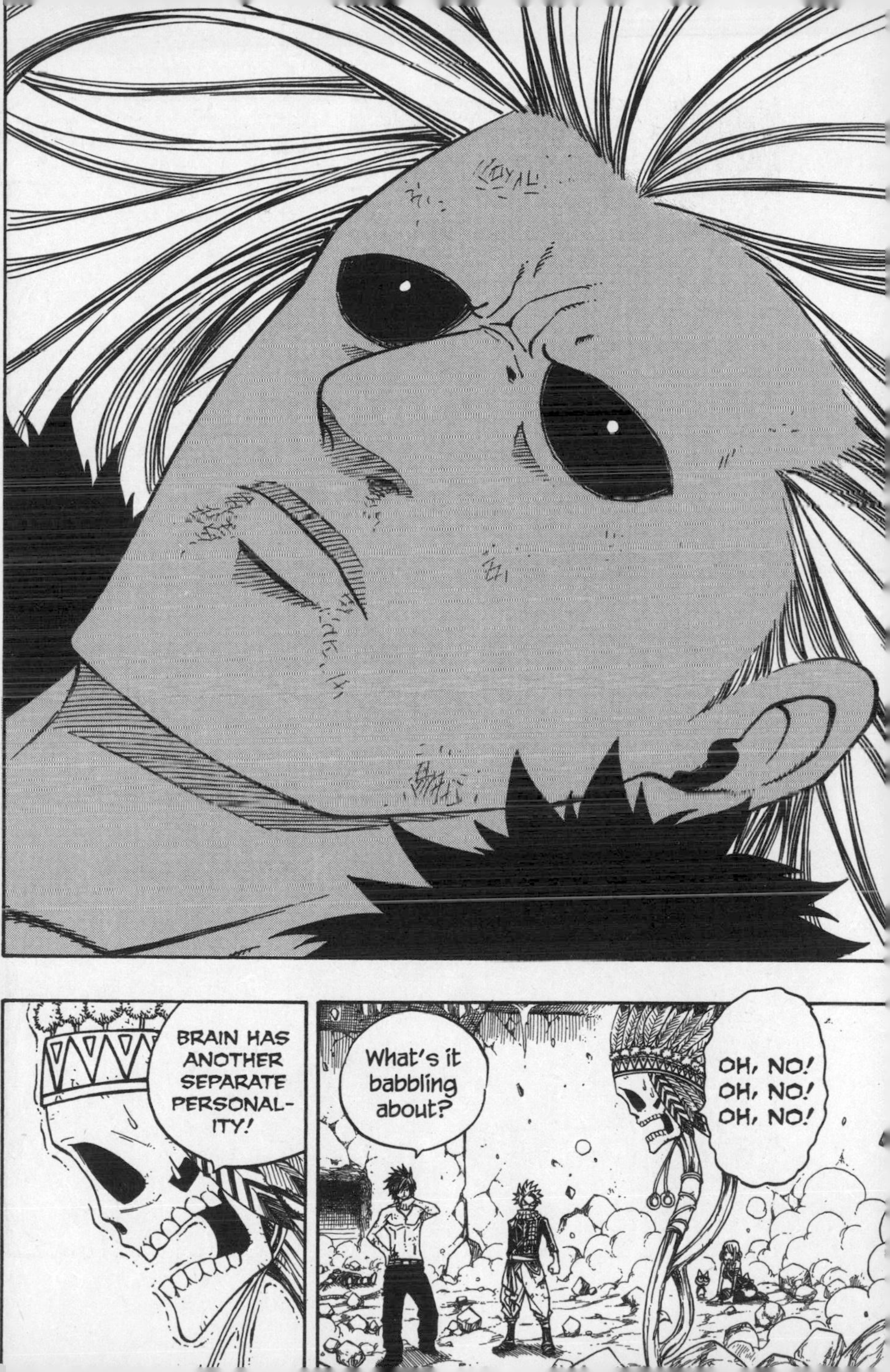
OH, NO! OH, NO! OH, NO!
What's it babbling about?
BRAIN HAS ANOTHER SEPARATE PERSONAL-ITY!

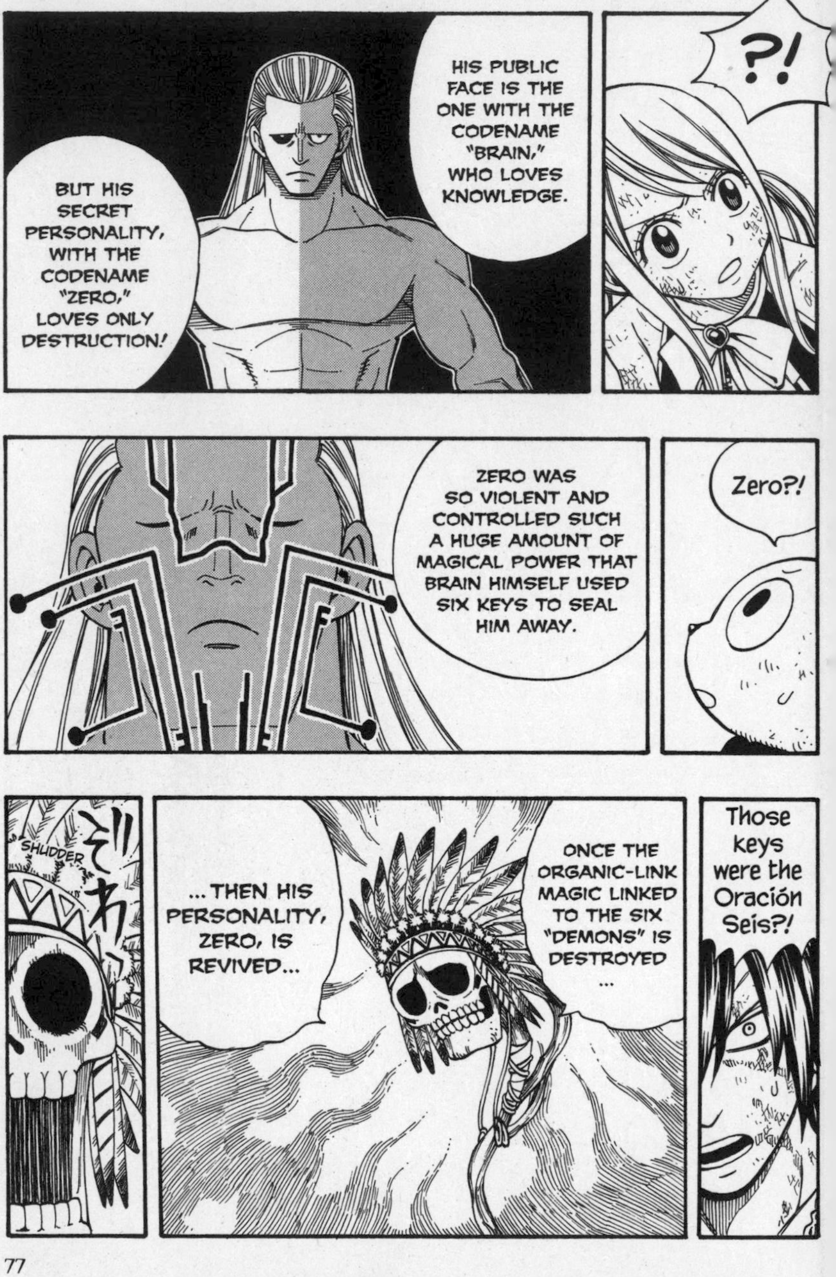
?!
HIS PUBLIC FACE IS THE ONE WITH THE CODENAME "BRAIN," WHO LOVES KNOWLEDGE.
BUT HIS SECRET PERSONALITY, WITH THE CODENAME "ZERO," LOVES ONLY DESTRUCTION!
Zero?!
ZERO WAS SO VIOLENT AND CONTROLLED SUCH A HUGE AMOUNT OF MAGICAL POWER THAT BRAIN HIMSELF USED SIX KEYS TO SEAL HIM AWAY.
Those keys were the Oración Seis?!
ONCE THE ORGANIC-LINK MAGIC LINKED TO THE SIX "DEMONS" IS DESTROYED ...
...THEN HIS PERSONALITY, ZERO, IS REVIVED...
SHUDDER

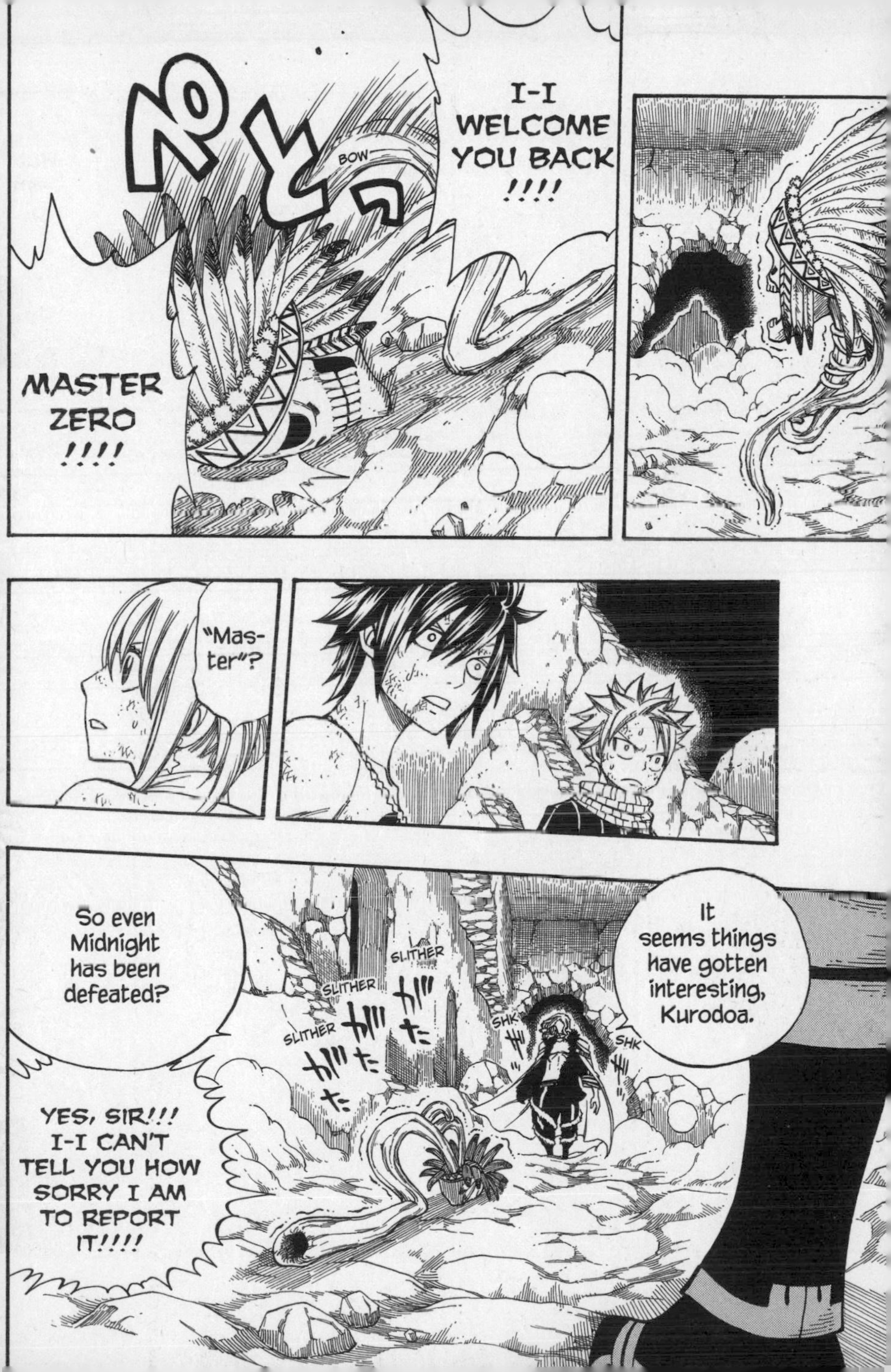

I-I WELCOME YOU BACK !!!!
BOW
MASTER ZERO !!!!
"Master"?
It seems things have gotten interesting, Kurodoa.
SHK
SHK
SLITHER
SLITHER
SLITHER
So even Midnight has been defeated?
YES, SIR!!! I-I CAN'T TELL YOU HOW SORRY I AM TO REPORT IT!!!!

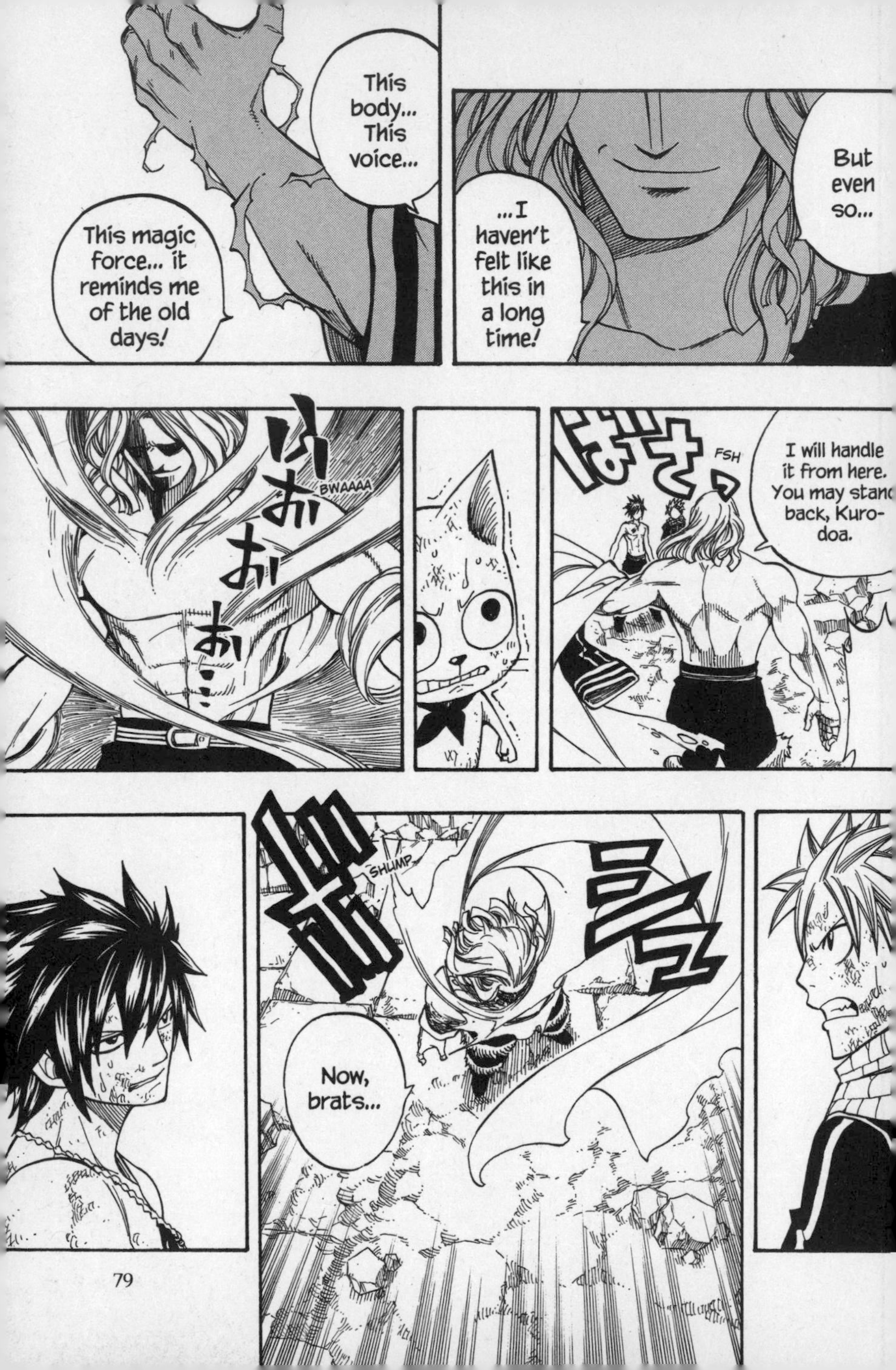
But even so...
...I haven't felt like this in a long time!
This body... This voice...
This magic force... it reminds me of the old days!
FSH
I will handle it from here. You may stand back, Kuro-doa.
BWAAAA
SHUMP
Now, brats...

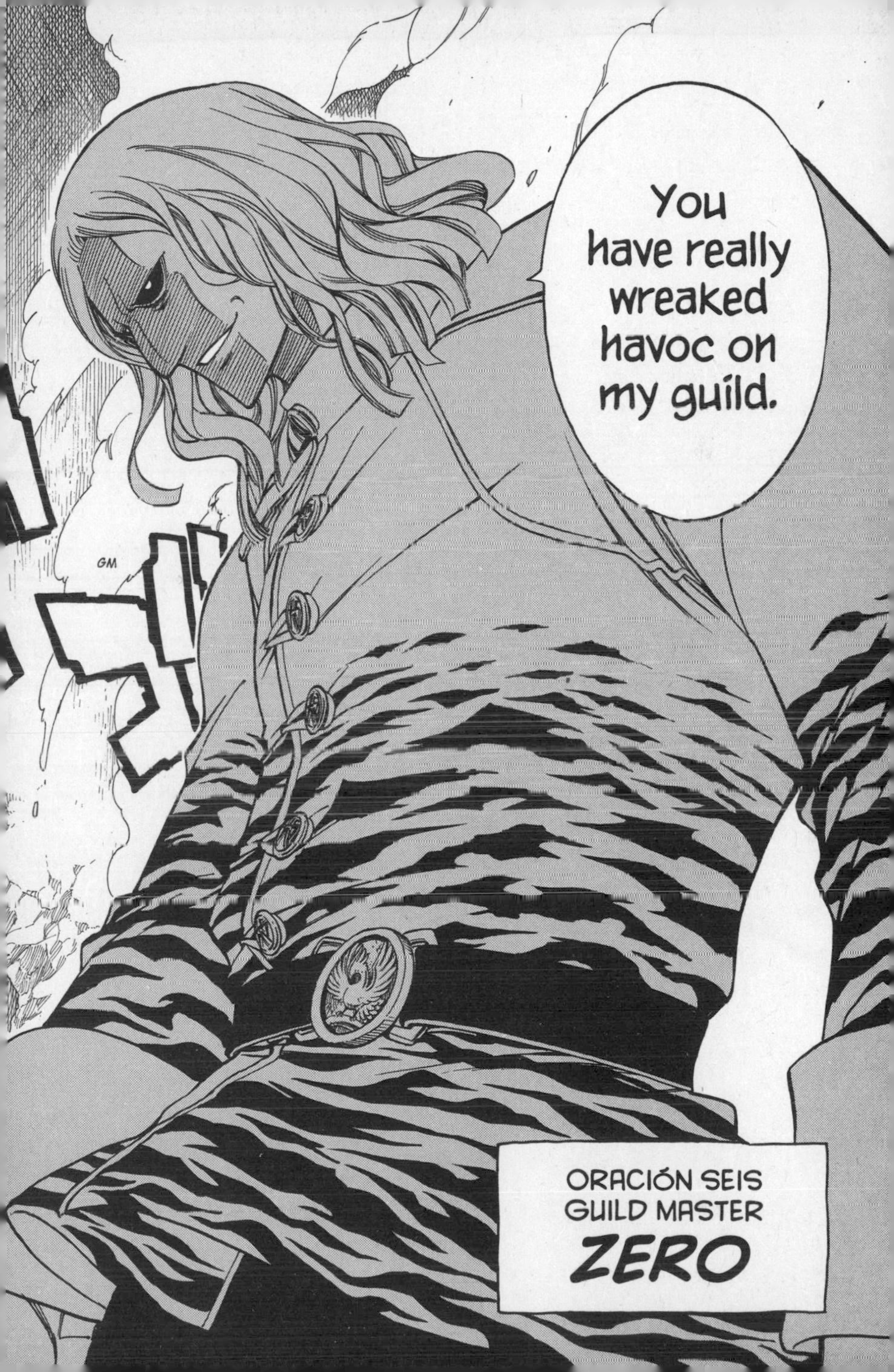
You have really wreaked havoc on my guild.
GM
ORACIÓN SEIS GUILD MASTER ZERO

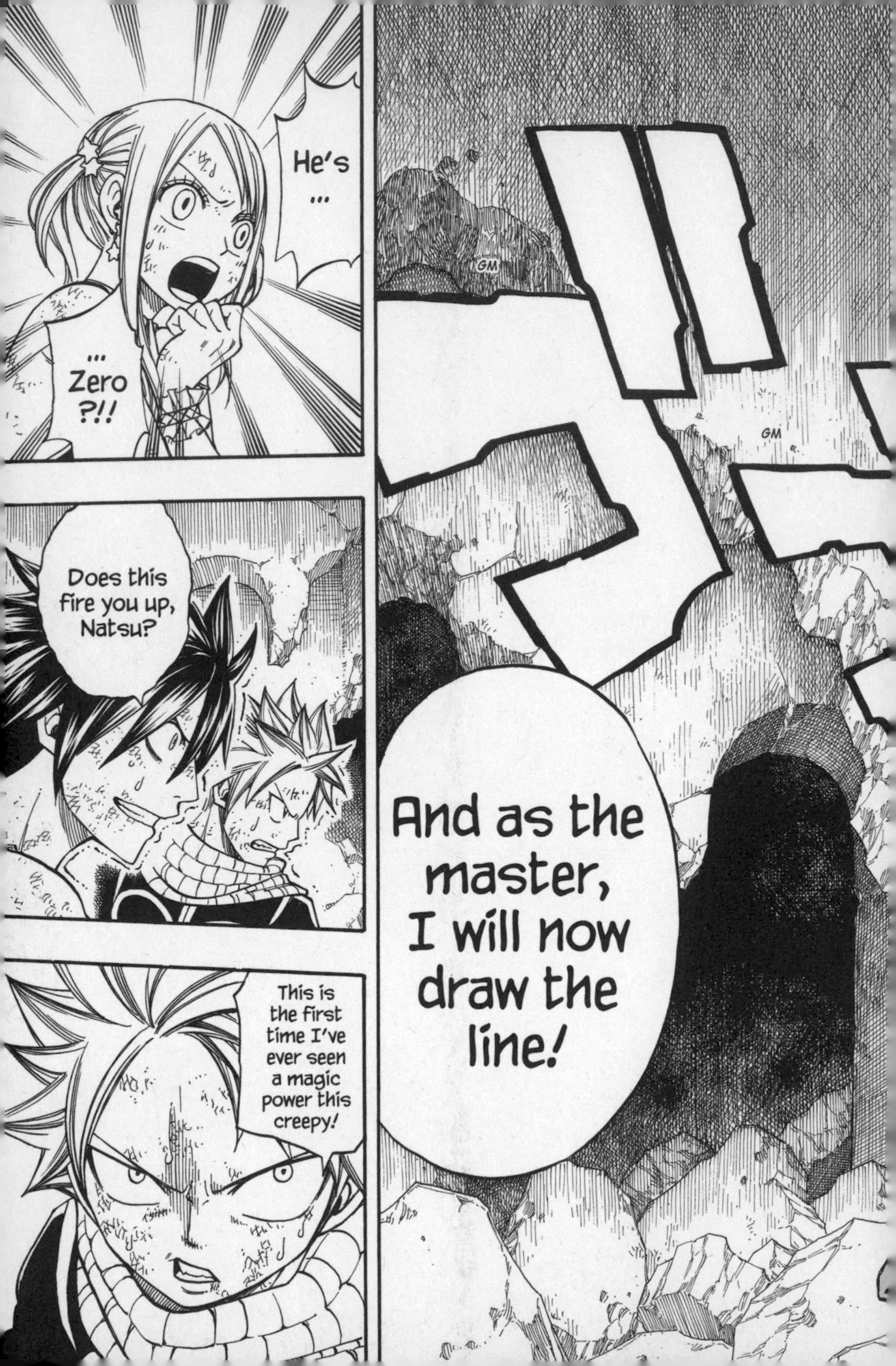
GM
GM
And as the master, I will now draw the line!
He's ...
... Zero ?!!
Does this fire you up, Natsu?
This is the first time I've ever seen a magic power this creepy!

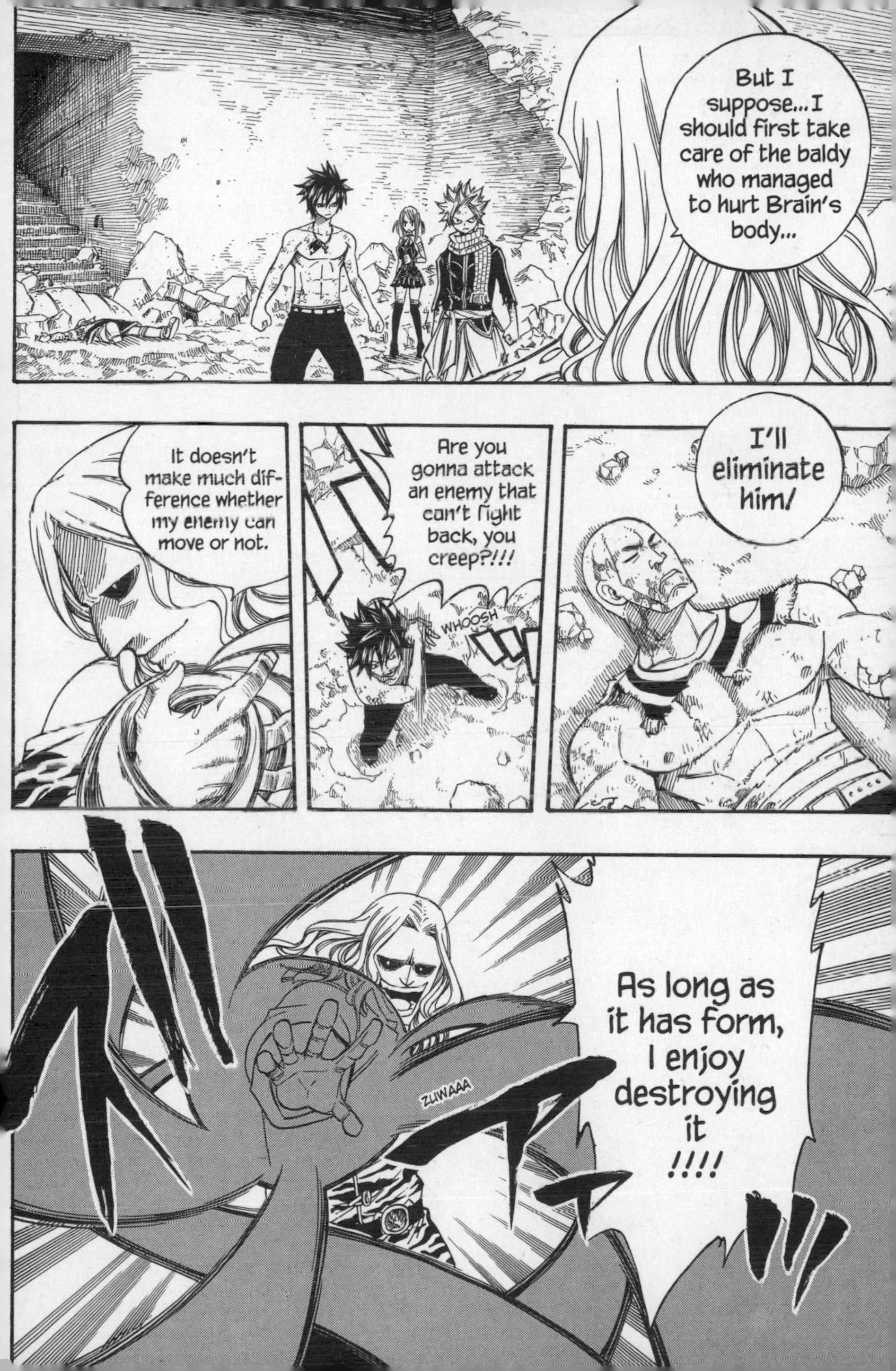
But I suppose...I should first take care of the baldy who managed to hurt Brain's body...
I'll eliminate him!
Are you gonna attack an enemy that can't fight back, you creep?!!!
WHOOSH
It doesn't make much difference whether my enemy can move or not.
As long as it has form, I enjoy destroying it !!!!
ZUWAAA

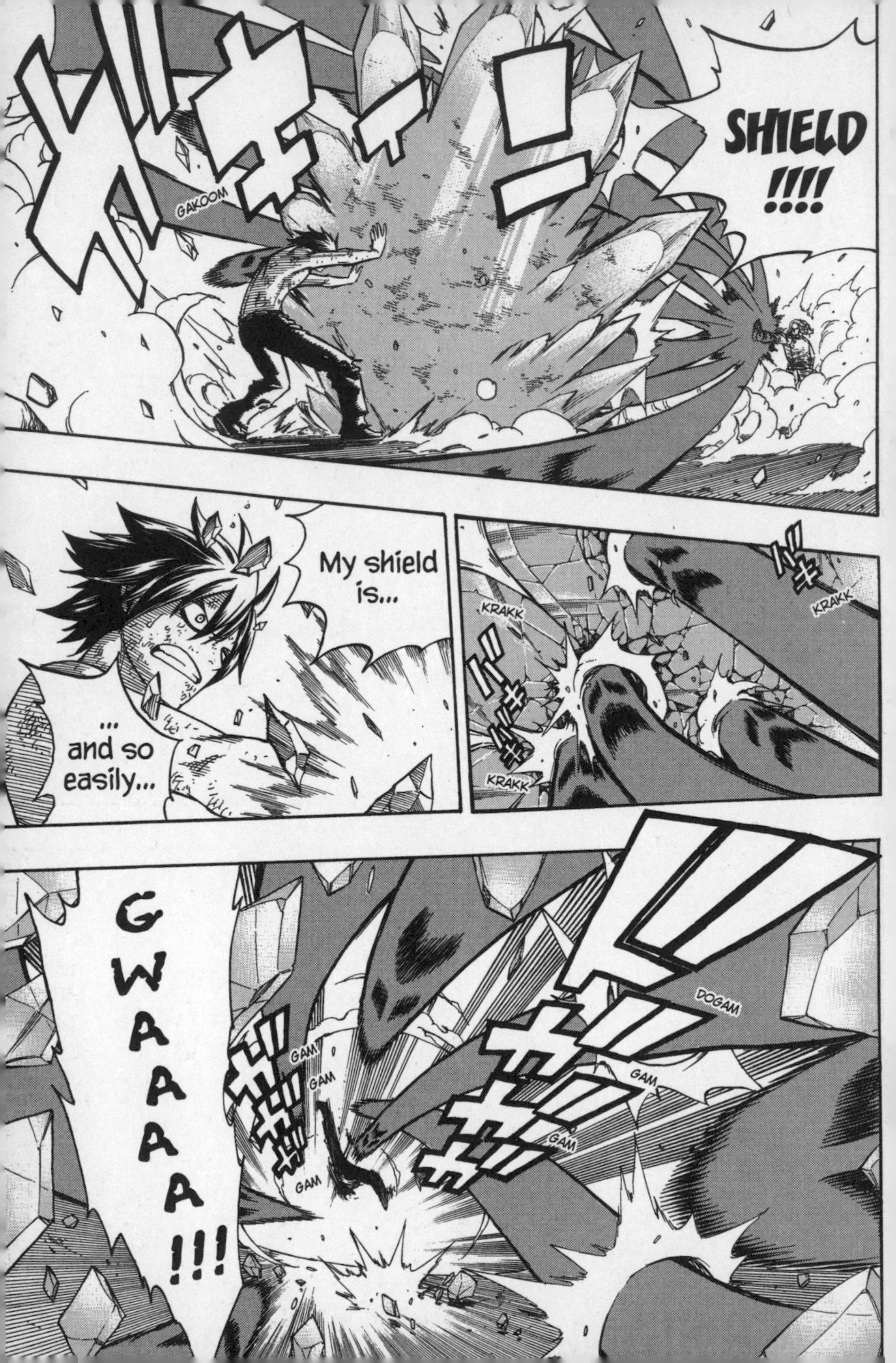
SHIELD !!!!
GAKOOM
KRAKK
KRAKK
KRAKK
My shield is...
... and so easily...
DOGAM
GAM
GAM
GAM
GAM
GAM
GWAAAA !!!

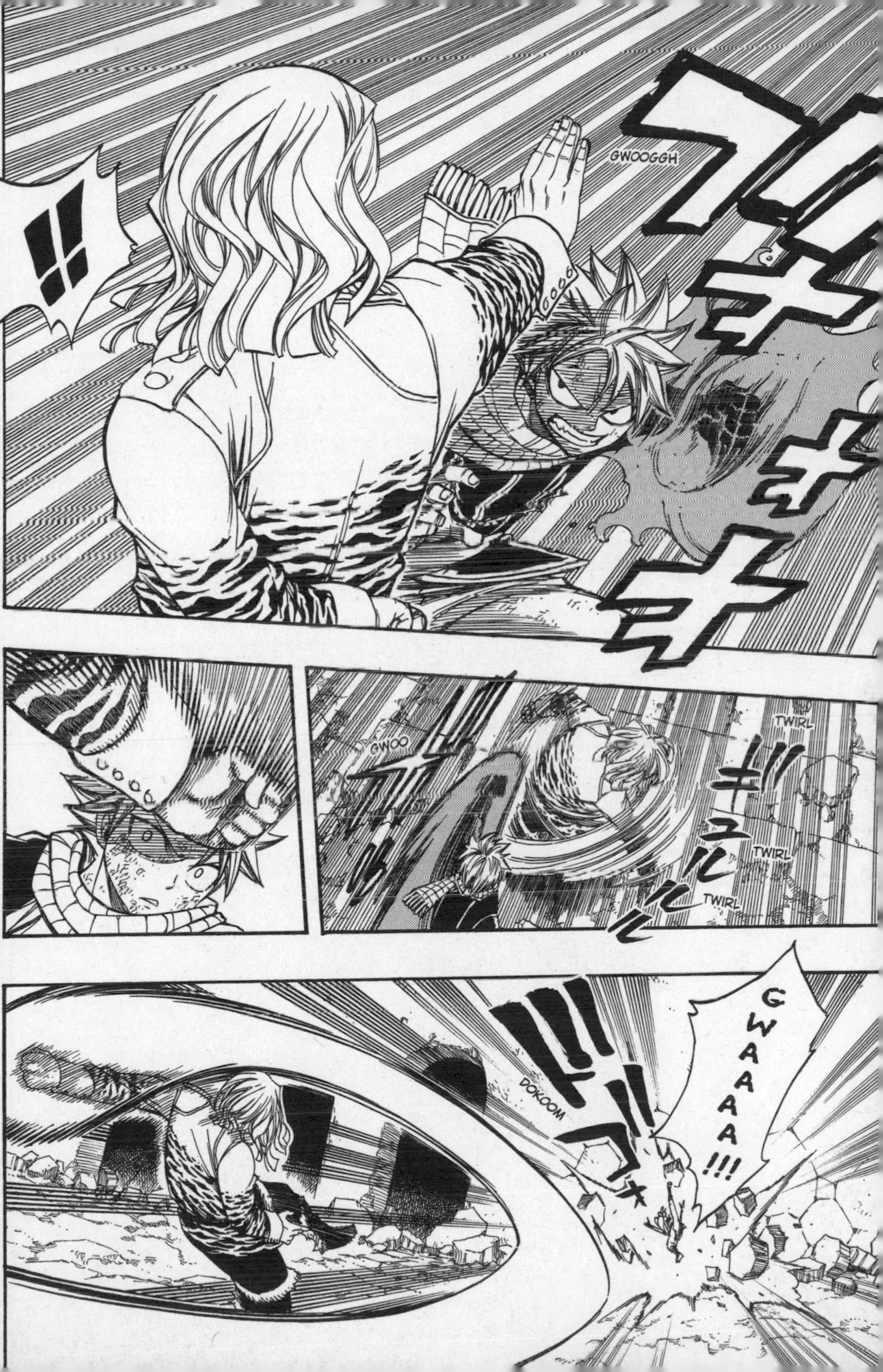
GWOOGGH
!!
TWIRL
TWIRL
TWIRL
GWOO
GWAAAAA!!!
DOKOOM

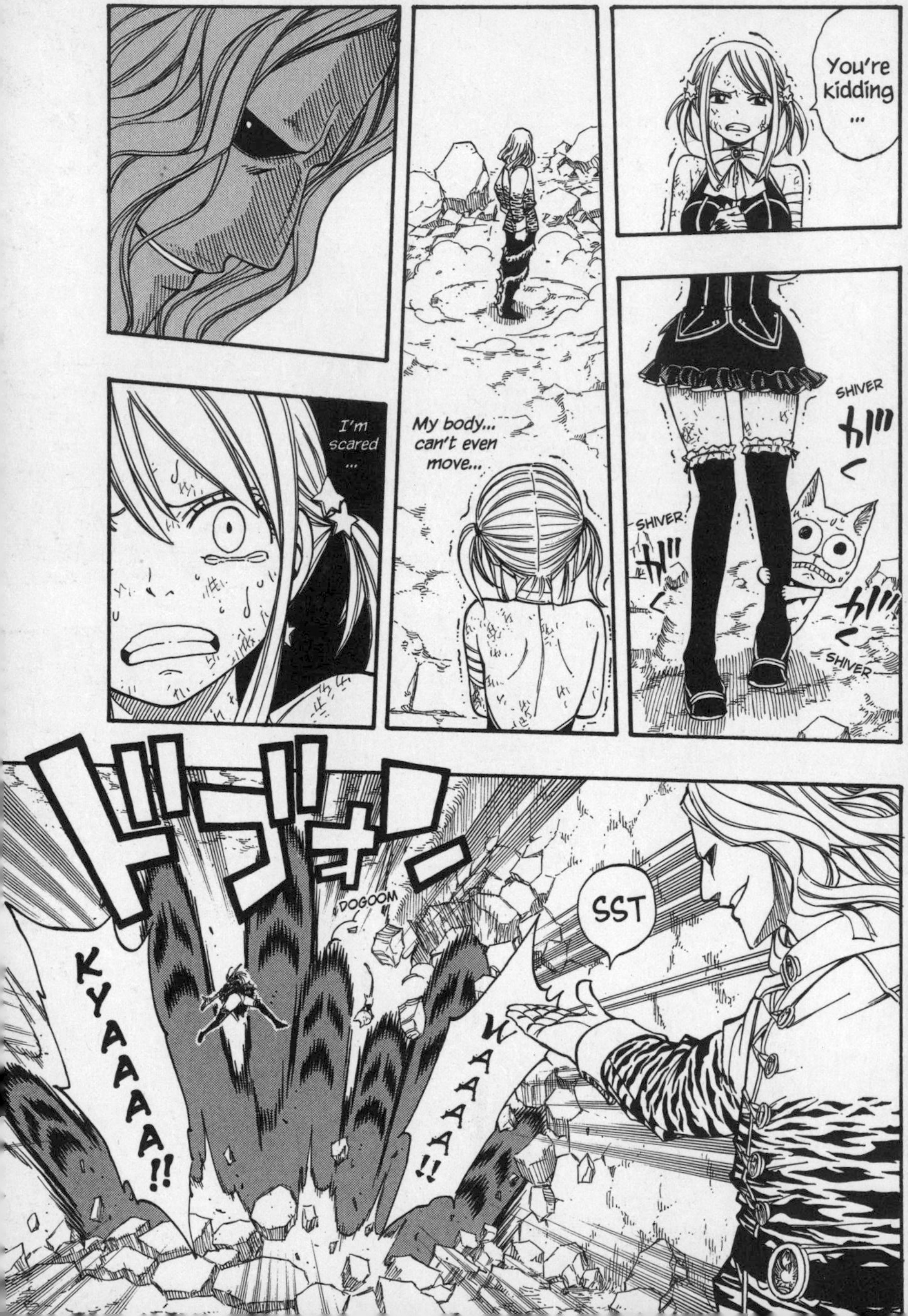
You're kidding ...
SHIVER
SHIVER
SHIVER
My body... can't even move...
I'm scared ...
SST
DOGOOM
WAAAAA!!
KYAAAA!!

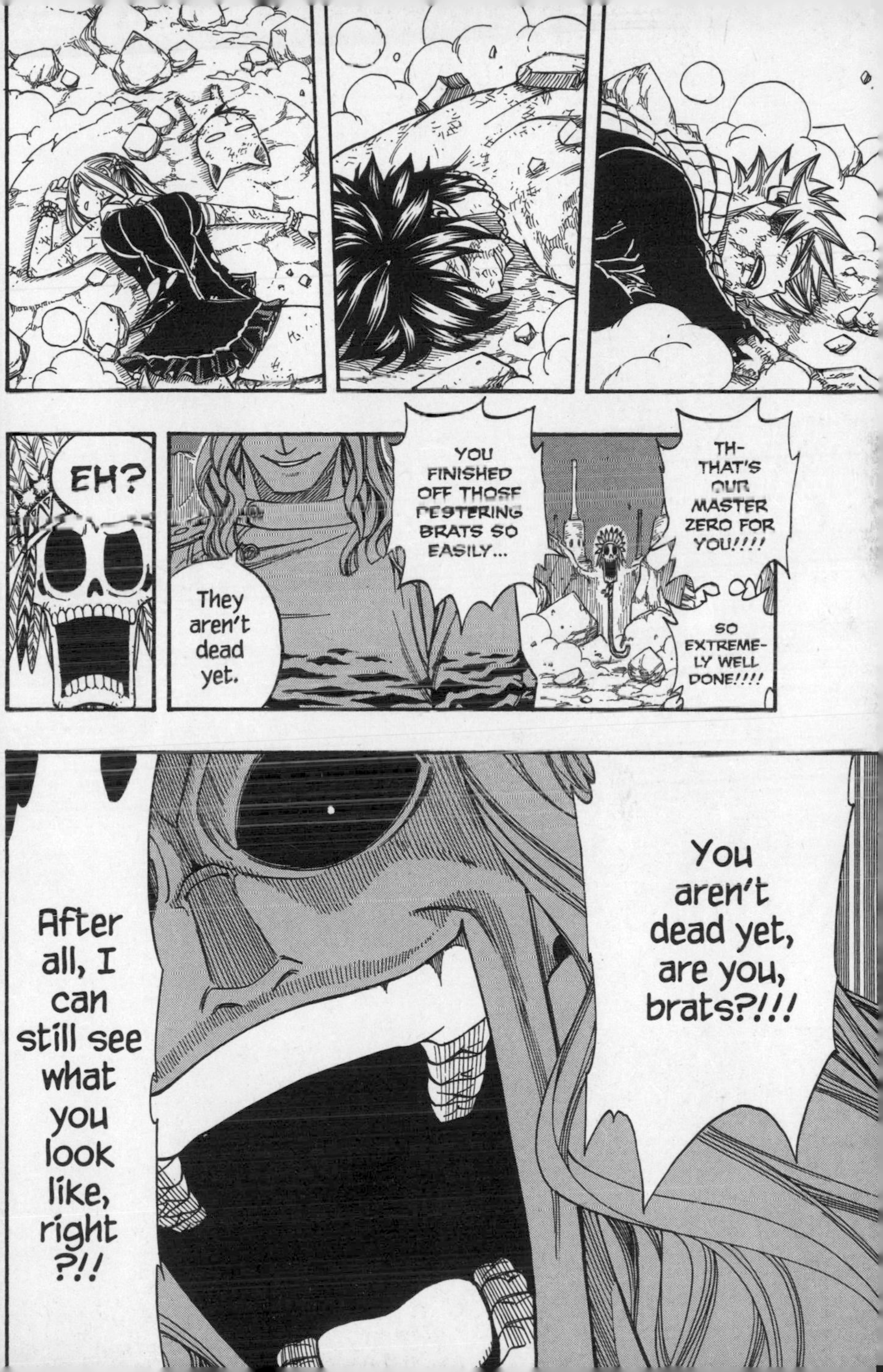
TH-THAT'S OUR MASTER ZERO FOR YOU!!!!
SO EXTREMELY WELL DONE!!!!
YOU FINISHED OFF THOSE PESTERING BRATS SO EASILY...
They aren't dead yet.
EH?
You aren't dead yet, are you, brats?!!!
After all, I can still see what you look like, right?!!

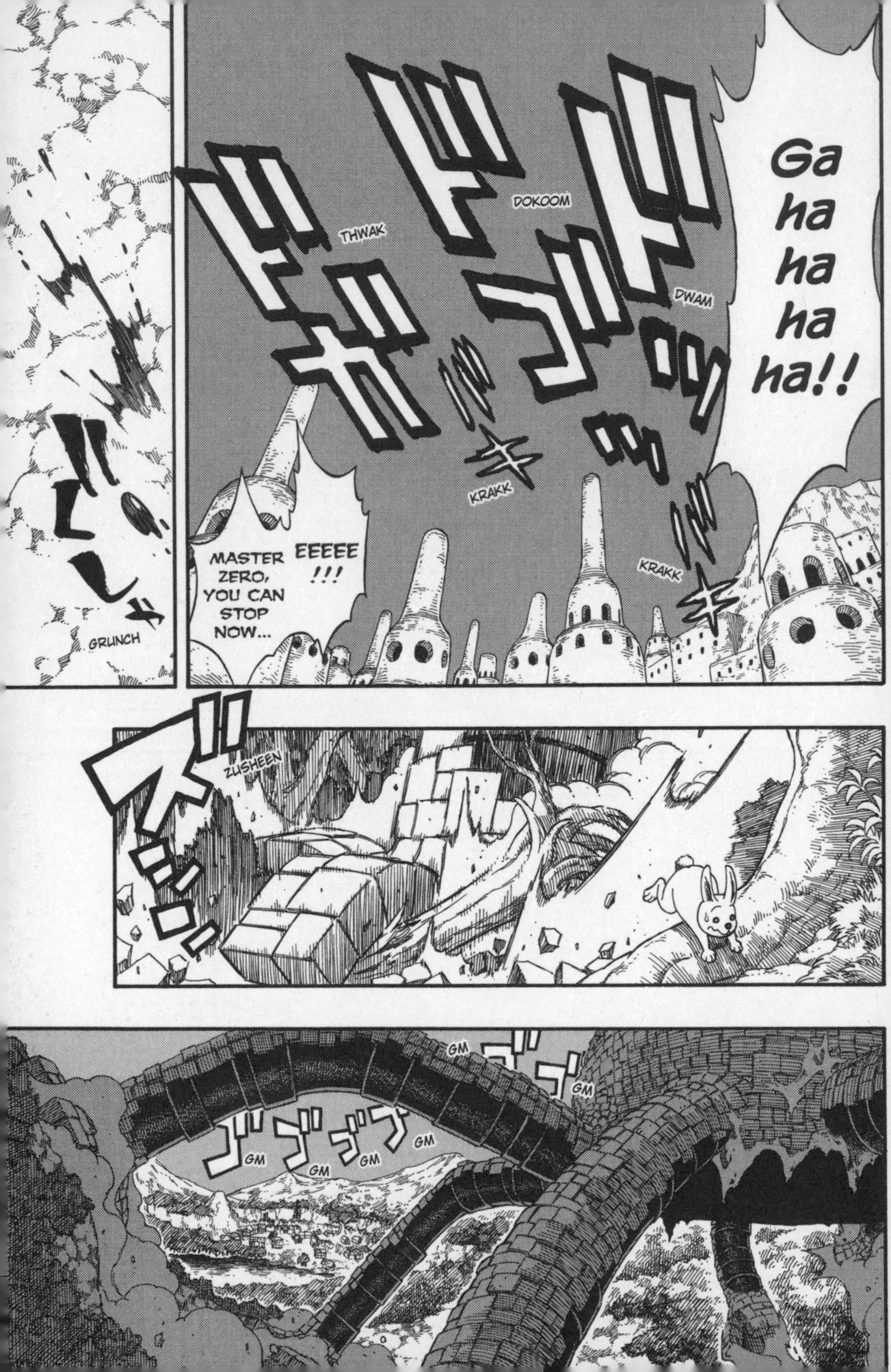
Ga ha ha ha ha!!
DOKOOM
DWAM
THWAK
KRAKK
KRAKK
EEEEE!!!
MASTER ZERO, YOU CAN STOP NOW...
GRUNCH
ZUSHEEN
GM
GM
GM
GM
GM
GM

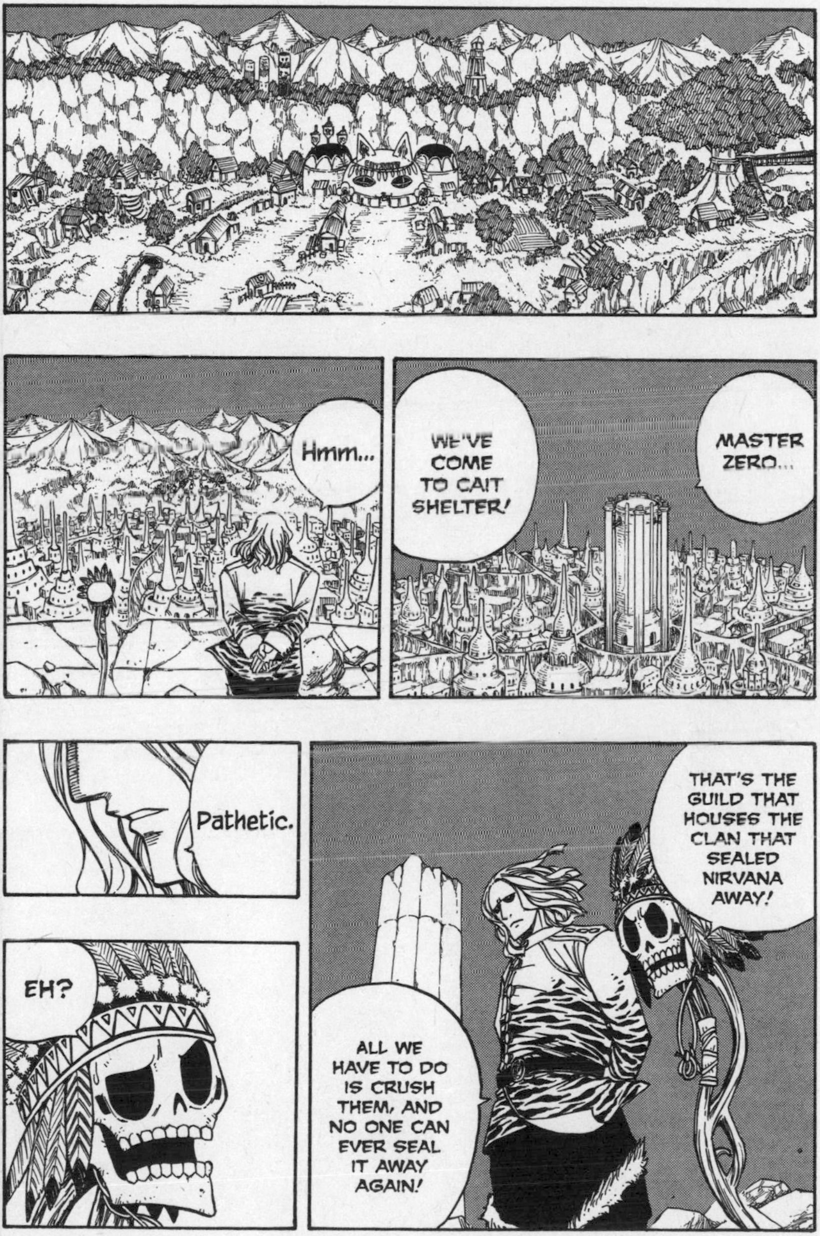
MASTER ZERO...
WE'VE COME TO CAIT SHELTER!
Hmm...
THAT'S THE GUILD THAT HOUSES THE CLAN THAT SEALED NIRVANA AWAY!
ALL WE HAVE TO DO IS CRUSH THEM, AND NO ONE CAN EVER SEAL IT AWAY AGAIN!
Pathetic.
EH?

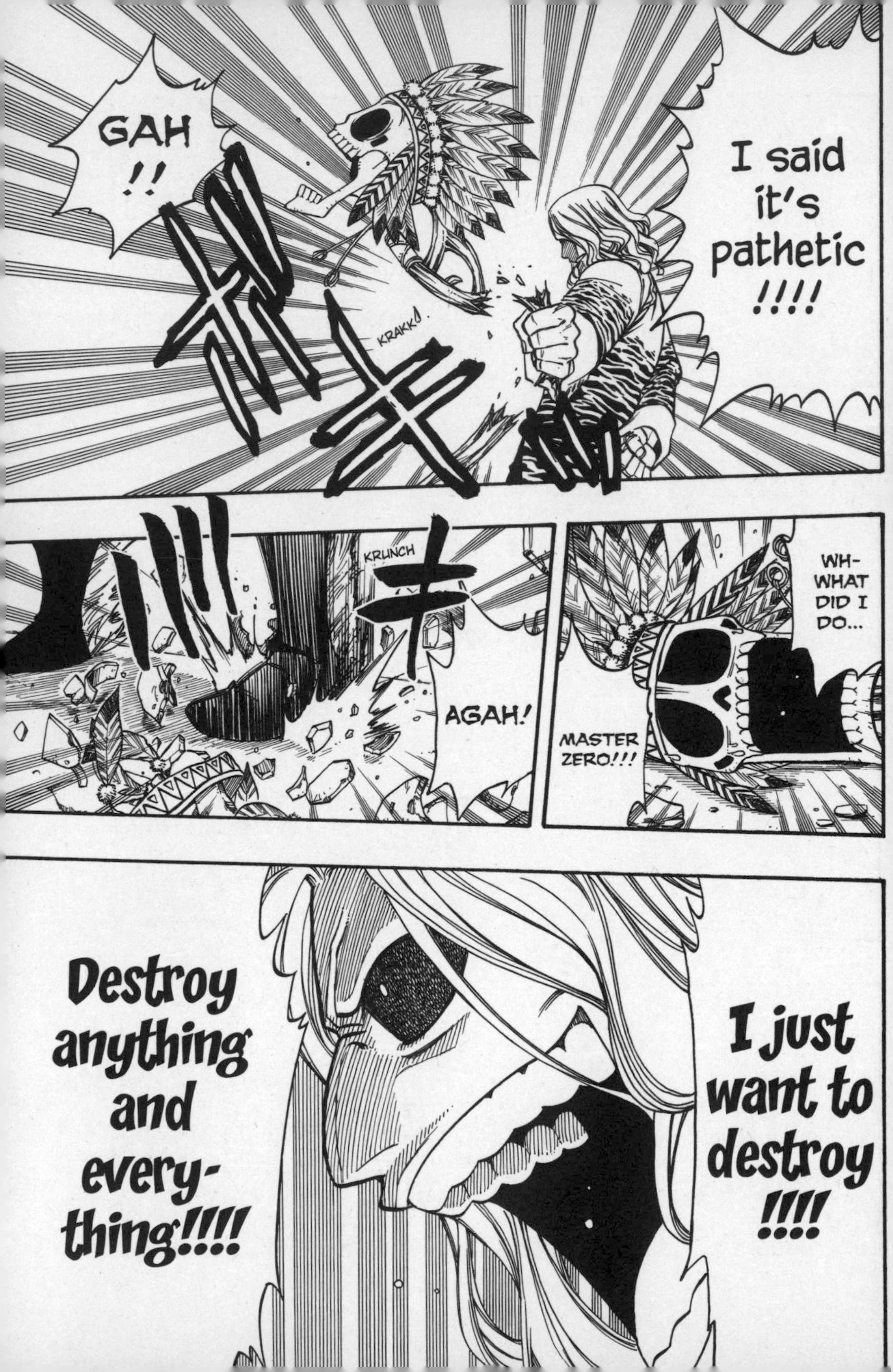
I said it's pathetic!!!!
KRAKK
GAH!!
WH-WHAT DID I DO...
MASTER ZERO!!!
KRUNCH
AGAH!
I just want to destroy!!!!
Destroy anything and every-thing!!!!

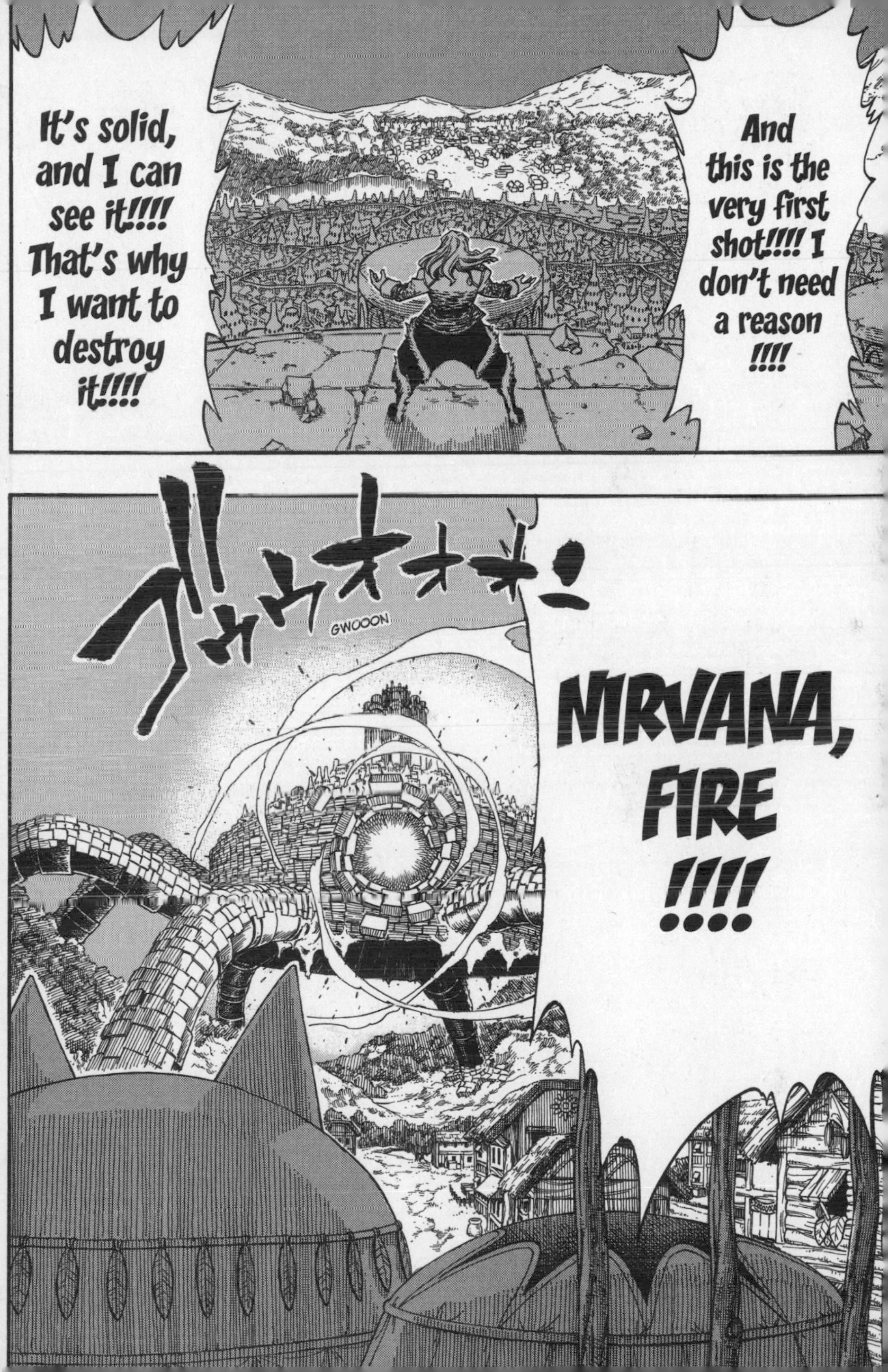
And this is the very first shot!!!! I don't need a reason !!!!
It's solid, and I can see it!!!! That's why I want to destroy it!!!!
GWOOON
NIRVANA, FIRE !!!!

FAIRY TAIL

フェアリーテイル

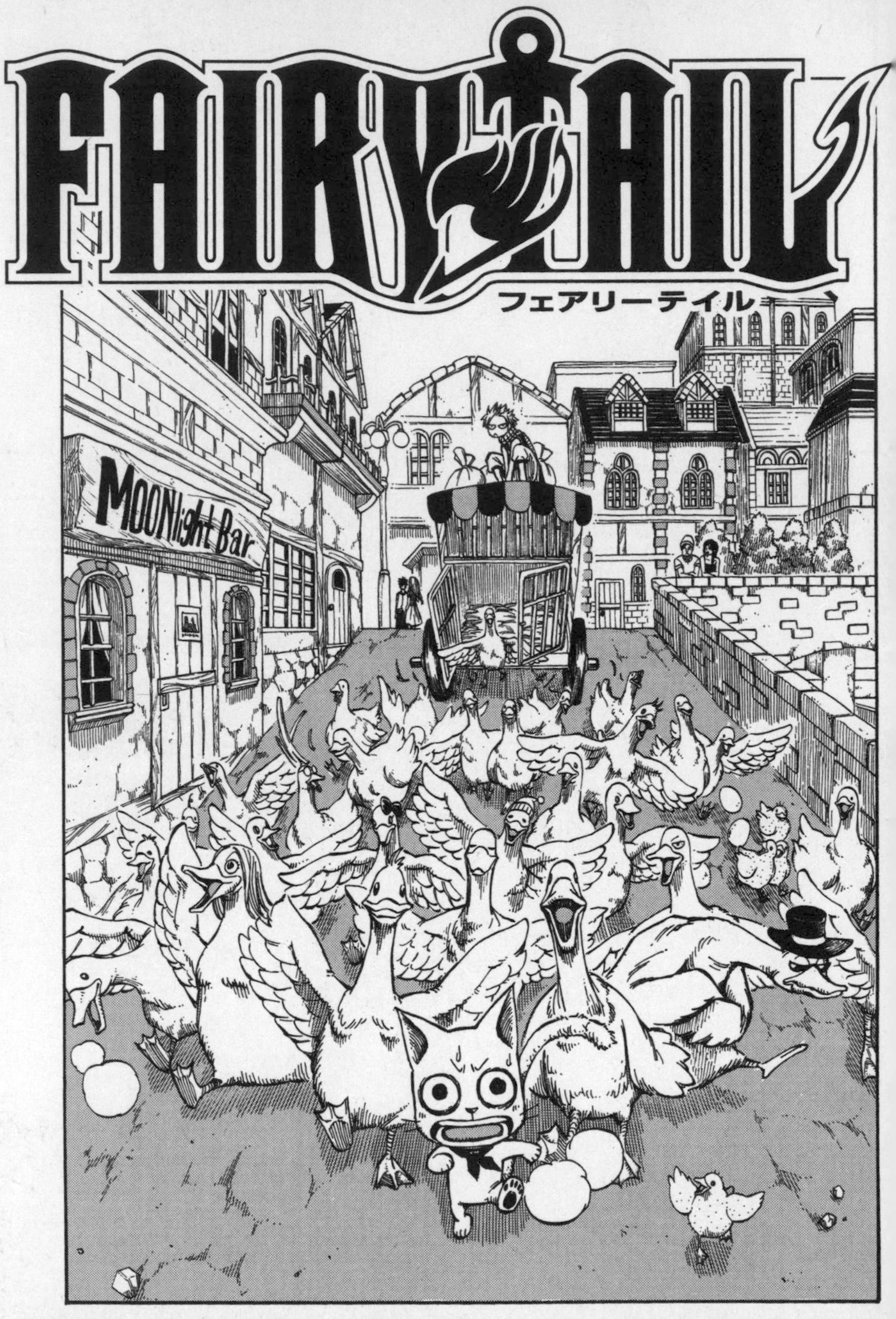
MOONlight Bar

Chapter 157: From Heaven's Steed to the Fairies

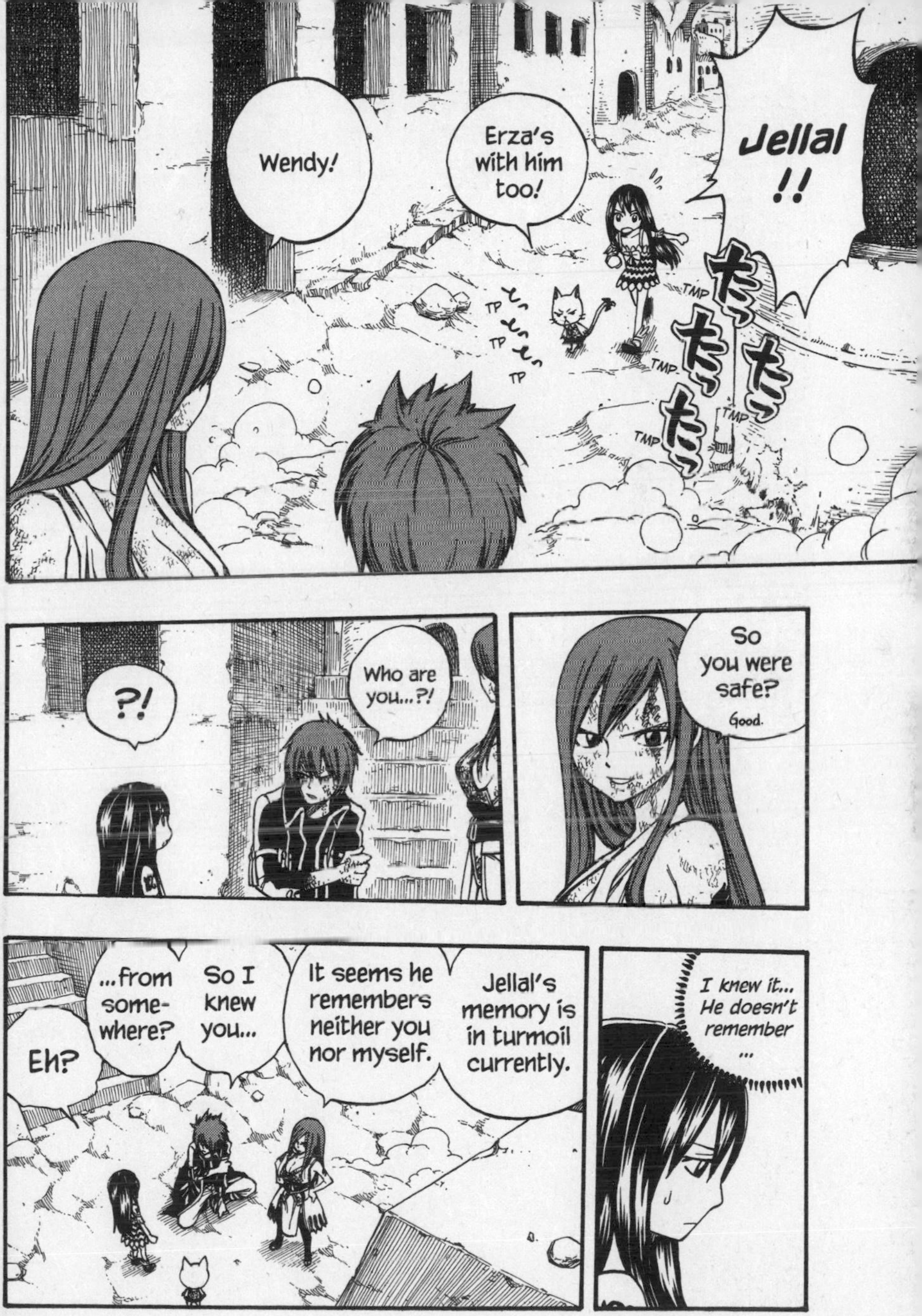

Jellal !!
たっ たっ たっ
TMP TMP TMP TMP
Erza's with him too!
Wendy!
TP TP TP
So you were safe?
Good.
Who are you...?!
?!
I knew it... He doesn't remember ...
Jellal's memory is in turmoil currently.
It seems he remembers neither you nor myself.
So I knew you...
...from some- where?
Eh?

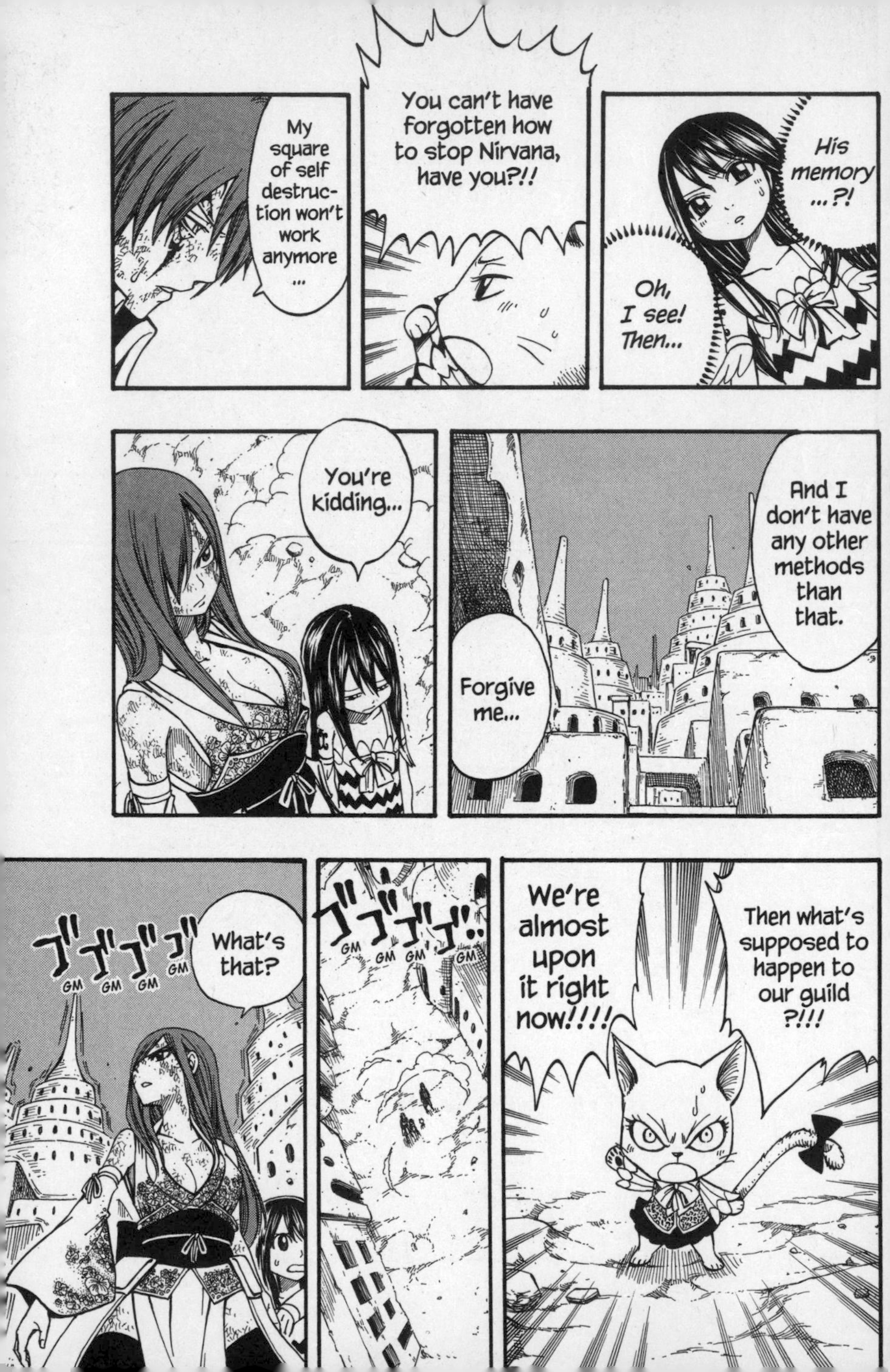
His memory ...?!
Oh, I see! Then...
You can't have forgotten how to stop Nirvana, have you?!!
My square of self destruction won't work anymore ...
And I don't have any other methods than that.
Forgive me...
You're kidding...
Then what's supposed to happen to our guild ?!!!
We're almost upon it right now!!!!
ゴゴゴゴ
GM GM GM GM
What's that?
ゴゴゴゴ
GM GM GM GM

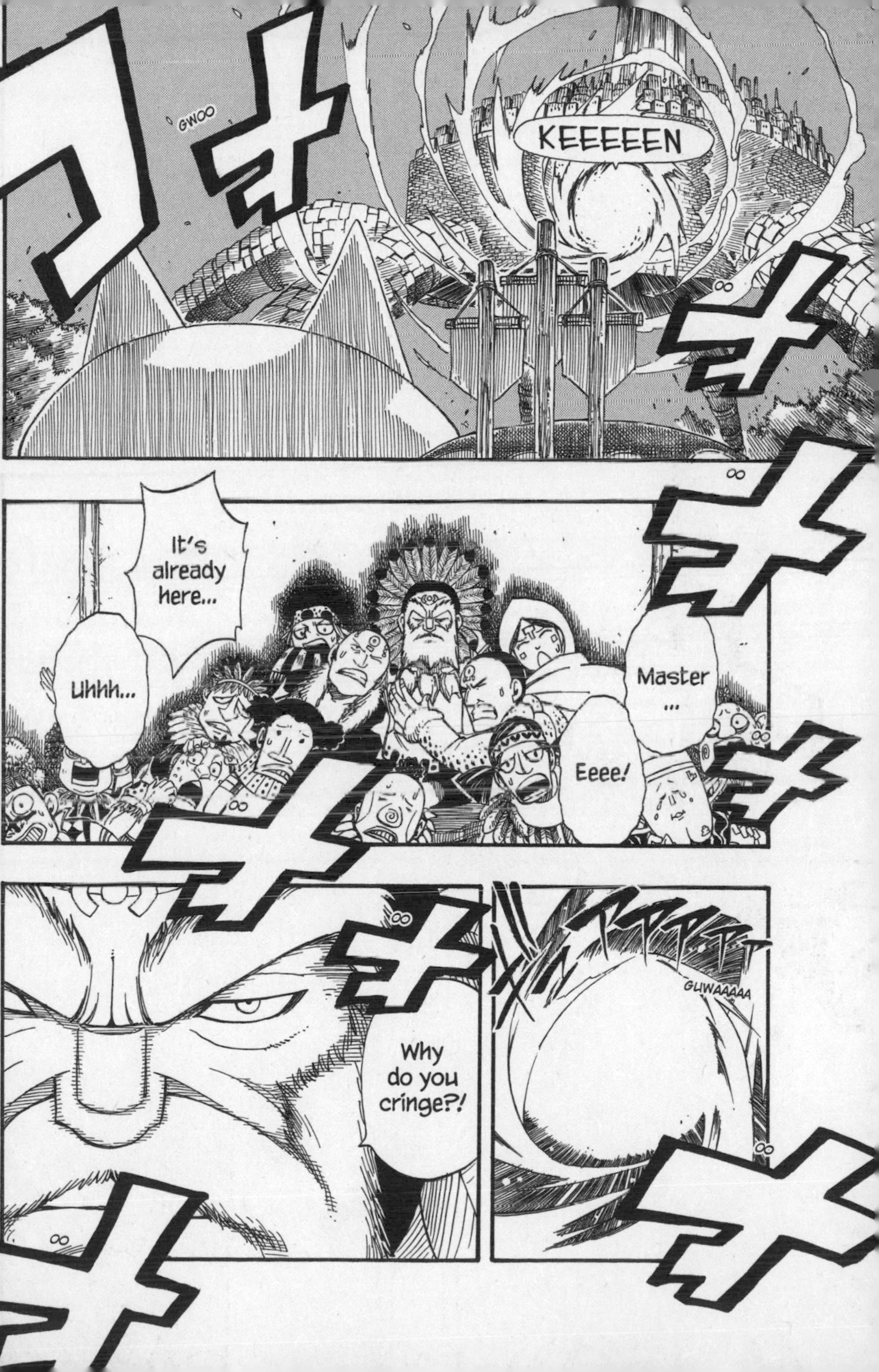
KEEEEEN
GWOO
Master ...
Eeee!
It's already here...
Uhhh...
GUWAAAAA
Why do you cringe?!

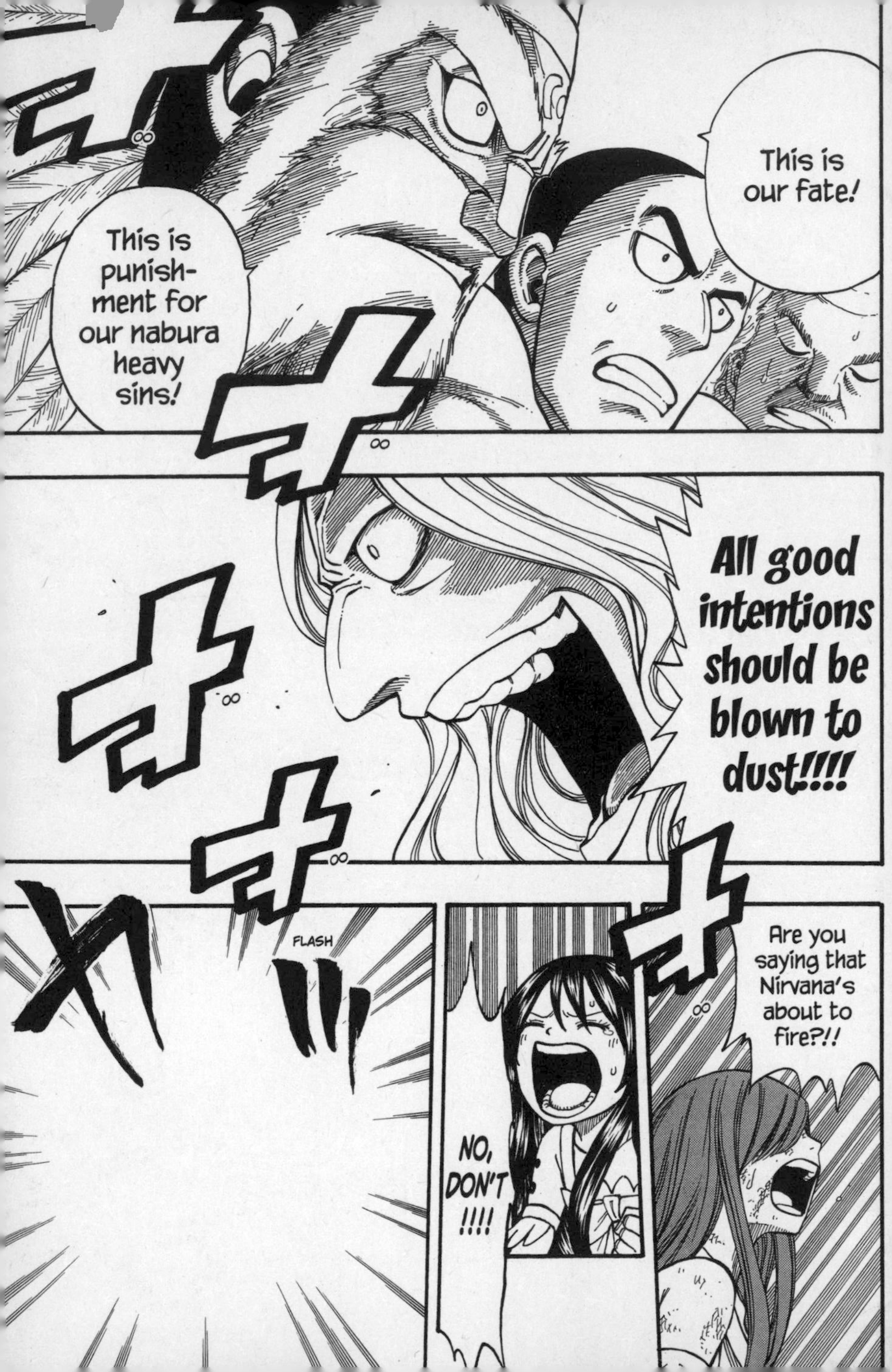
This is our fate!
This is punishment for our nabura heavy sins!
All good intentions should be blown to dust!!!!
Are you saying that Nirvana's about to fire?!!
NO, DON'T !!!!
FLASH

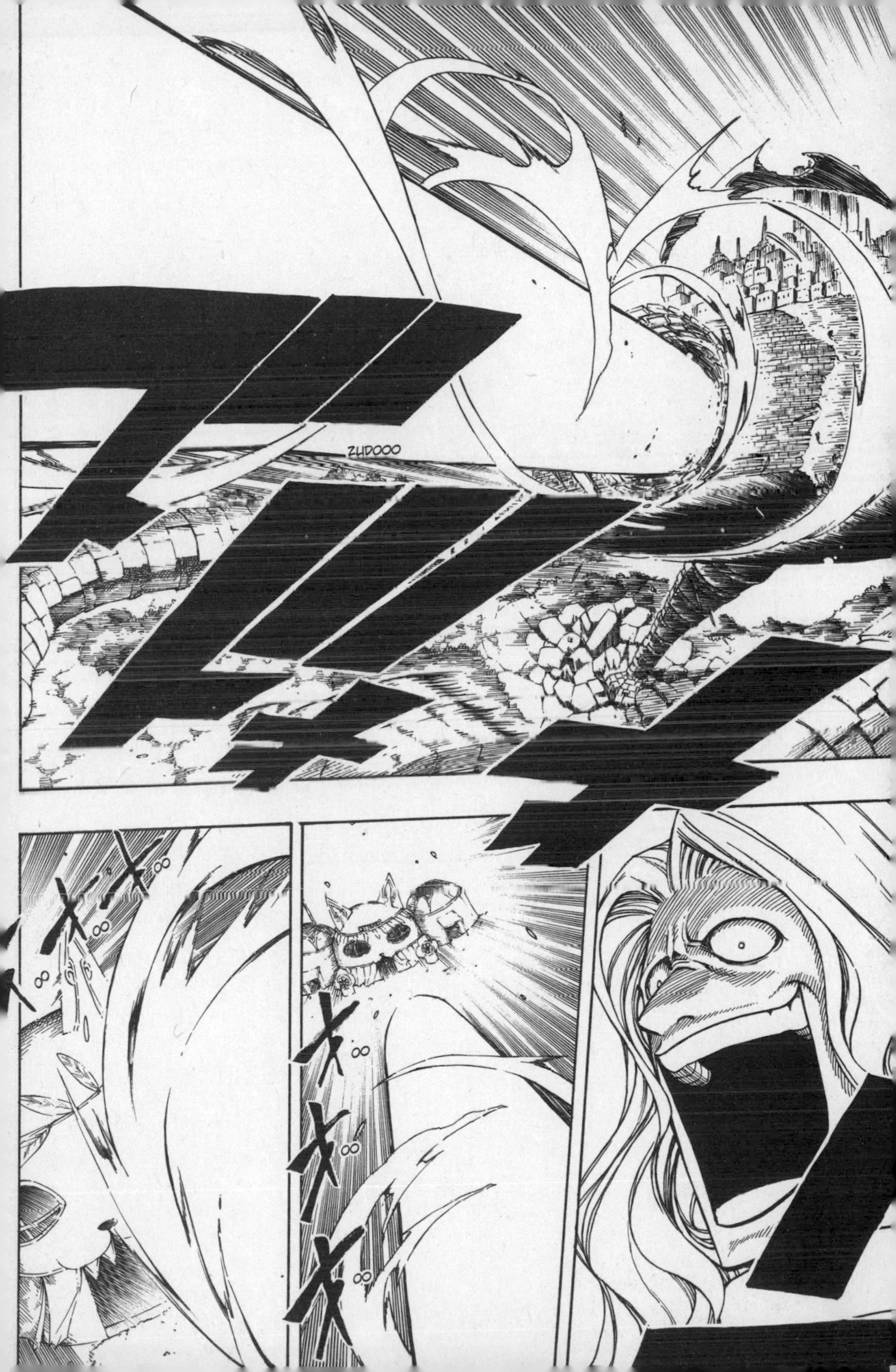
ZUDOOO

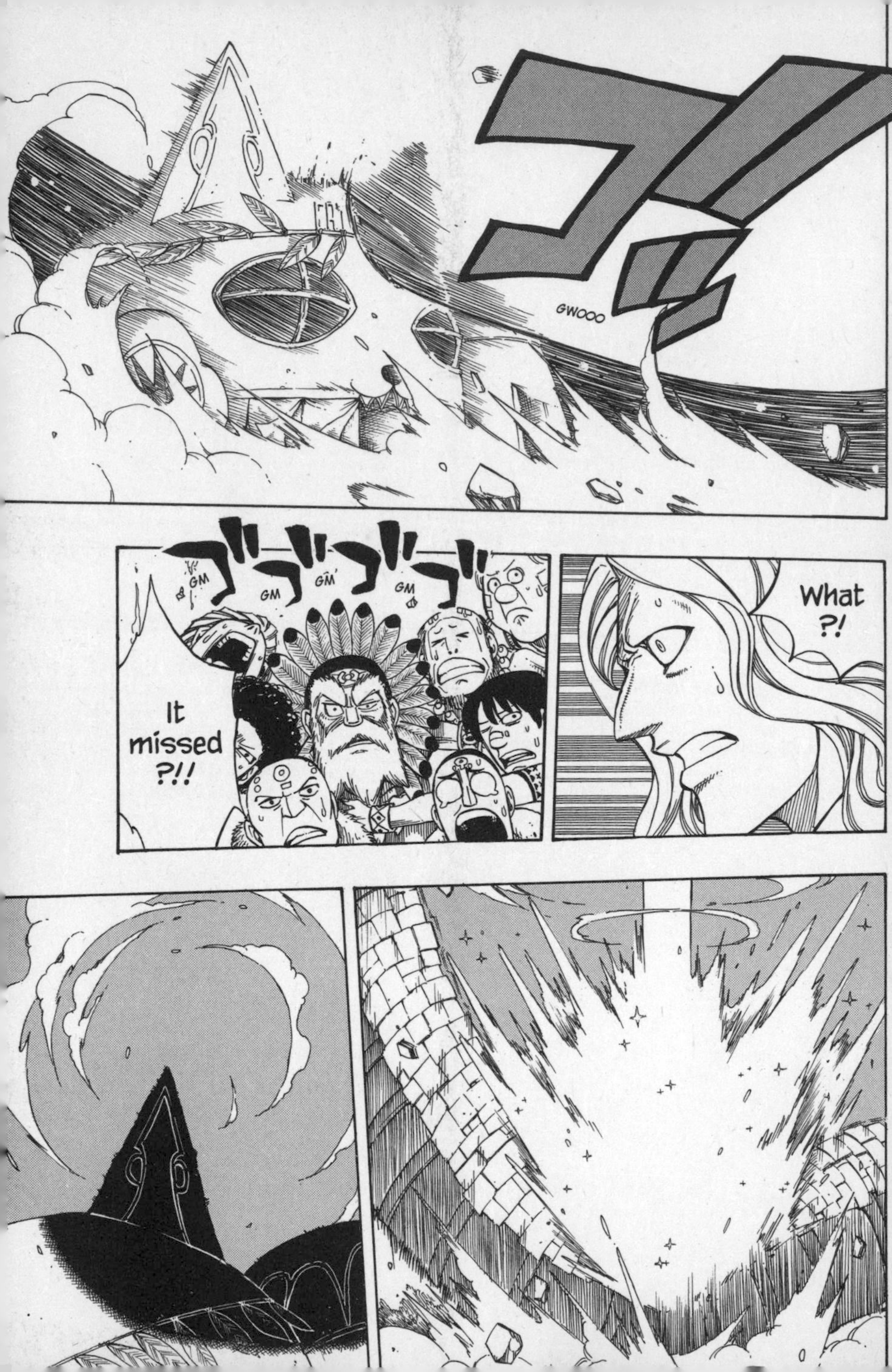
GWOOO
What ?!
GM
GM
GM
GM
It missed ?!!

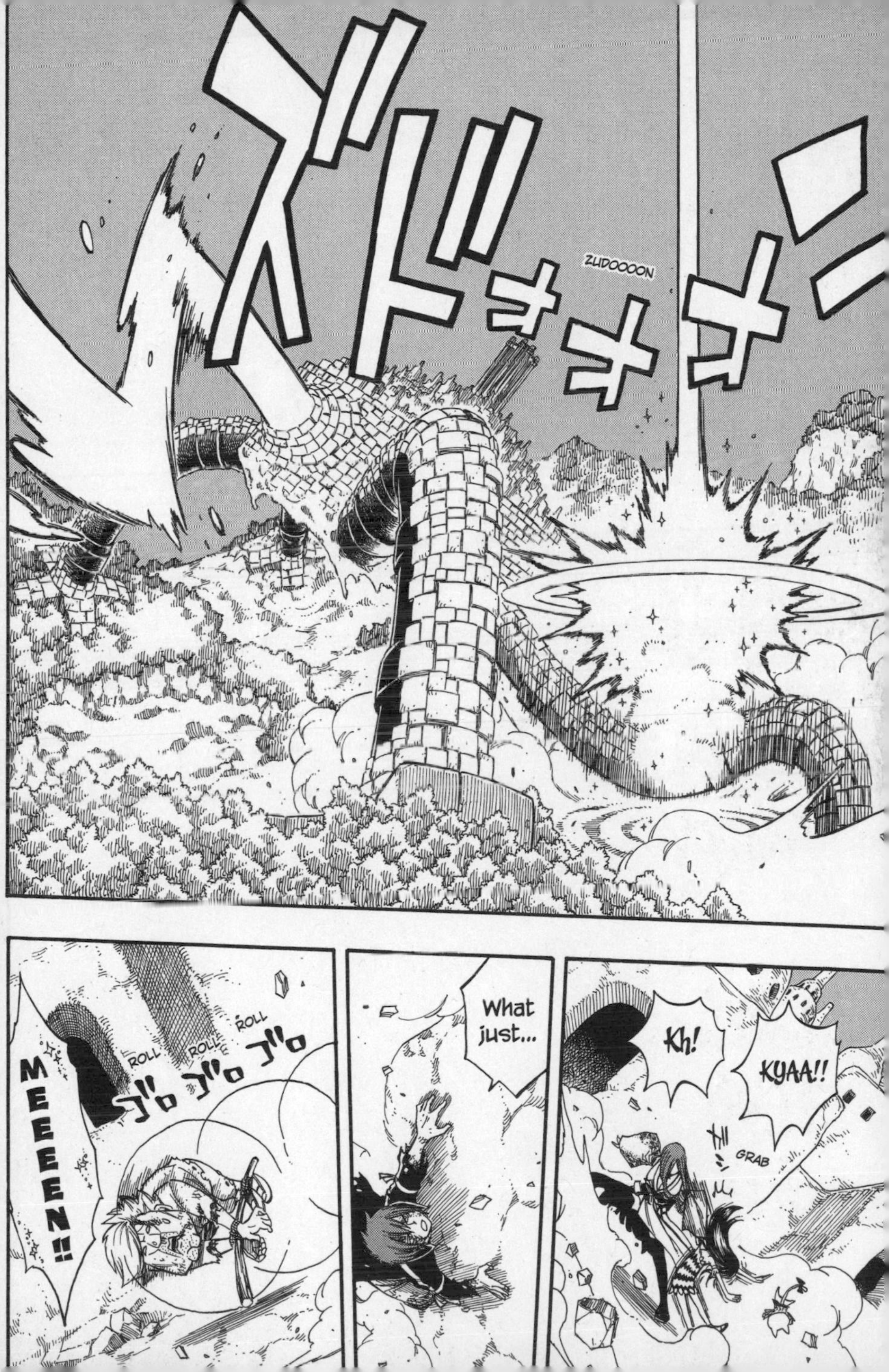
ズドォォオン
ZUDOOOON
KYAA!!
Kh!
GRAB
What just...
ROLL
ROLL
ROLL
MEEEEN!!

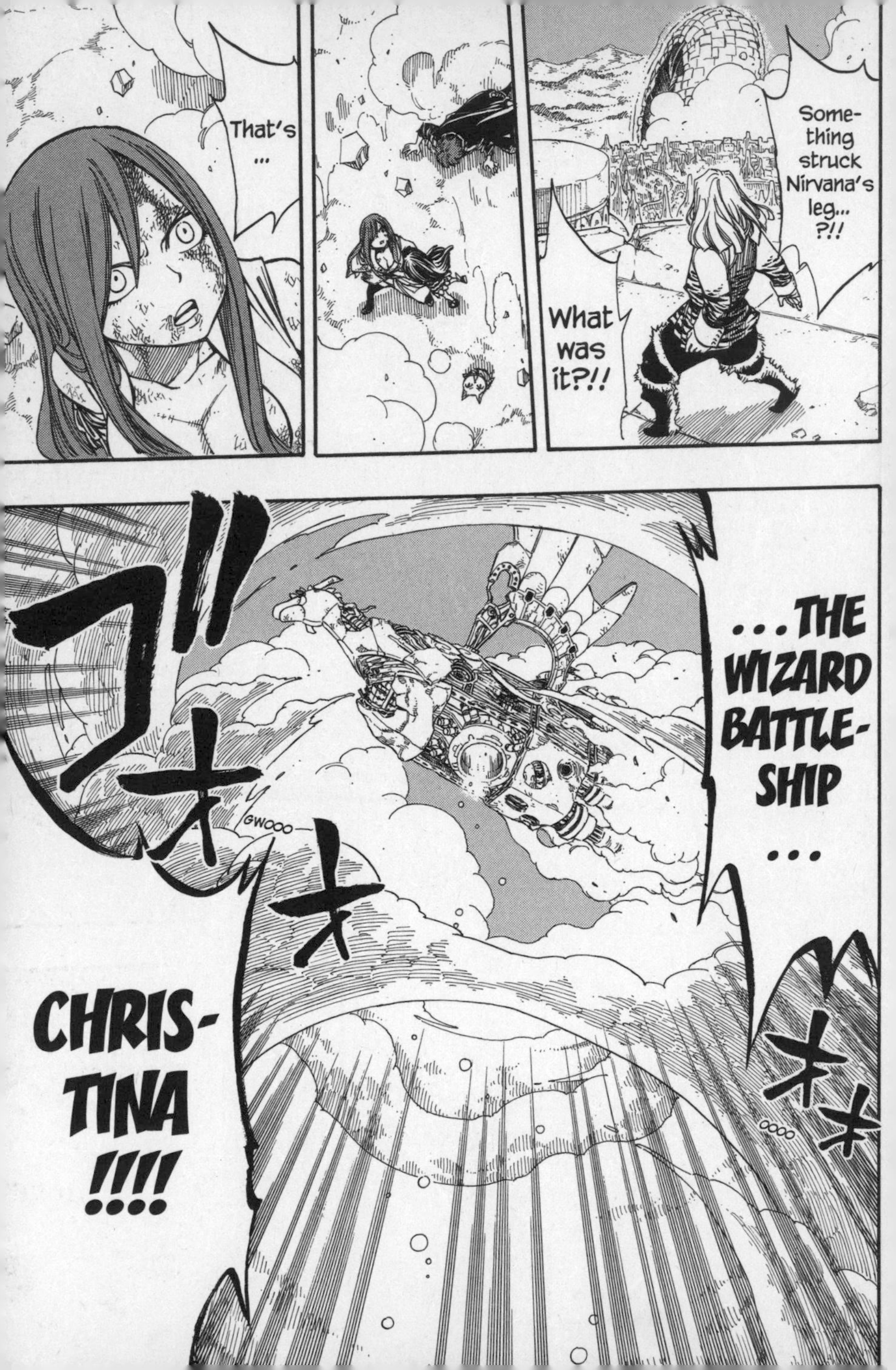
Something struck Nirvana's leg...?!!
What was it?!!
That's ...
...THE WIZARD BATTLE-SHIP ...
GWOOO—
CHRIS-TINA!!!!
OOOO

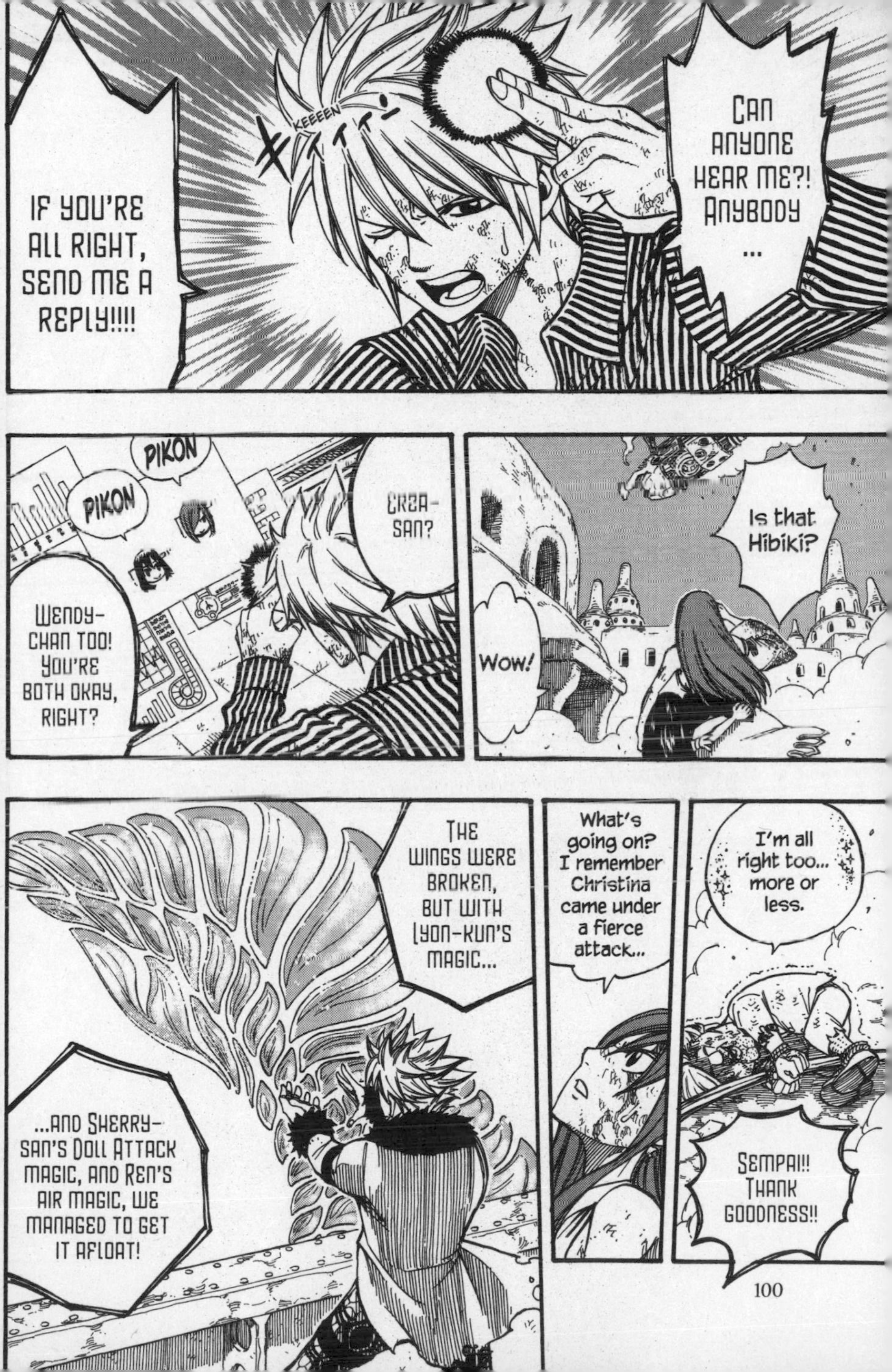
CAN ANYONE HEAR ME?! ANYBODY ...
KEEEEN
IF YOU'RE ALL RIGHT, SEND ME A REPLY!!!!
Is that Hibiki?
Wow!
ERZA-SAN?
PIKON
PIKON
WENDY-CHAN TOO! YOU'RE BOTH OKAY, RIGHT?
I'm all right too... more or less.
SEMPAI!! THANK GOODNESS!!
What's going on? I remember Christina came under a fierce attack...
THE WINGS WERE BROKEN, BUT WITH LYON-KUN'S MAGIC...
...AND SHERRY-SAN'S DOLL ATTACK MAGIC, AND REN'S AIR MAGIC, WE MANAGED TO GET IT AFLOAT!

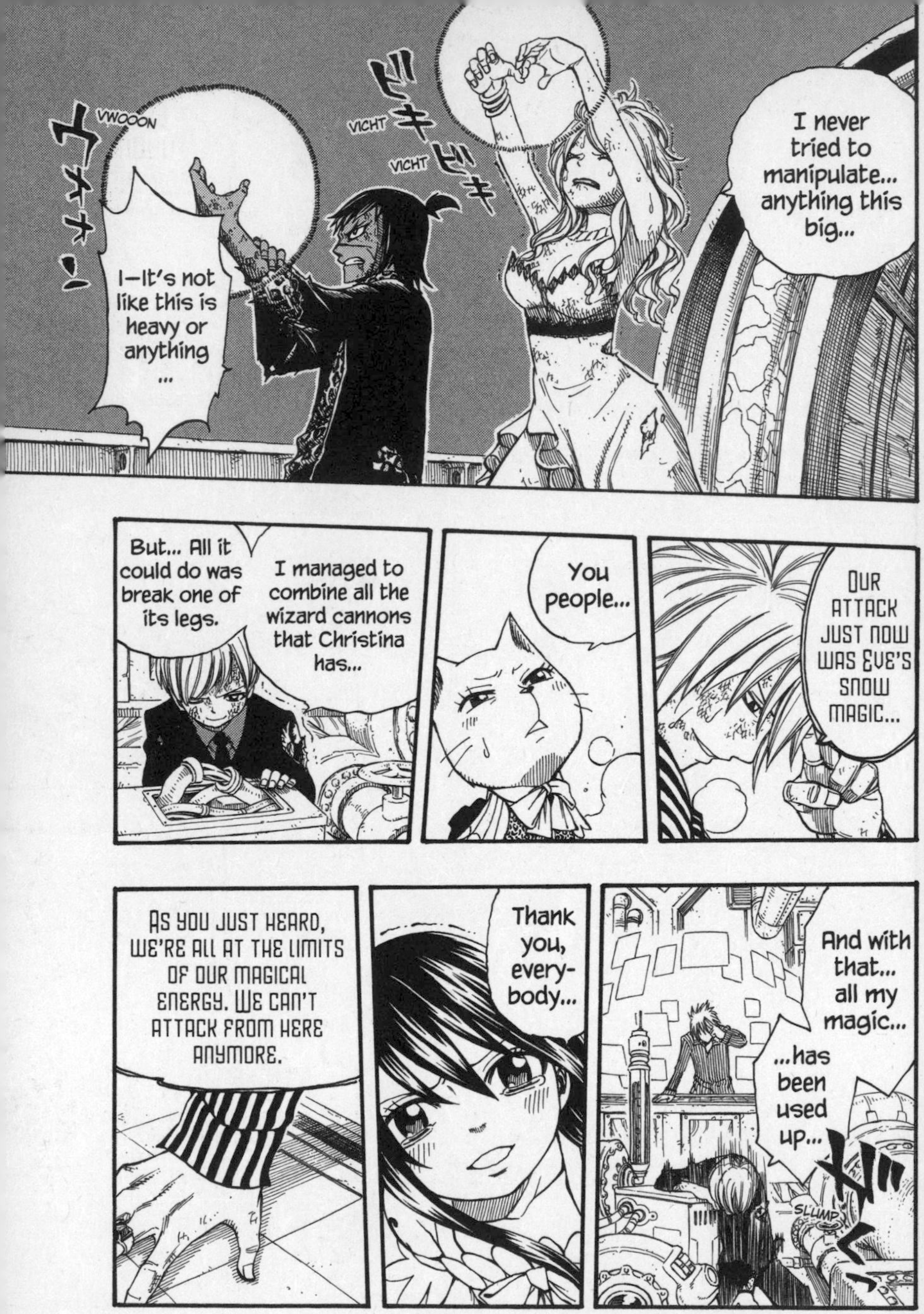
I never tried to manipulate... anything this big...
VICHT
VICHT
VWOOON
I—It's not like this is heavy or anything...
Our attack just now was Eve's snow magic...
You people...
I managed to combine all the wizard cannons that Christina has...
But... All it could do was break one of its legs.
And with that... all my magic...
...has been used up...
SLUMP
Thank you, everybody...
As you just heard, we're all at the limits of our magical energy. We can't attack from here anymore.

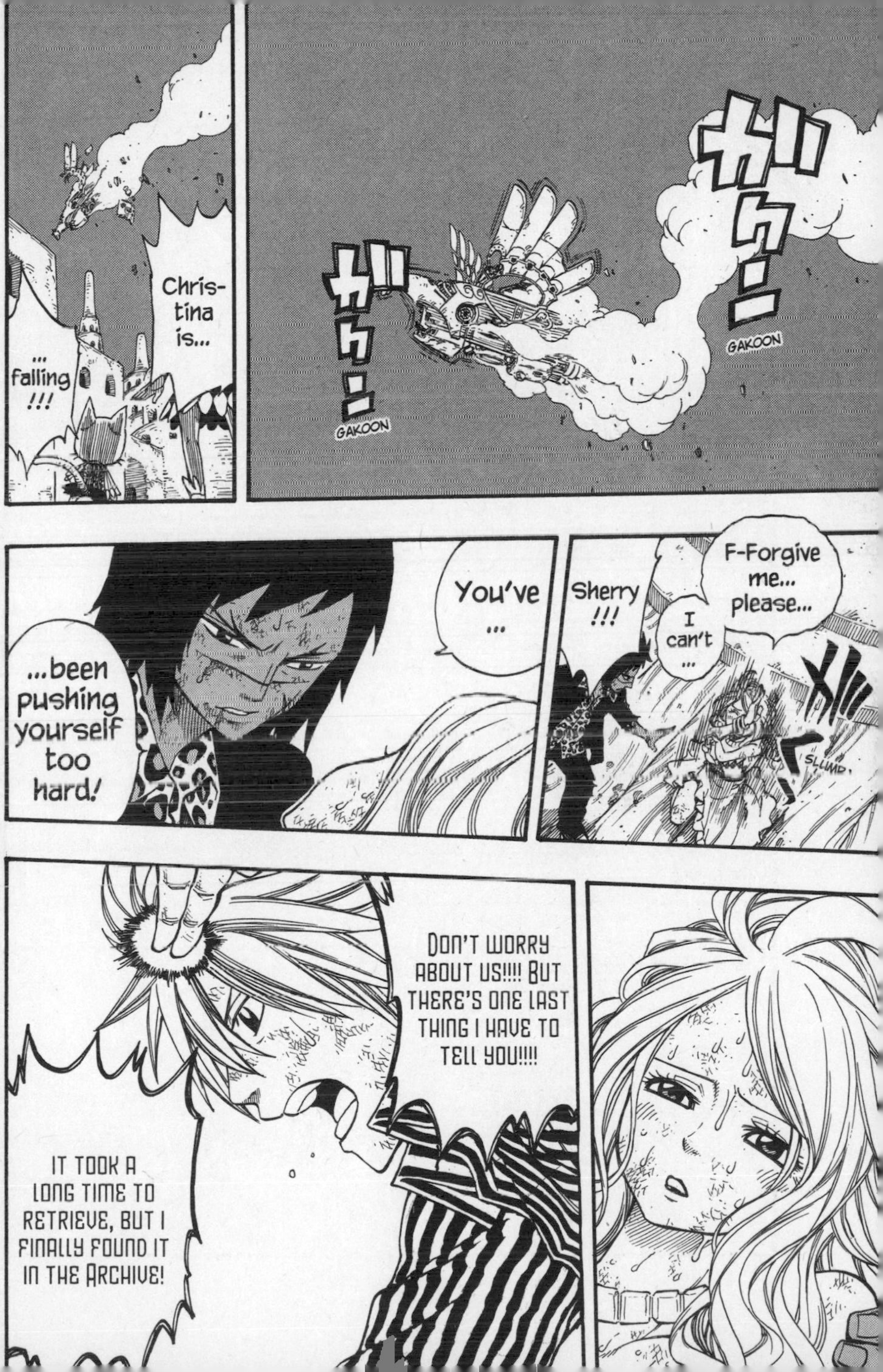
GAKOON
GAKOON
Chris-tina is...
...falling!!!
F-Forgive me... please...
I can't ...
Sherry!!!
SLUMP
You've ...
...been pushing yourself too hard!
DON'T WORRY ABOUT US!!!! BUT THERE'S ONE LAST THING I HAVE TO TELL YOU!!!!
IT TOOK A LONG TIME TO RETRIEVE, BUT I FINALLY FOUND IT IN THE ARCHIVE!

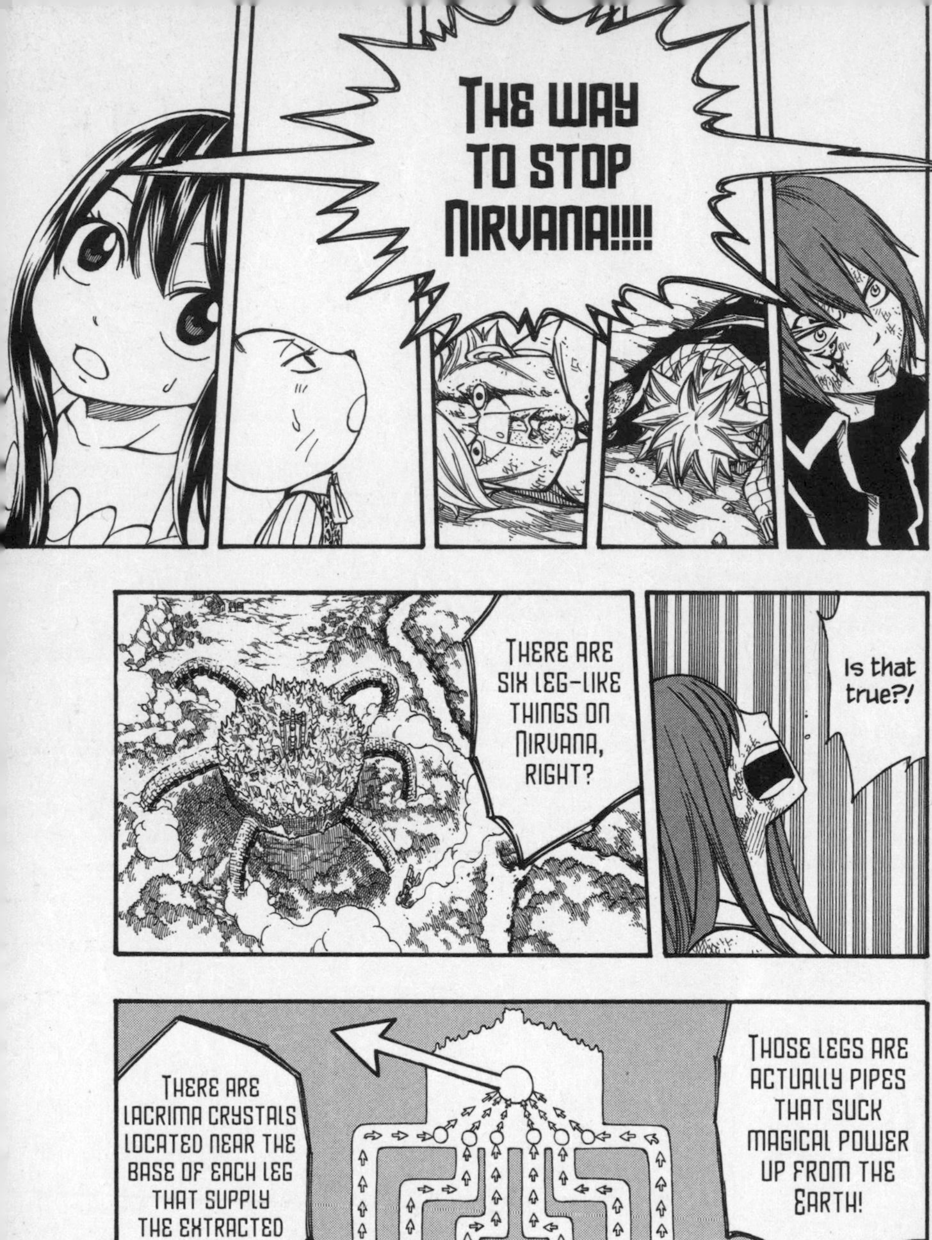
THE WAY TO STOP NIRVANA!!!!
Is that true?!
THERE ARE SIX LEG-LIKE THINGS ON NIRVANA, RIGHT?
THOSE LEGS ARE ACTUALLY PIPES THAT SUCK MAGICAL POWER UP FROM THE EARTH!
THERE ARE LACRIMA CRYSTALS LOCATED NEAR THE BASE OF EACH LEG THAT SUPPLY THE EXTRACTED POWER!

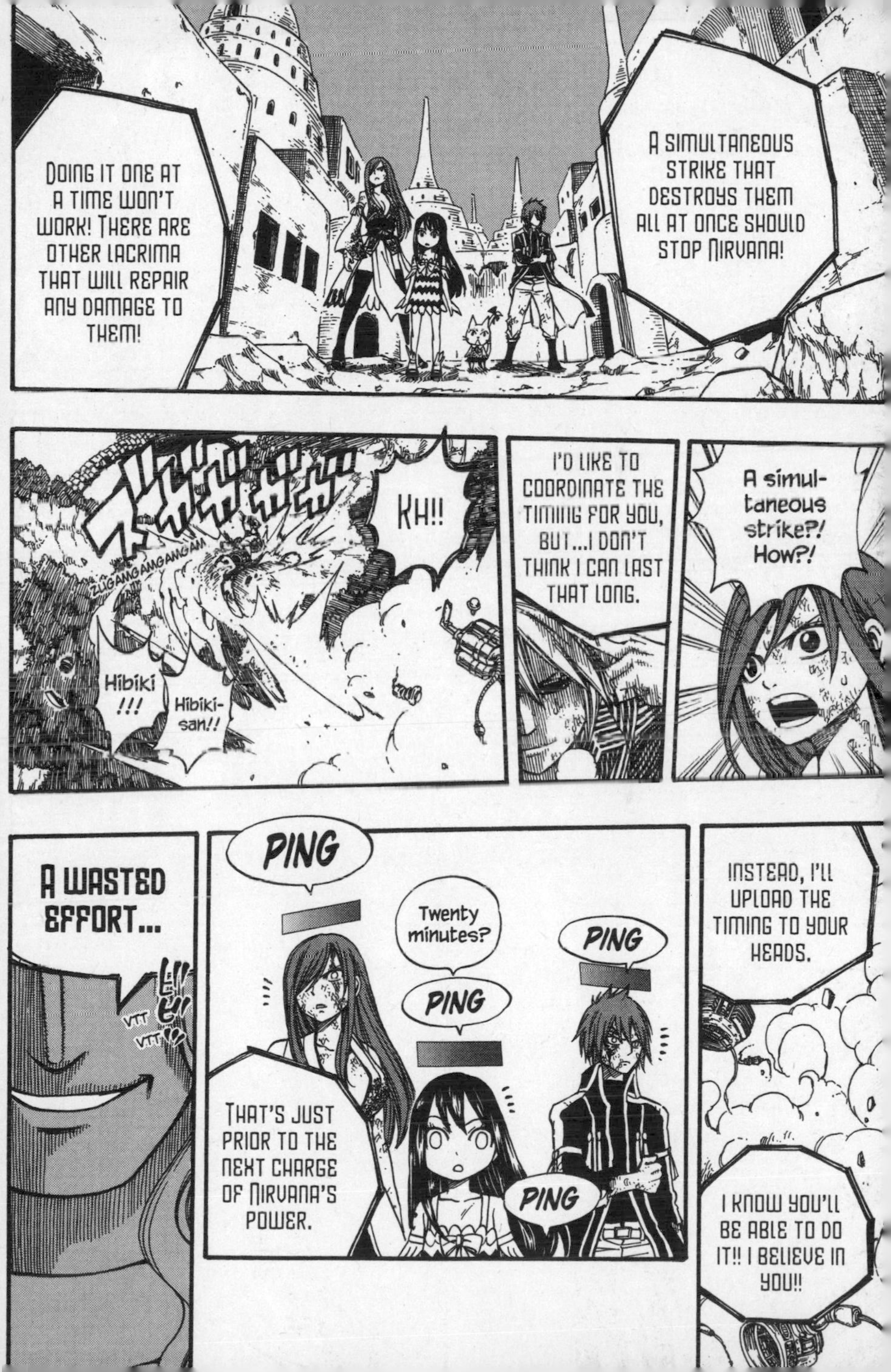

A simultaneous strike that destroys them all at once should stop Nirvana!
Doing it one at a time won't work! There are other lacrima that will repair any damage to them!
A simul-taneous strike?! How?!
I'd like to coordinate the timing for you, but...I don't think I can last that long.
KH!!
ZUGAMGAMGAMGAM
Hibiki!!!
Hibiki-san!!
Instead, I'll upload the timing to your heads.
I know you'll be able to do it!! I believe in you!!
PING
Twenty minutes?
PING
PING
PING
That's just prior to the next charge of Nirvana's power.
A wasted effort...
VTT
VTT

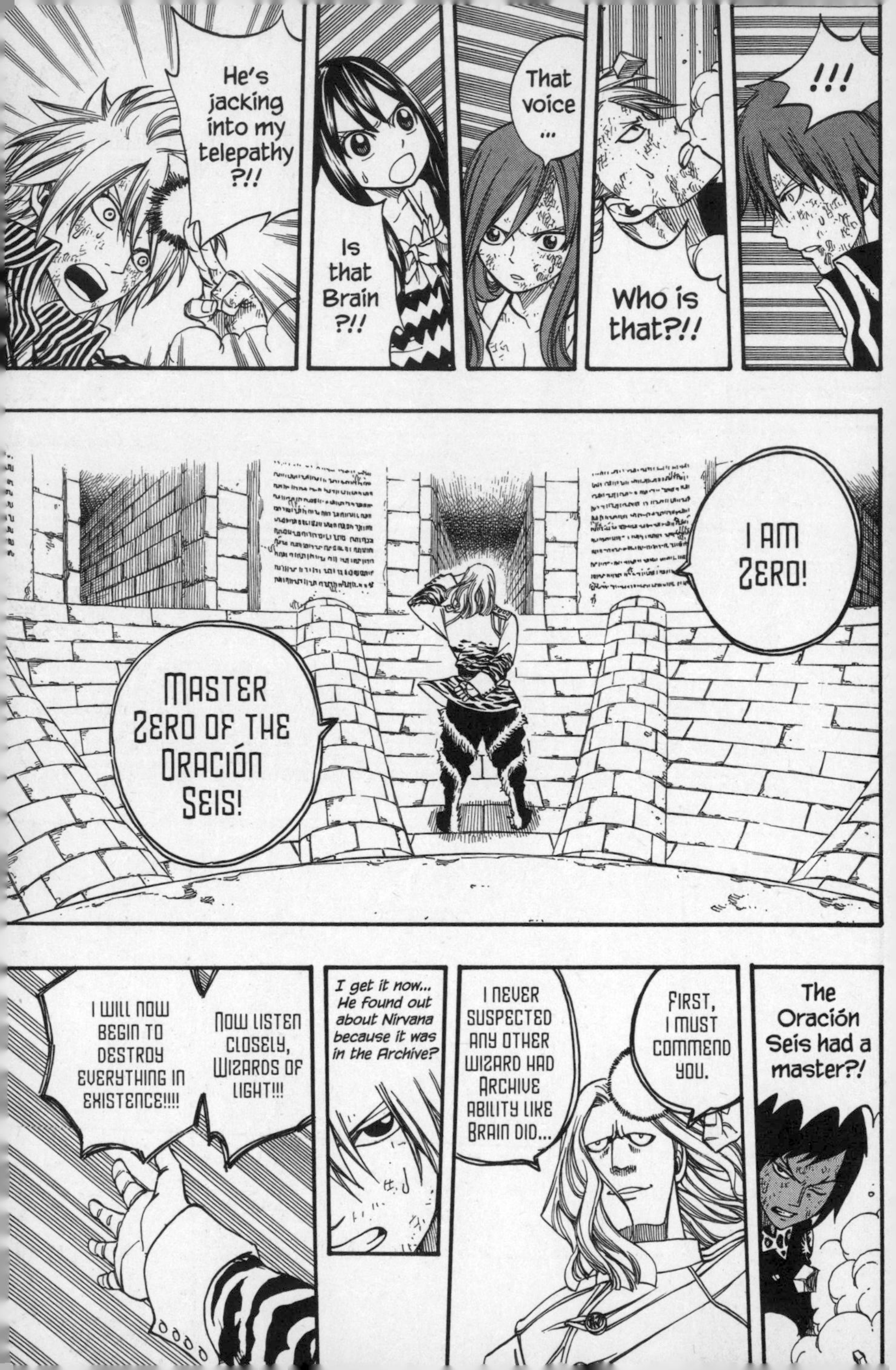
!!!
Who is that?!!
That voice ...
Is that Brain ?!!
He's jacking into my telepathy ?!!
I AM ZERO!
MASTER ZERO OF THE ORACIÓN SEIS!
The Oración Seis had a master?!
FIRST, I MUST COMMEND YOU.
I NEVER SUSPECTED ANY OTHER WIZARD HAD ARCHIVE ABILITY LIKE BRAIN DID...
I get it now... He found out about Nirvana because it was in the Archive?
NOW LISTEN CLOSELY, WIZARDS OF LIGHT!!!
I WILL NOW BEGIN TO DESTROY EVERYTHING IN EXISTENCE!!!!

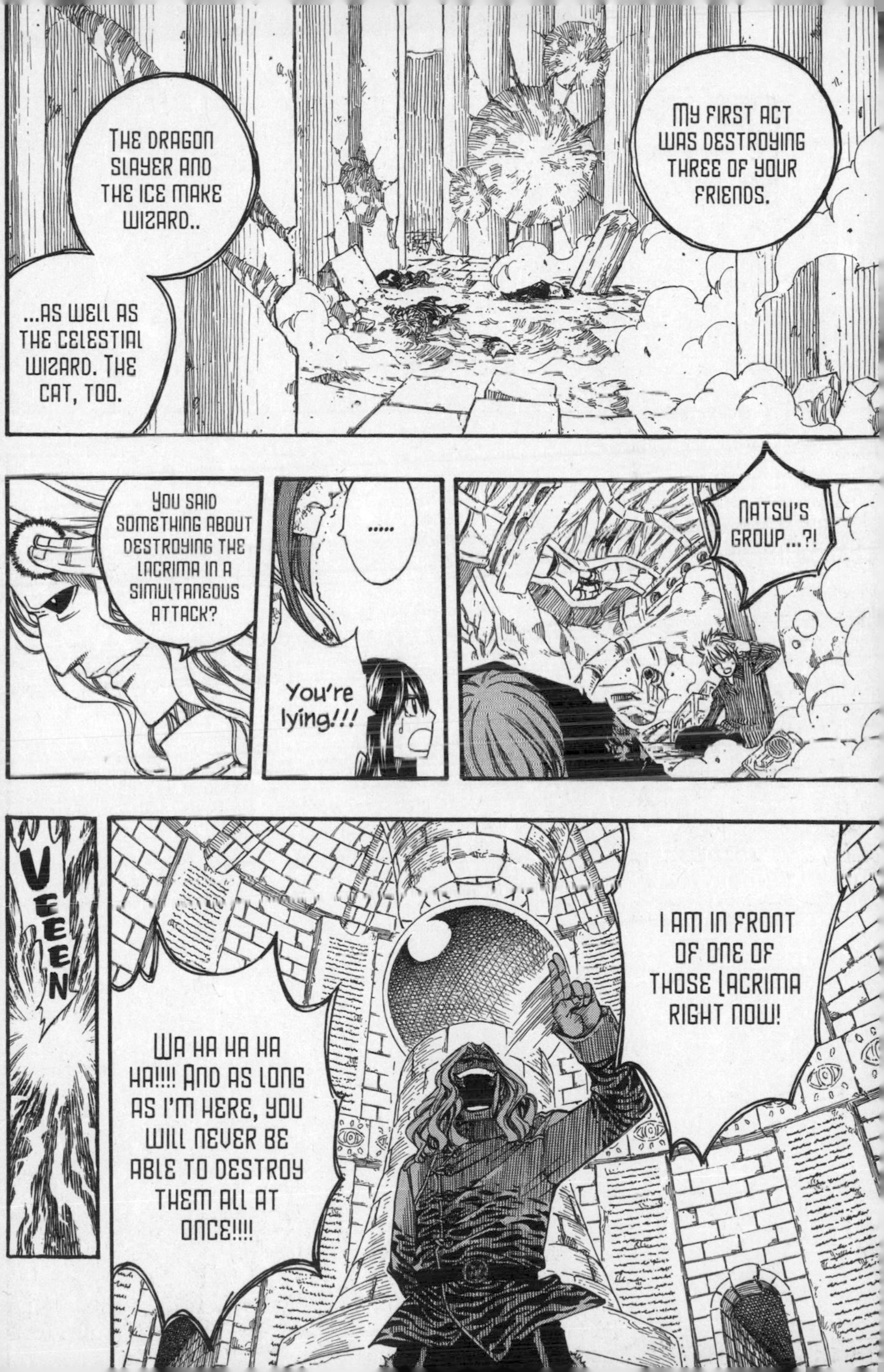
My first act was destroying three of your friends.
The dragon slayer and the ice make wizard..
...as well as the celestial wizard. The cat, too.
Natsu's group...?!
.....
You're lying!!!
You said something about destroying the lacrima in a simultaneous attack?
I am in front of one of those Lacrima right now!
Wa ha ha ha ha!!!! And as long as I'm here, you will never be able to destroy them all at once!!!!
VEEEN

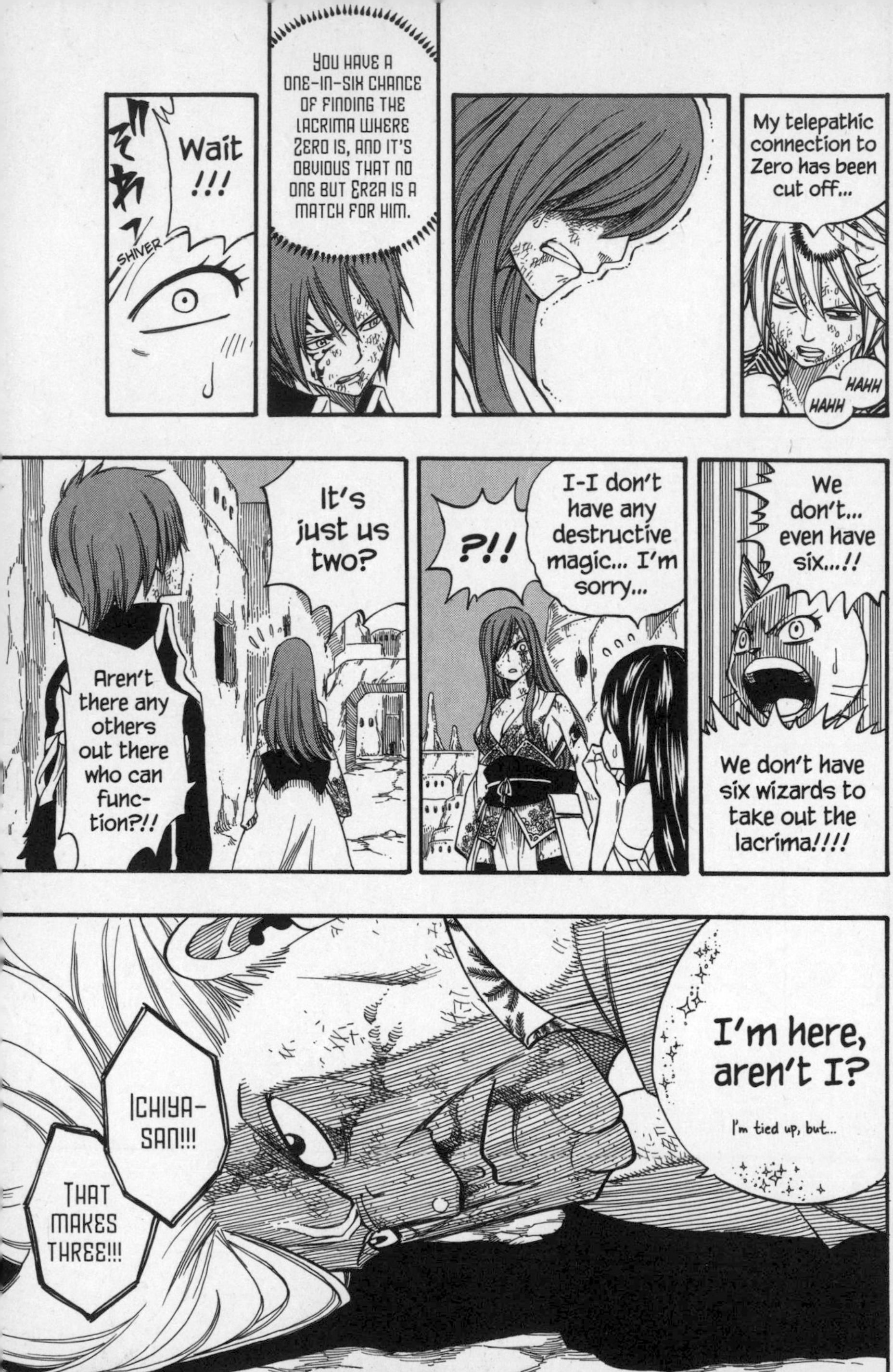
My telepathic connection to Zero has been cut off...
HAHH
HAHH
YOU HAVE A ONE-IN-SIX CHANCE OF FINDING THE LACRIMA WHERE ZERO IS, AND IT'S OBVIOUS THAT NO ONE BUT ERZA IS A MATCH FOR HIM.
Wait!!!
SHIVER
We don't... even have six...!!
We don't have six wizards to take out the lacrima!!!!
I-I don't have any destructive magic... I'm sorry...
?!!
It's just us two?
Aren't there any others out there who can function?!!
I'm here, aren't I?
I'm tied up, but...
ICHIYA-SAN!!!
THAT MAKES THREE!!!

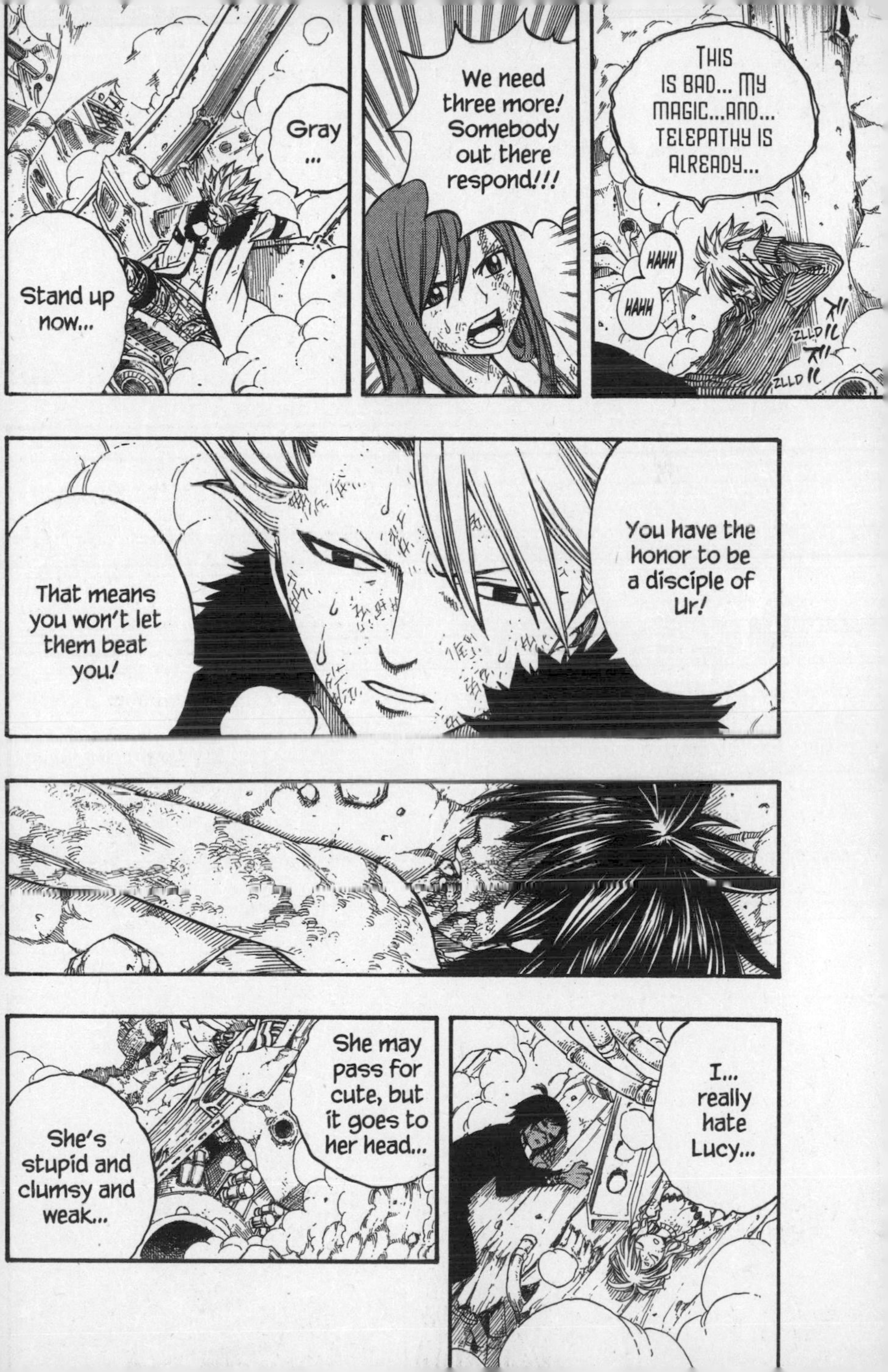
THIS IS BAD... MY MAGIC...AND... TELEPATHY IS ALREADY...
HAHH
HAHH
ZLLD
ZLLD
We need three more! Somebody out there respond!!!
Gray ...
Stand up now...
You have the honor to be a disciple of Ur!
That means you won't let them beat you!
I... really hate Lucy...
She may pass for cute, but it goes to her head...
She's stupid and clumsy and weak...

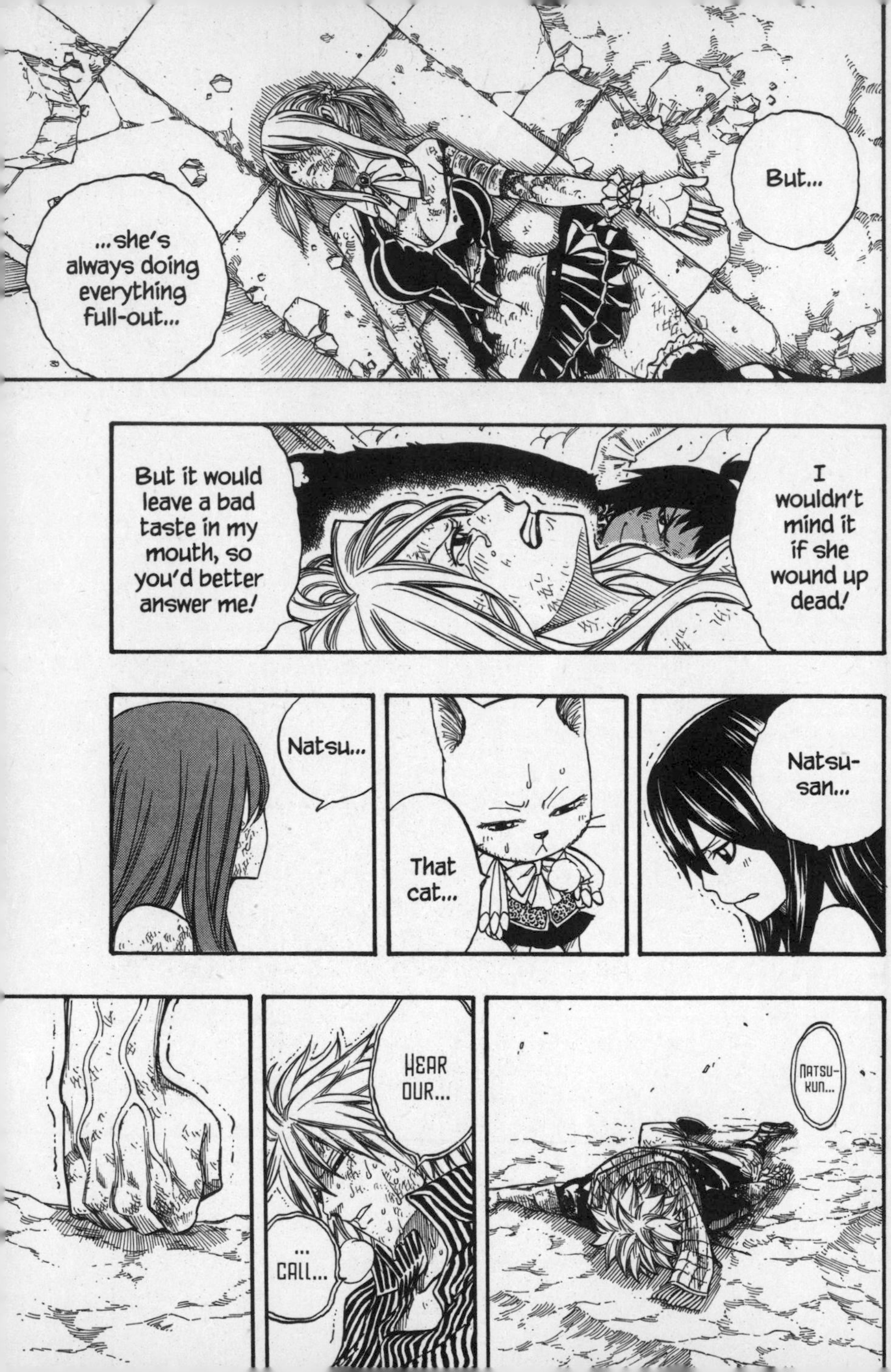
But...
...she's always doing everything full-out...
I wouldn't mind it if she wound up dead!
But it would leave a bad taste in my mouth, so you'd better answer me!
Natsu-san...
That cat...
Natsu...
NATSU-KUN...
HEAR OUR...
...CALL...

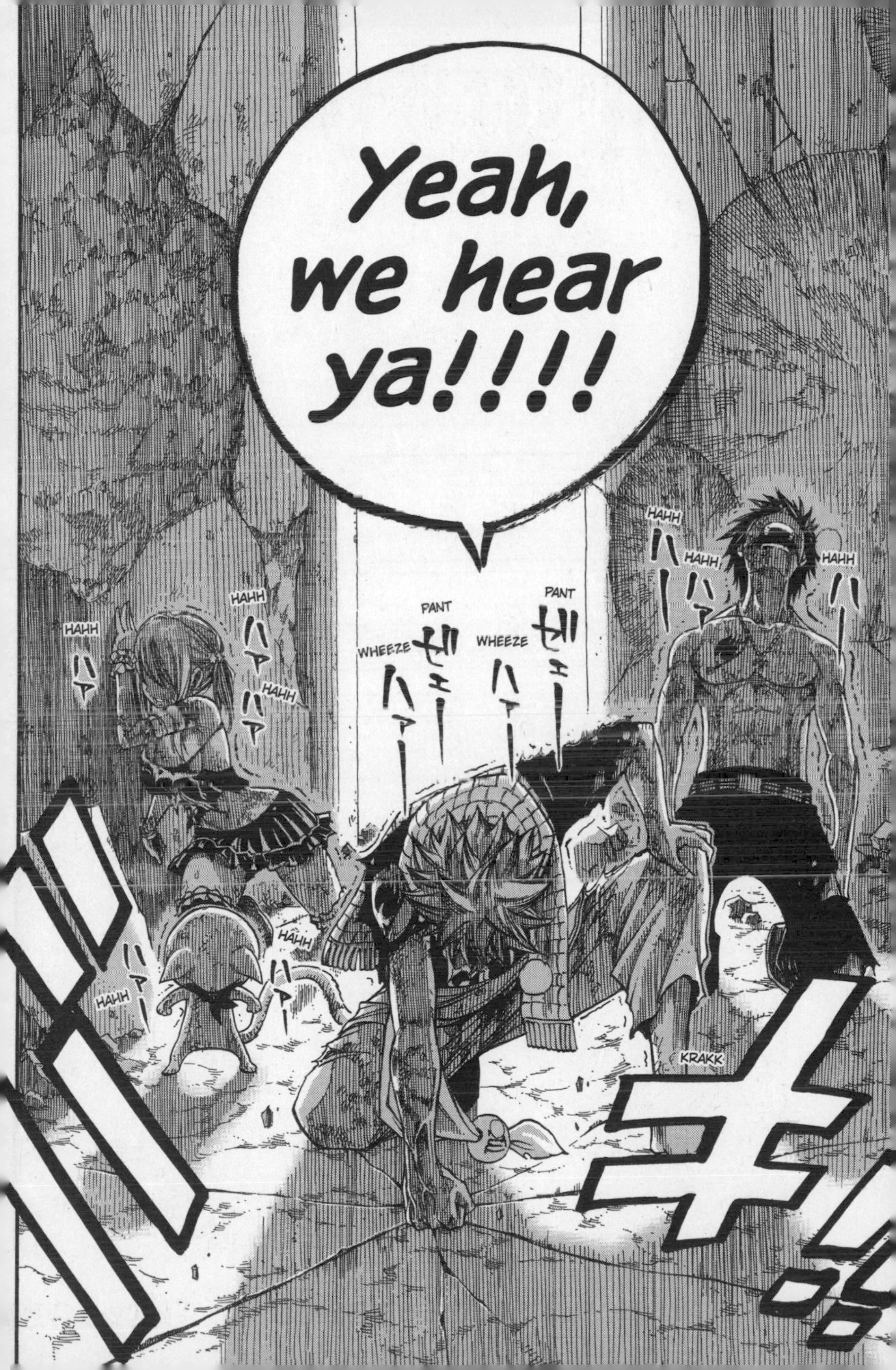

Yeah, we hear ya!!!!
HAHH
HAHH
HAHH
KRAKK
PANT
WHEEZE
PANT
WHEEZE
HAHH
HAHH
HAHH
HAHH
HAHH

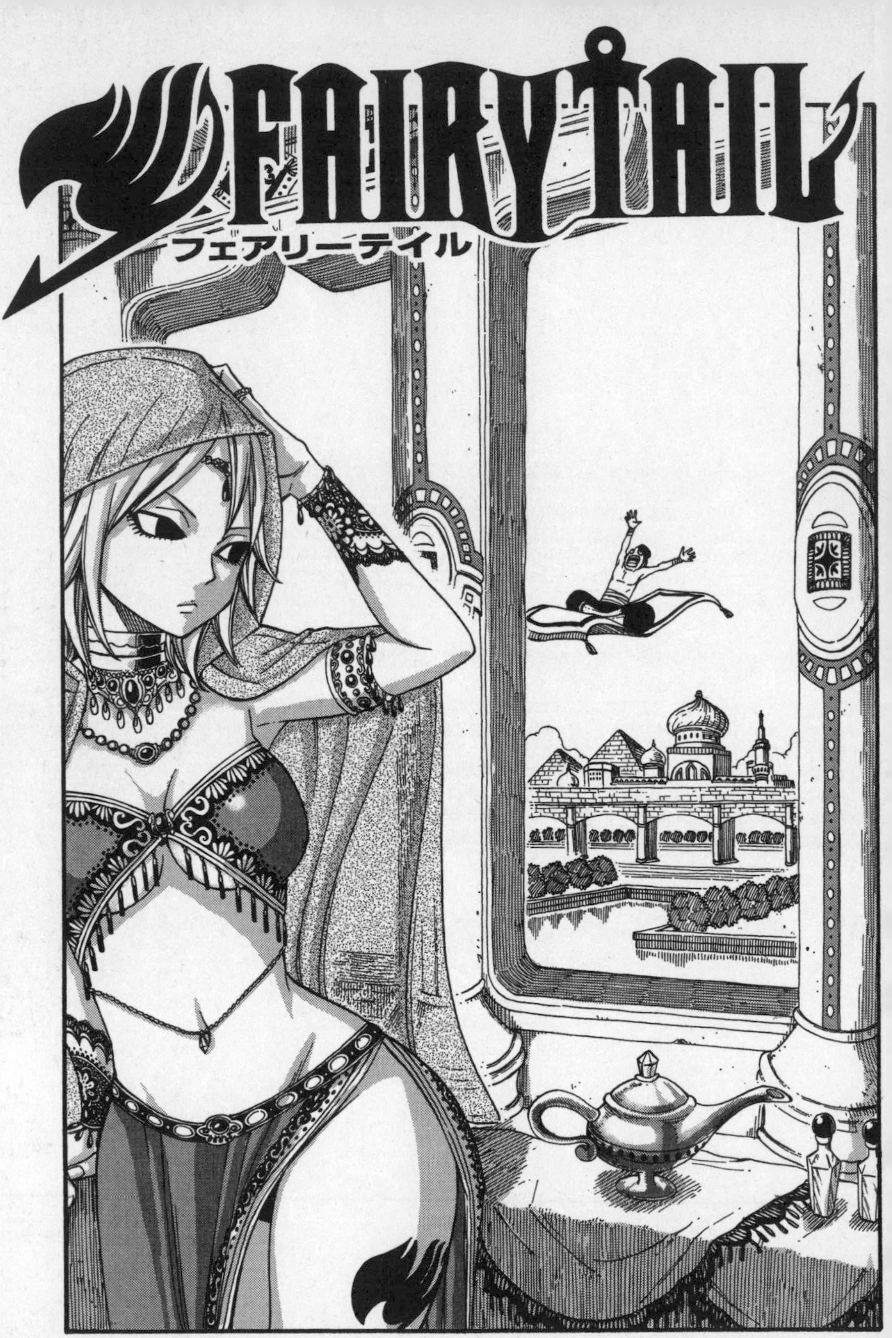
FAIRY TAIL
フェアリーテイル

Chapter 158: The Door to Memory

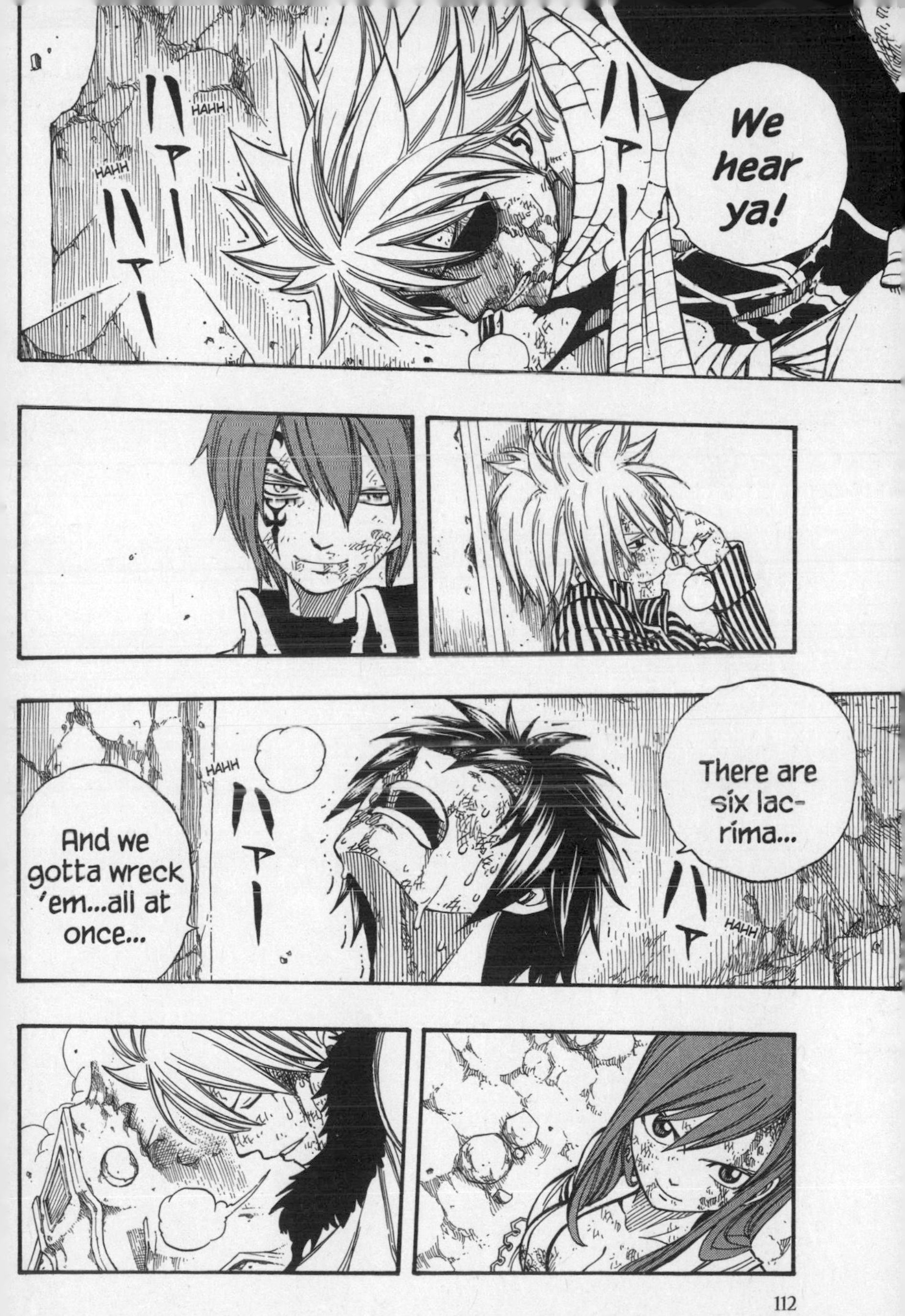
We hear ya!
HAHH
HAHH
There are six lac-rima...
HAHH
HAHH
And we gotta wreck 'em...all at once...

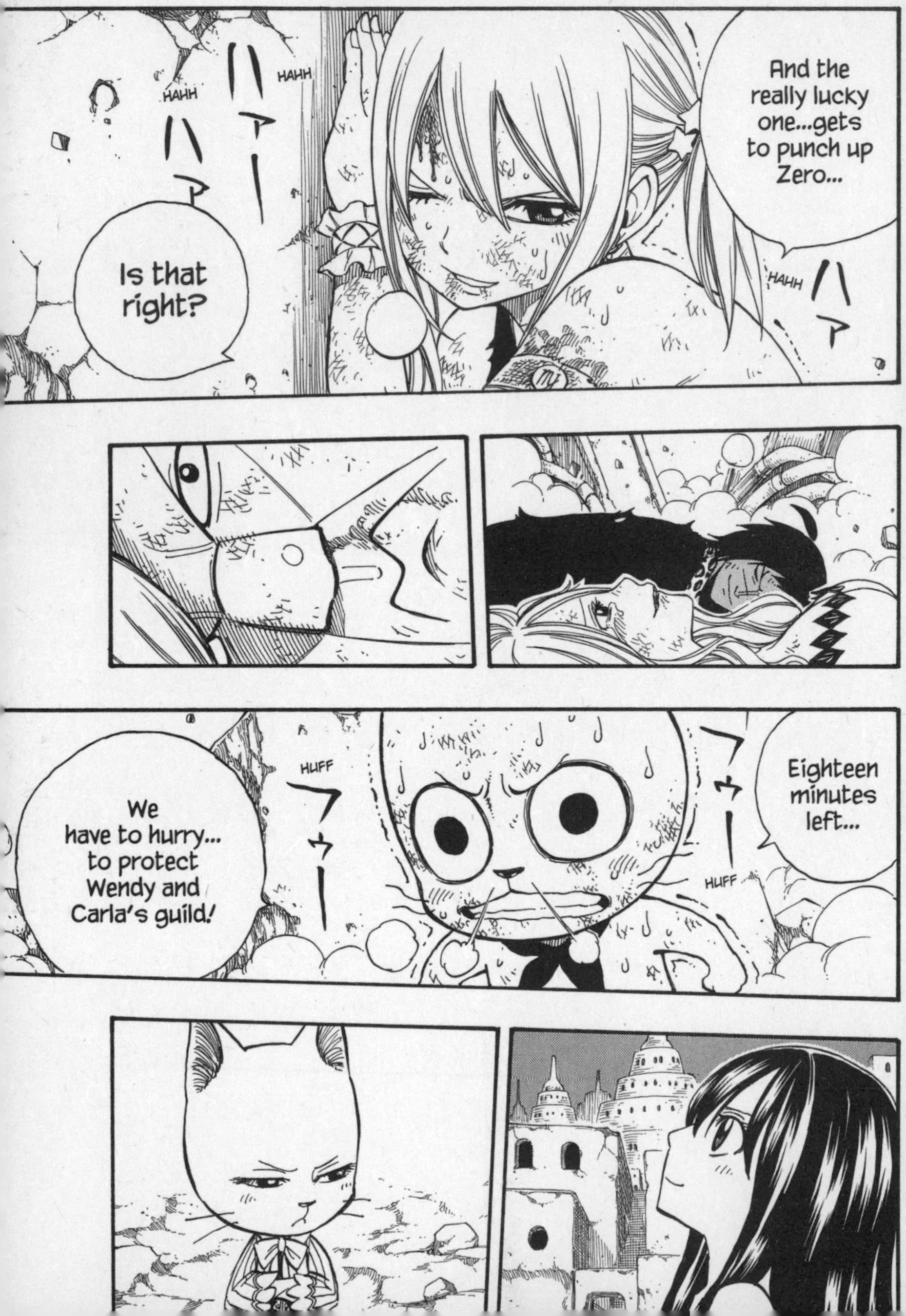
And the really lucky one...gets to punch up Zero...
HAHH
HAHH
HAHH
Is that right?
Eighteen minutes left...
HUFF
HUFF
We have to hurry... to protect Wendy and Carla's guild!

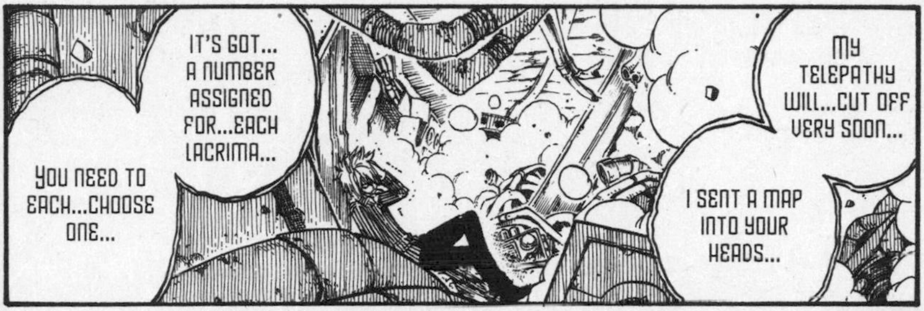
MY TELEPATHY WILL...CUT OFF VERY SOON...
I SENT A MAP INTO YOUR HEADS...
IT'S GOT... A NUMBER ASSIGNED FOR...EACH LACRIMA...
YOU NEED TO EACH...CHOOSE ONE...

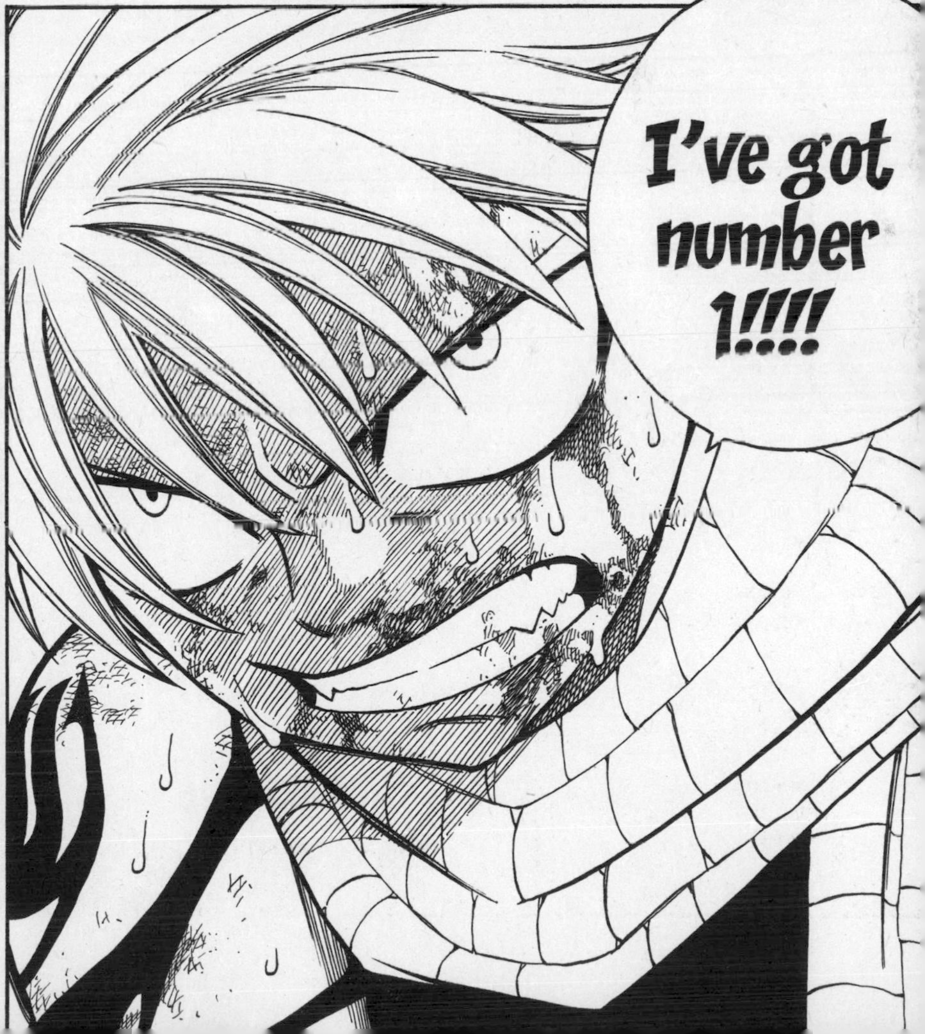
I've got number 1!!!!

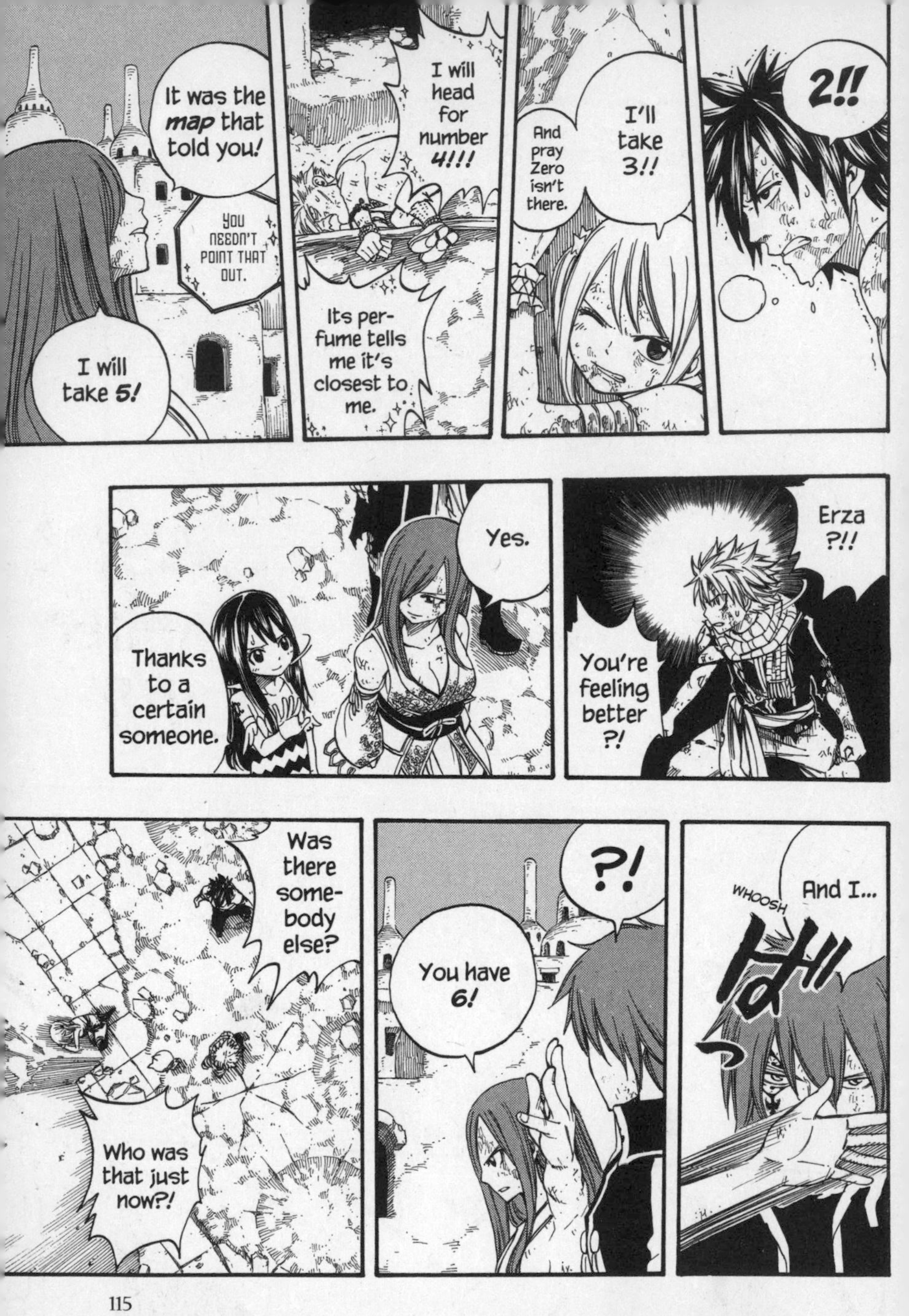
2!!
I'll take 3!!
And pray Zero isn't there.
I will head for number 4!!!
Its per-fume tells me it's closest to me.
It was the map that told you!
You needn't point that out.
I will take 5!
Erza?!!
You're feeling better?!
Yes.
Thanks to a certain someone.
And I...
WHOOSH
?!
You have 6!
Was there some-body else?
Who was that just now?!

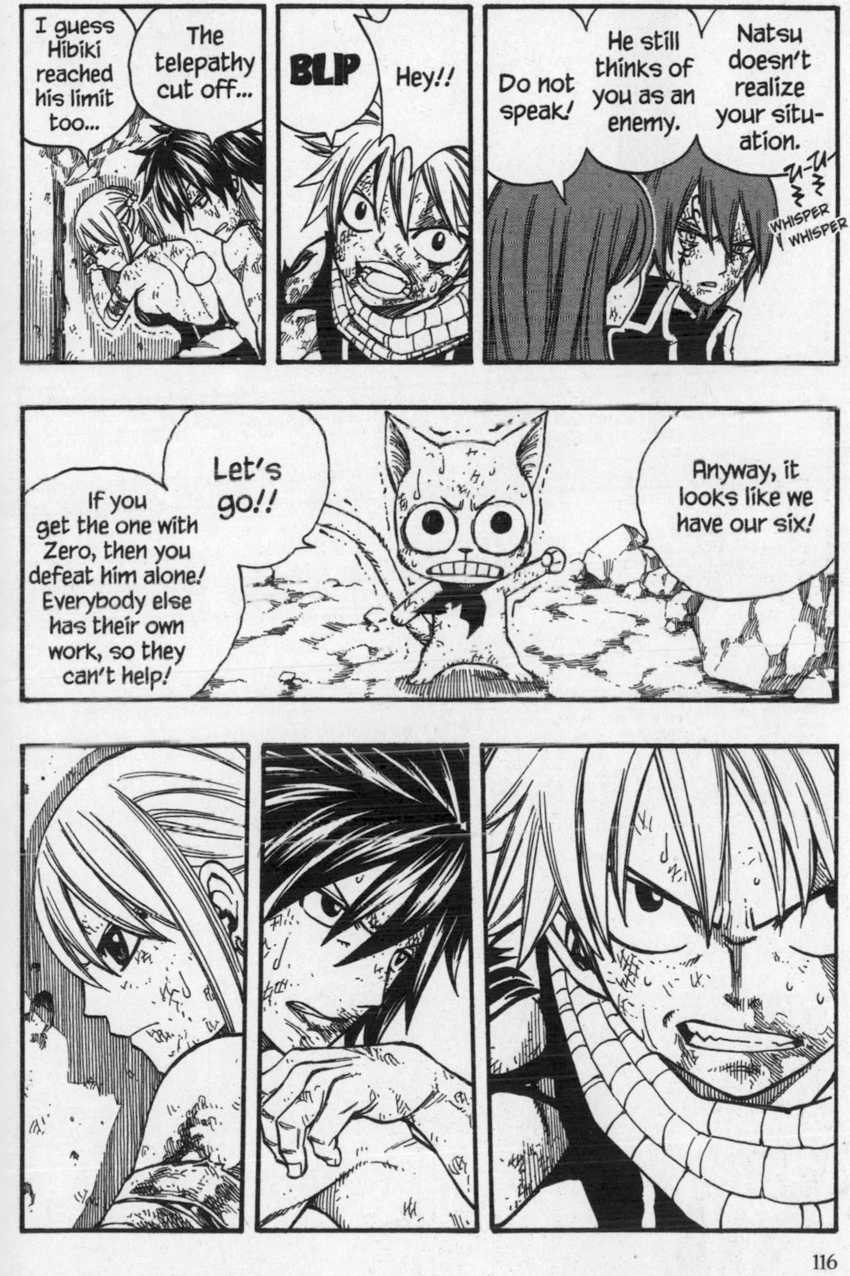
Natsu doesn't realize your situation.
He still thinks of you as an enemy.
Do not speak!
WHISPER WHISPER
Hey!!
BLIP
The telepathy cut off...
I guess Hibiki reached his limit too...
Anyway, it looks like we have our six!
Let's go!!
If you get the one with Zero, then you defeat him alone! Everybody else has their own work, so they can't help!

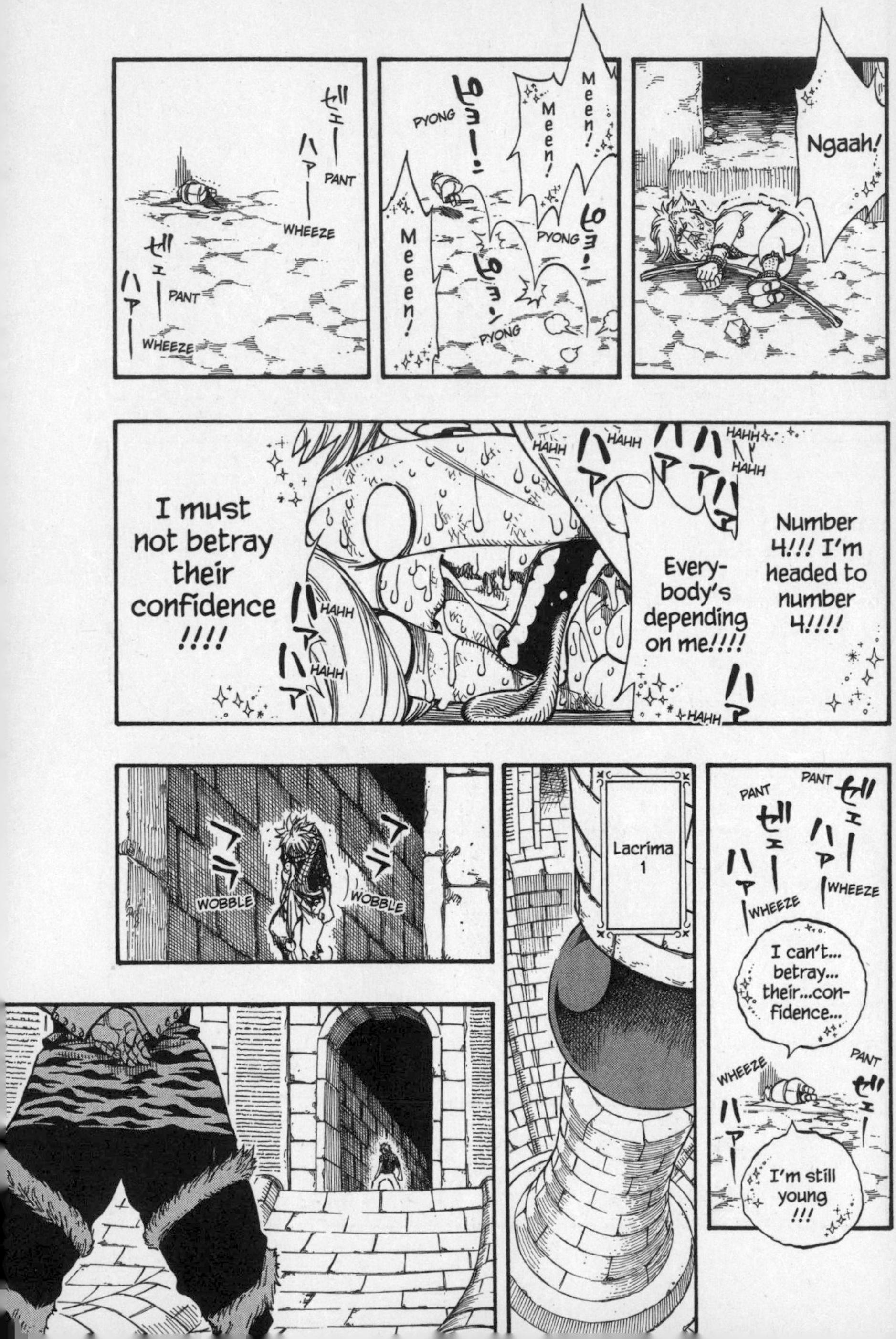

Ngaah!
Meen!
Meen!
PYONG
PYONG
PYONG
Meeen!
PANT
WHEEZE
PANT
WHEEZE
Number 4!!! I'm headed to number 4!!!!
Every-body's depending on me!!!!
HAHH
HAHH
HAHH
HAHH
I must not betray their confidence!!!!
HAHH
HAHH
HAHH
PANT
WHEEZE
PANT
WHEEZE
I can't... betray... their...con-fidence...
PANT
WHEEZE
I'm still young!!!
Lacrima 1
WOBBLE
WOBBLE

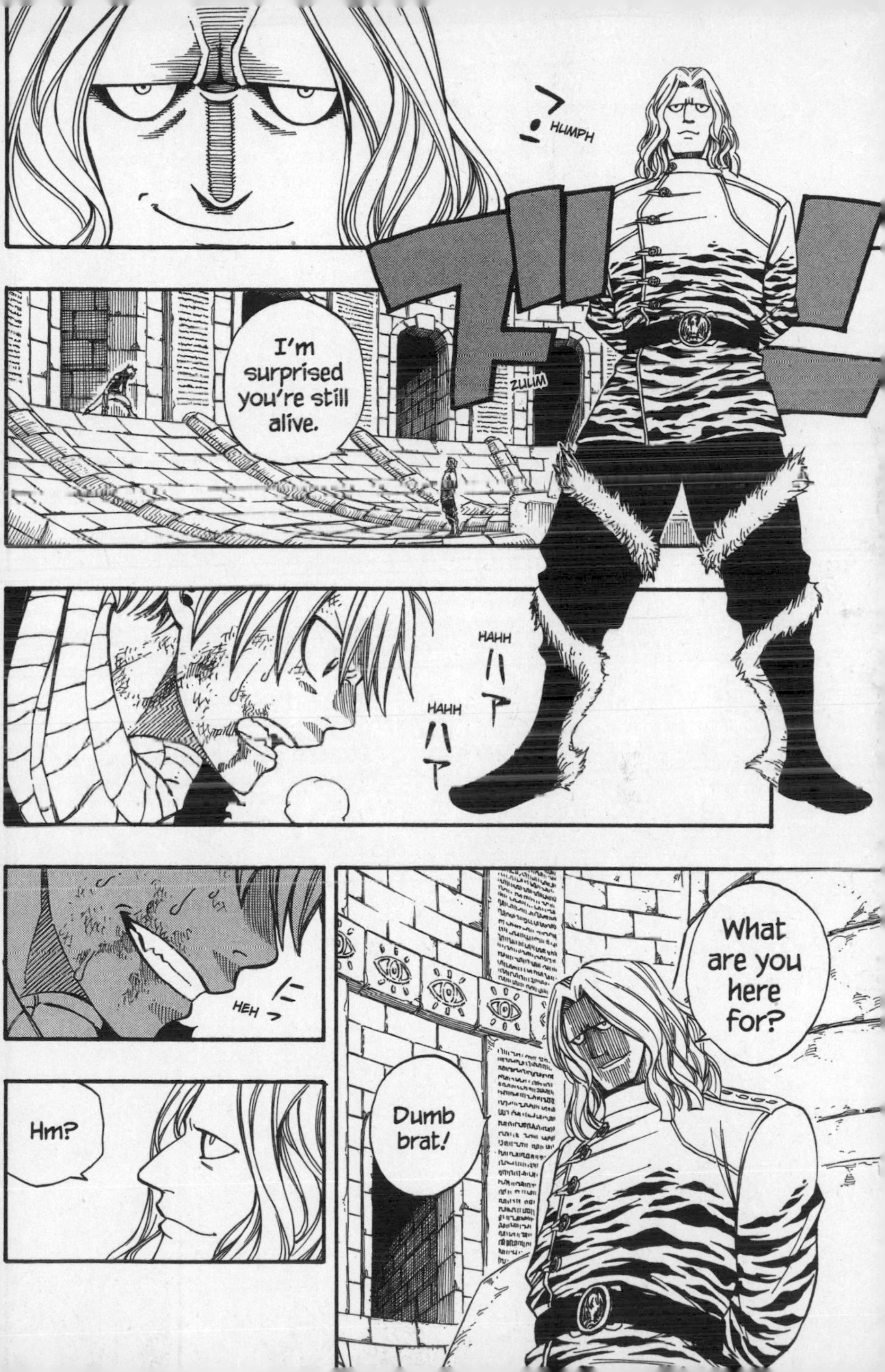
HUMPH
ZULUM
I'm surprised you're still alive.
HAHH ハア
HAHH ハア
What are you here for?
Dumb brat!
HEH
Hm?

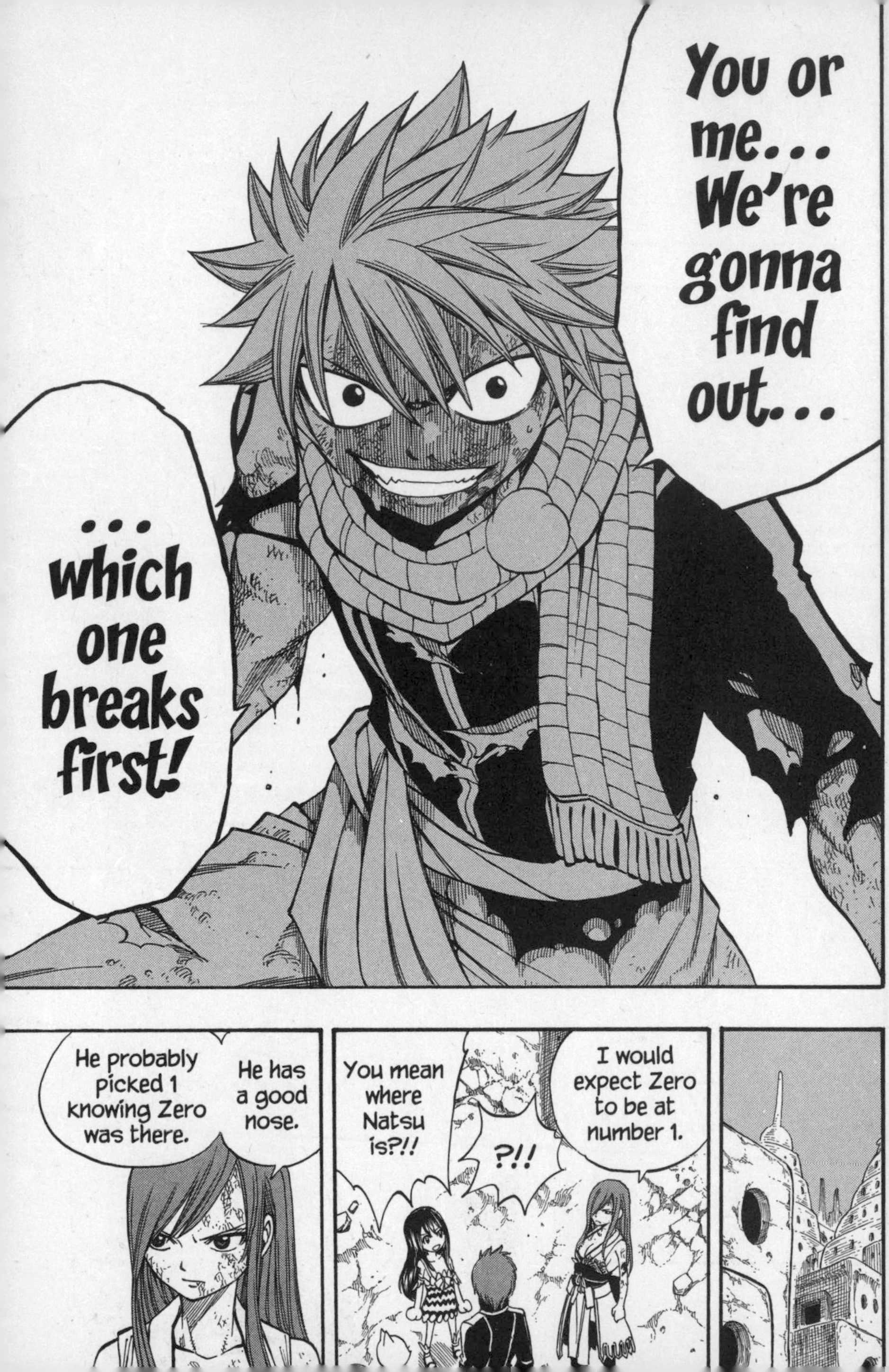

You or me... We're gonna find out...
...which one breaks first!
I would expect Zero to be at number 1.
?!!
You mean where Natsu is?!!
He has a good nose.
He probably picked 1 knowing Zero was there.

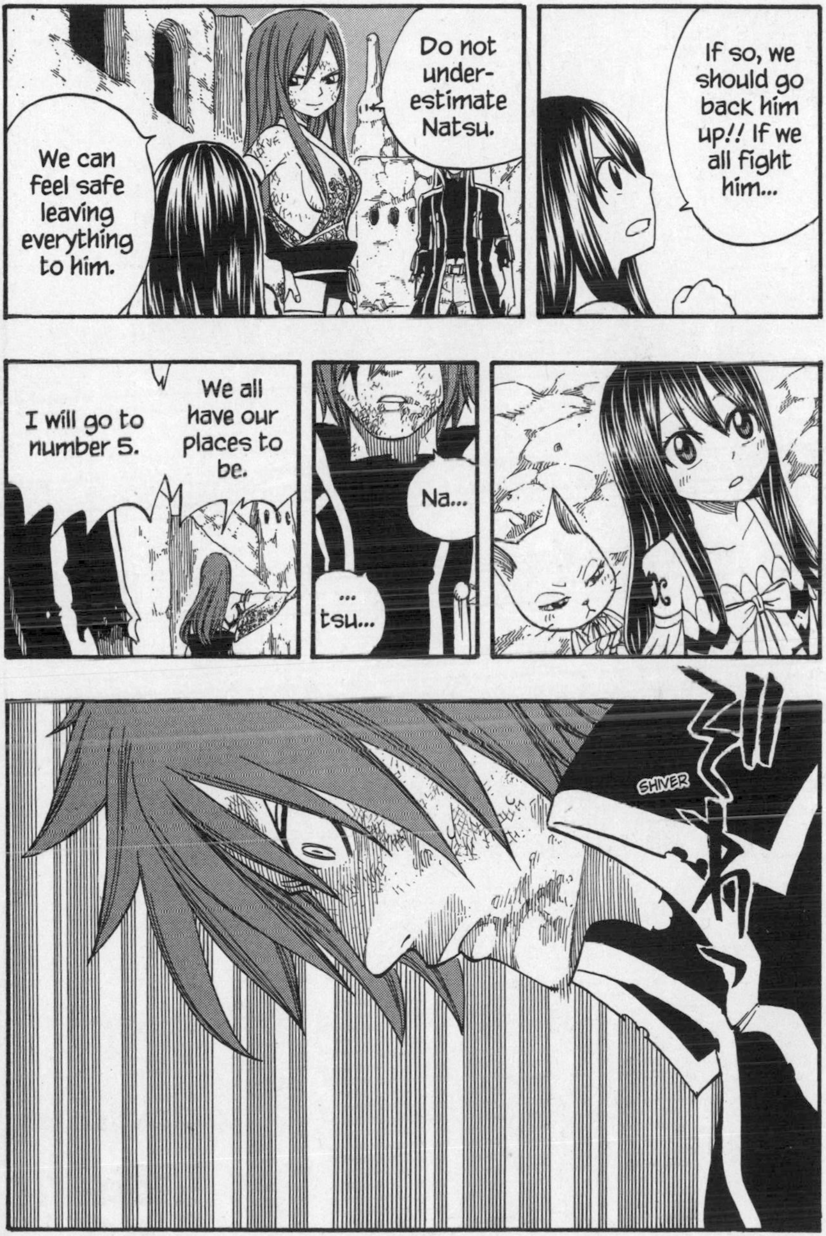
If so, we should go back him up!! If we all fight him...
Do not under-estimate Natsu.
We can feel safe leaving everything to him.
Na...
... tsu...
We all have our places to be.
I will go to number 5.
SHIVER

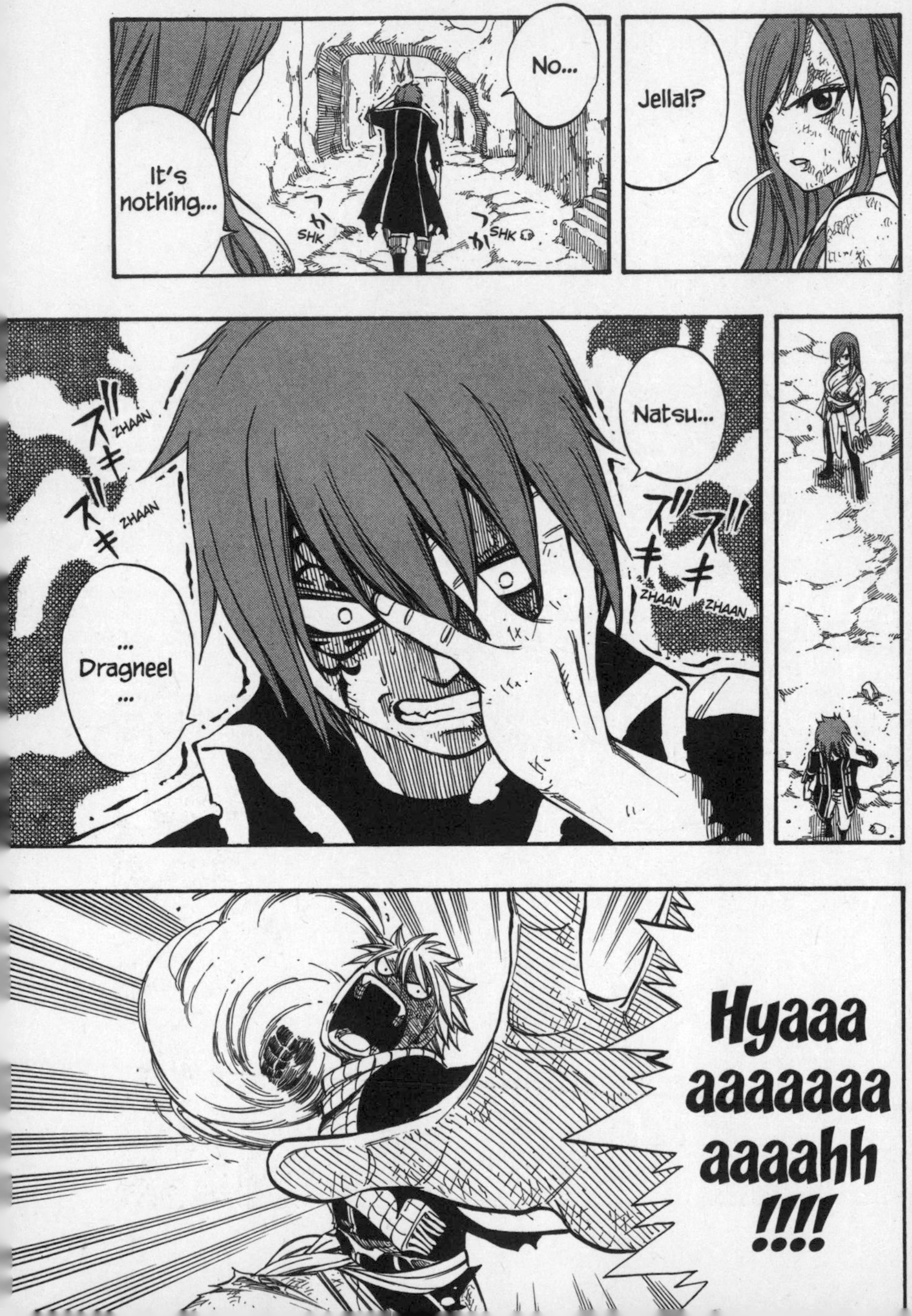

Jellal?
No...
It's nothing...
つか SHK
つか SHK
Natsu...
ズキ ZHAAN
ズキ ZHAAN
ズキ ZHAAN
ズキ ZHAAN
... Dragneel ...
Hyaaa aaaaaaa aaaahh !!!!

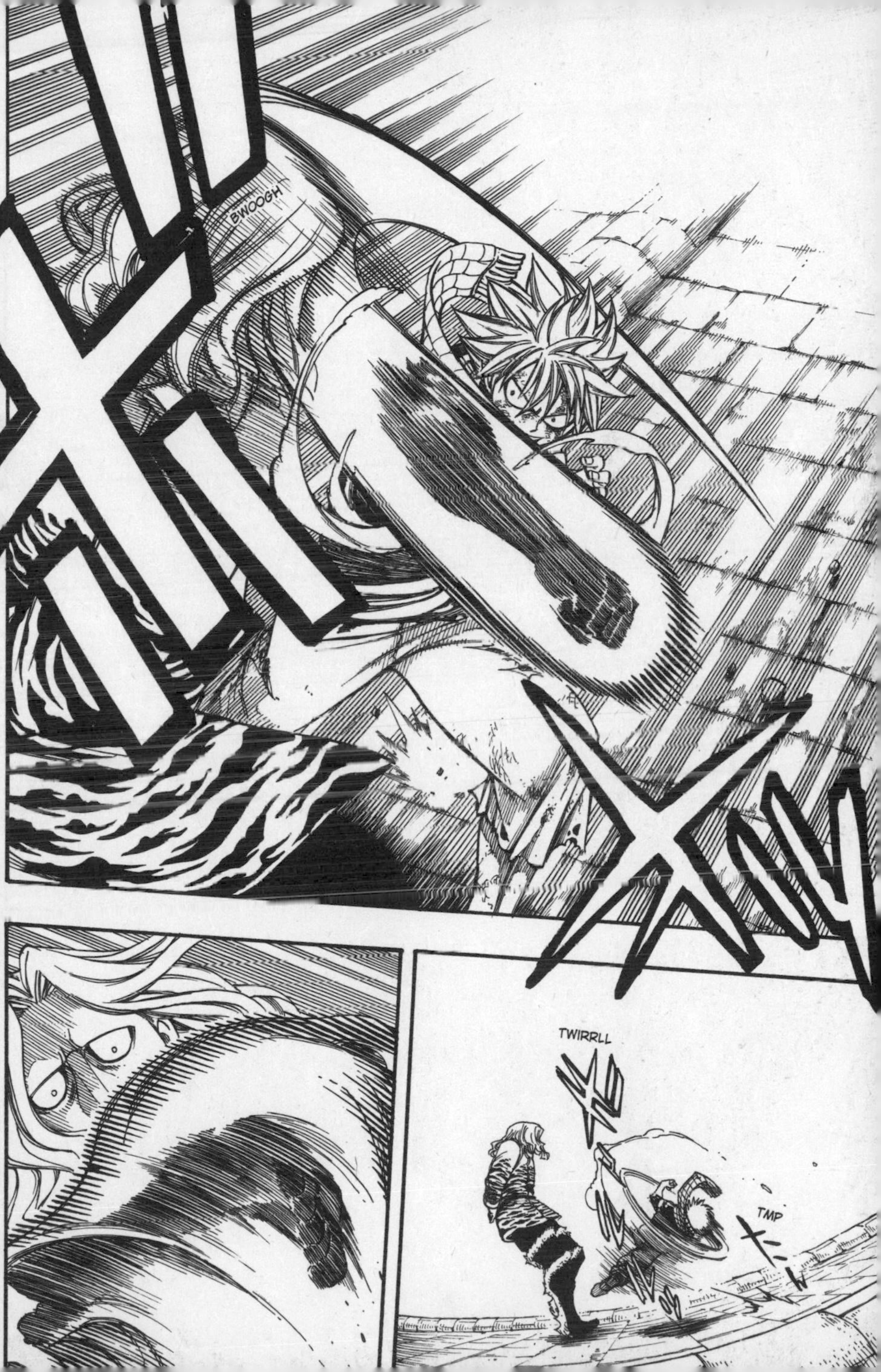
BWOOGH
TWIRRLL
TMP

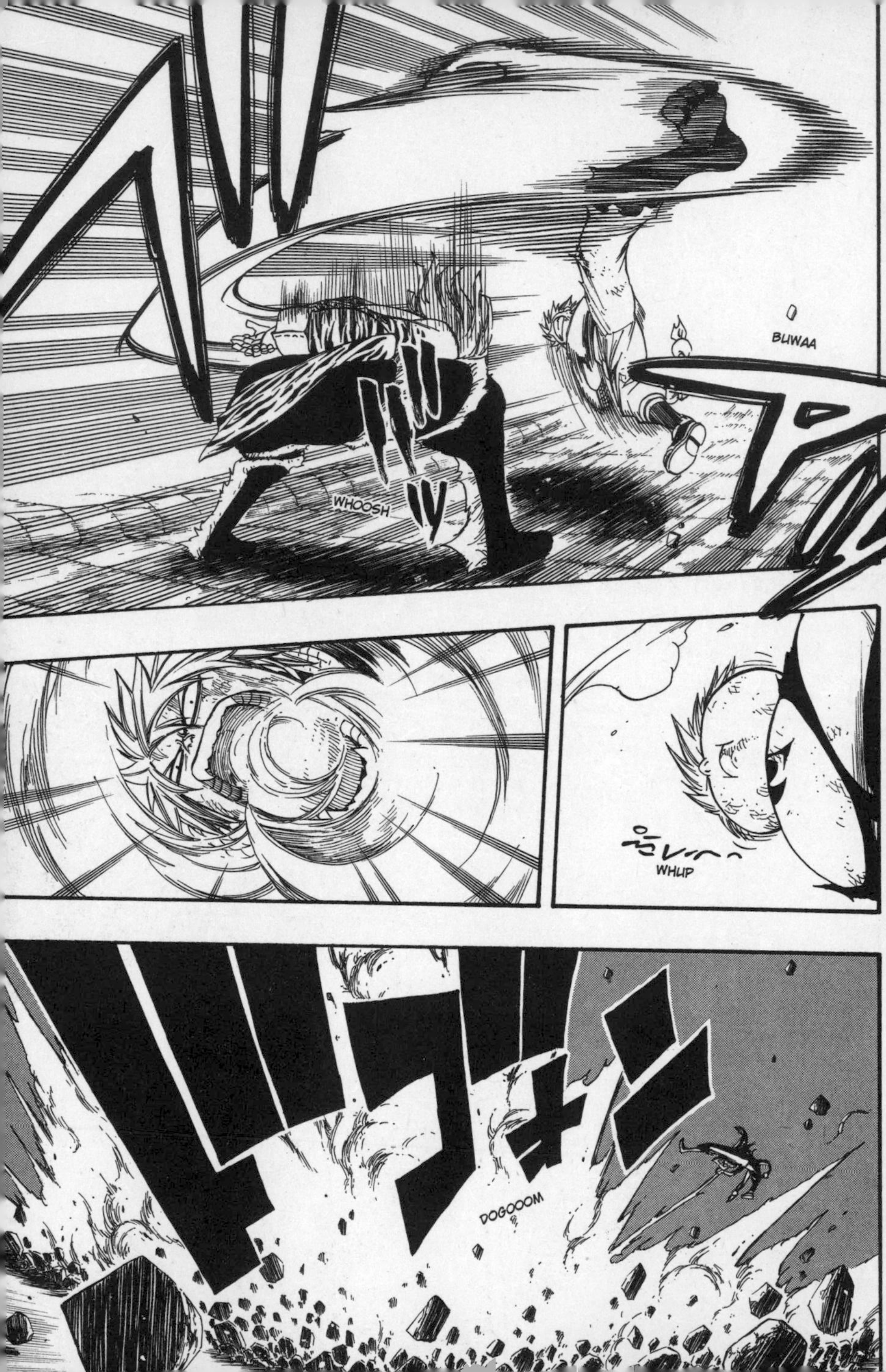
BUWAA
WHOOSH
WHUP
DOGOOOM

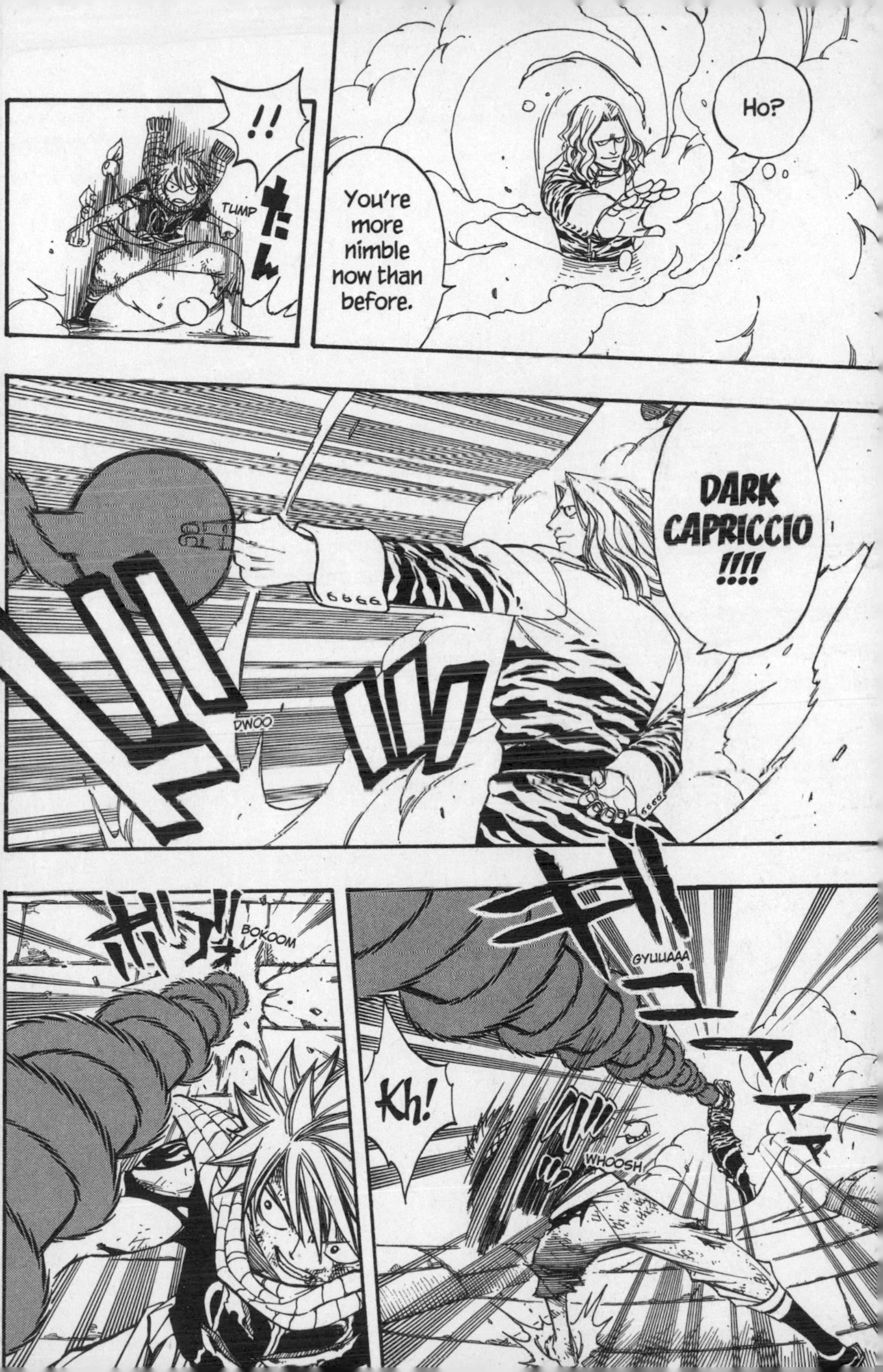
Ho?
You're more nimble now than before.
!!
TUMP
たん
DARK CAPRICCIO!!!!
DWOO
GYUUAAA
Kh!
WHOOSH
BOKOOM

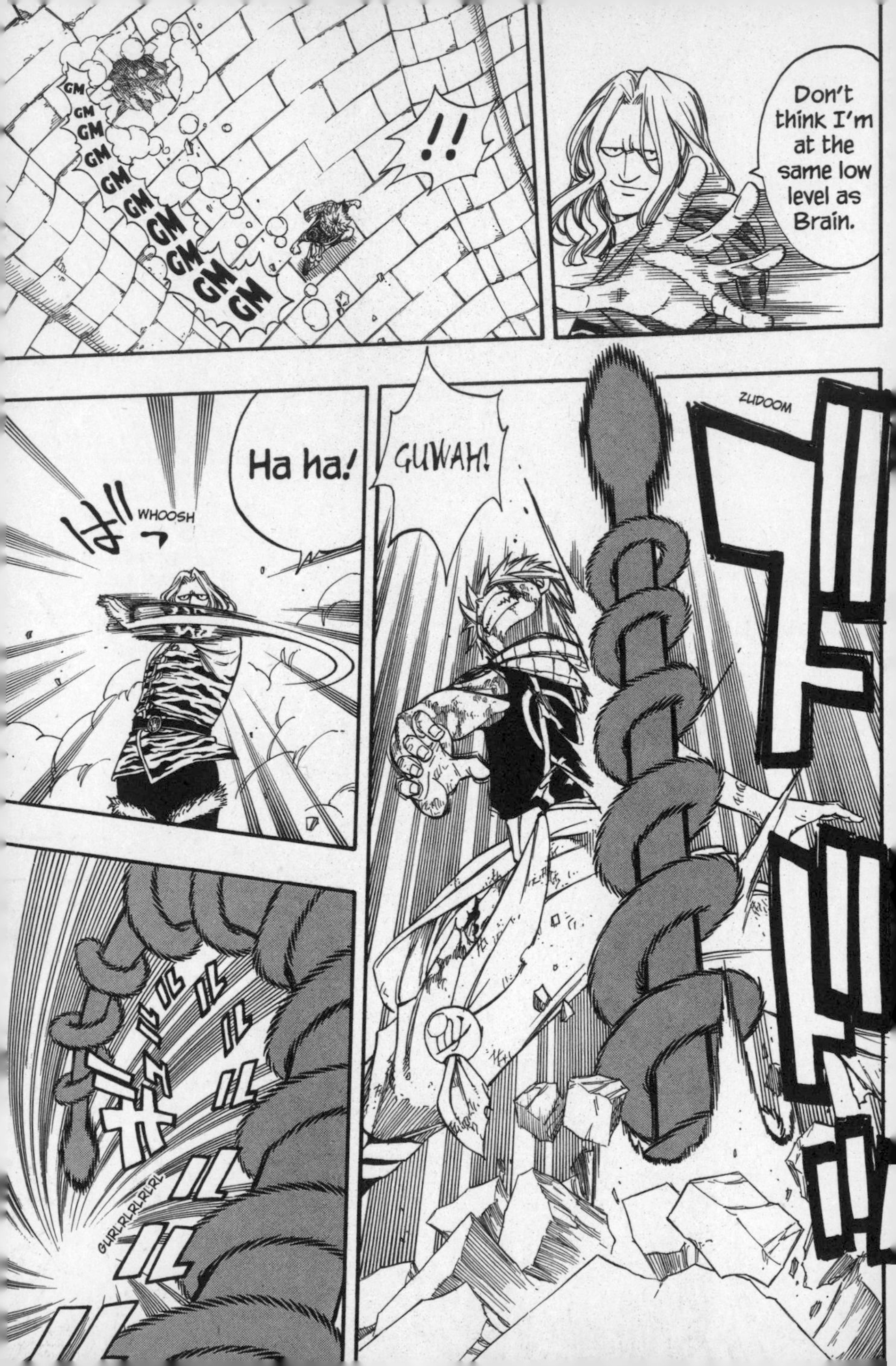
Don't think I'm at the same low level as Brain.
!!
GM GM GM GM GM GM GM GM GM GM
ZUDOOM
GUWAH!
Ha ha!
WHOOSH
GURLRLRLRL

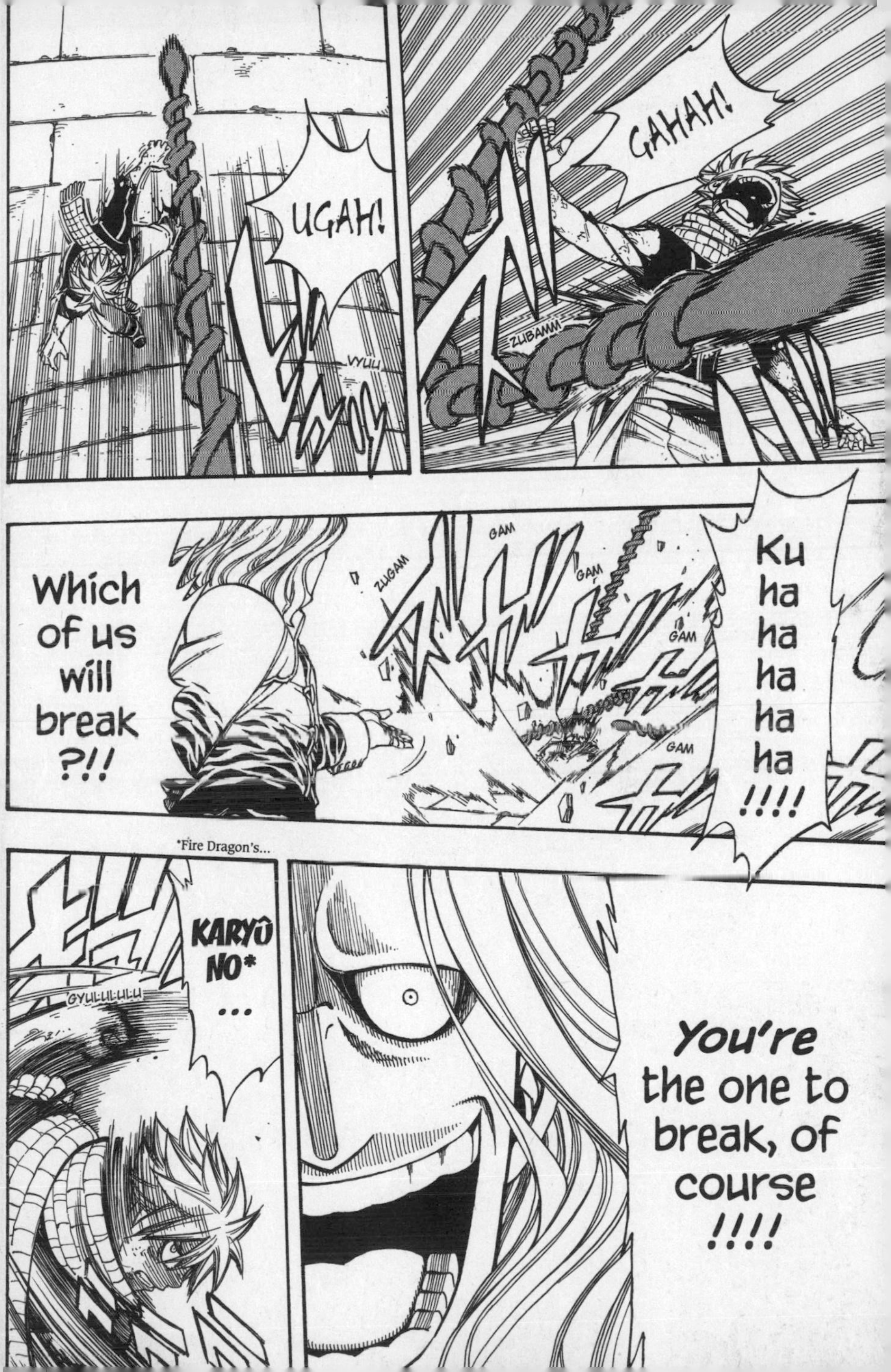
GAHAH!
ZUBAMM
UGAH!
VYUU
Ku ha ha ha ha ha !!!!
GAM
GAM
GAM
GAM
ZUGAM
Which of us will break ?!!
You're the one to break, of course !!!!
KARYÛ NO* ...
GYULULULU

*Fire Dragon's...

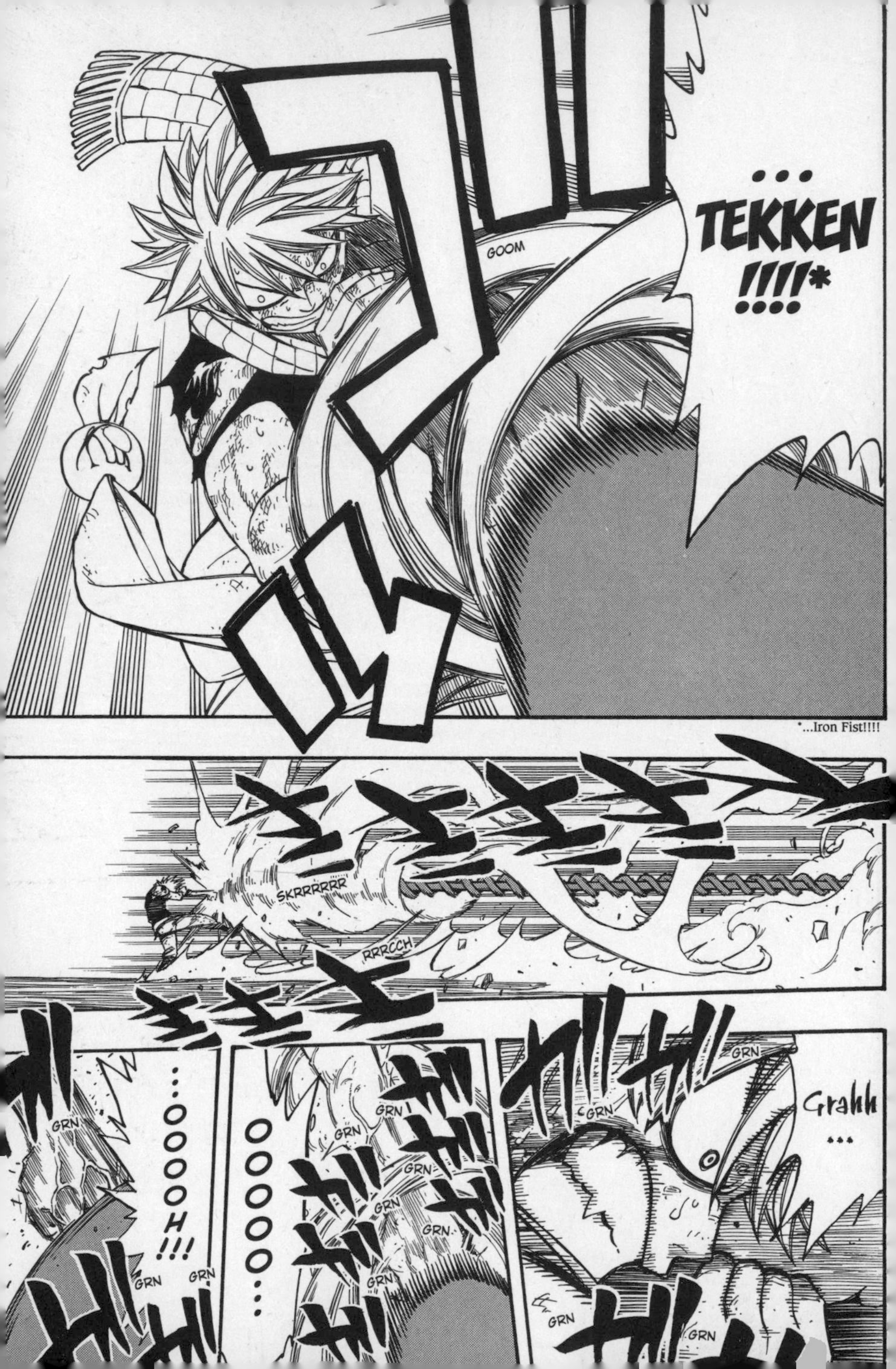
...TEKKEN !!!!*
GOOM
*...Iron Fist!!!!
SKRRRRRR
RRRCCH
Grahh ...
GRN
GRN
GRN
...OOOOOO...
GRN
GRN
GRN
GRN
GRN
GRN
...OOOOH!!!
GRN
GRN
GRN

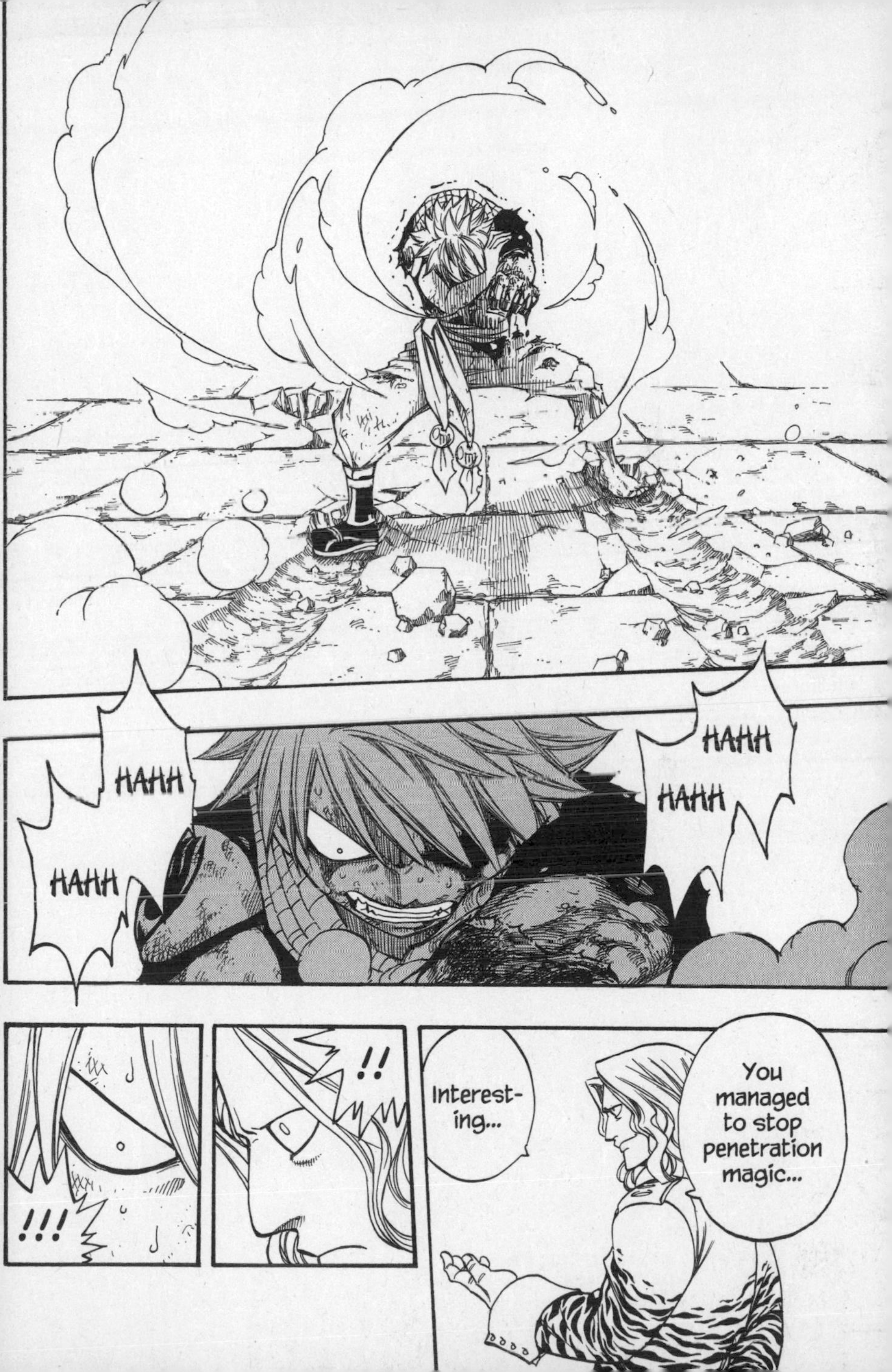
HAHH
HAHH
HAHH
HAHH
You managed to stop penetration magic...
Interest-ing...
!!
!!!

DOOOM.

GWAAH !!!

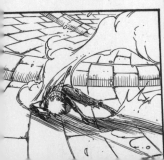

WHO ?!

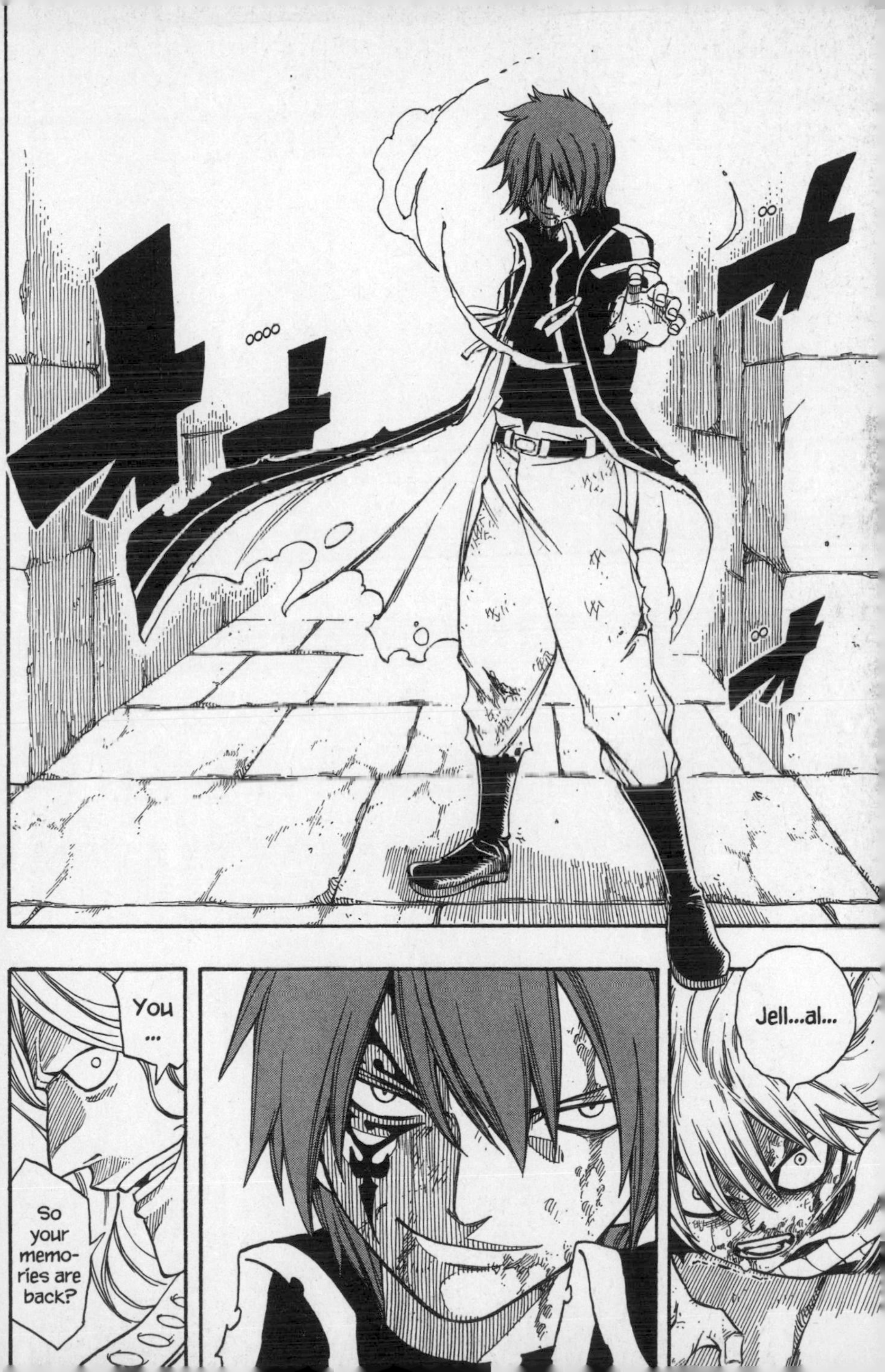
Jell...al...
You ...
So your memories are back?

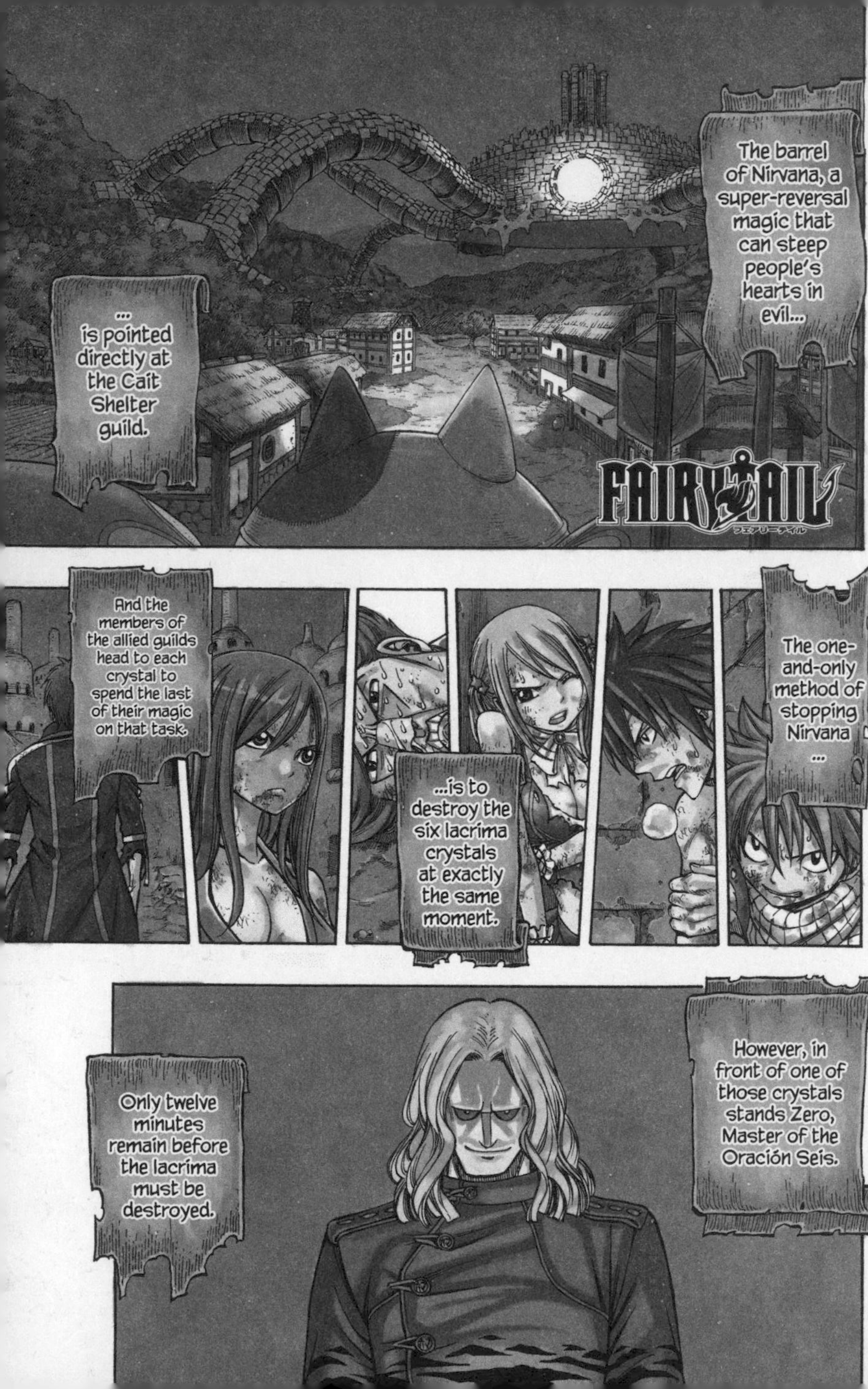
The barrel of Nirvana, a super-reversal magic that can steep people's hearts in evil...
FAIRY TAIL
...is pointed directly at the Cait Shelter guild.
The one-and-only method of stopping Nirvana...
...is to destroy the six lacrima crystals at exactly the same moment.
And the members of the allied guilds head to each crystal to spend the last of their magic on that task.
However, in front of one of those crystals stands Zero, Master of the Oración Seis.
Only twelve minutes remain before the lacrima must be destroyed.

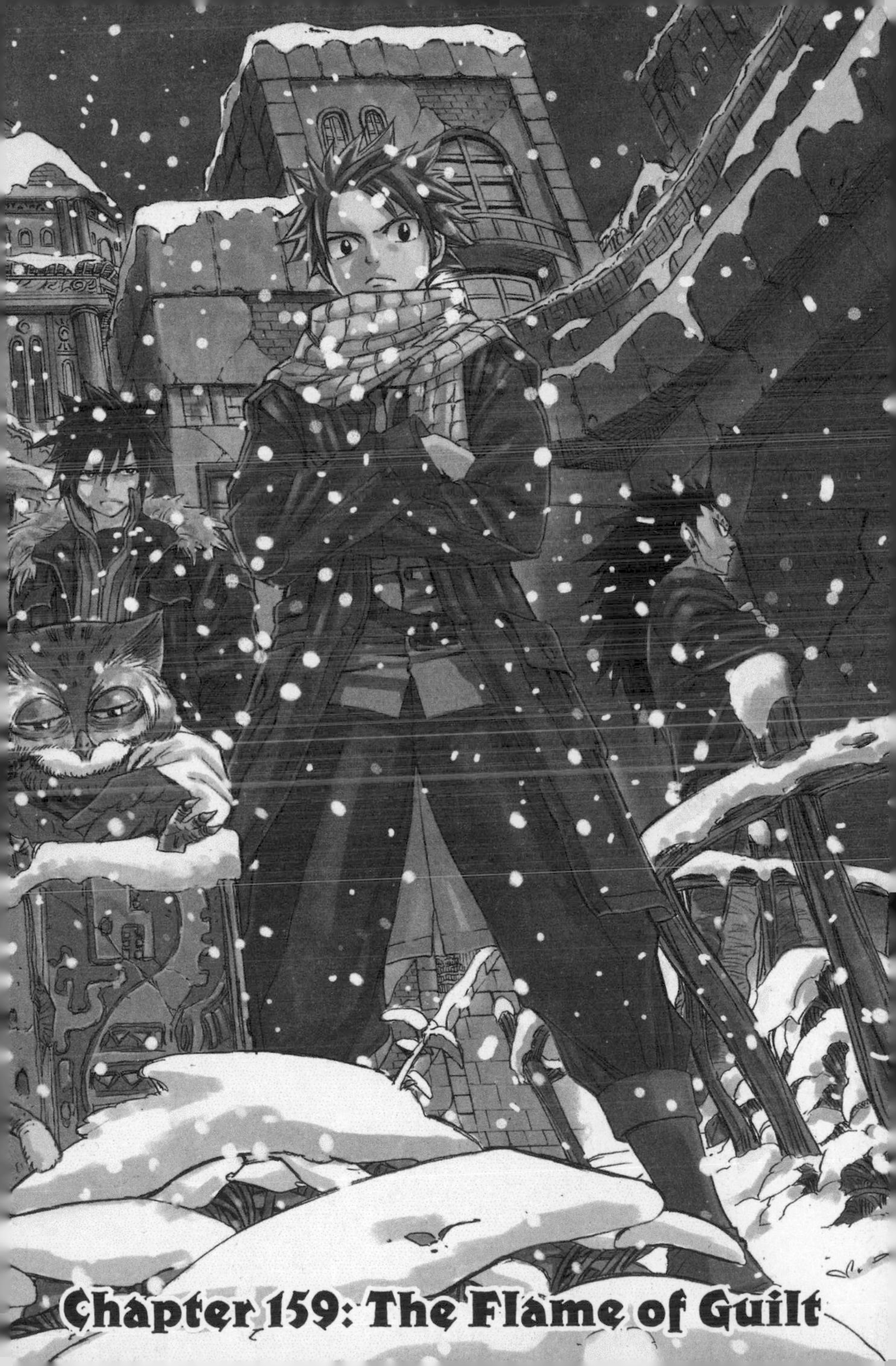
Chapter 159: The Flame of Guilt

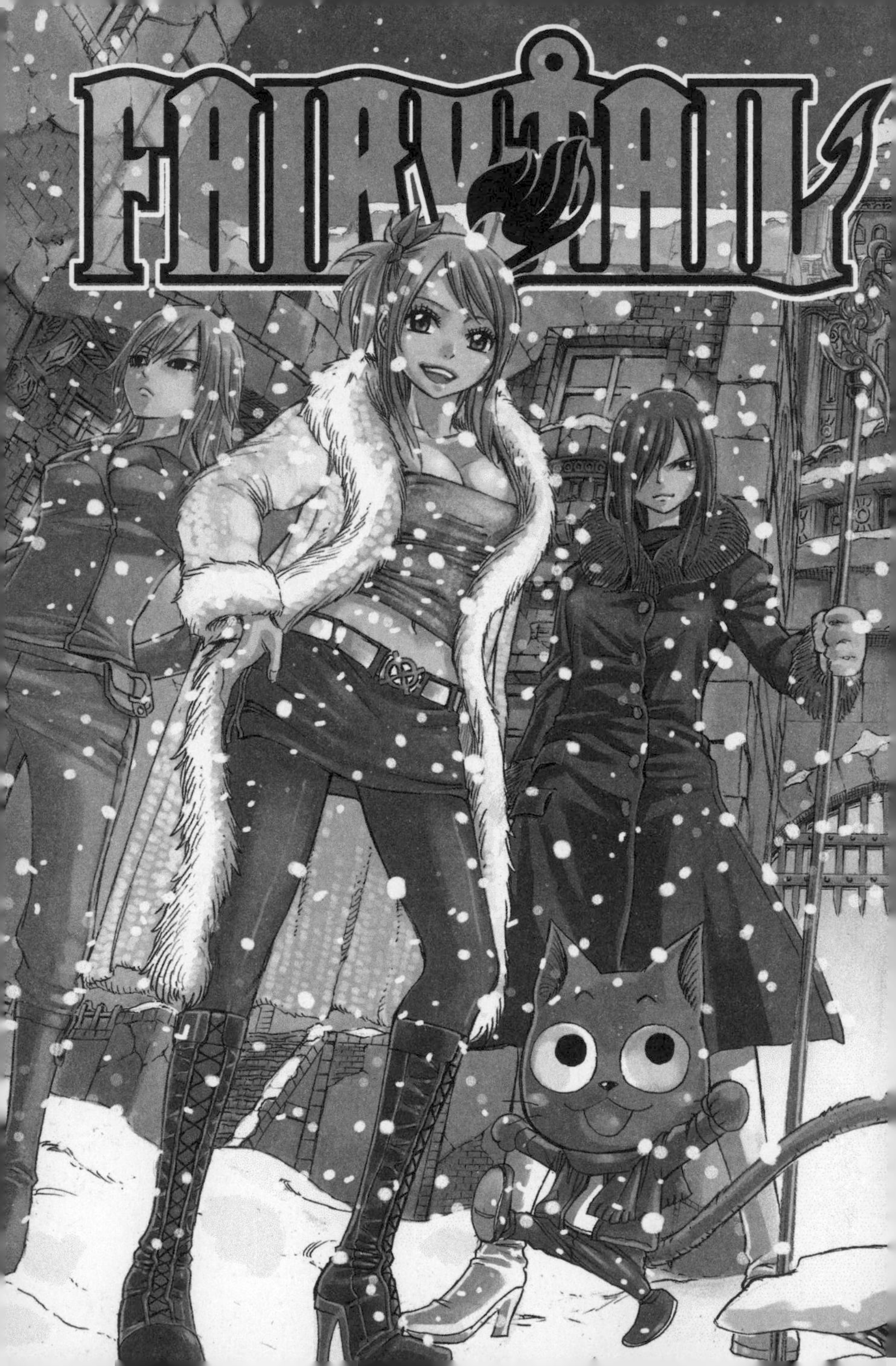
FAIRY TAIL

FAIRY TAIL

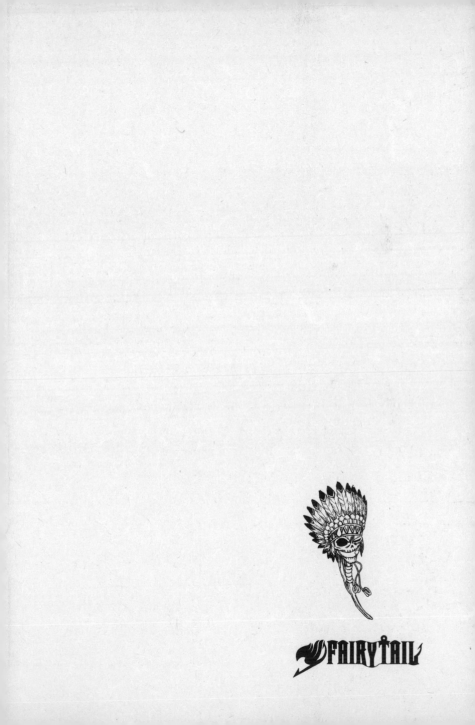

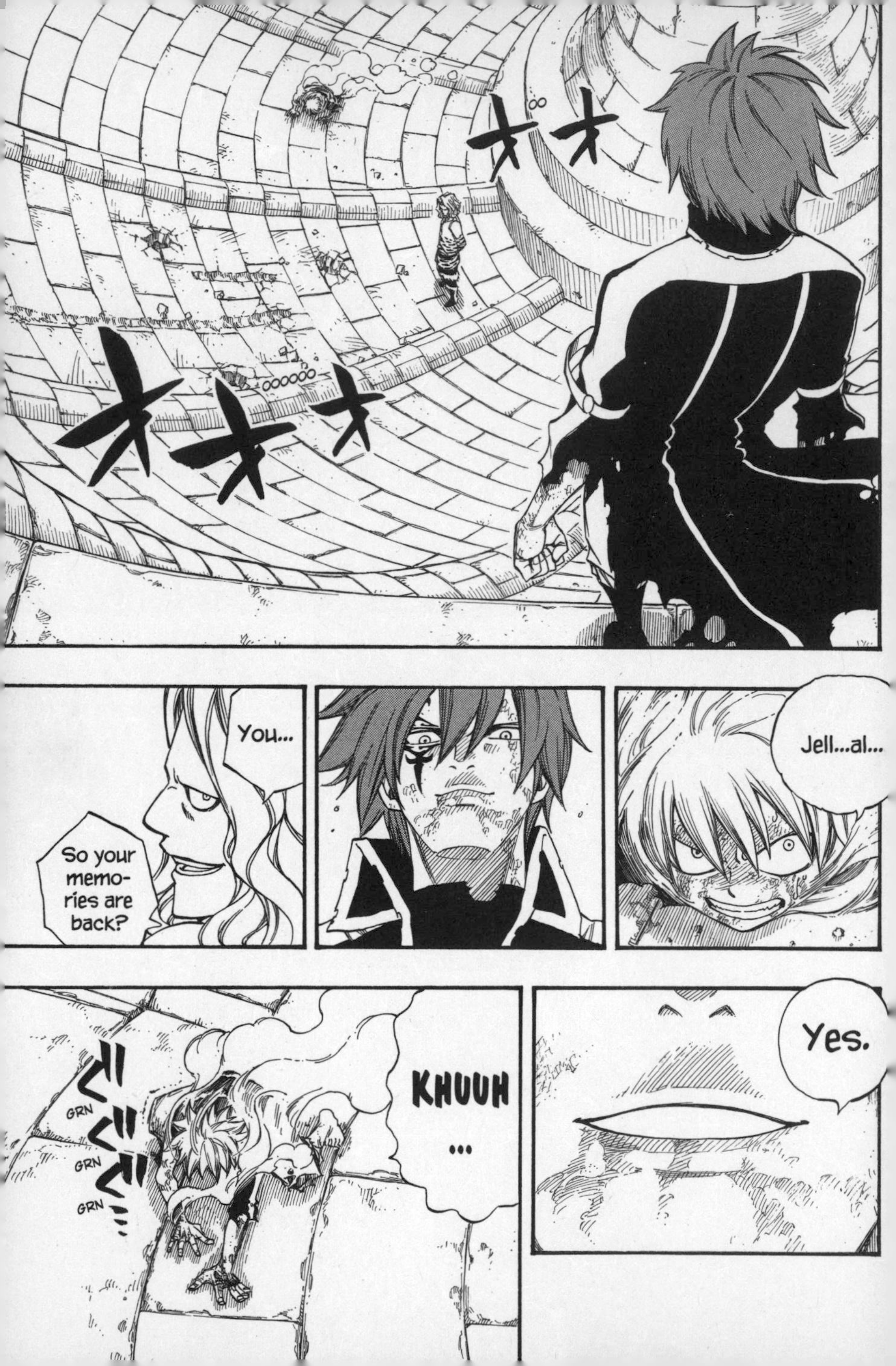
オオ
オオオ
OOOOOO
Jell...al...
You...
So your memories are back?
Yes.
KHUUH ...
GRN
GRN
GRN

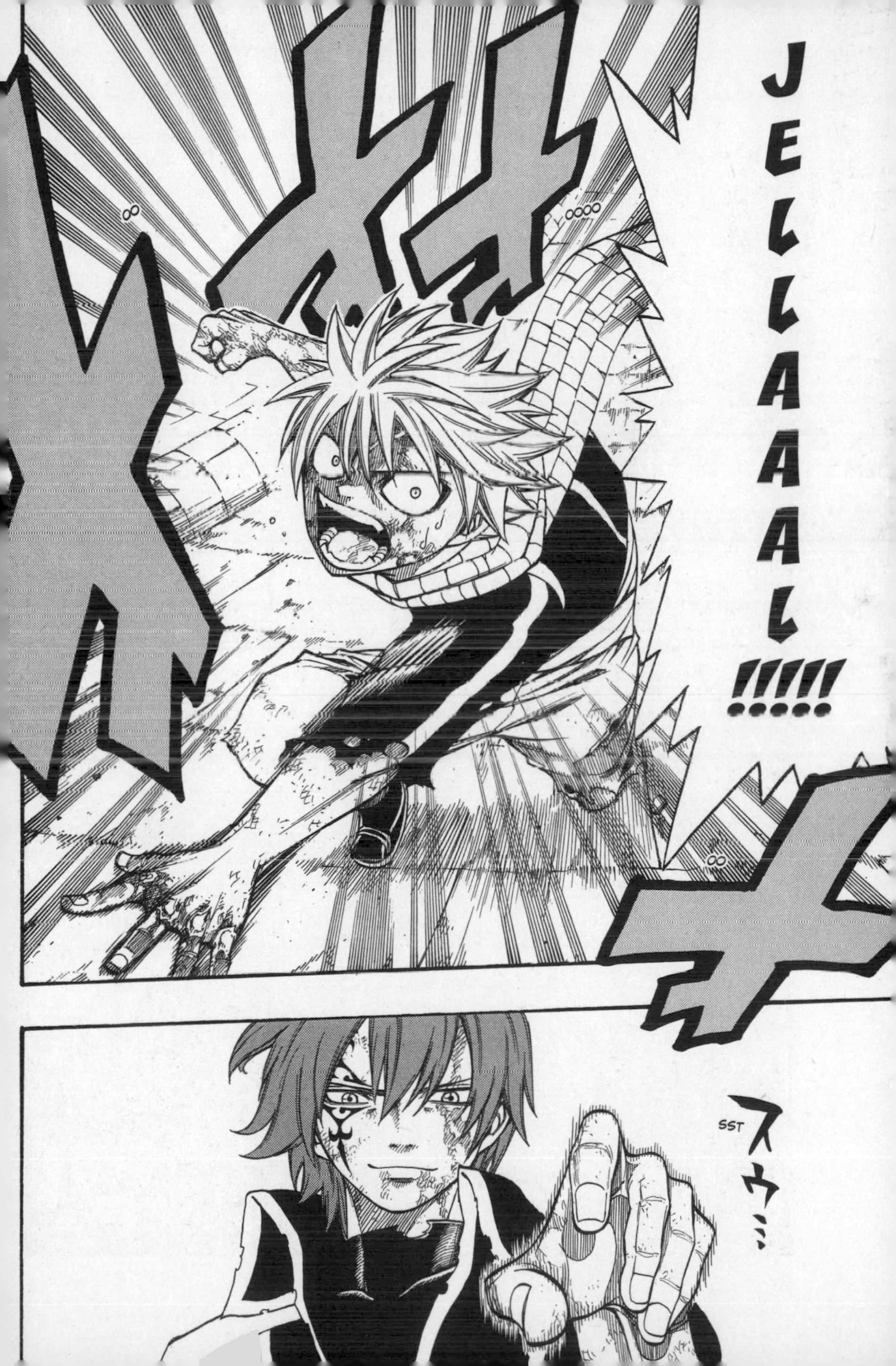
JELLAAAL!!!!!
SST
スゥ

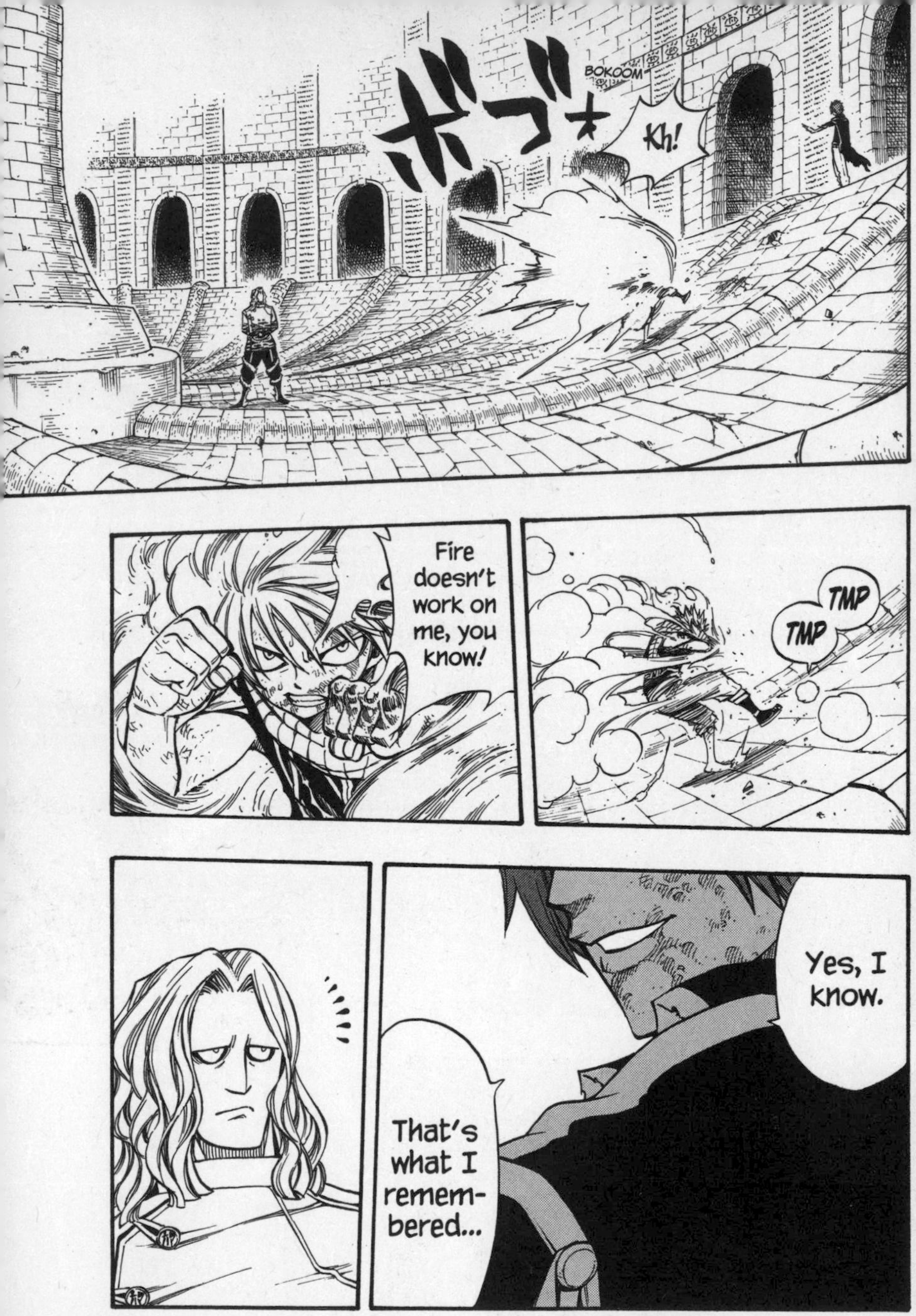
Kh!
BOKOOM
TMP
TMP
Fire doesn't work on me, you know!
Yes, I know.
That's what I remem-bered...

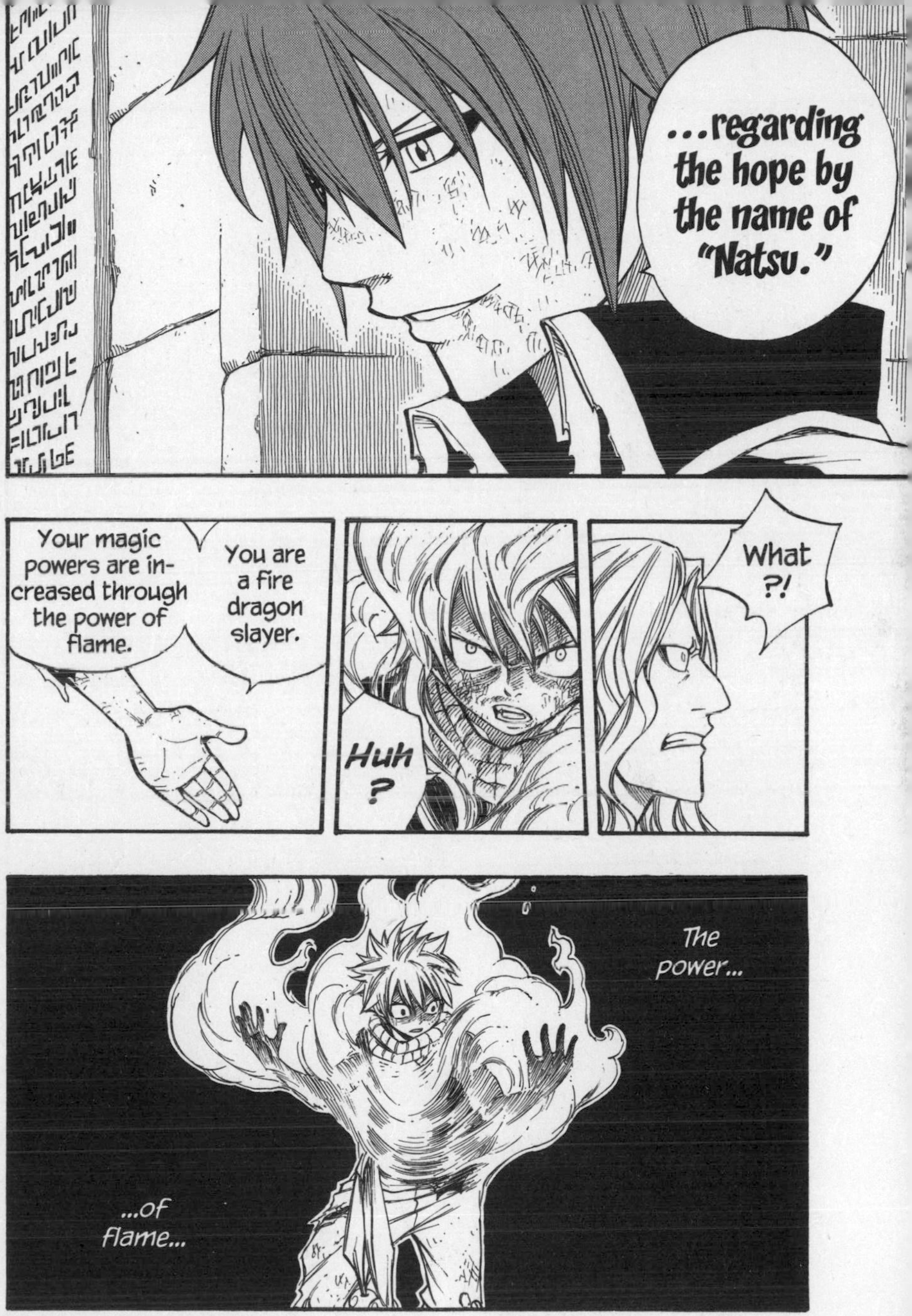
...regarding the hope by the name of "Natsu."
What?!
Huh?
You are a fire dragon slayer.
Your magic powers are increased through the power of flame.
The power...
...of flame...

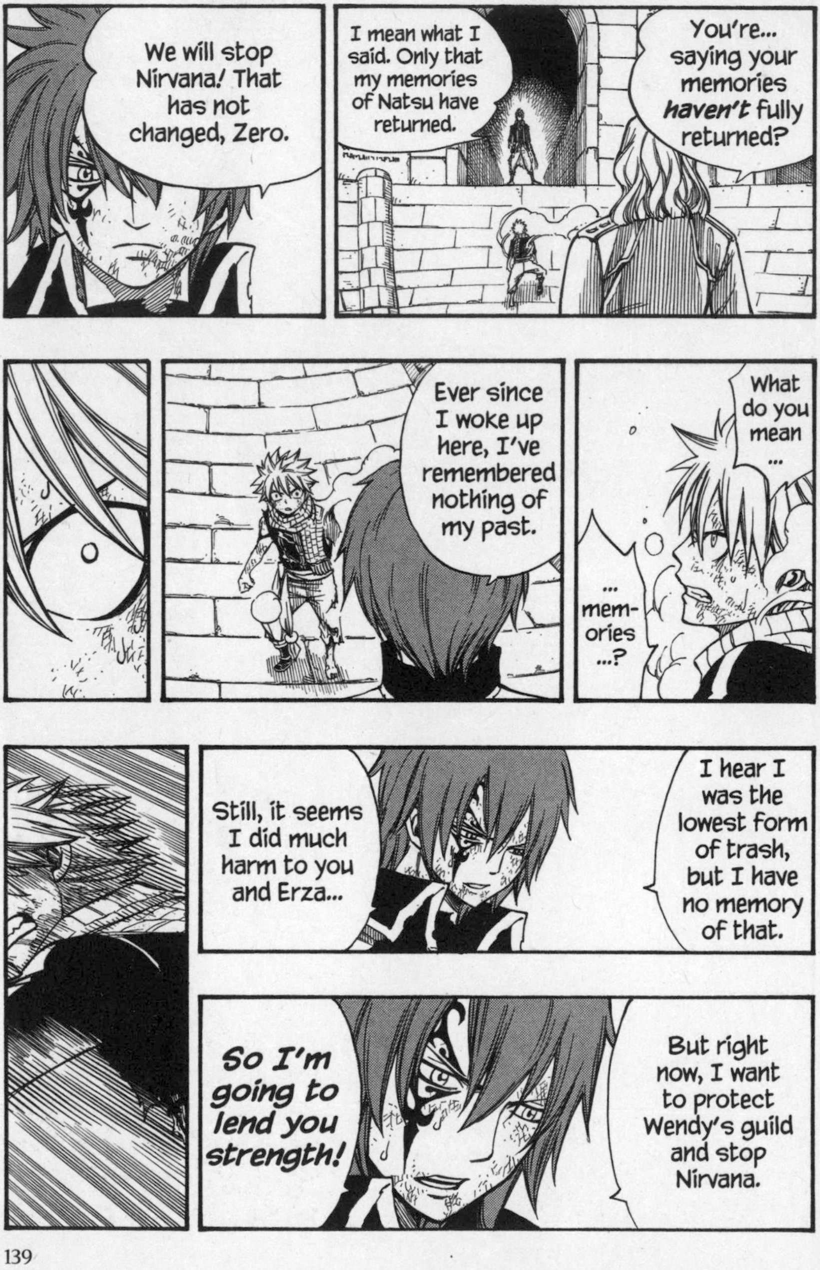
You're... saying your memories *haven't* fully returned?
I mean what I said. Only that my memories of Natsu have returned.
We will stop Nirvana! That has not changed, Zero.
What do you mean ...
... memories ...?
Ever since I woke up here, I've remembered nothing of my past.
I hear I was the lowest form of trash, but I have no memory of that.
Still, it seems I did much harm to you and Erza...
But right now, I want to protect Wendy's guild and stop Nirvana.
So I'm going to lend you strength!

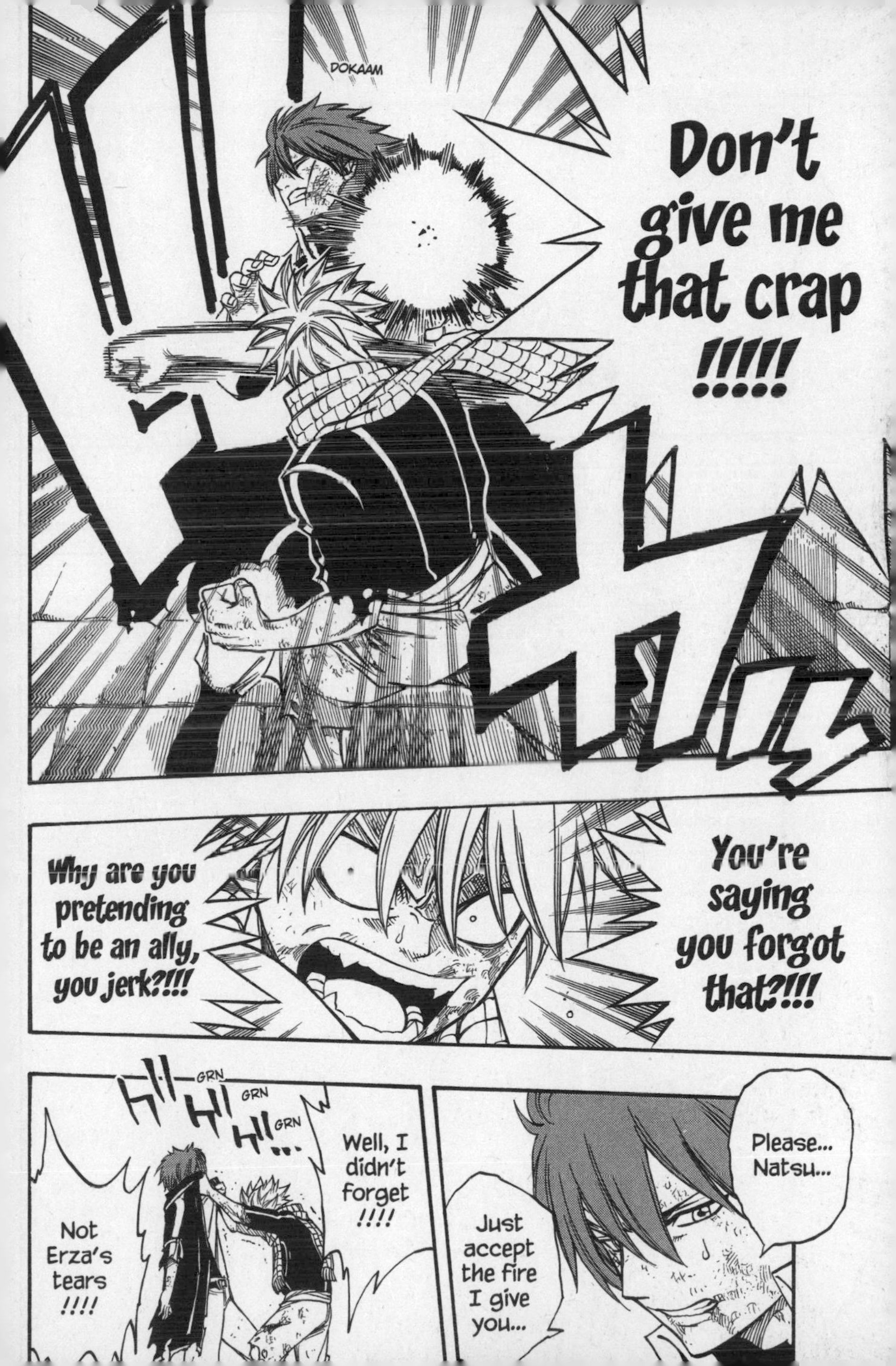
DOKAAM
Don't give me that crap!!!!!
You're saying you forgot that?!!!
Why are you pretending to be an ally, you jerk?!!!
Please... Natsu...
Just accept the fire I give you...
Well, I didn't forget!!!!
GRN
GRN
GRN
Not Erza's tears!!!!

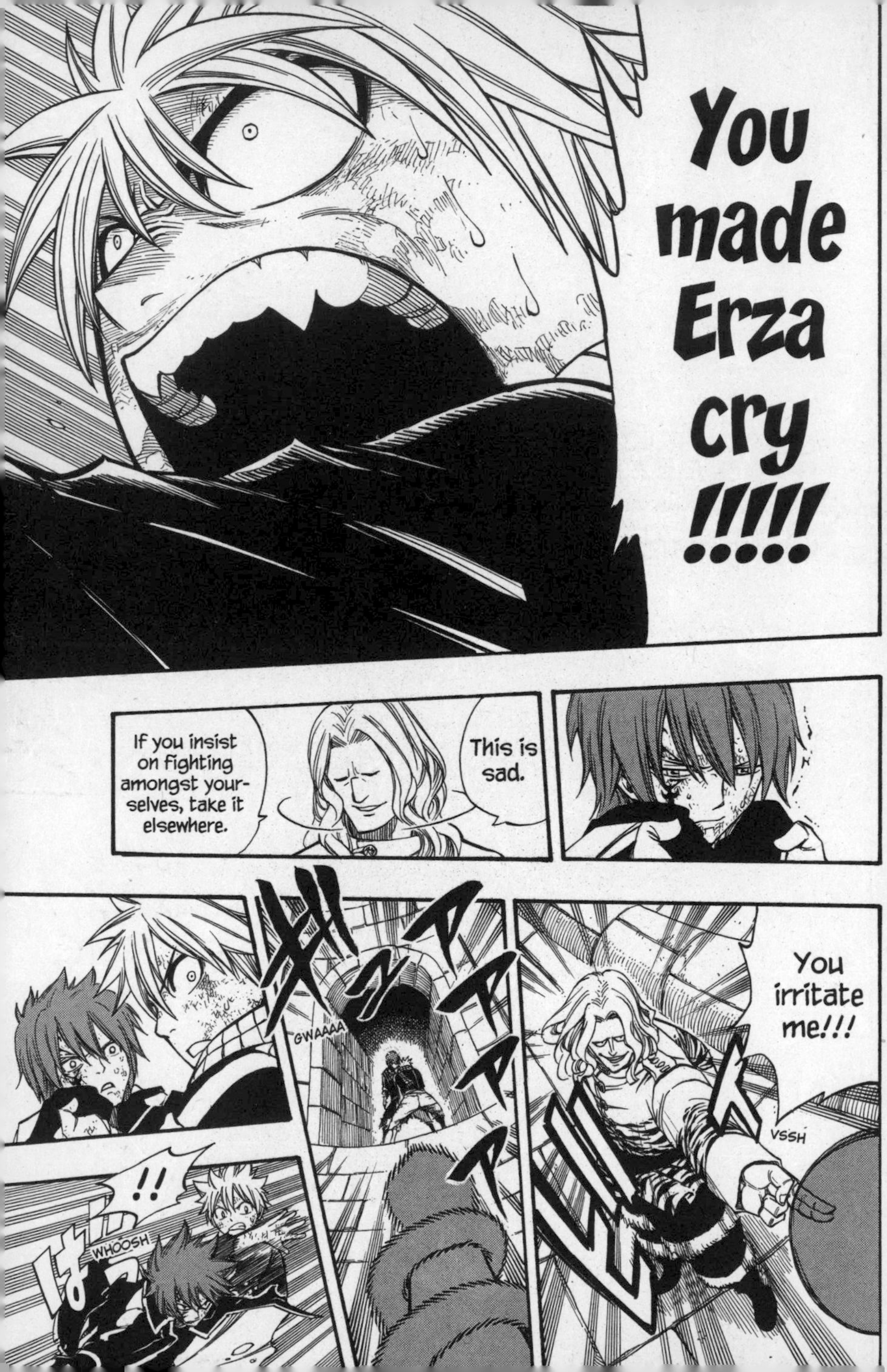

You made Erza cry!!!!!
This is sad.
If you insist on fighting amongst yourselves, take it elsewhere.
You irritate me!!!
VSSH
GWAAAA
!!
WHOOSH

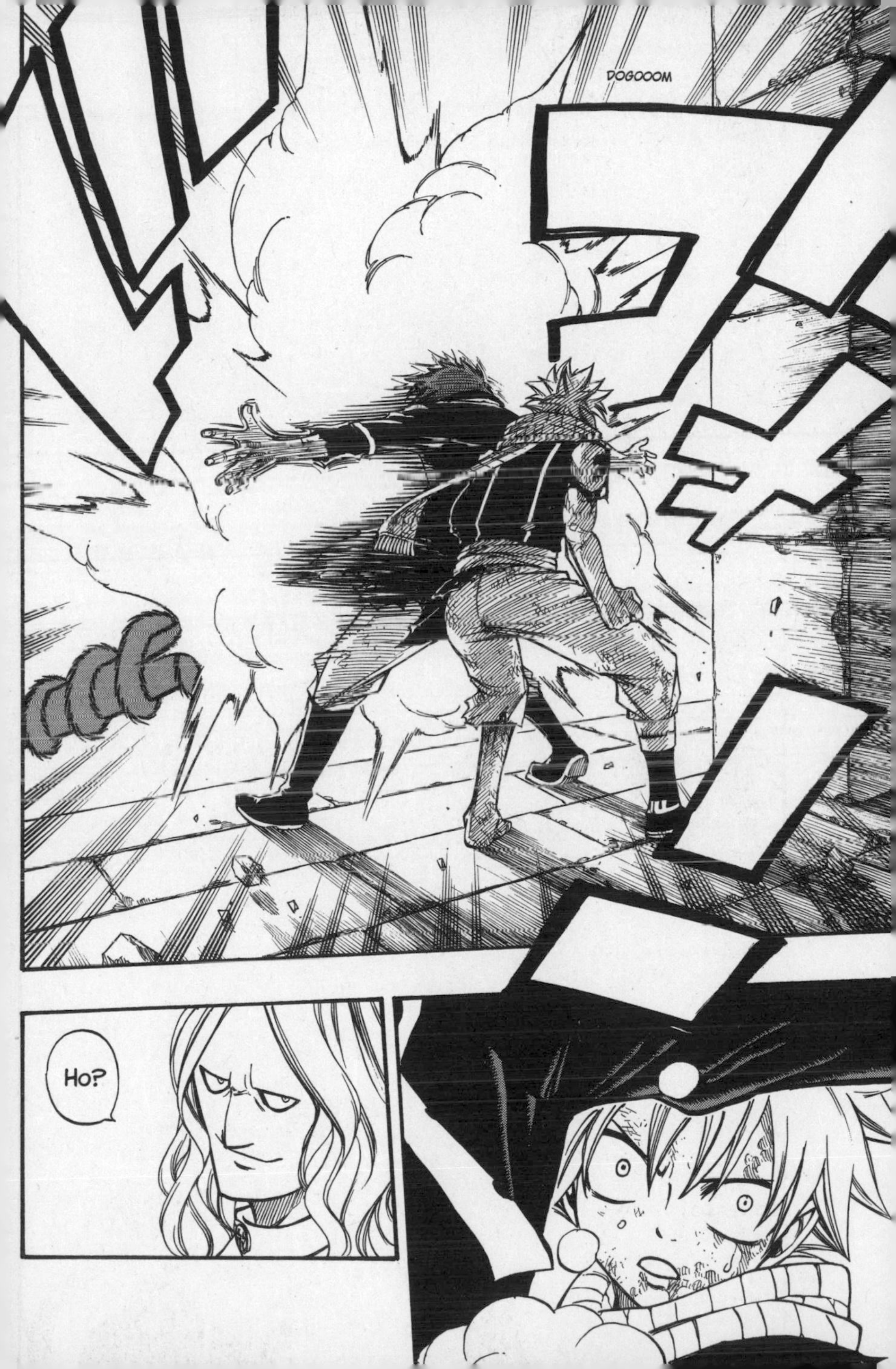
DOGOOOM
Ho?

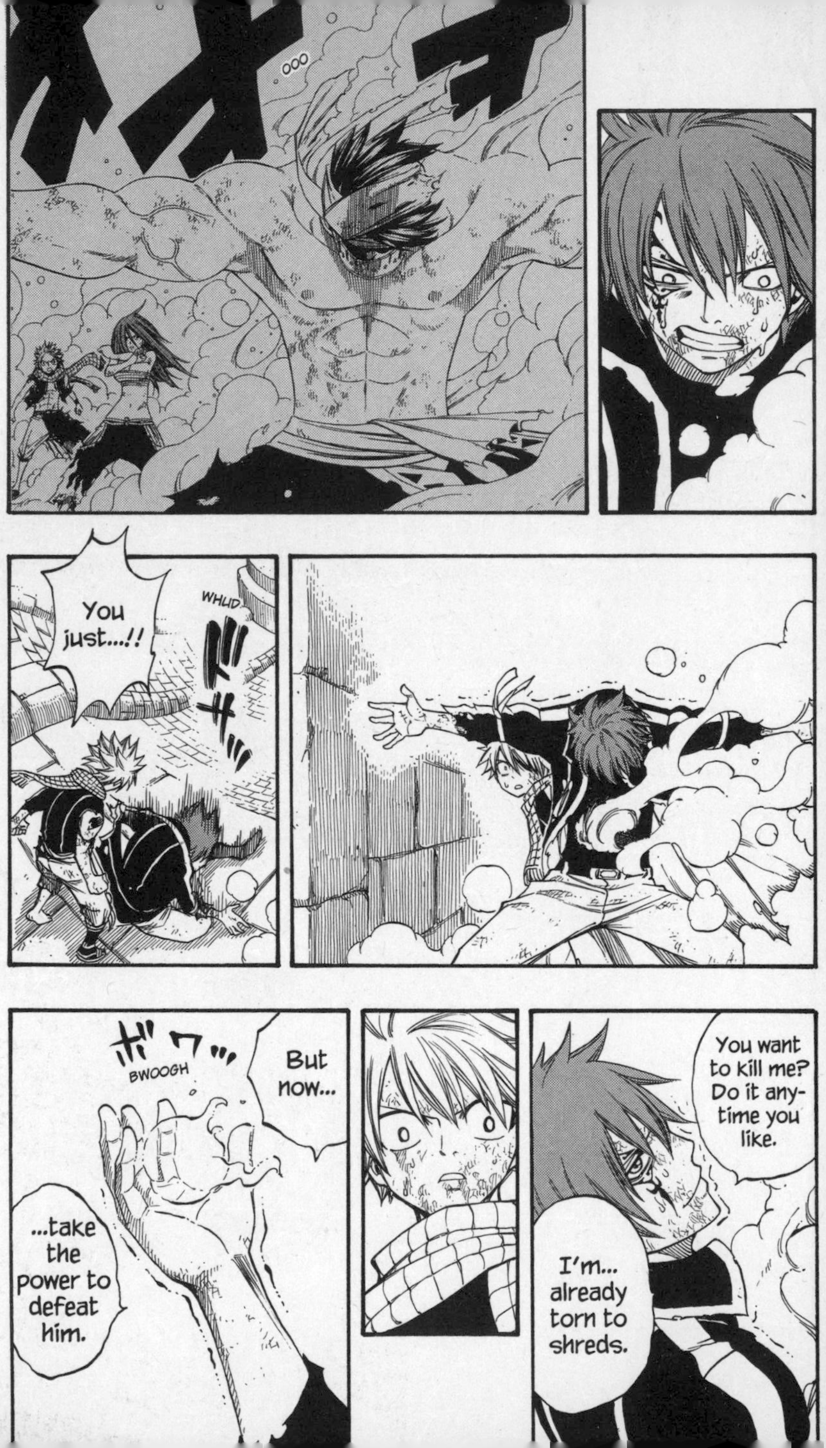

オオオ
ooo
ドサッ
WHUD
You just...!!
You want to kill me? Do it any-time you like.
I'm... already torn to shreds.
But now...
ボワッ
BWOOGH
...take the power to defeat him.

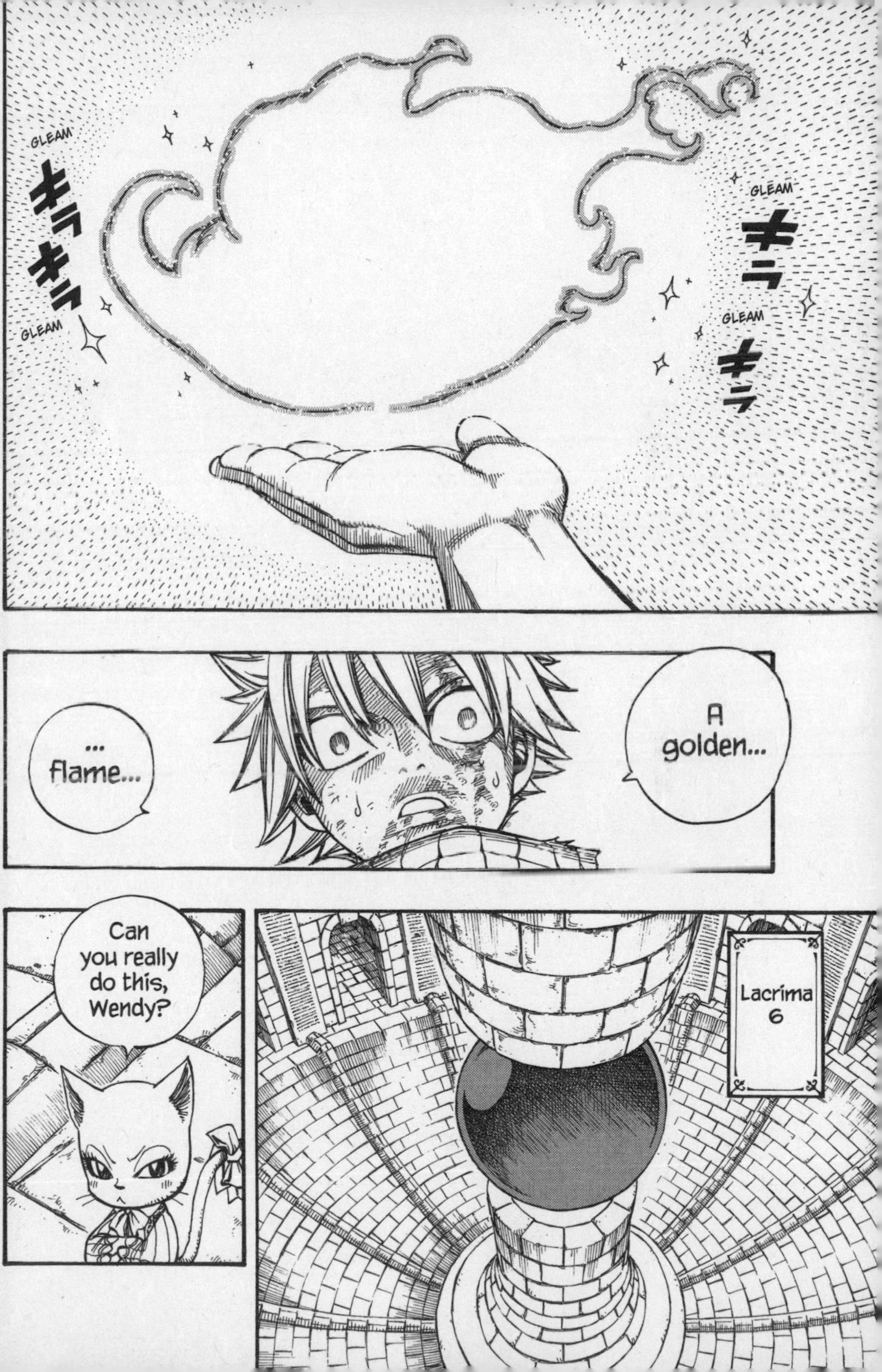
GLEAM
キラ
GLEAM
キラ
GLEAM
キラキラ
GLEAM
A golden...
... flame...
Lacrima 6
Can you really do this, Wendy?

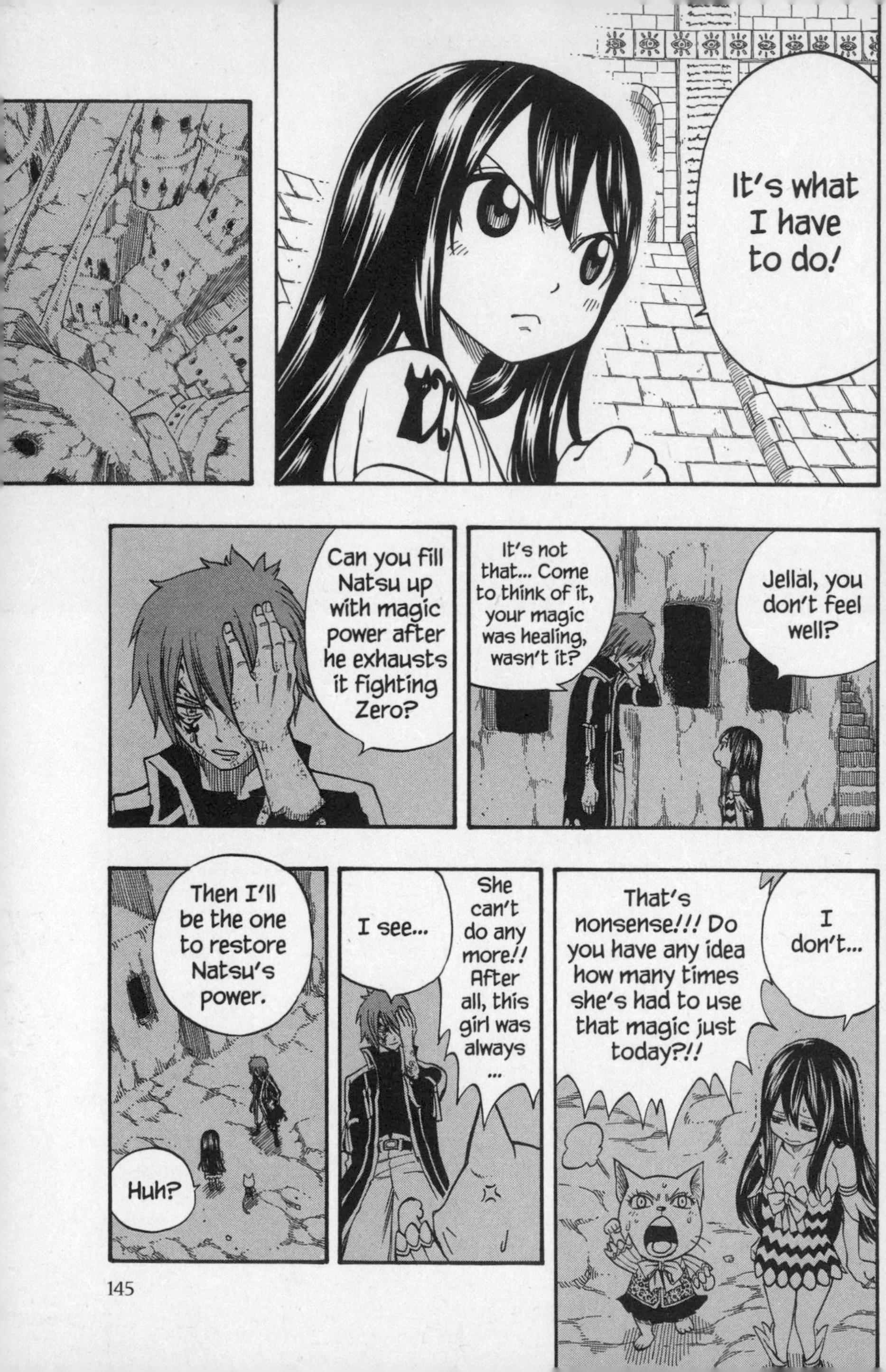
It's what I have to do!
Jellal, you don't feel well?
It's not that... Come to think of it, your magic was healing, wasn't it?
Can you fill Natsu up with magic power after he exhausts it fighting Zero?
I don't...
That's nonsense!!! Do you have any idea how many times she's had to use that magic just today?!!
She can't do any more!! After all, this girl was always ...
I see...
Then I'll be the one to restore Natsu's power.
Huh?

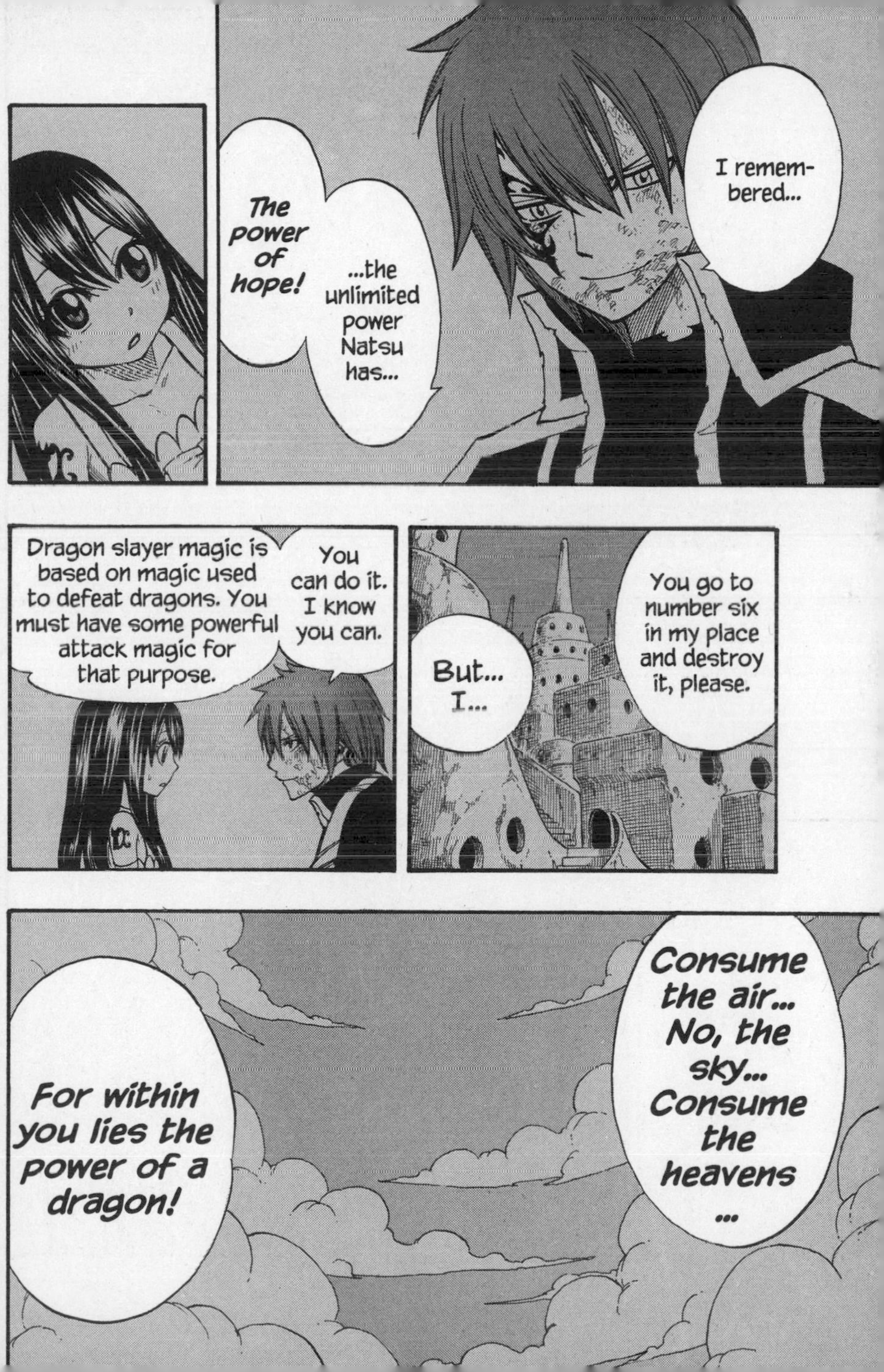
I remembered...
...the unlimited power Natsu has...
The power of hope!
You go to number six in my place and destroy it, please.
But... I...
You can do it. I know you can.
Dragon slayer magic is based on magic used to defeat dragons. You must have some powerful attack magic for that purpose.
Consume the air... No, the sky... Consume the heavens...
For within you lies the power of a dragon!

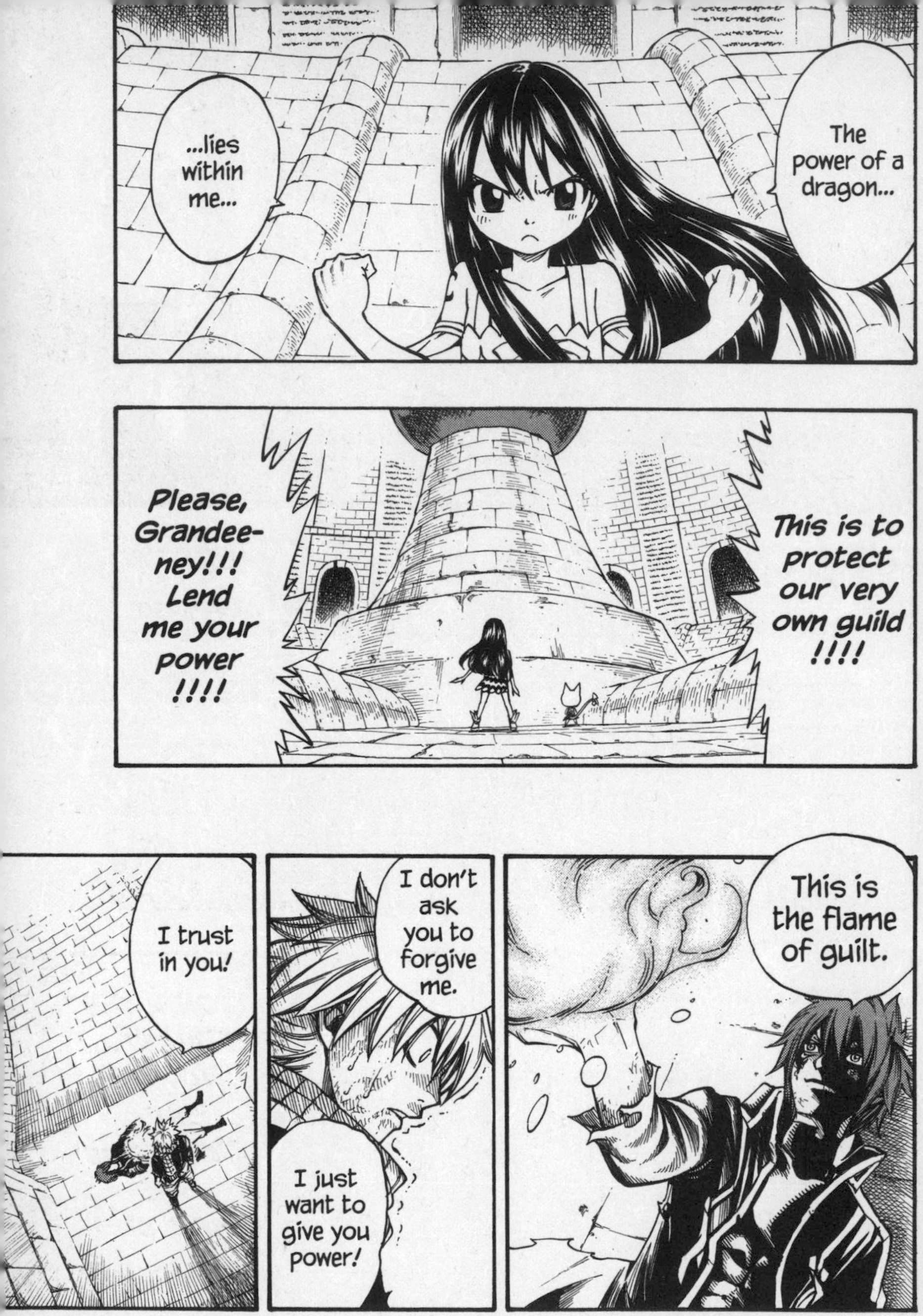
The power of a dragon...
...lies within me...
This is to protect our very own guild!!!!
Please, Grandeeney!!! Lend me your power!!!!
This is the flame of guilt.
I don't ask you to forgive me.
I just want to give you power!
I trust in you!

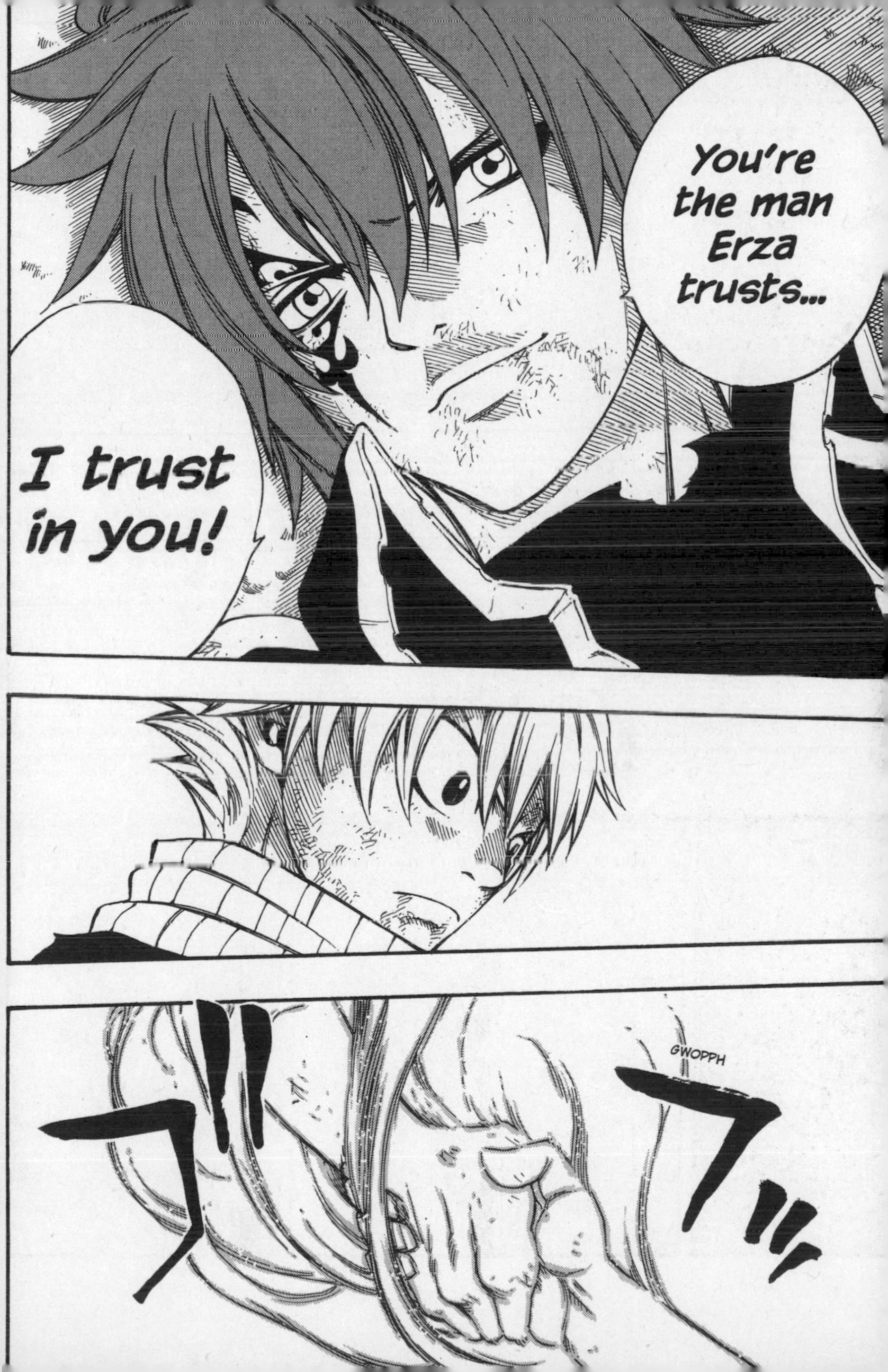
You're the man Erza trusts...
I trust in you!
GWOPPH

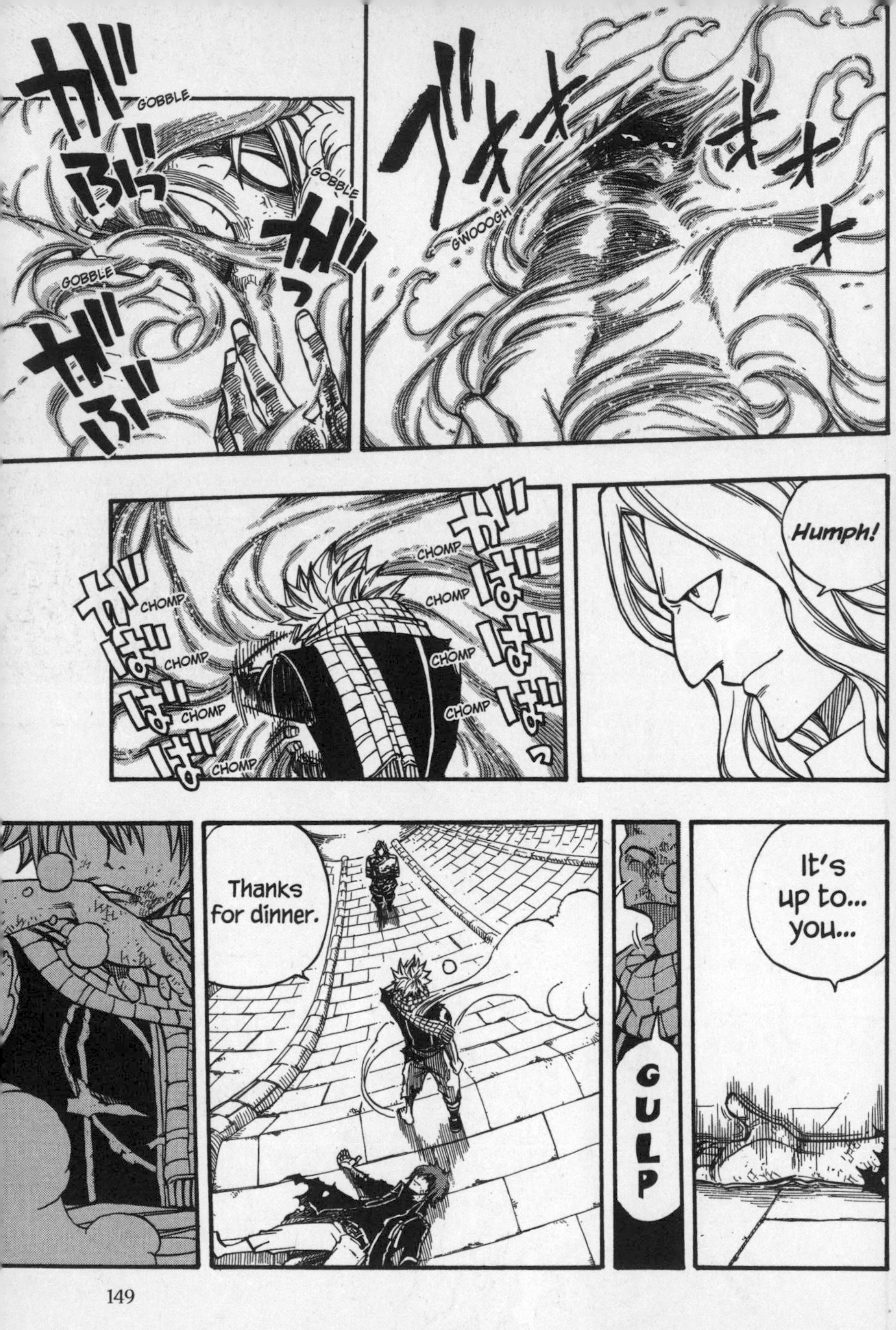
GWOOOGH
GOBBLE
GOBBLE
GOBBLE
Humph!
CHOMP
CHOMP
CHOMP
CHOMP
CHOMP
CHOMP
CHOMP
CHOMP
It's up to... you...
GULP
Thanks for dinner.

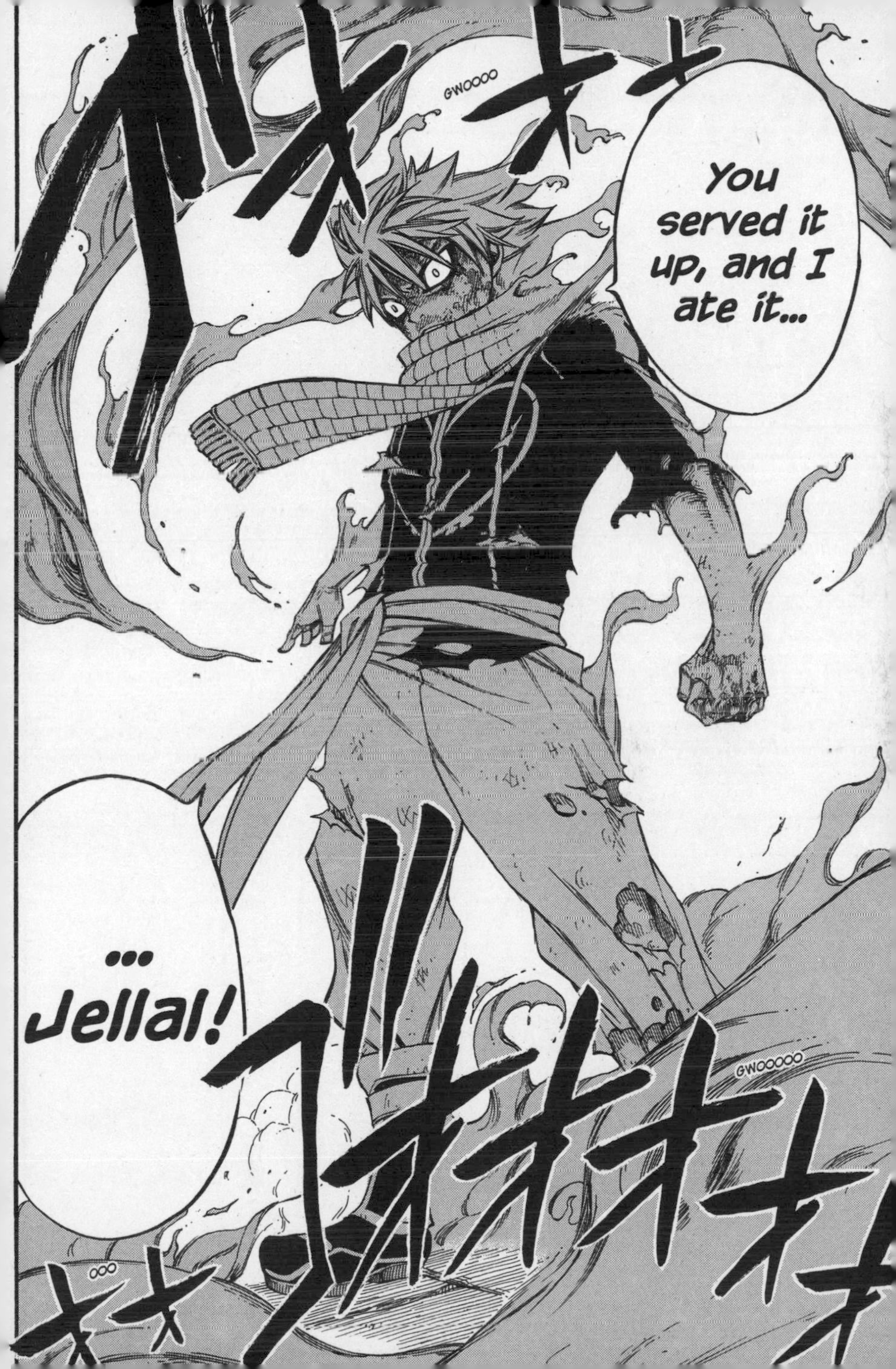
You served it up, and I ate it...
GWOOOO
GWOOOOO
...Jellal!
OOO

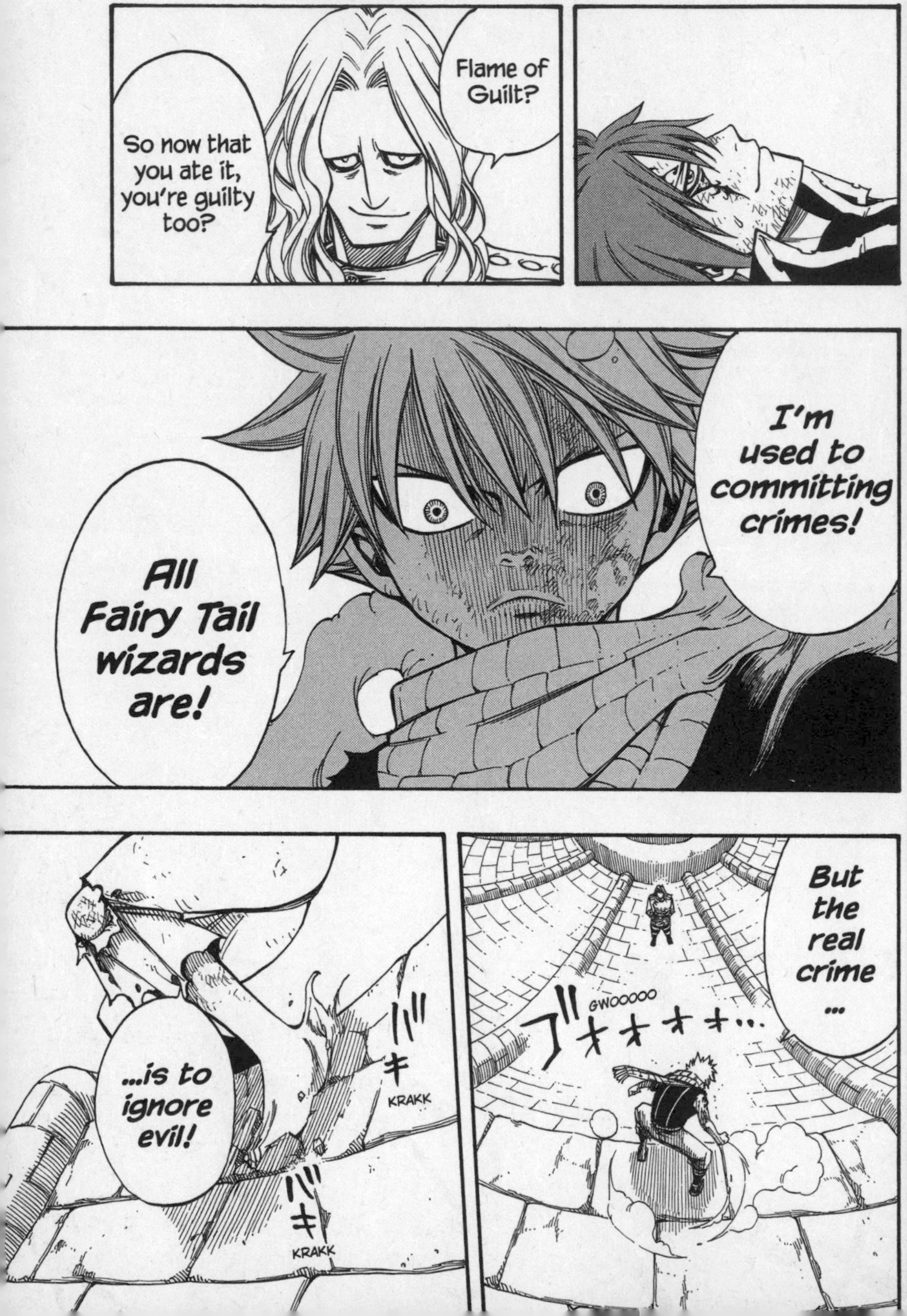

Flame of Guilt?
So now that you ate it, you're guilty too?
I'm used to committing crimes!
All Fairy Tail wizards are!
But the real crime ...
GWOOOOO
...is to ignore evil!
バキ
KRAKK
バキ
KRAKK

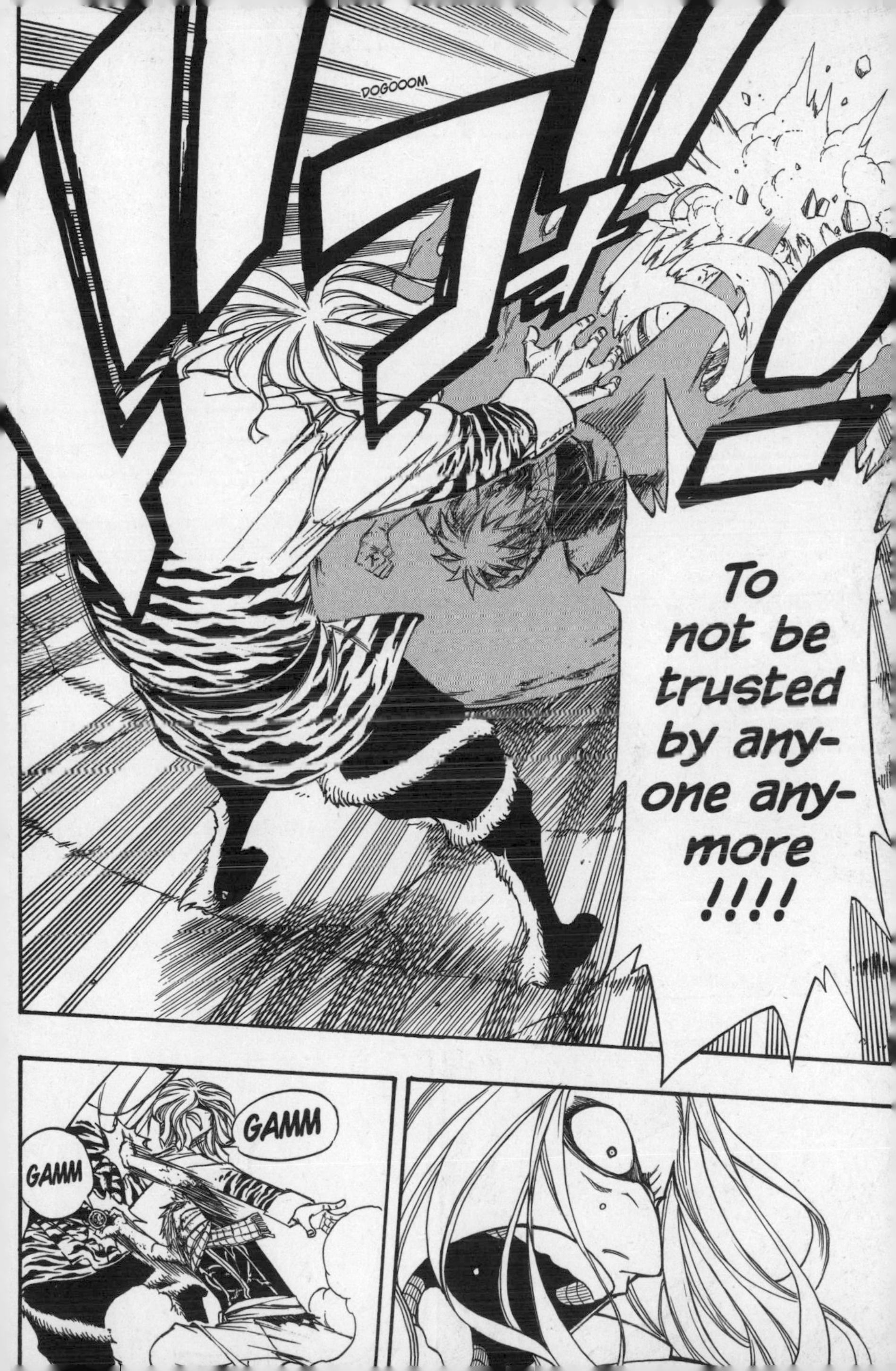
DOGOOOM
To not be trusted by any-one any-more !!!!
GAMM
GAMM

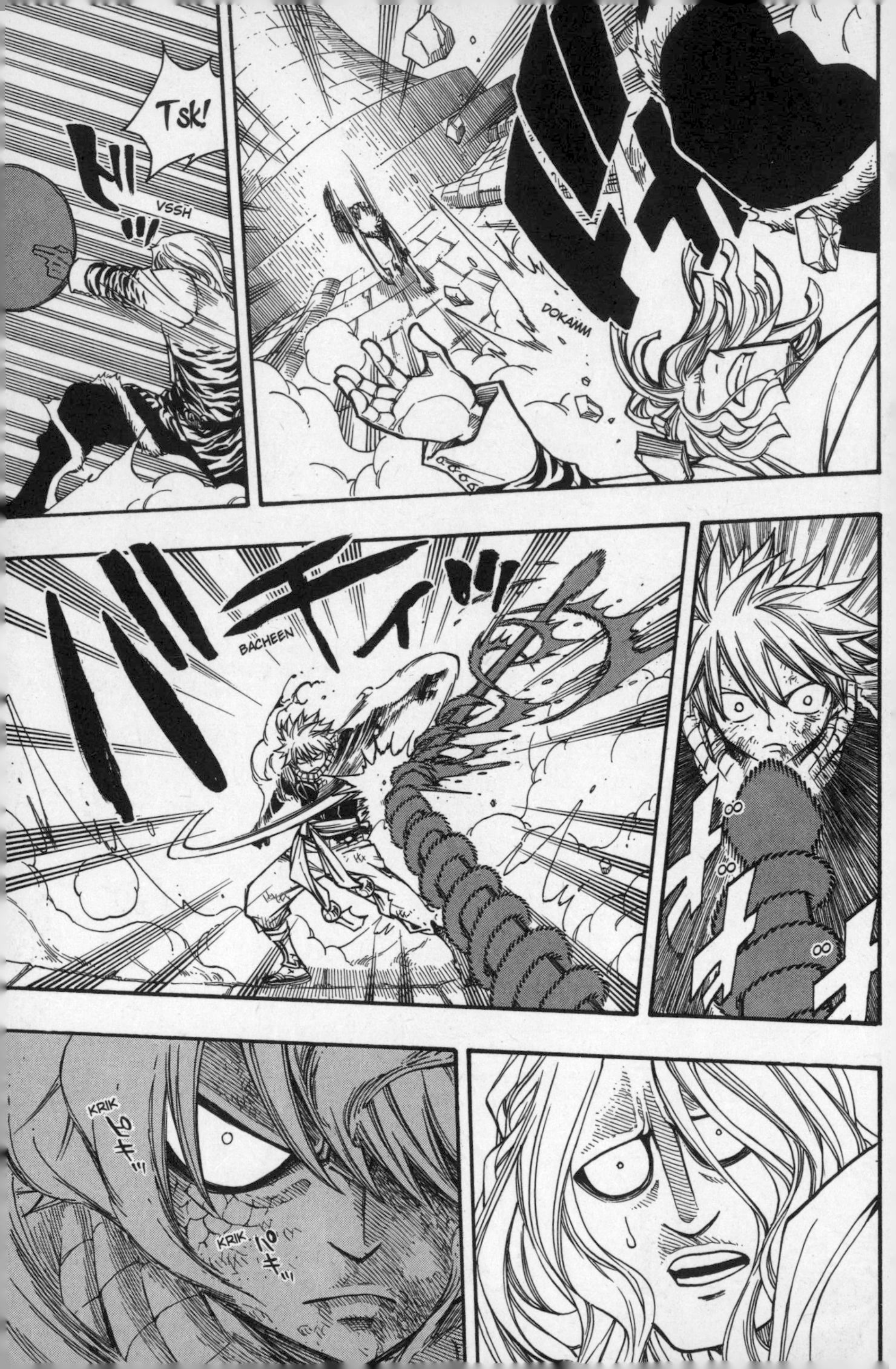
DOKAMM
Tsk!
VSSH
BACHEEN
KRIK
KRIK

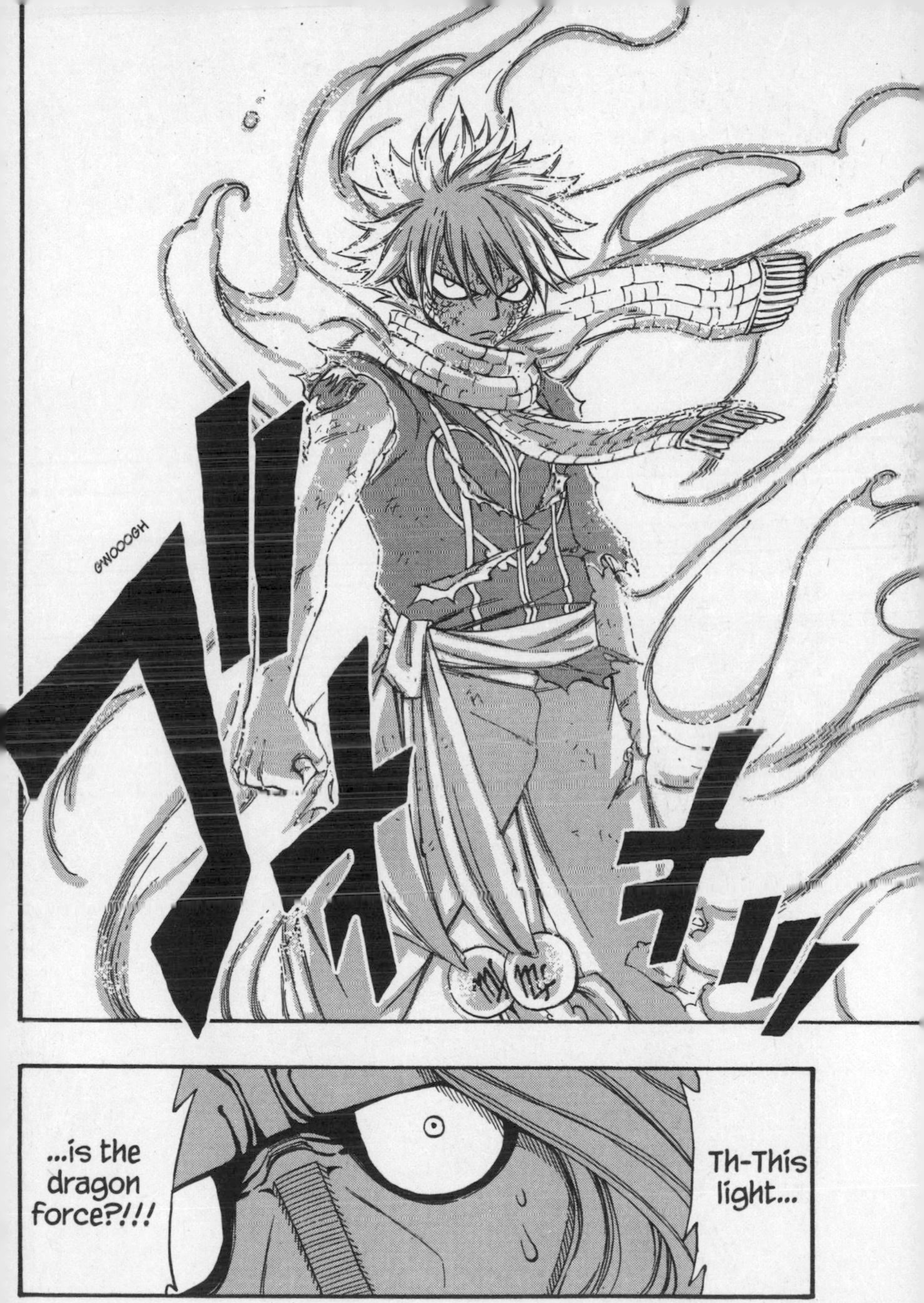
GWOOOGH
Th-This light...
...is the dragon force?!!!

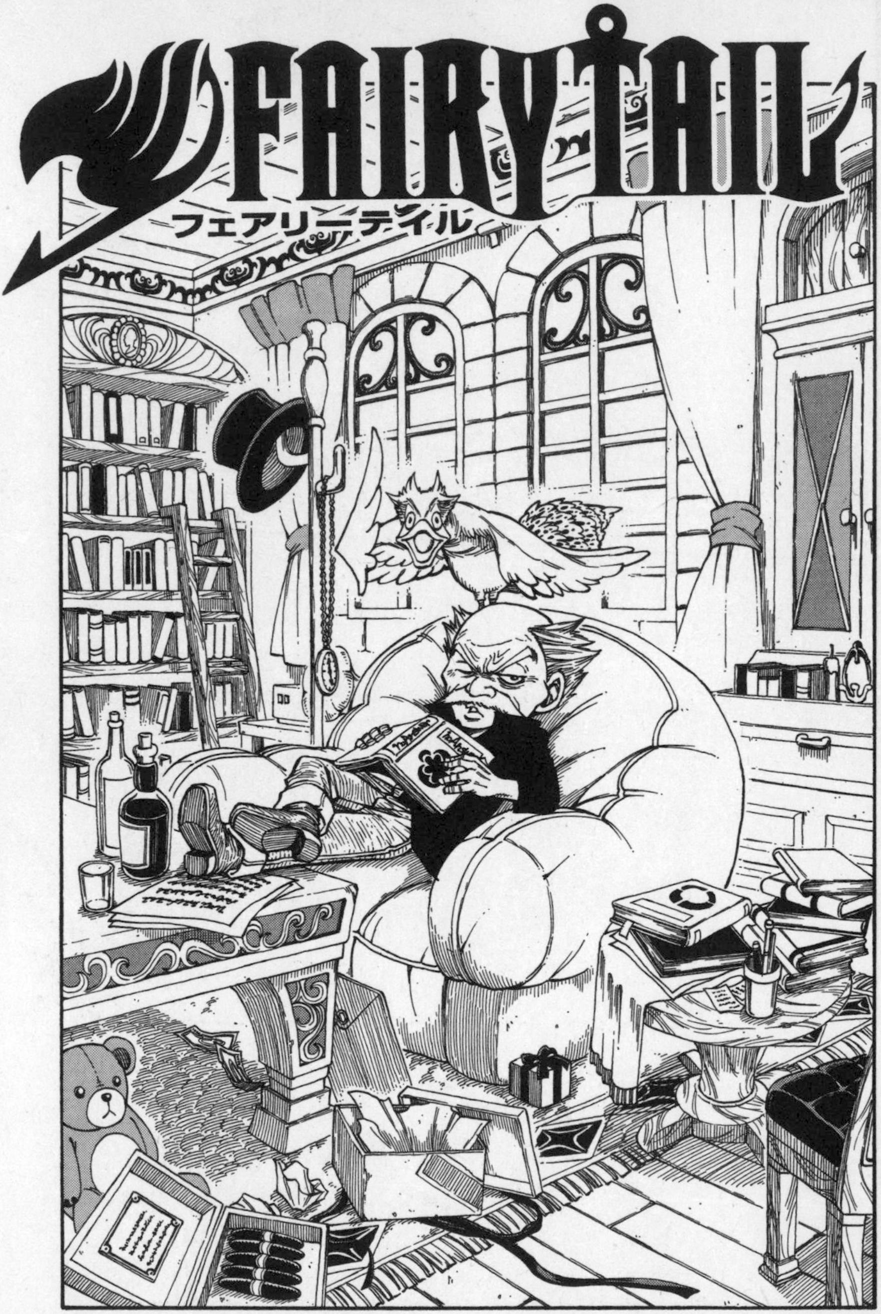
FAIRY TAIL
フェアリーテイル

Chapter 160: The Power of Emotion

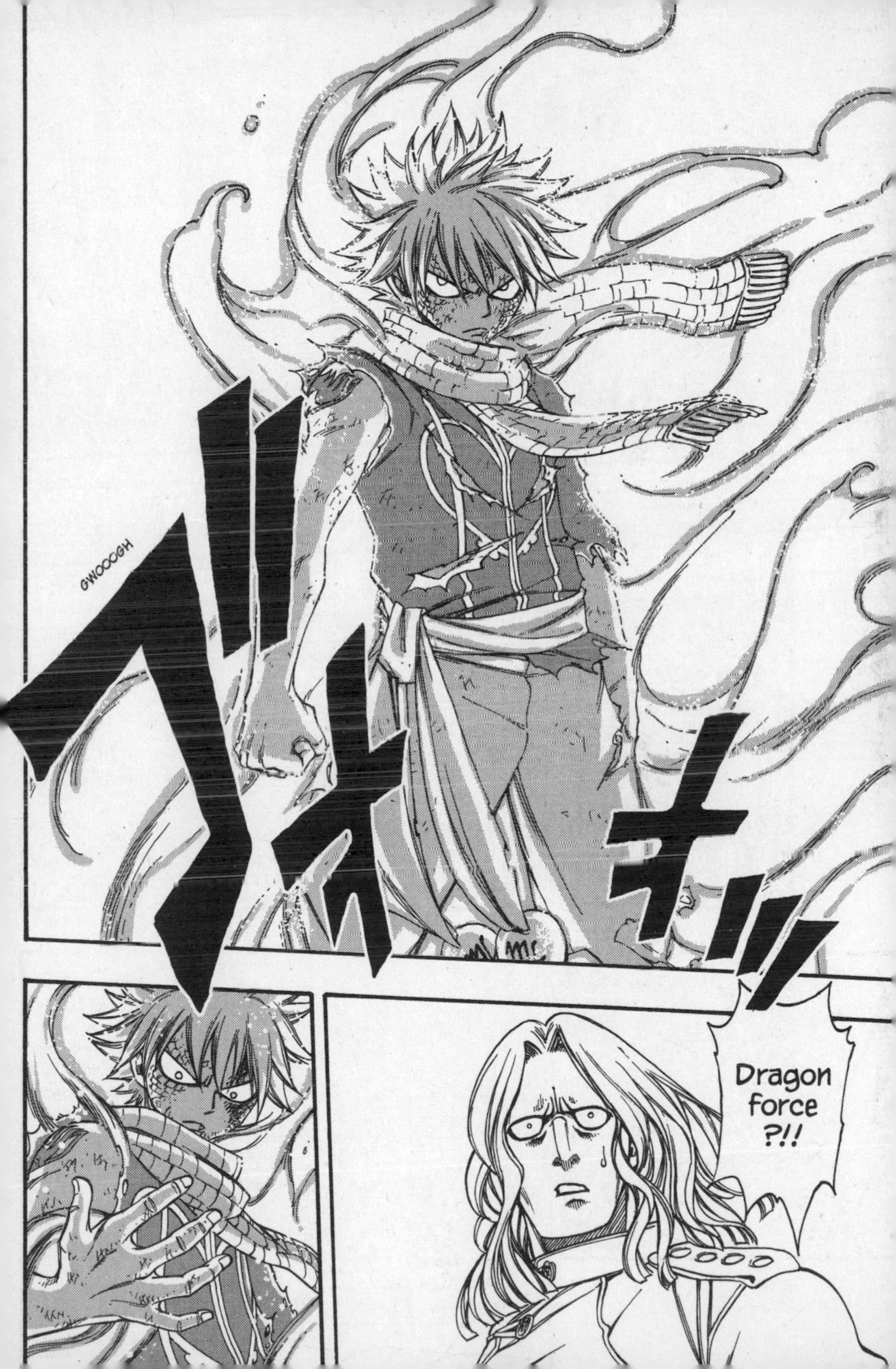
GWOOOGH
Dragon force ?!!

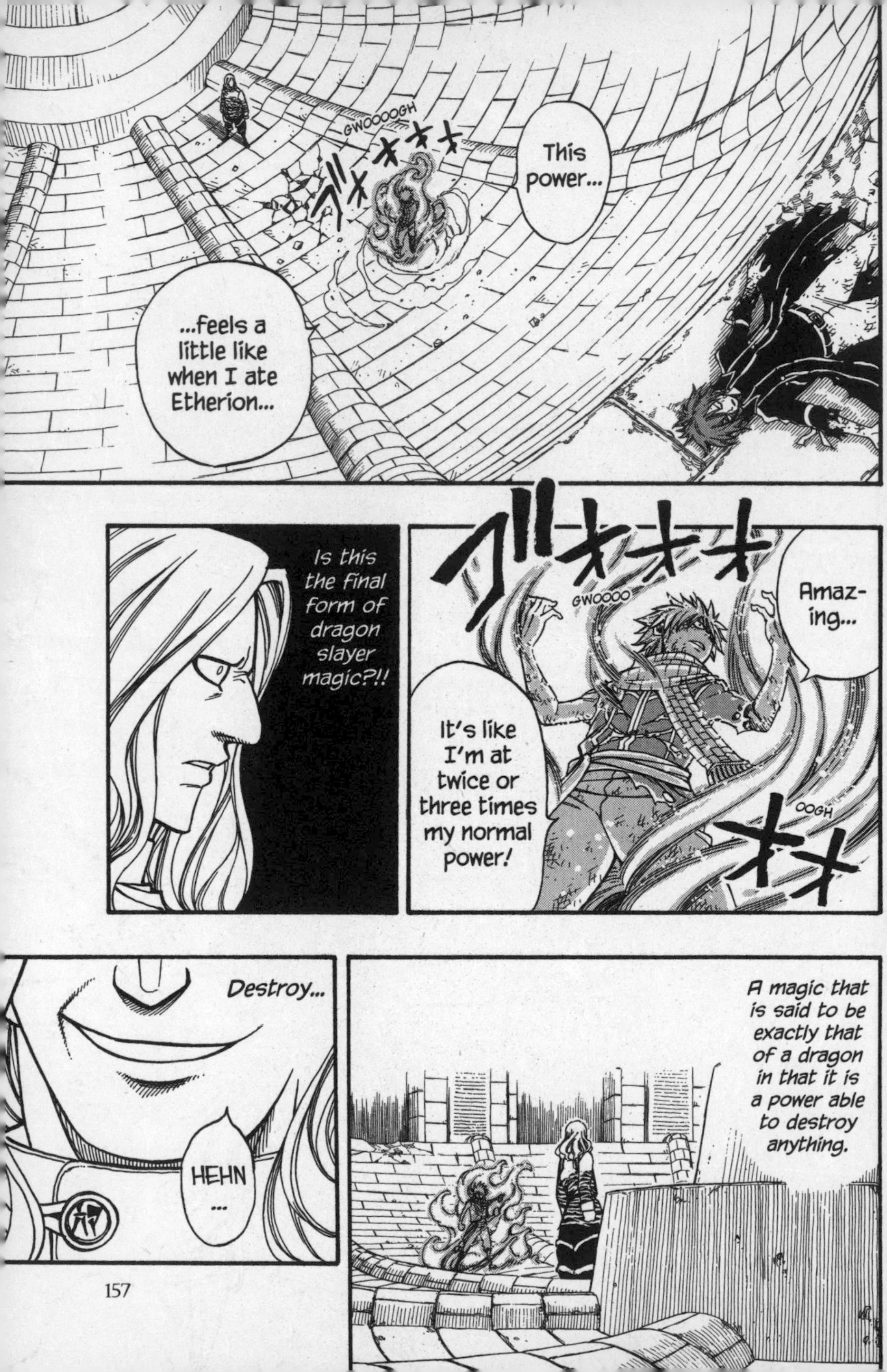
GWOOOOGH
This power...
...feels a little like when I ate Etherion...
GWOOOO
Amaz-ing...
It's like I'm at twice or three times my normal power!
OOGH
Is this the final form of dragon slayer magic?!!
A magic that is said to be exactly that of a dragon in that it is a power able to destroy anything.
Destroy...
HEHN ...

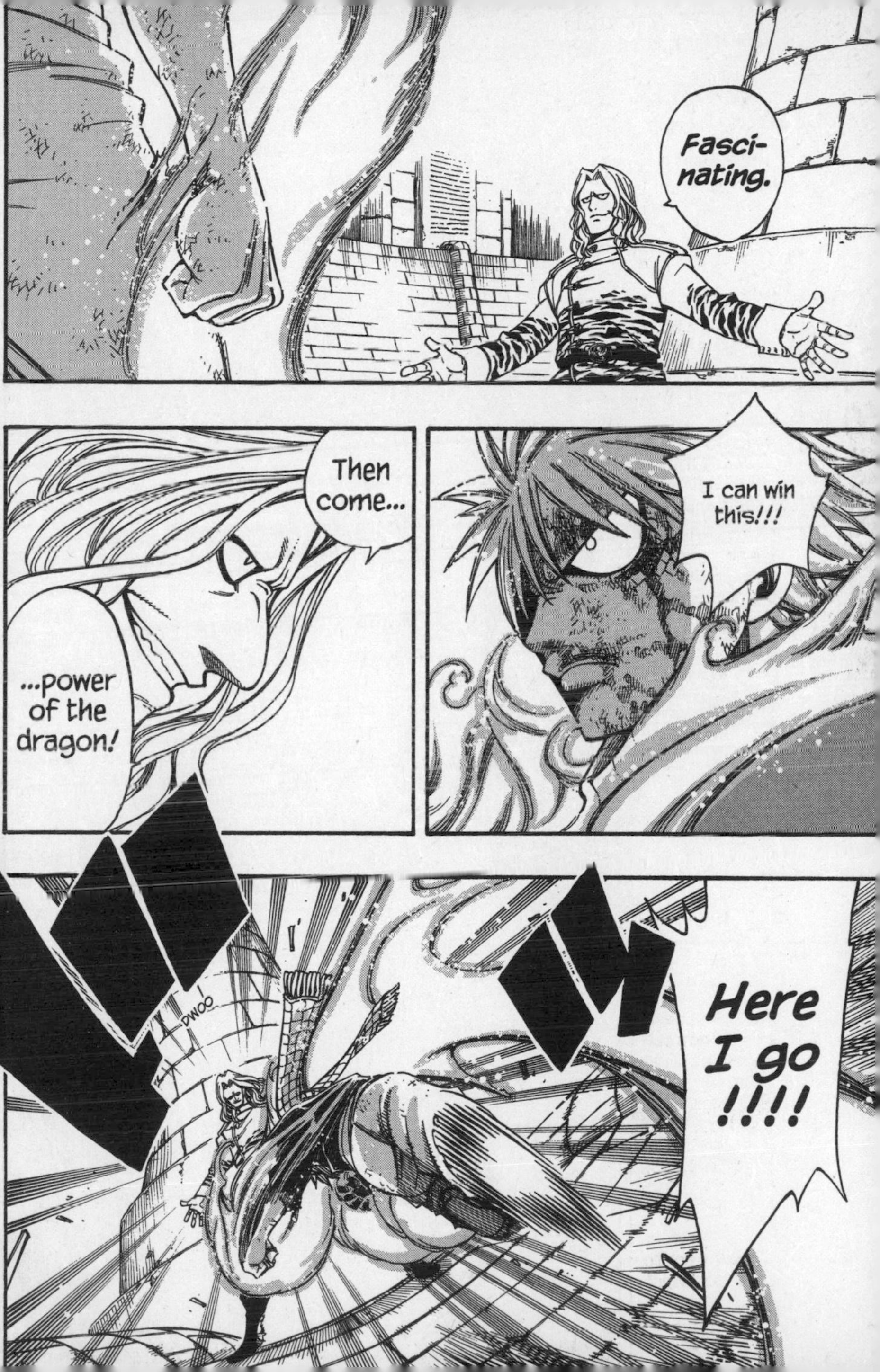
Fascinating.
I can win this!!!
Then come...
...power of the dragon!
DWOO
Here I go!!!!

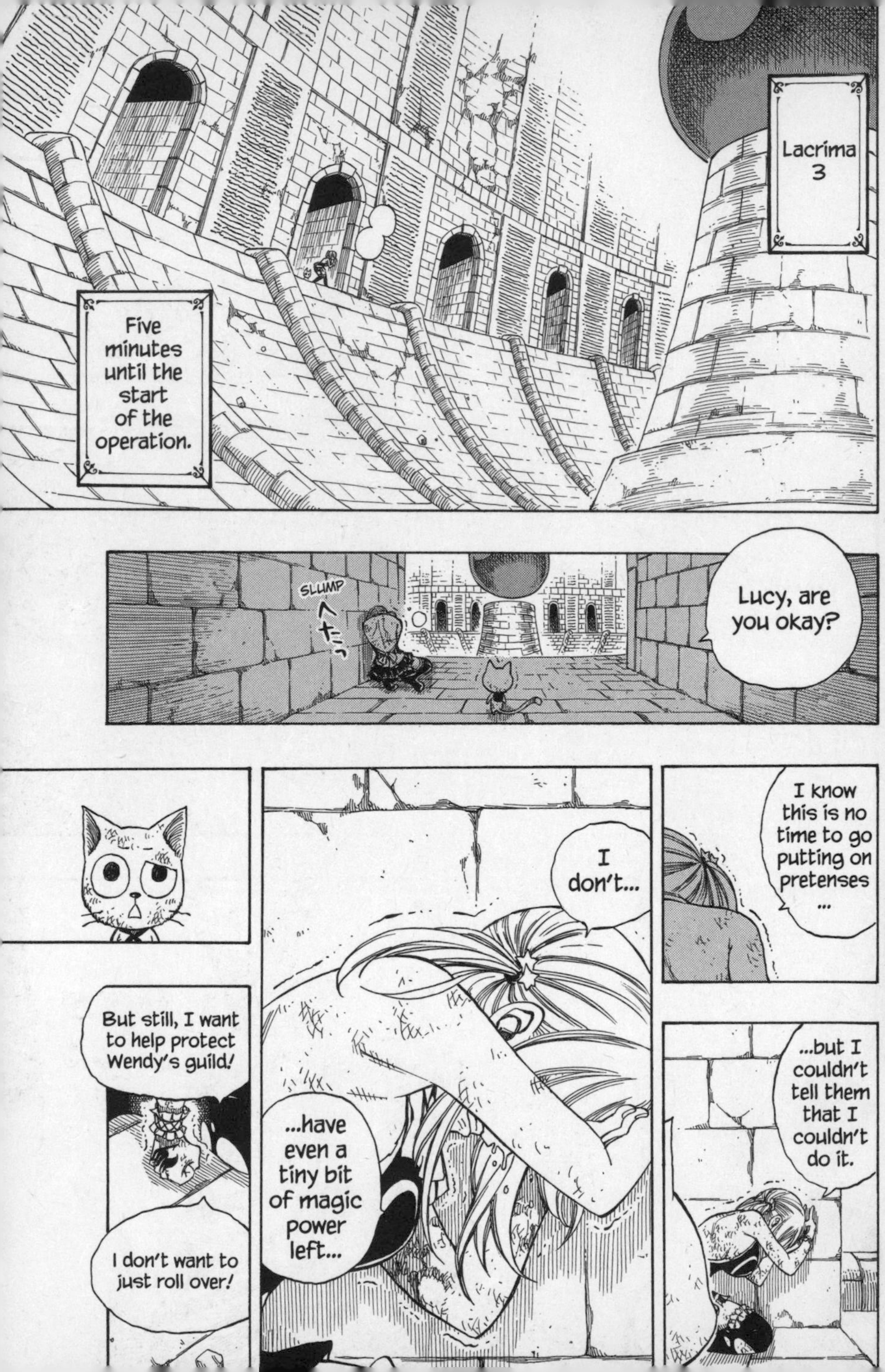
Lacrima 3
Five minutes until the start of the operation.
Lucy, are you okay?
SLUMP
I know this is no time to go putting on pretenses...
...but I couldn't tell them that I couldn't do it.
I don't...
...have even a tiny bit of magic power left...
But still, I want to help protect Wendy's guild!
I don't want to just roll over!

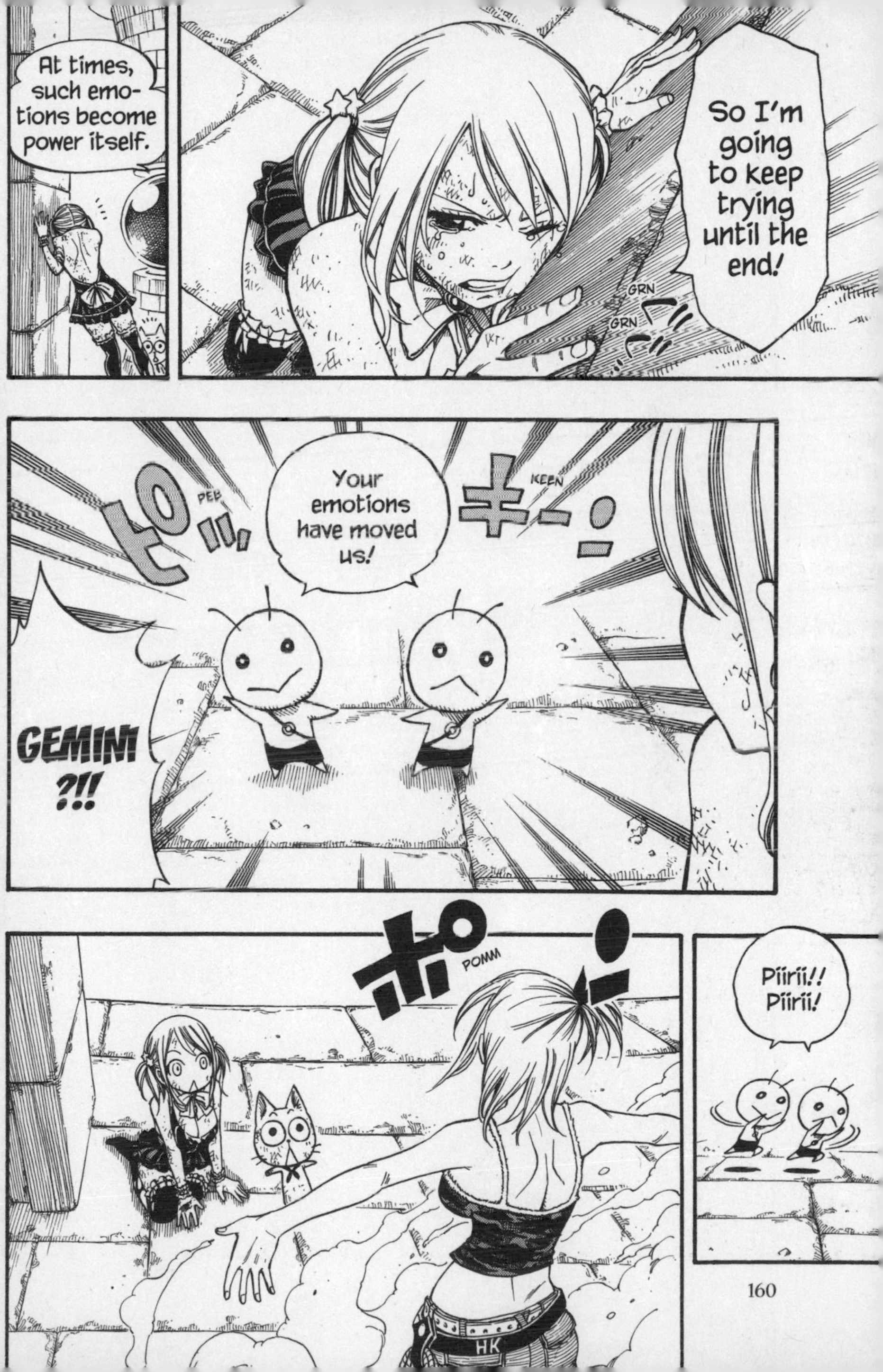

So I'm going to keep trying until the end!
GRN
GRN
At times, such emotions become power itself.
KEEN
Your emotions have moved us!
PEE
GEMINI ?!!
Piirii!! Piirii!
POMM

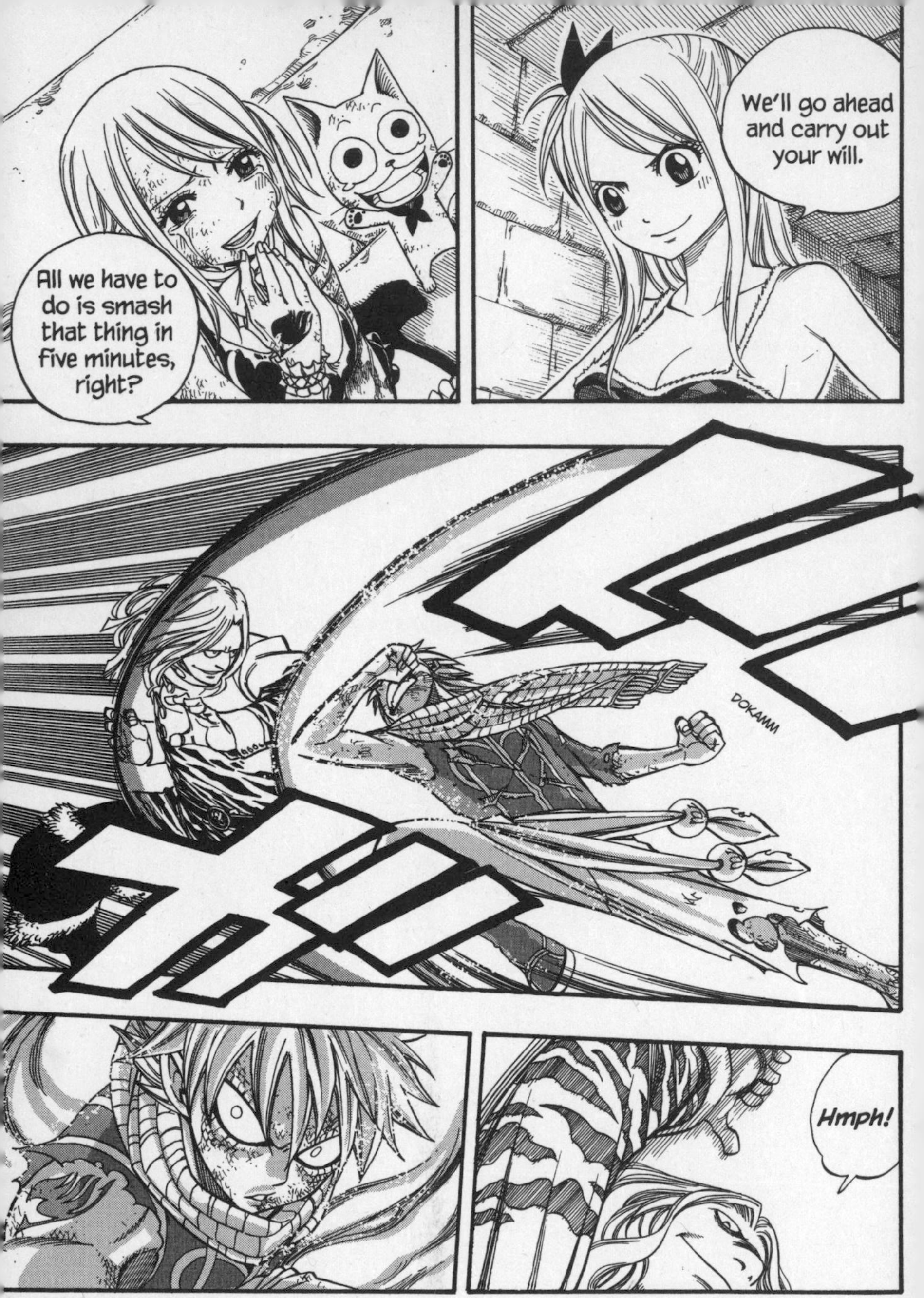
We'll go ahead and carry out your will.
All we have to do is smash that thing in five minutes, right?
DOKAMM
Hmph!

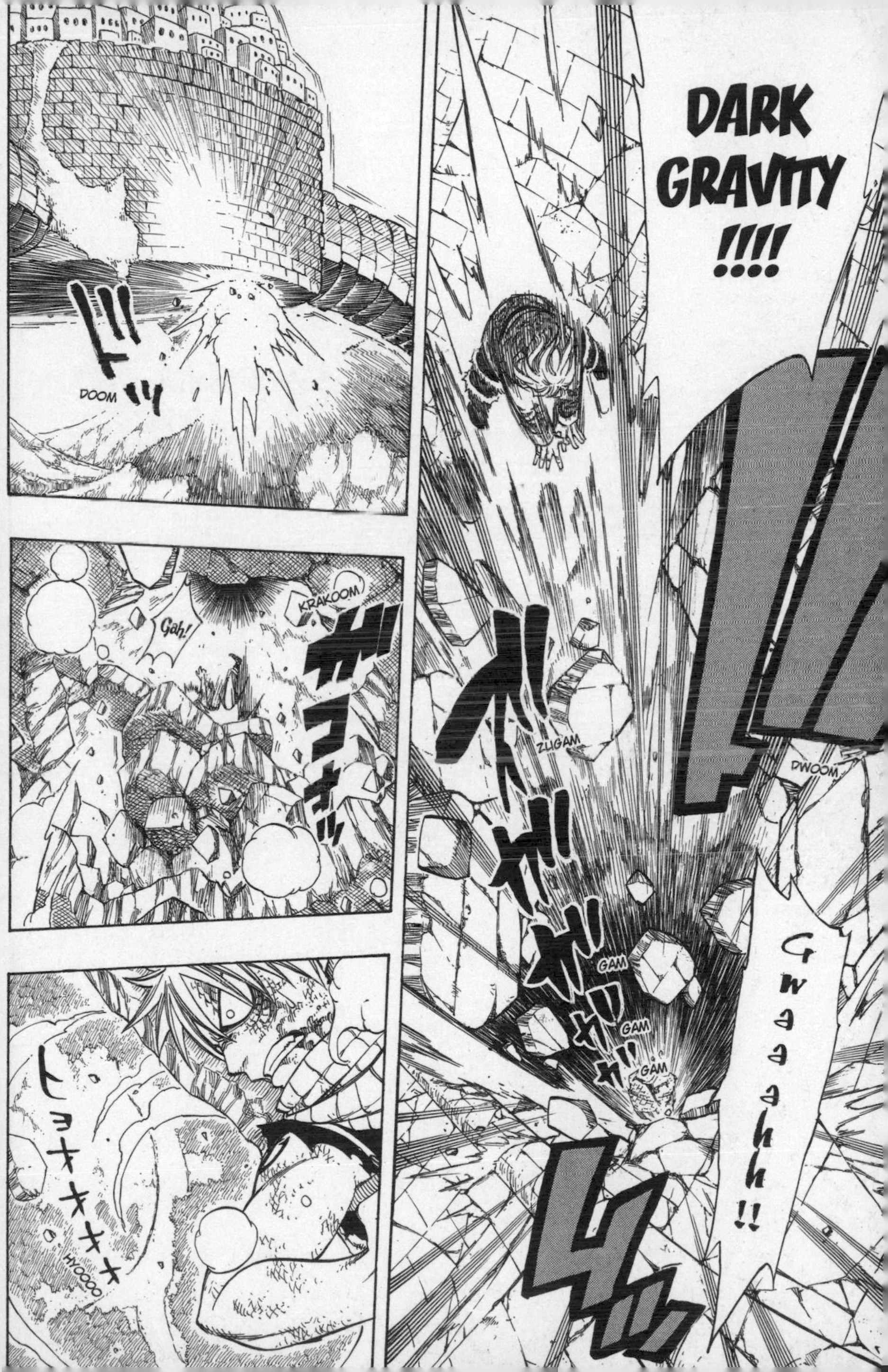
DARK GRAVITY!!!!
DWOOM
ZUGAM
Gwaaaahh!!
GAM
GAM
GAM
DOOM
KRAKOOM
Gah!
HYOOOO

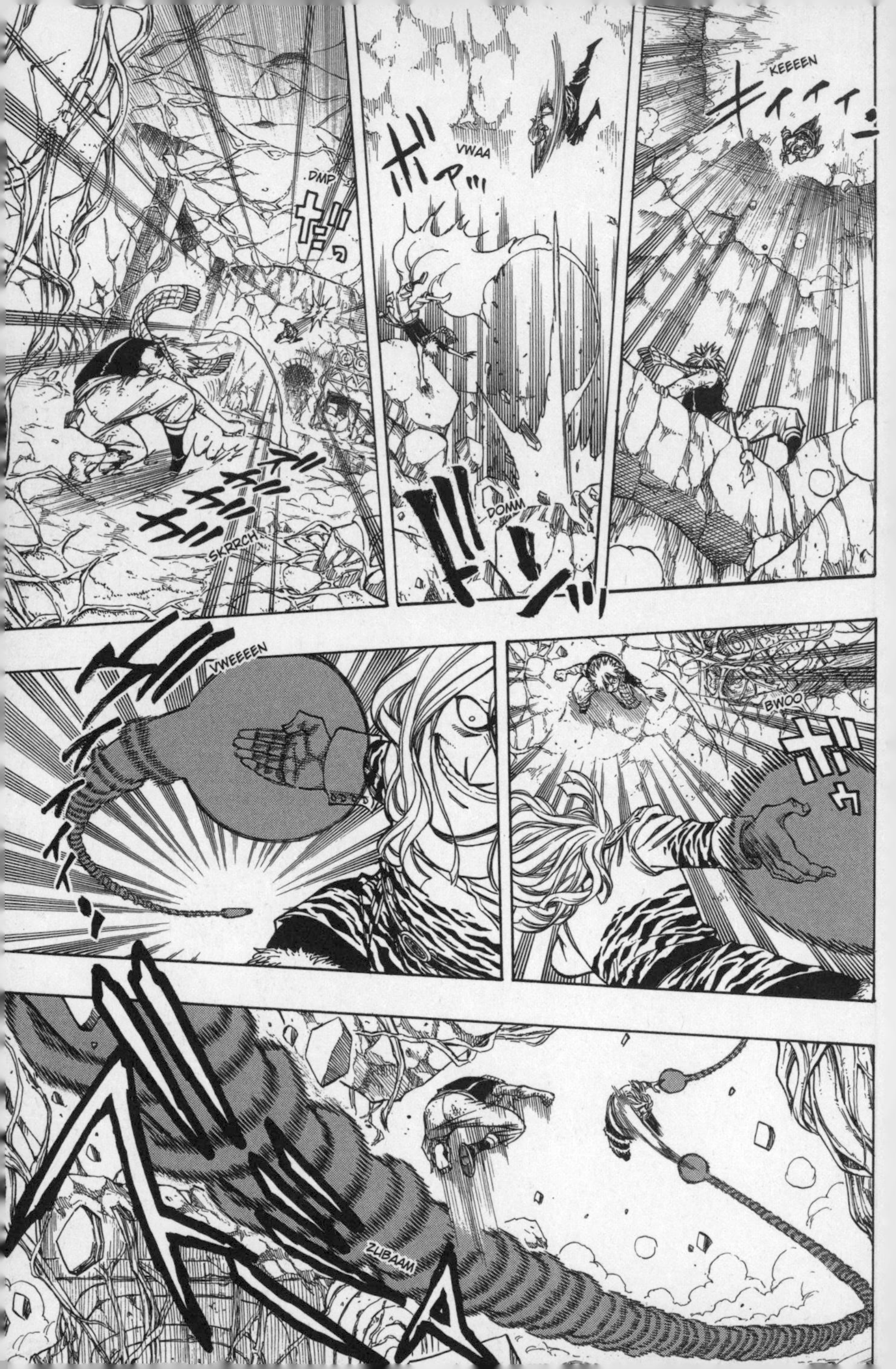
KEEEEN
VWAA
DOMM
DMP
SKRRCH
BWOO
VWEEEEN
ZUBAAM

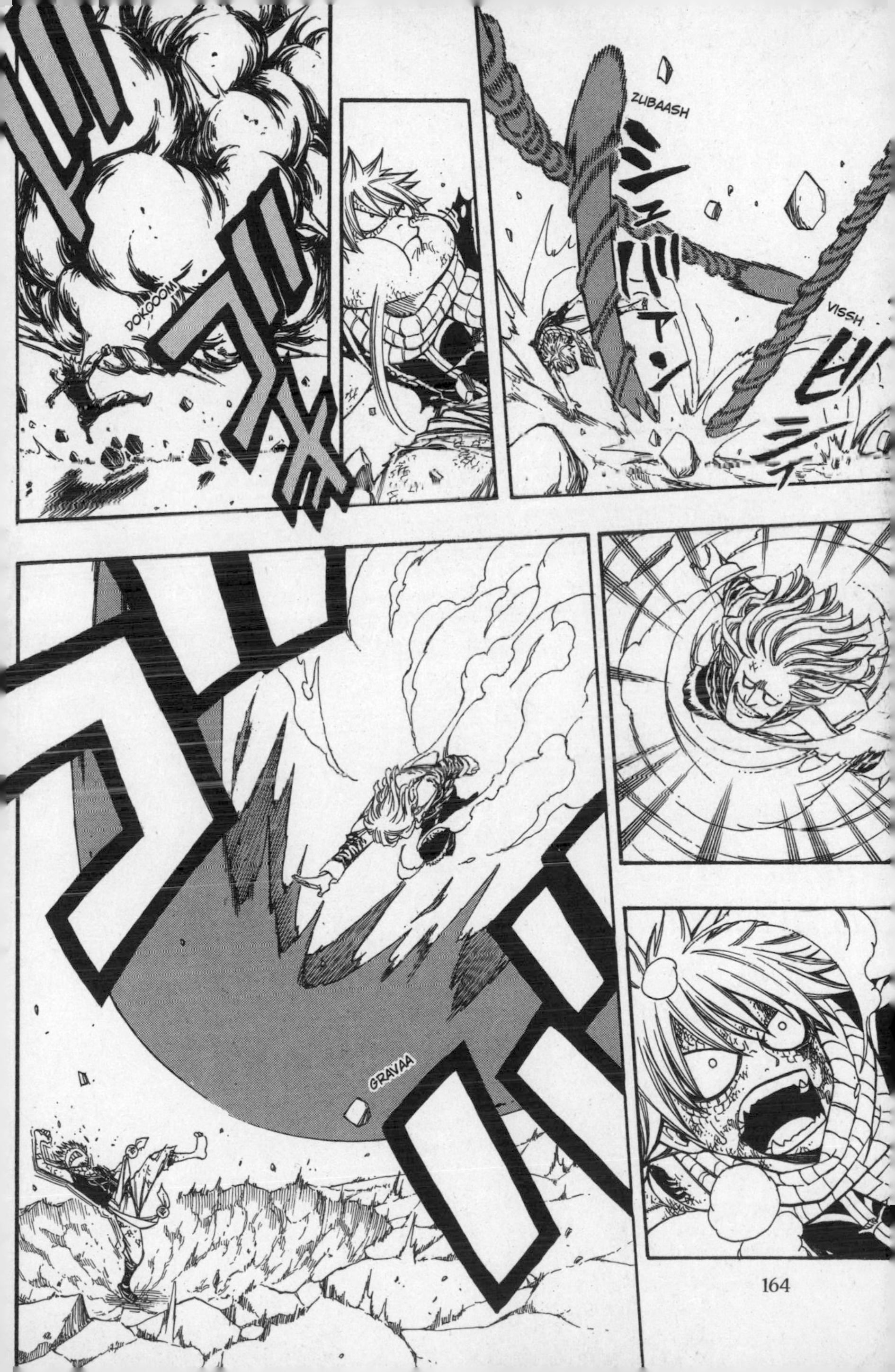
ZUBAASH
VISSH
DOKOOOM
GRAVAA

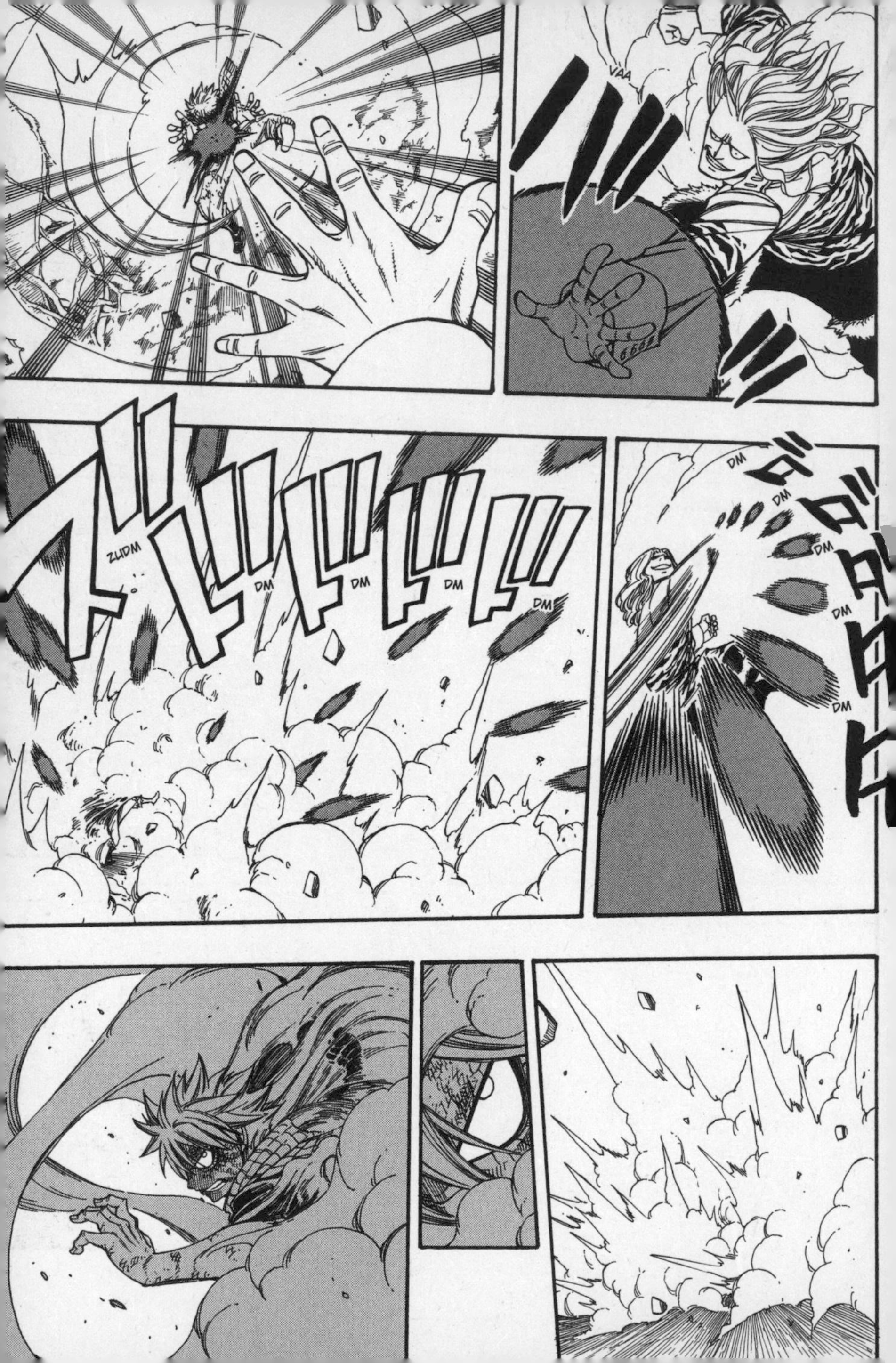
VAA
DM
DM
DM
DM
DM
ZUDM
DM
DM
DM
DM

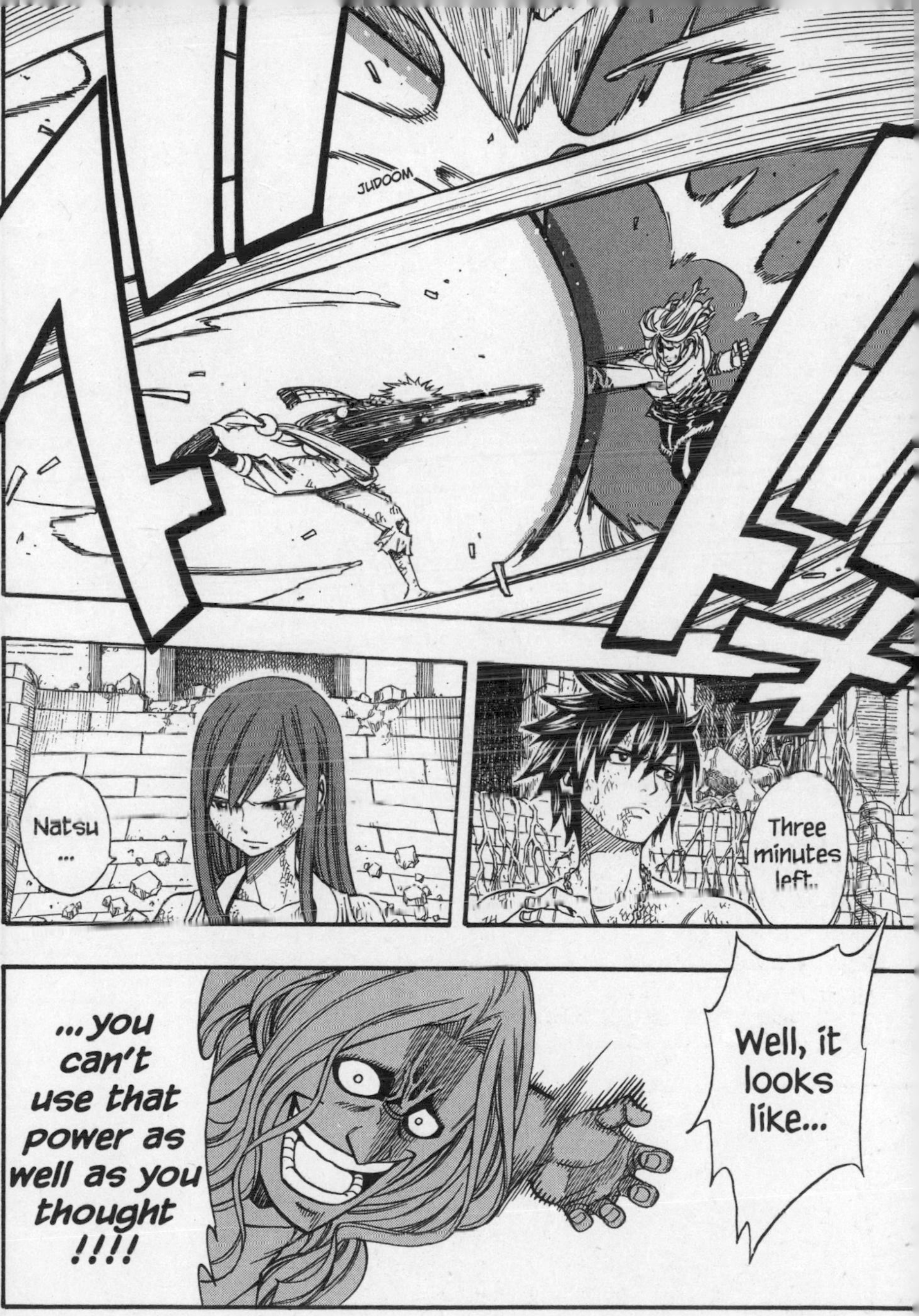
JUDOOM
Three minutes left...
Natsu ...
Well, it looks like...
...you can't use that power as well as you thought!!!!

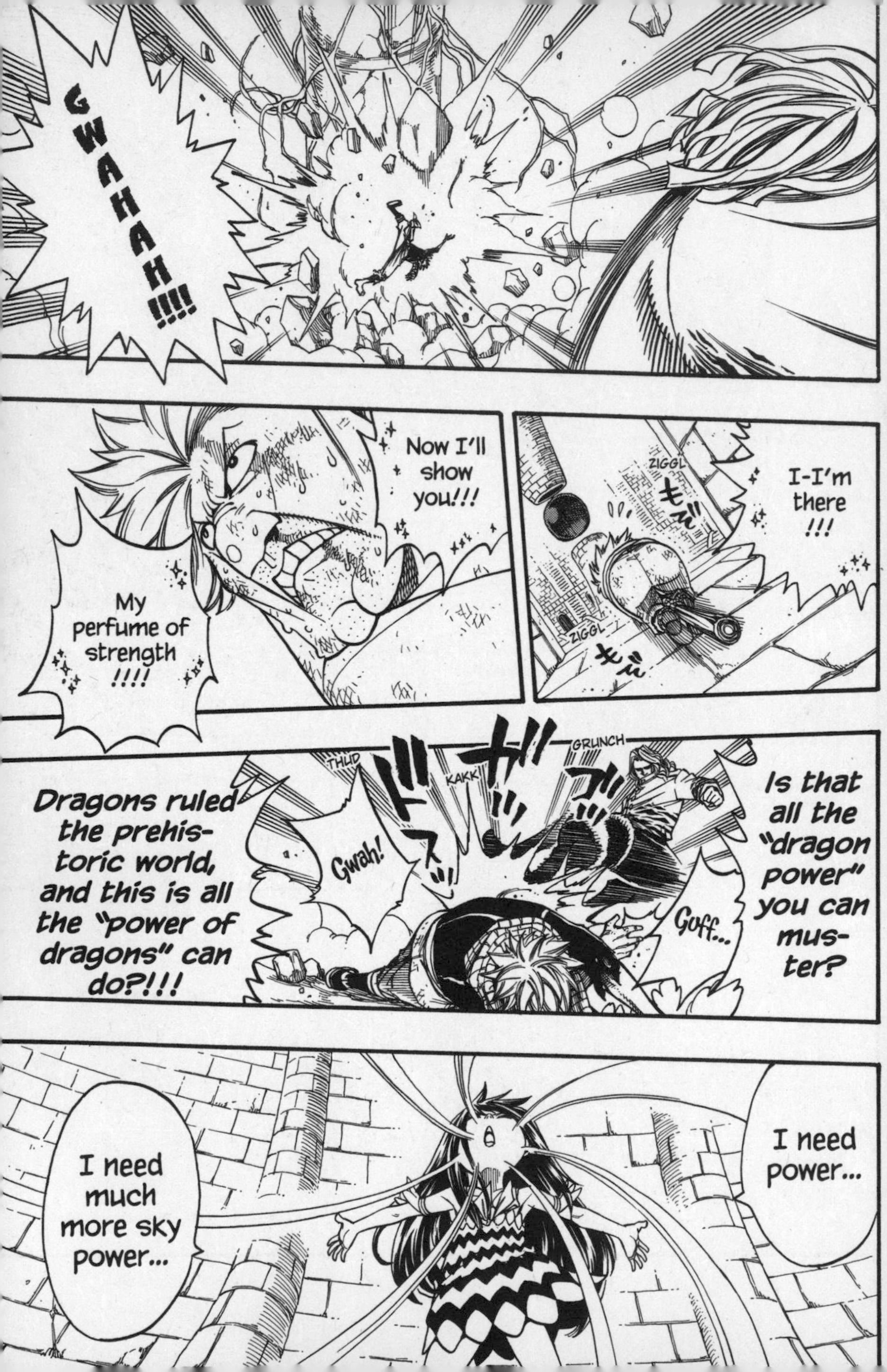
GWAHAH!!!!
ZIGGL
I-I'm there !!!
ZIGGL
Now I'll show you!!!
My perfume of strength !!!!
Is that all the "dragon power" you can muster?
GRUNCH
KAKK
Goff...
THUD
Gwah!
Dragons ruled the prehistoric world, and this is all the "power of dragons" can do?!!!
I need power...
I need much more sky power...

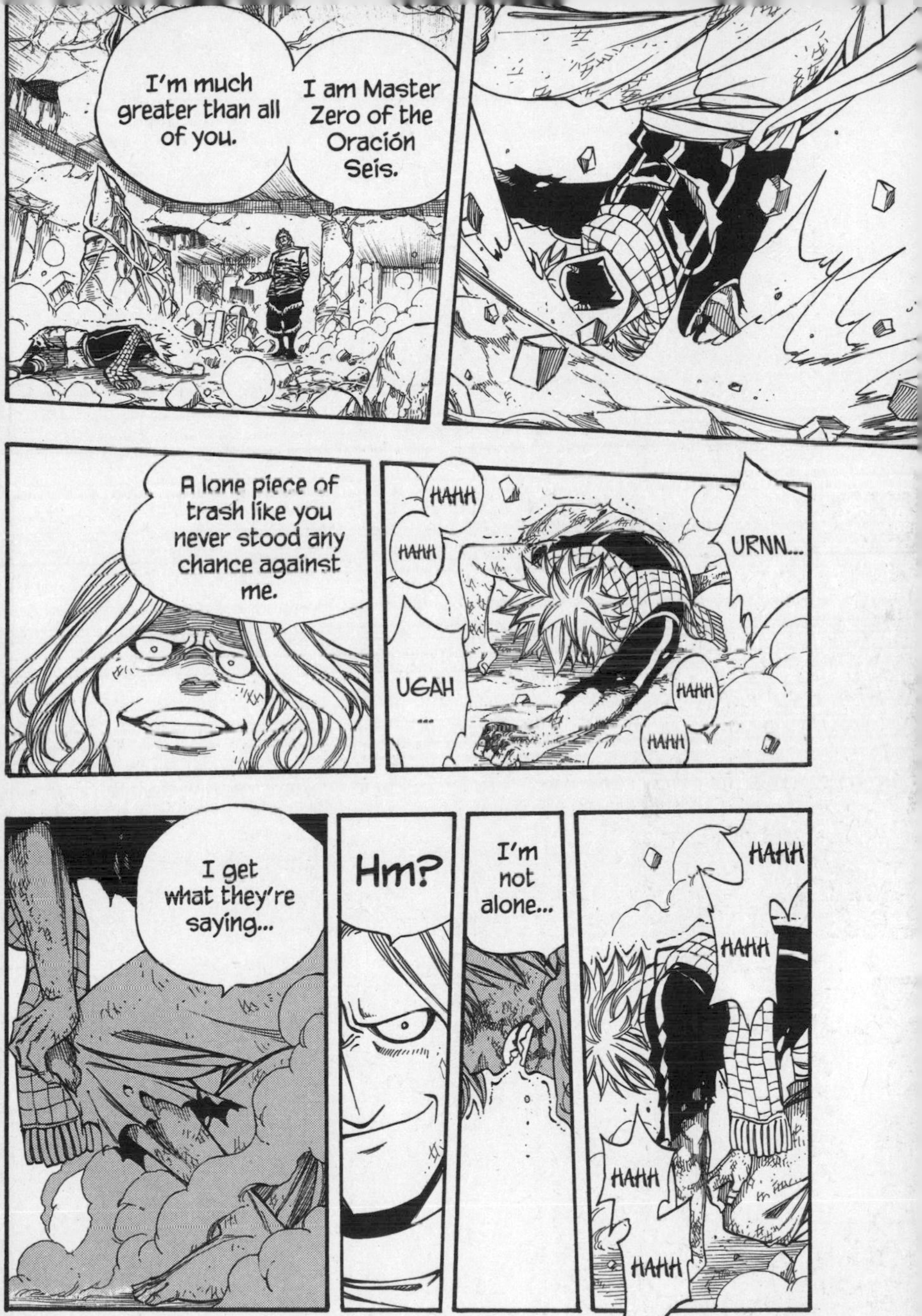
I am Master Zero of the Oración Seis.
I'm much greater than all of you.
URNN...
HAHH
HAHH
HAHH
HAHH
UGAH ...
A lone piece of trash like you never stood any chance against me.
HAHH
HAHH
HAHH
HAHH
I'm not alone...
Hm?
I get what they're saying...

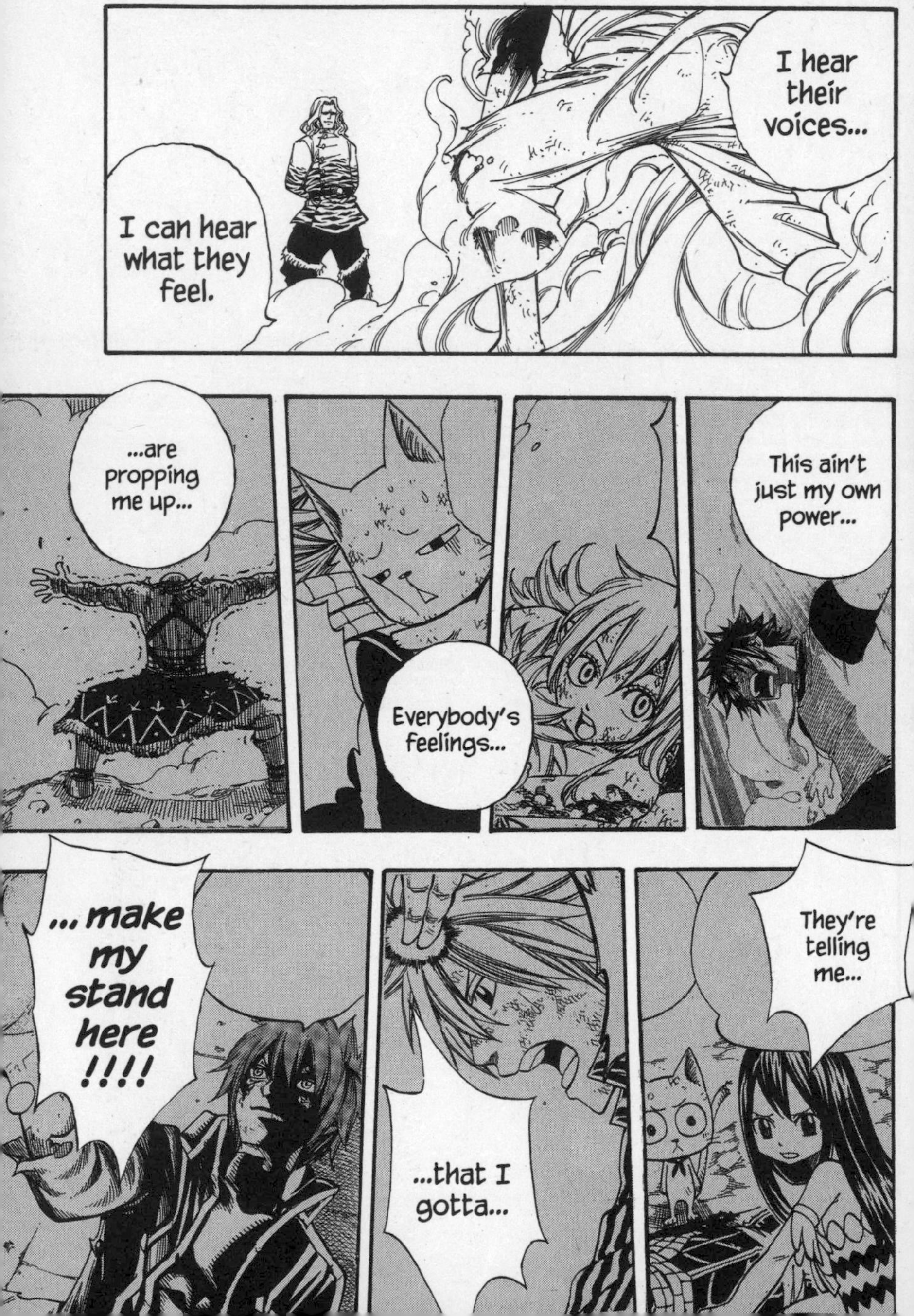
I hear their voices...
I can hear what they feel.
This ain't just my own power...
Everybody's feelings...
...are propping me up...
They're telling me...
...that I gotta...
...make my stand here!!!!

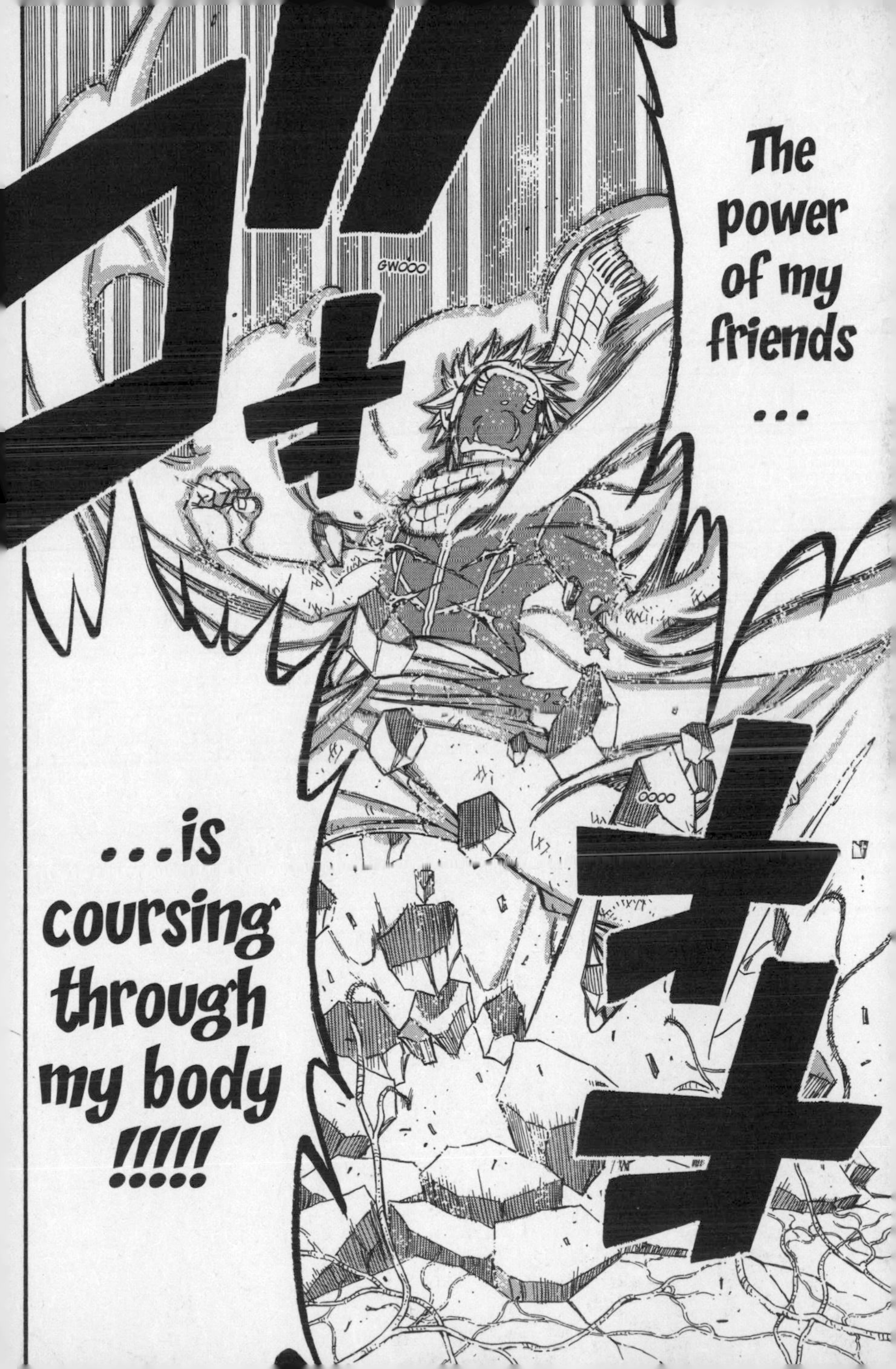
The power of my friends ...
GWOOO
...is coursing through my body !!!!!

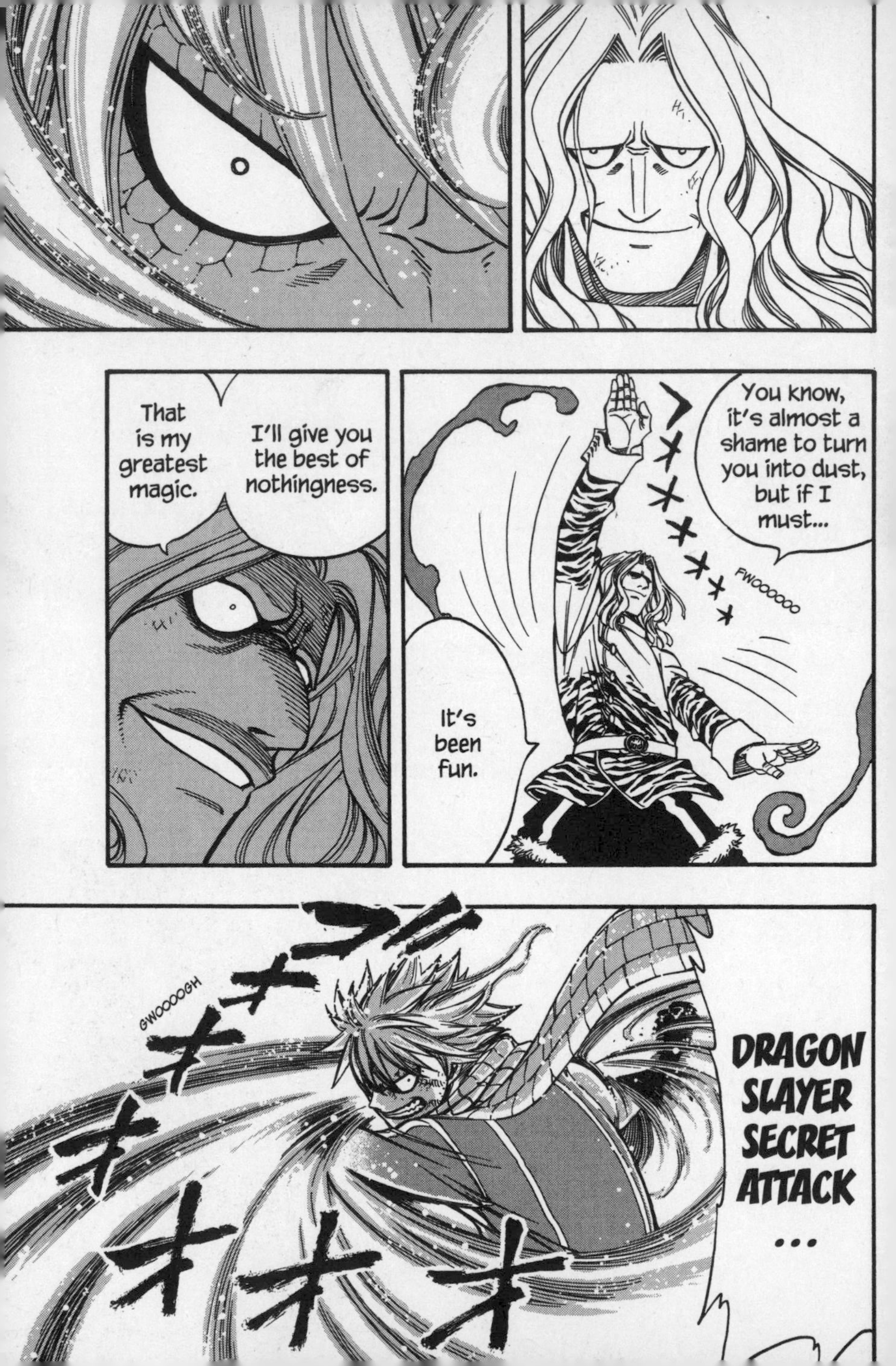
You know, it's almost a shame to turn you into dust, but if I must...
FWOOOOOO
It's been fun.
I'll give you the best of nothingness.
That is my greatest magic.
DRAGON SLAYER SECRET ATTACK ...
GWOOOOGH

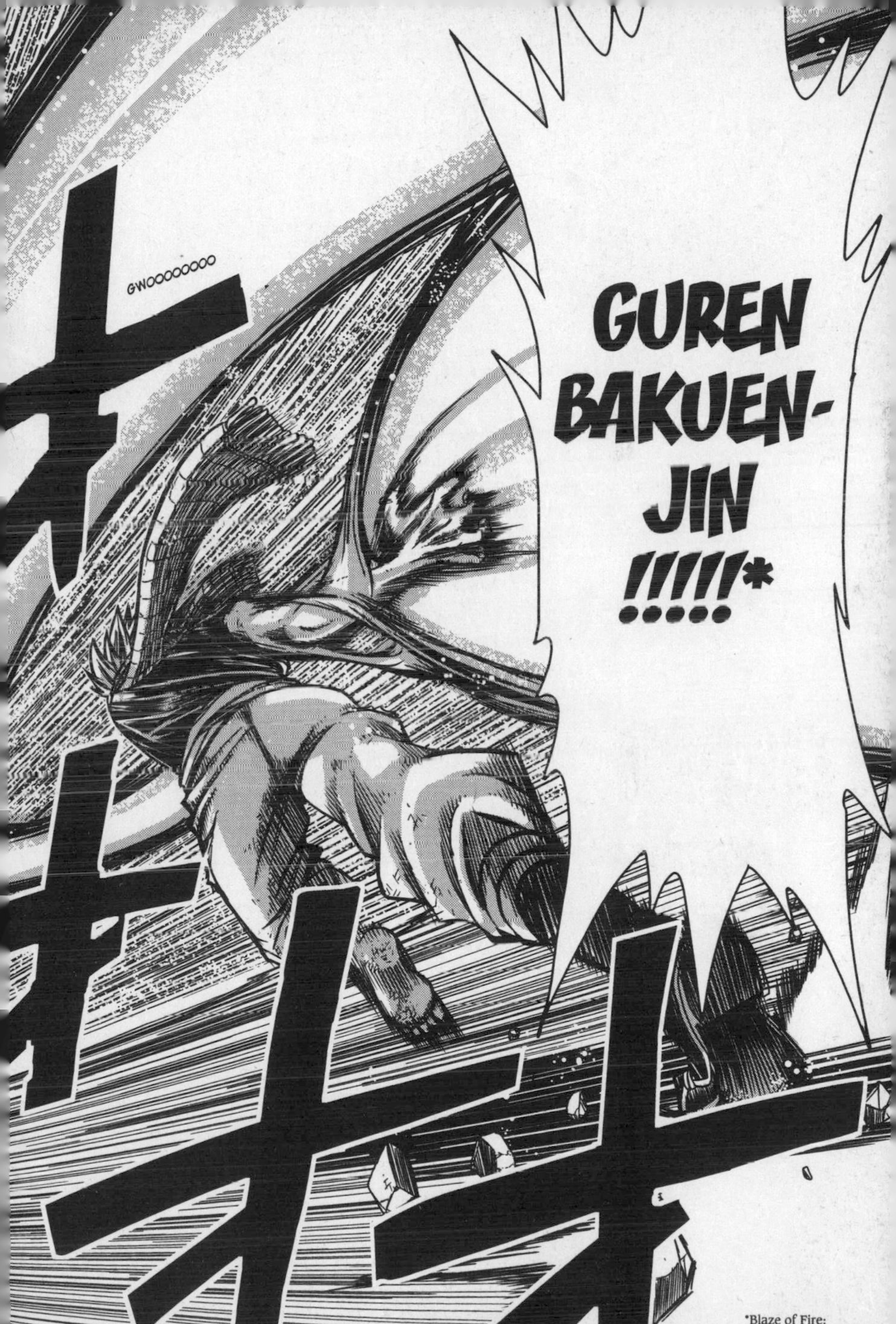
GUREN BAKUEN-JIN!!!!!*
GWOOOOOOOO

*Blaze of Fire: Exploding Blade!!!!!

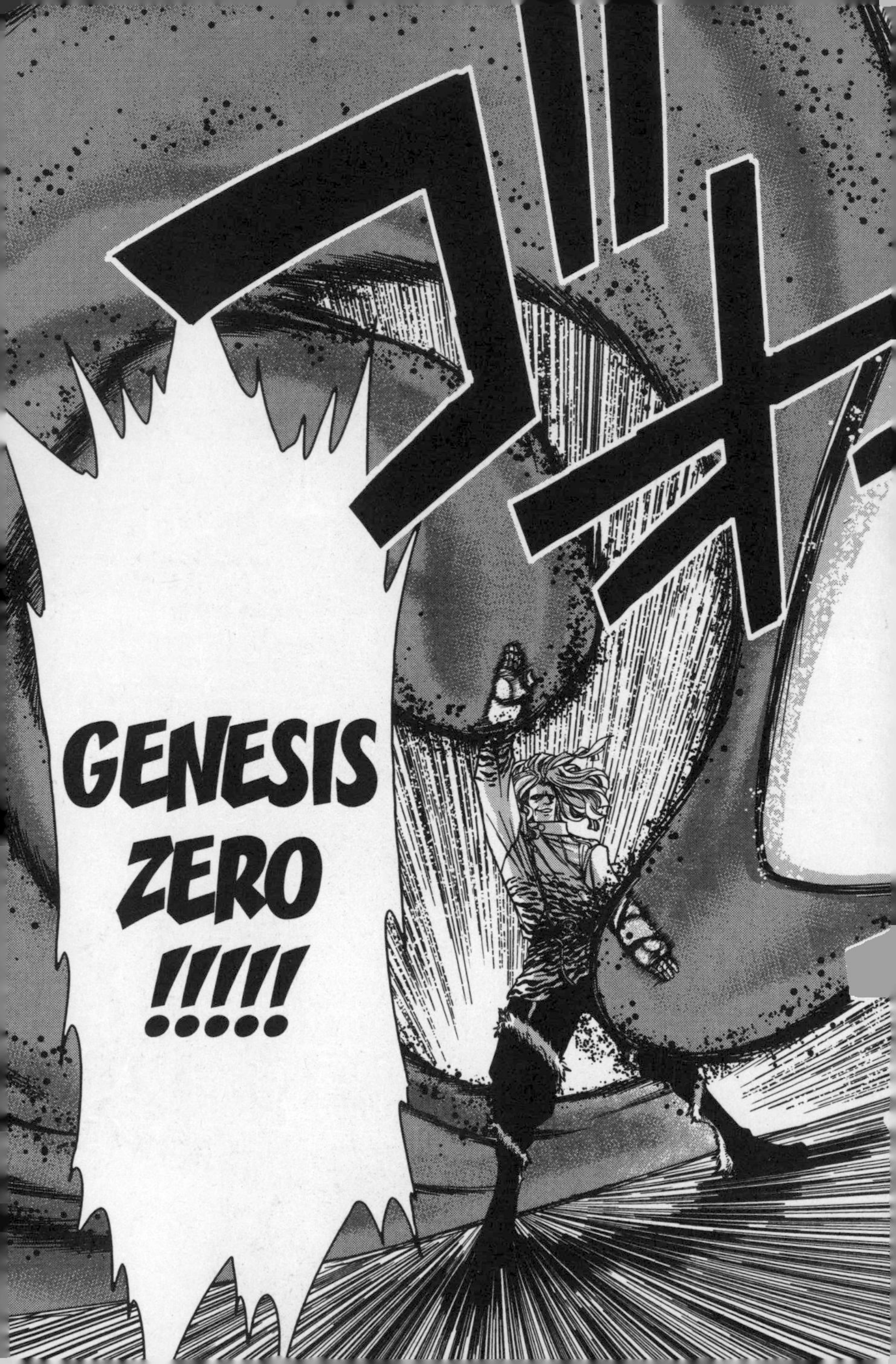
GENESIS ZERO !!!!!

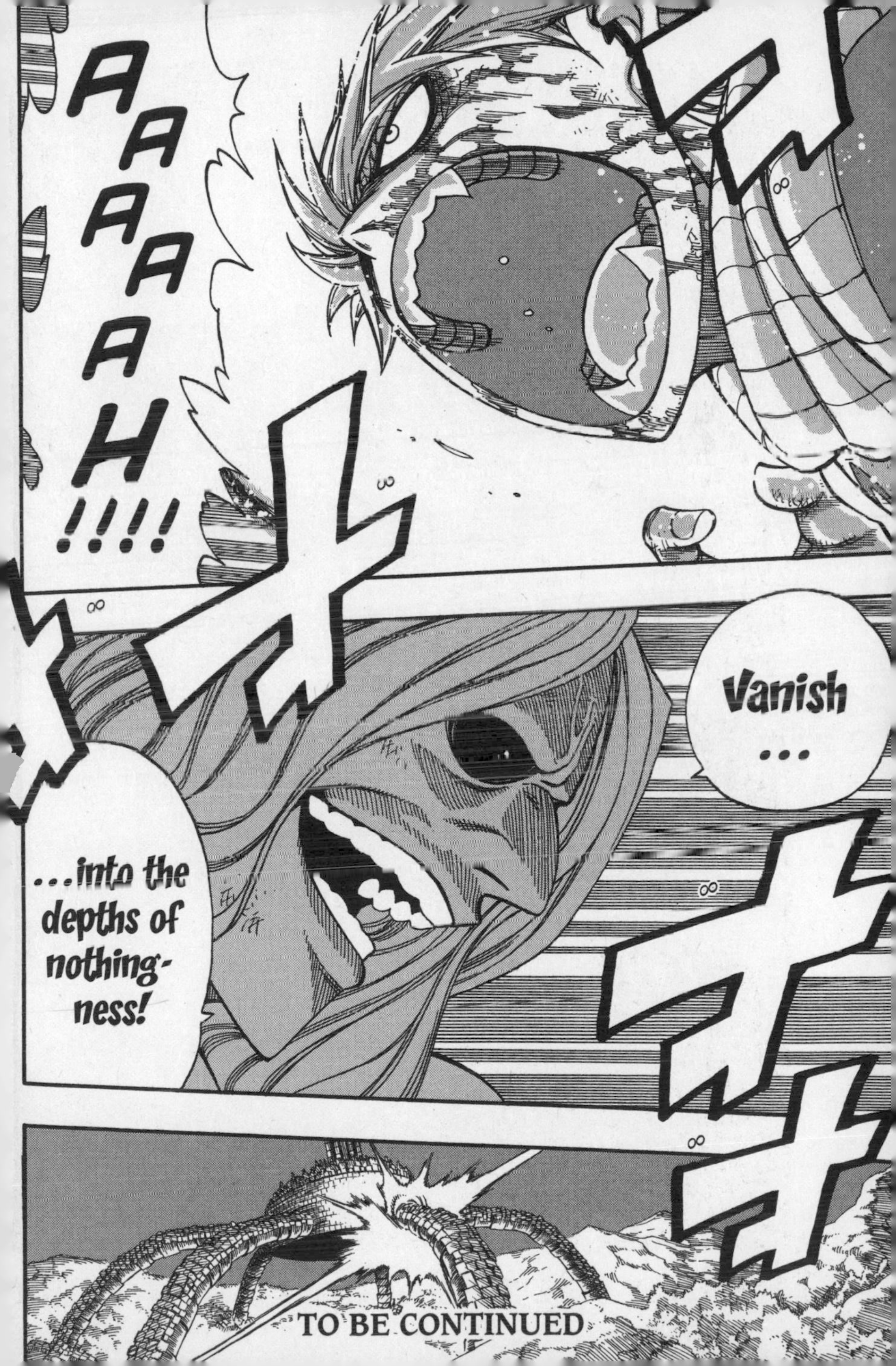
AAAAAH!!!!
Vanish...
...into the depths of nothing-ness!
TO BE CONTINUED

FAIRY TAIL

Side Story

フェアリーテイル

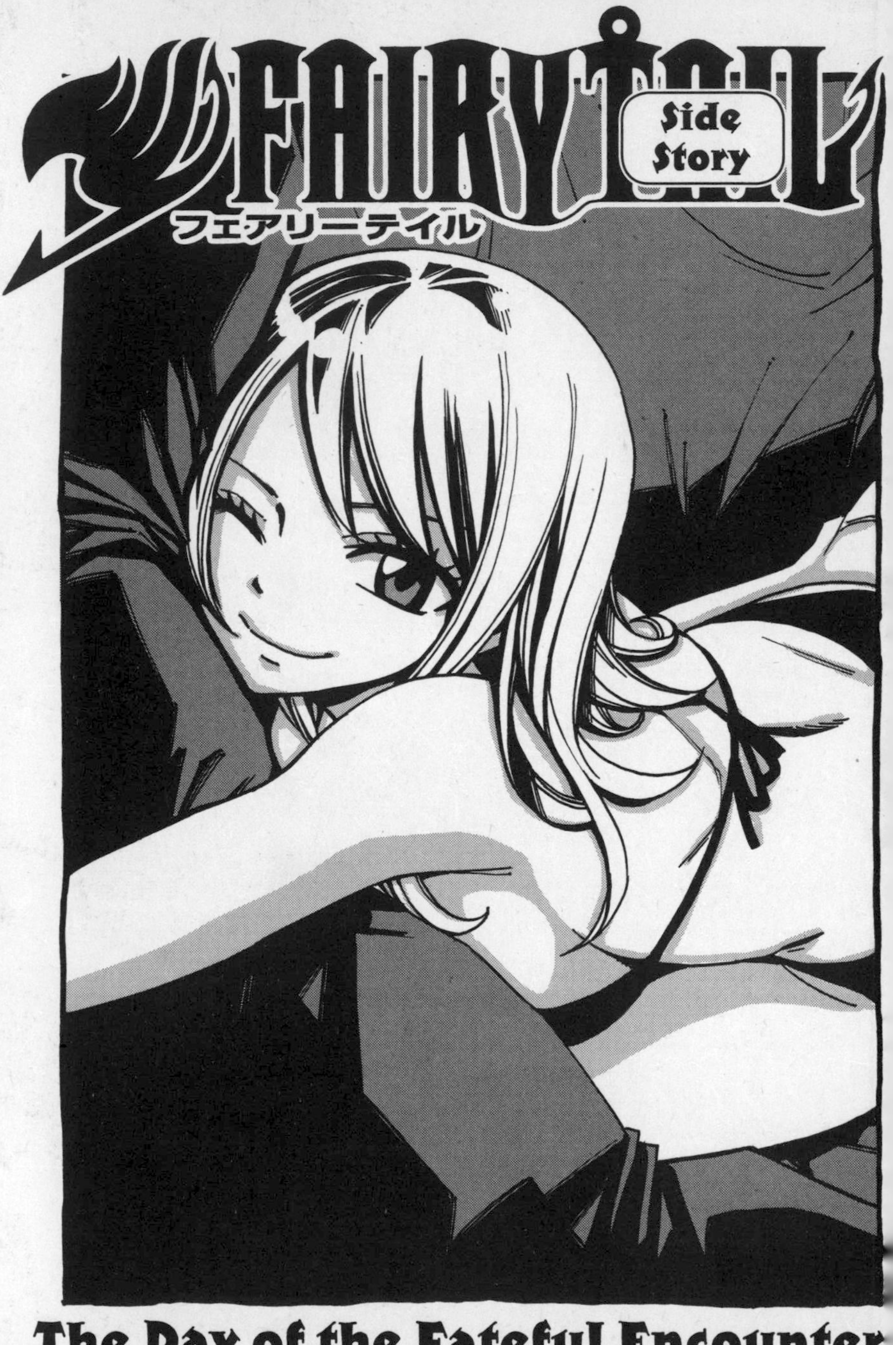

The Day of the Fateful Encounter

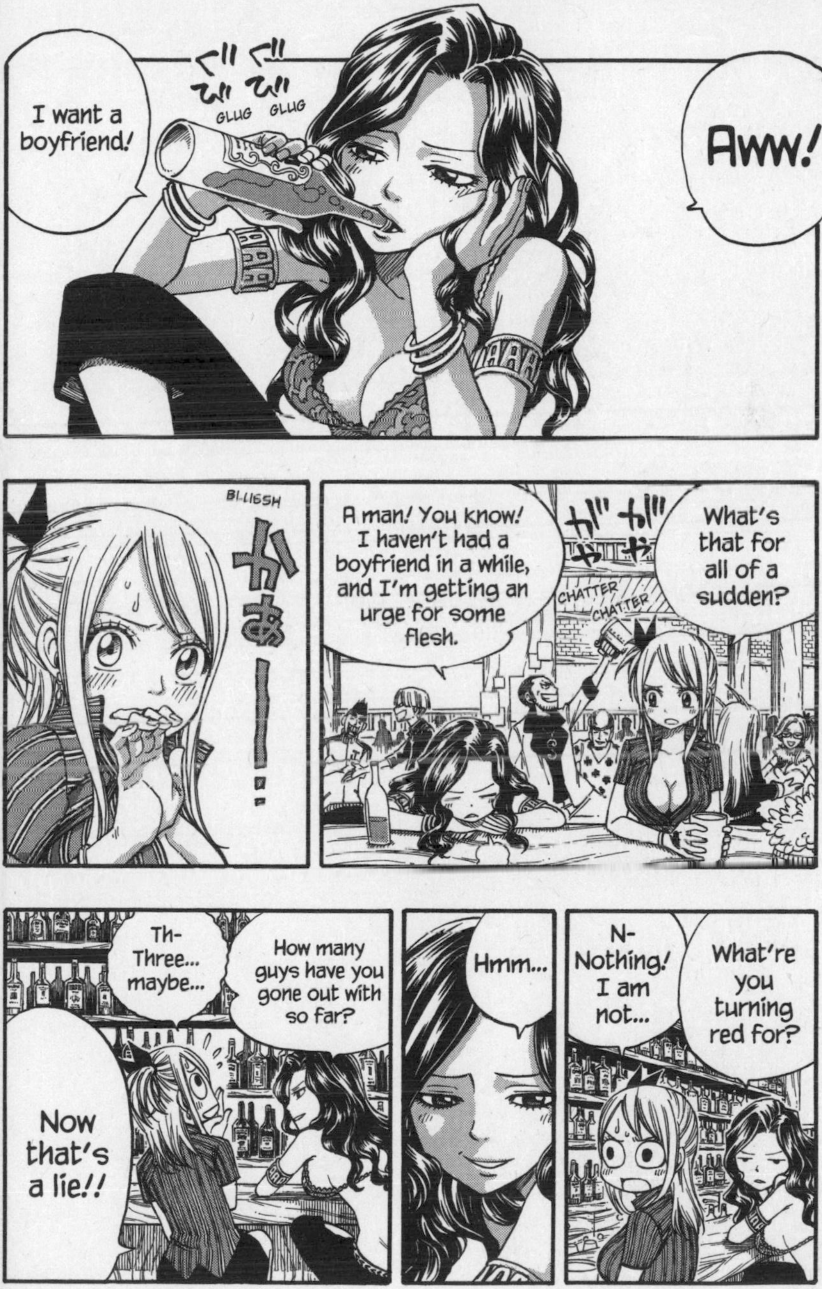
Aww!
GLUG GLUG
I want a boyfriend!
What's that for all of a sudden?
CHATTER CHATTER
A man! You know! I haven't had a boyfriend in a while, and I'm getting an urge for some flesh.
What're you turning red for?
N- Nothing! I am not...
Hmm...
How many guys have you gone out with so far?
Th- Three... maybe...
Now that's a lie!!

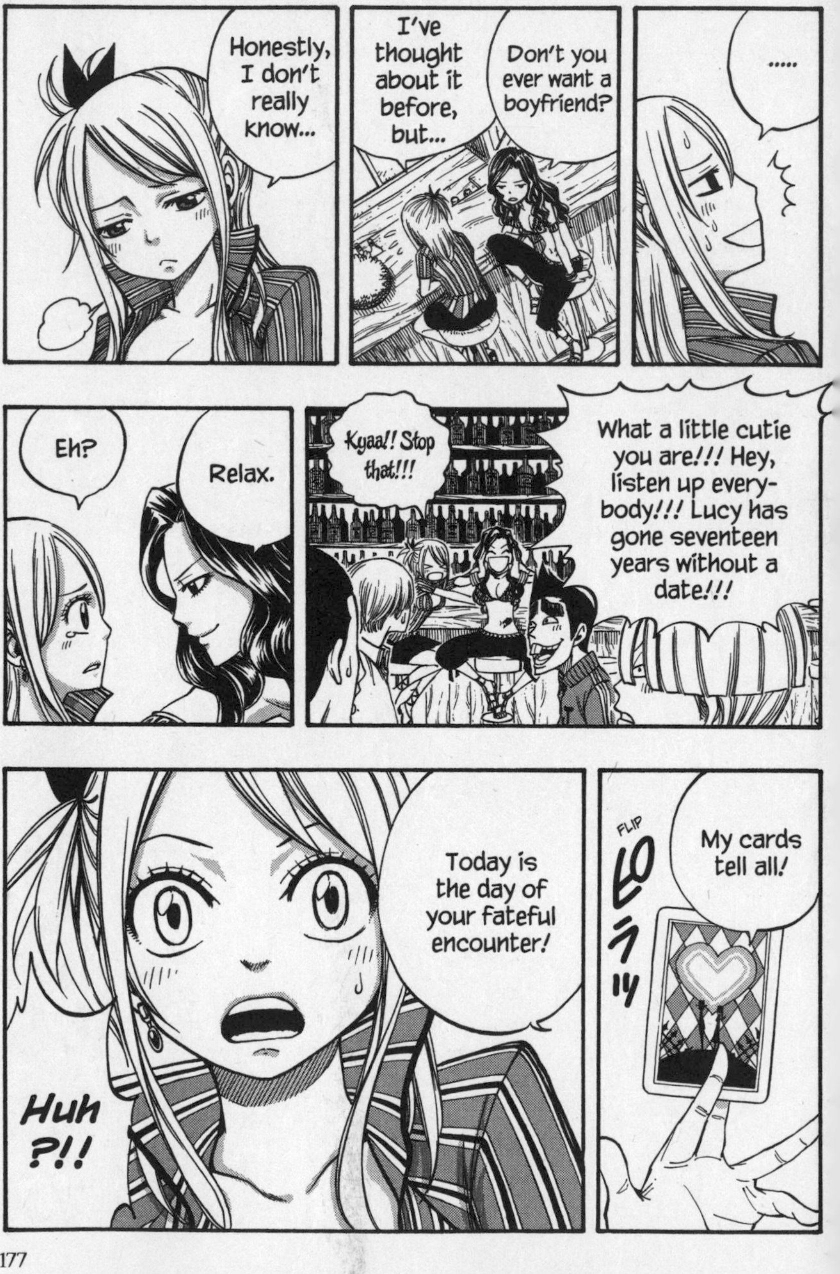
.....
Don't you ever want a boyfriend?
I've thought about it before, but...
Honestly, I don't really know...
What a little cutie you are!!! Hey, listen up every-body!!! Lucy has gone seventeen years without a date!!!
Kyaa!! Stop that!!!
Relax.
Eh?
My cards tell all!
FLIP
Today is the day of your fateful encounter!
Huh ?!!

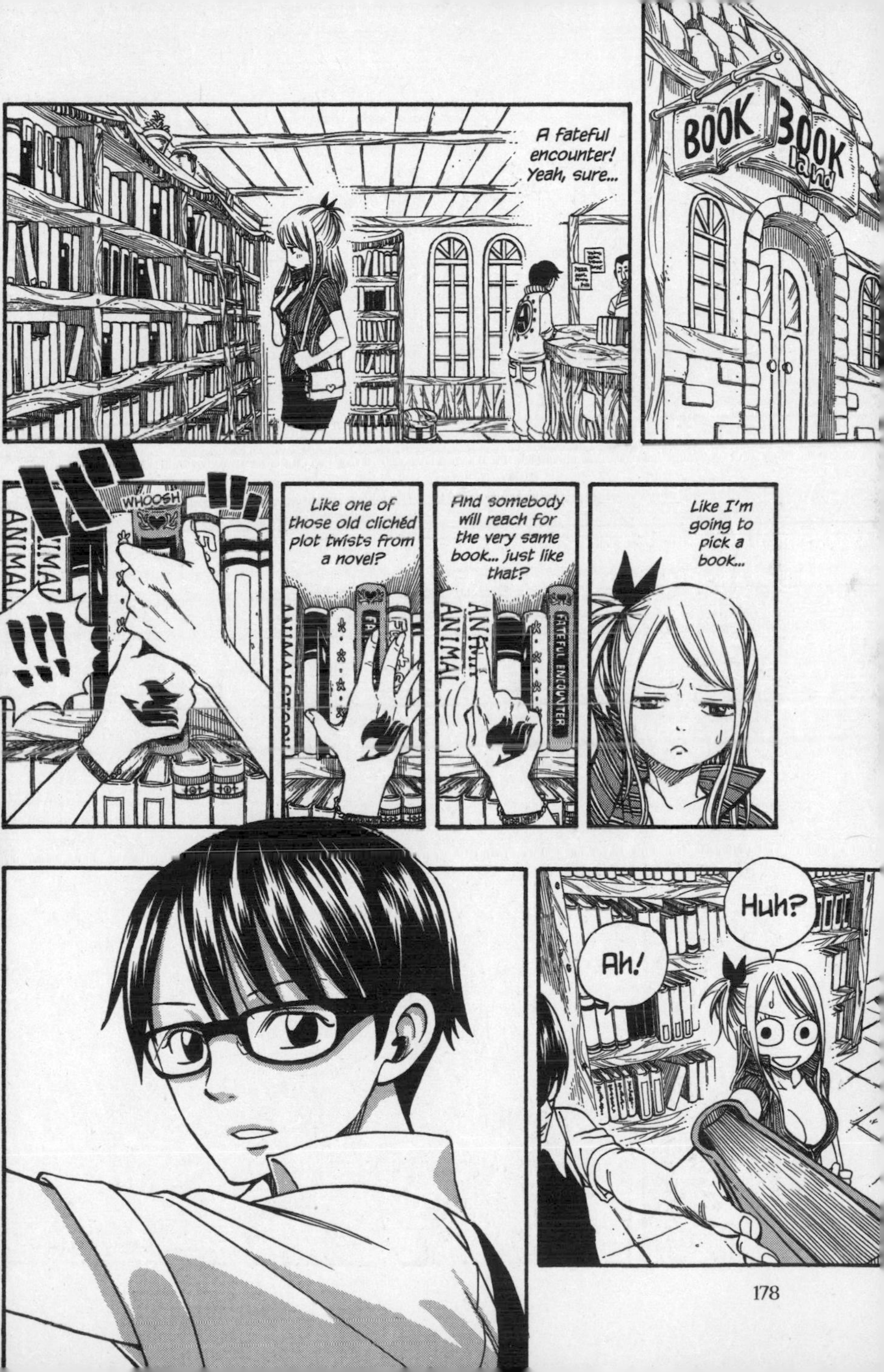
BOOK BOOK land
A fateful encounter! Yeah, sure...
Like I'm going to pick a book...
And somebody will reach for the very same book... just like that?
FATEFUL ENCOUNTER
Like one of those old clichéd plot twists from a novel?
WHOOSH
!!!
Huh?
Ah!

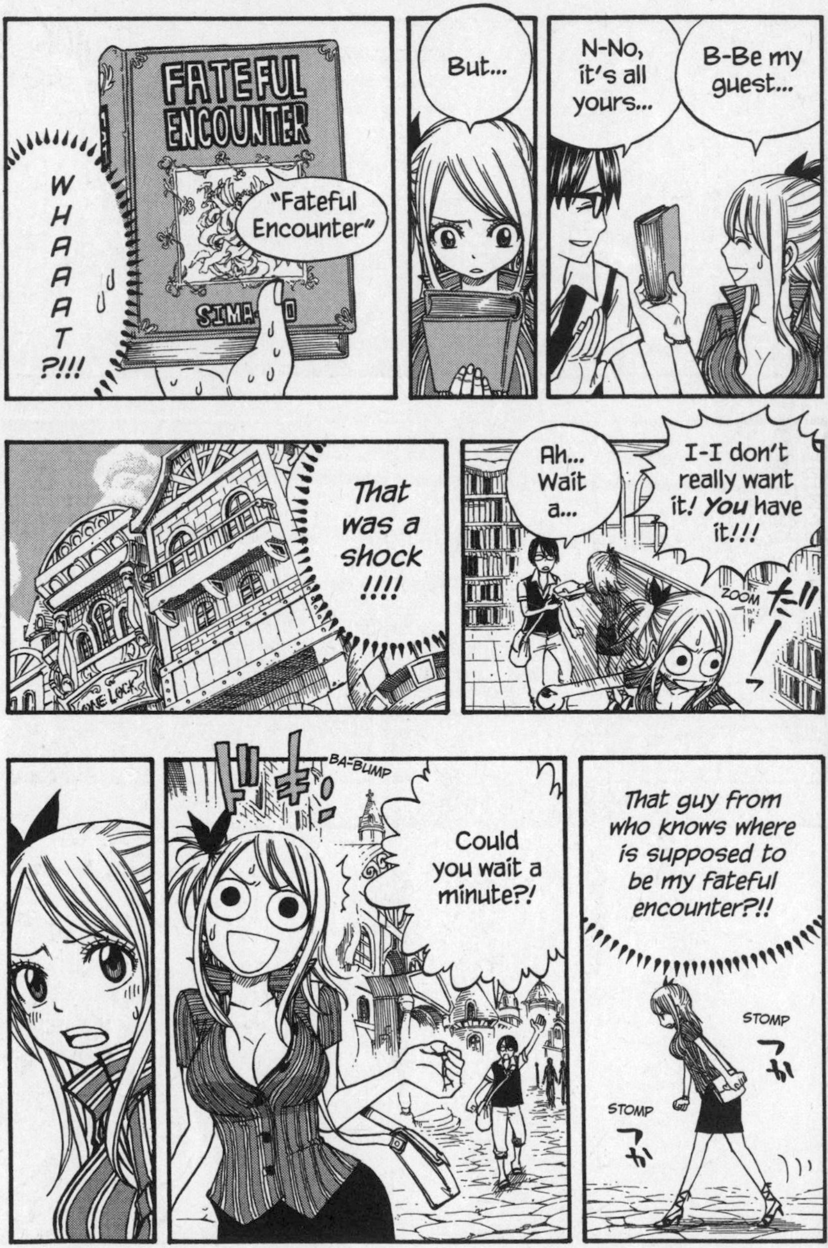
B-Be my guest...
N-No, it's all yours...
But...
FATEFUL ENCOUNTER
"Fateful Encounter"
WHAAAAT?!!!
I-I don't really want it! You have it!!!
Ah... Wait a...
ZOOM
That was a shock!!!!
That guy from who knows where is supposed to be my fateful encounter?!!
STOMP
STOMP
BA-BUMP
Could you wait a minute?!

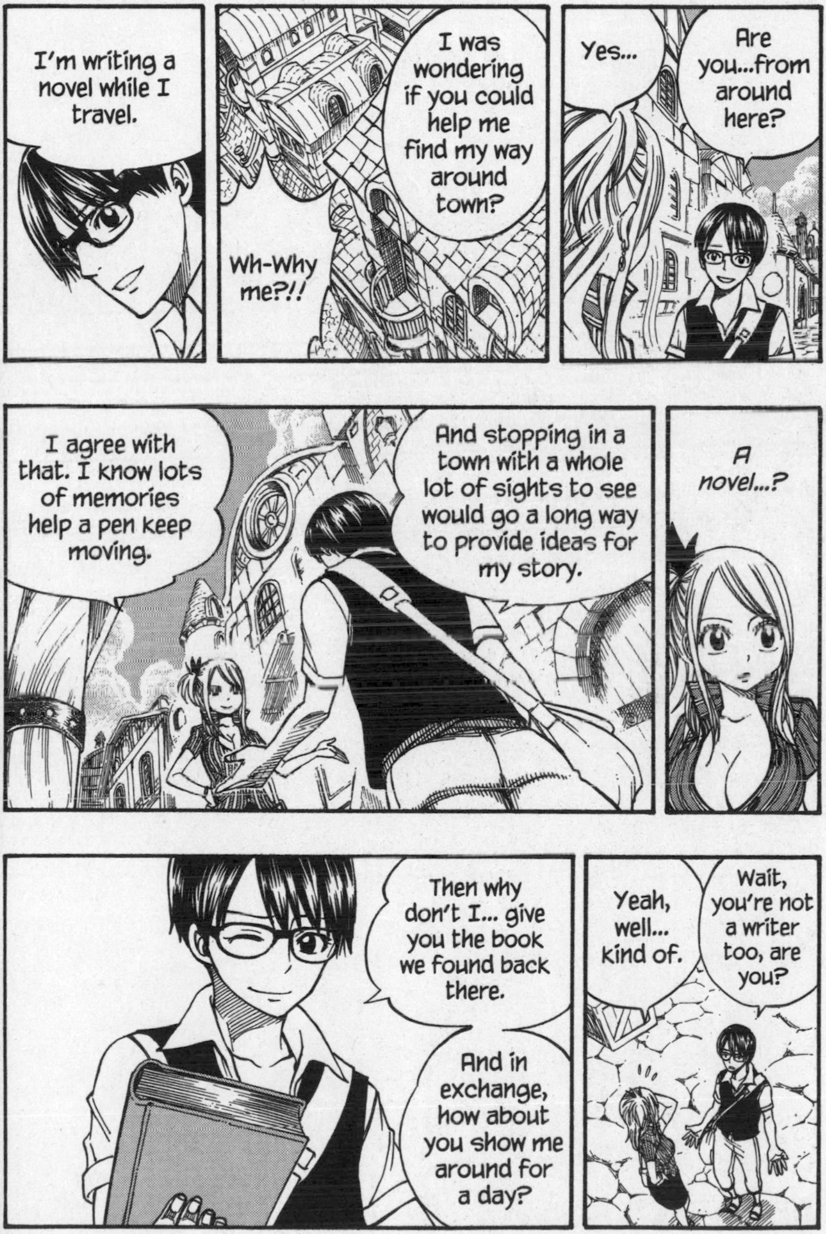
Are you...from around here?
Yes...
I was wondering if you could help me find my way around town?
Wh-Why me?!!
I'm writing a novel while I travel.
A novel...?
And stopping in a town with a whole lot of sights to see would go a long way to provide ideas for my story.
I agree with that. I know lots of memories help a pen keep moving.
Wait, you're not a writer too, are you?
Yeah, well... kind of.
Then why don't I... give you the book we found back there.
And in exchange, how about you show me around for a day?

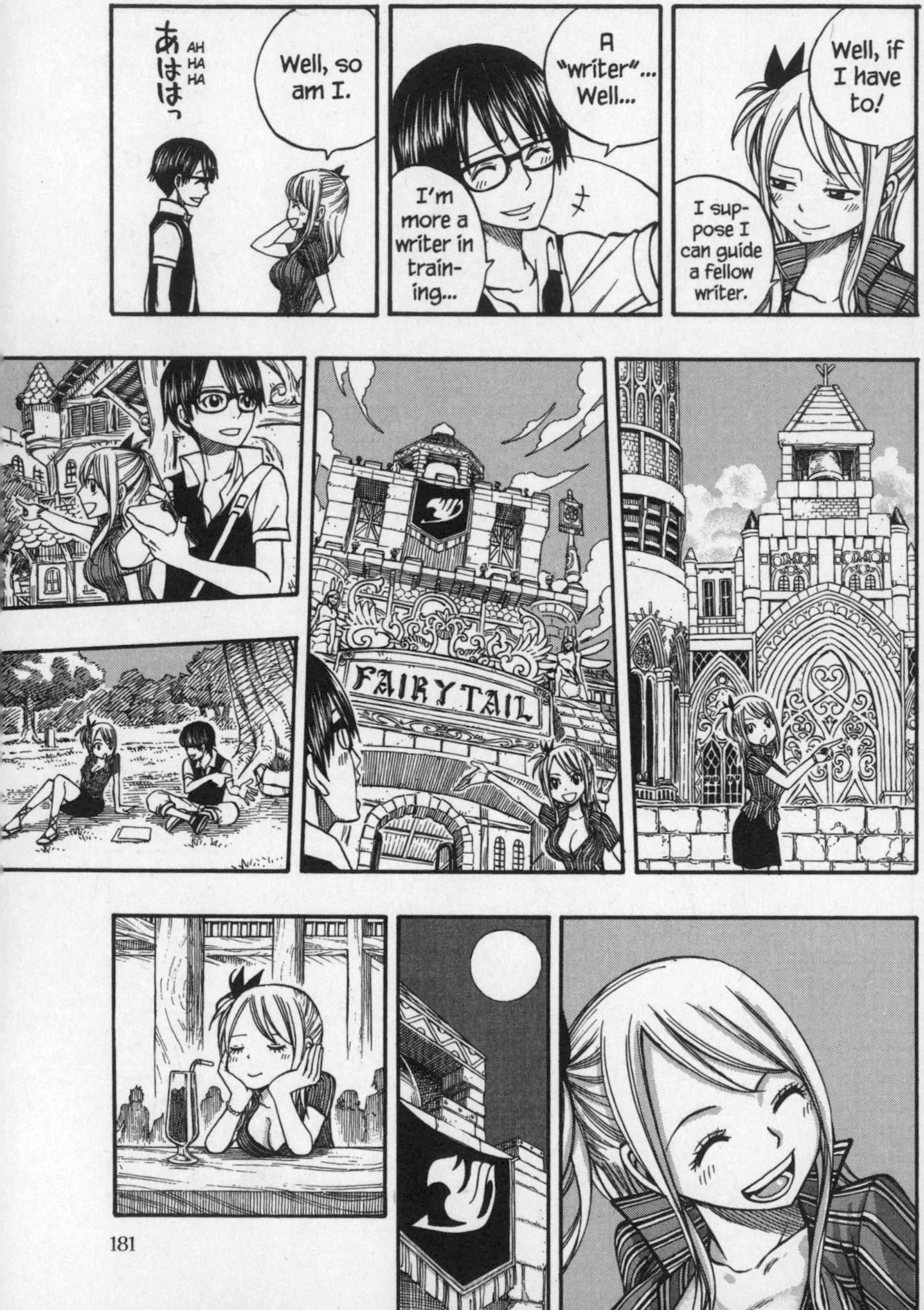
Well, if I have to!
I sup-pose I can guide a fellow writer.
A "writer"... Well...
I'm more a writer in train-ing...
Well, so am I.
あははっ
AH HA HA
FAIRY TAIL

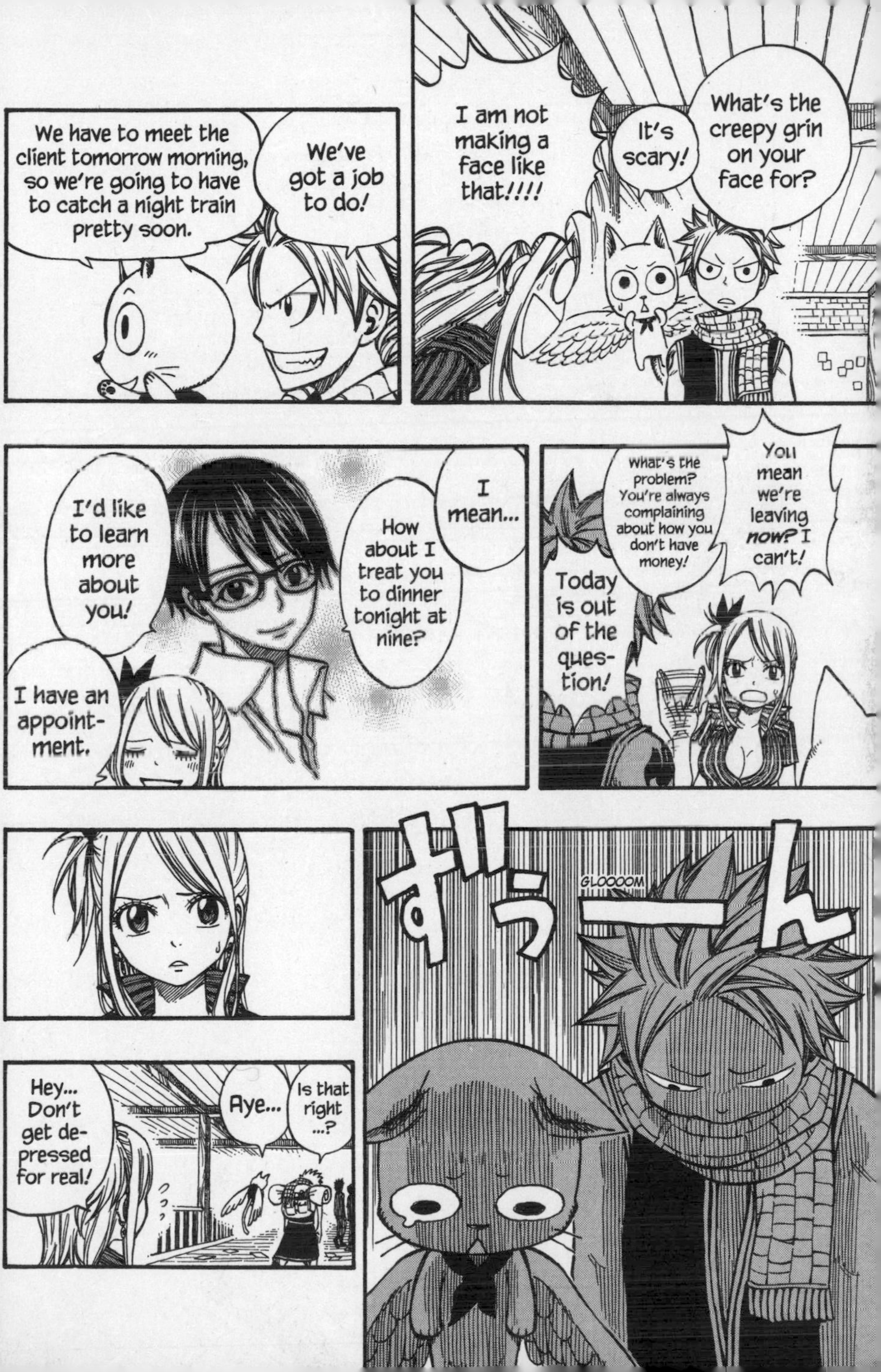
What's the creepy grin on your face for?
It's scary!
I am not making a face like that!!!!
We've got a job to do!
We have to meet the client tomorrow morning, so we're going to have to catch a night train pretty soon.
You mean we're leaving *now?* I can't!
What's the problem? You're always complaining about how you don't have money!
Today is out of the question!
I mean...
How about I treat you to dinner tonight at nine?
I'd like to learn more about you!
I have an appointment.
ずう一ん
GLOOOOM
Is that right ...?
Aye...
Hey... Don't get de-pressed for real!

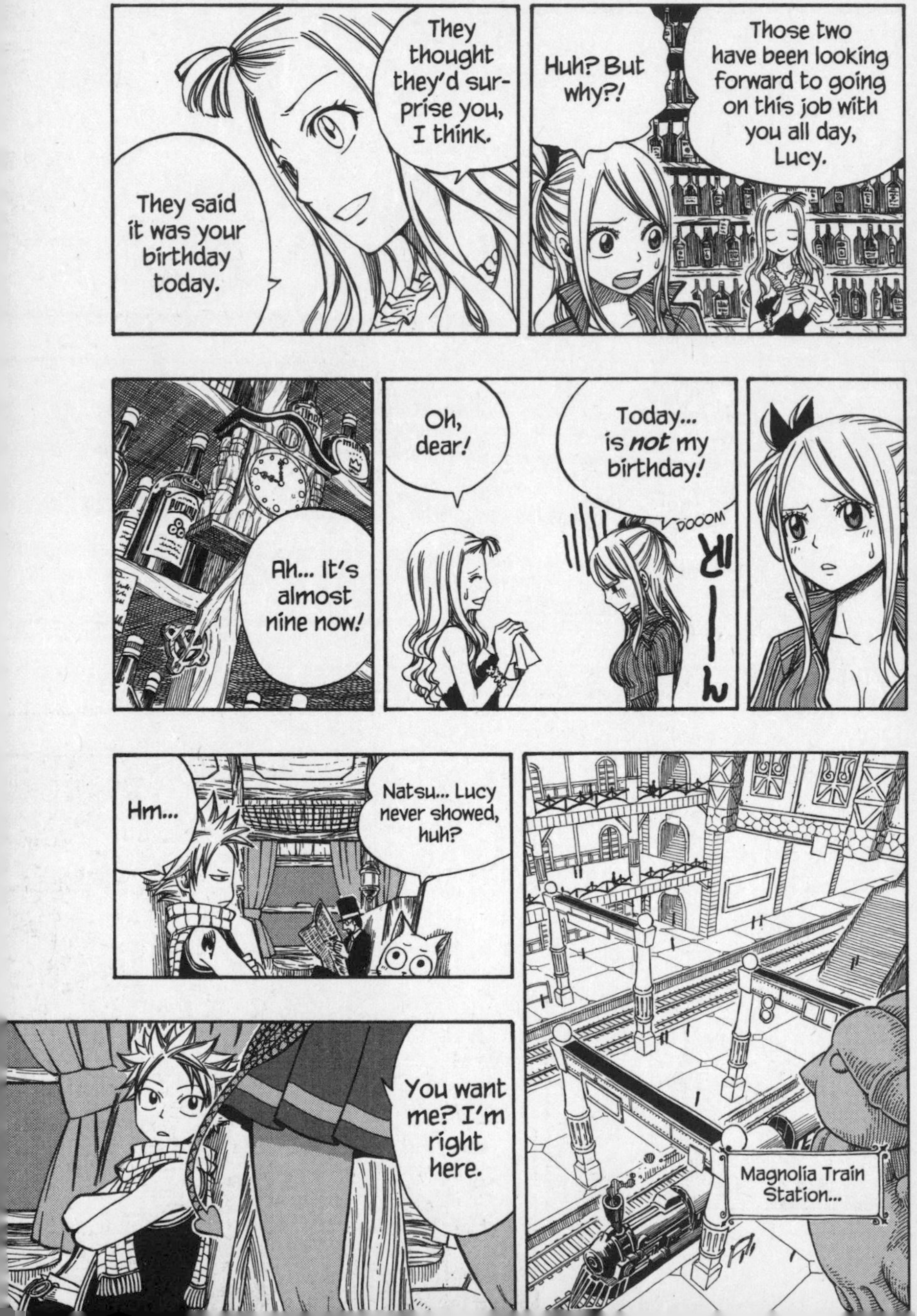
Those two have been looking forward to going on this job with you all day, Lucy.
Huh? But why?!
They thought they'd surprise you, I think.
They said it was your birthday today.
Today... is *not* my birthday!
DOOOM
どーん
Oh, dear!
Ah... It's almost nine now!
Magnolia Train Station...
Natsu... Lucy never showed, huh?
Hm...
You want me? I'm right here.

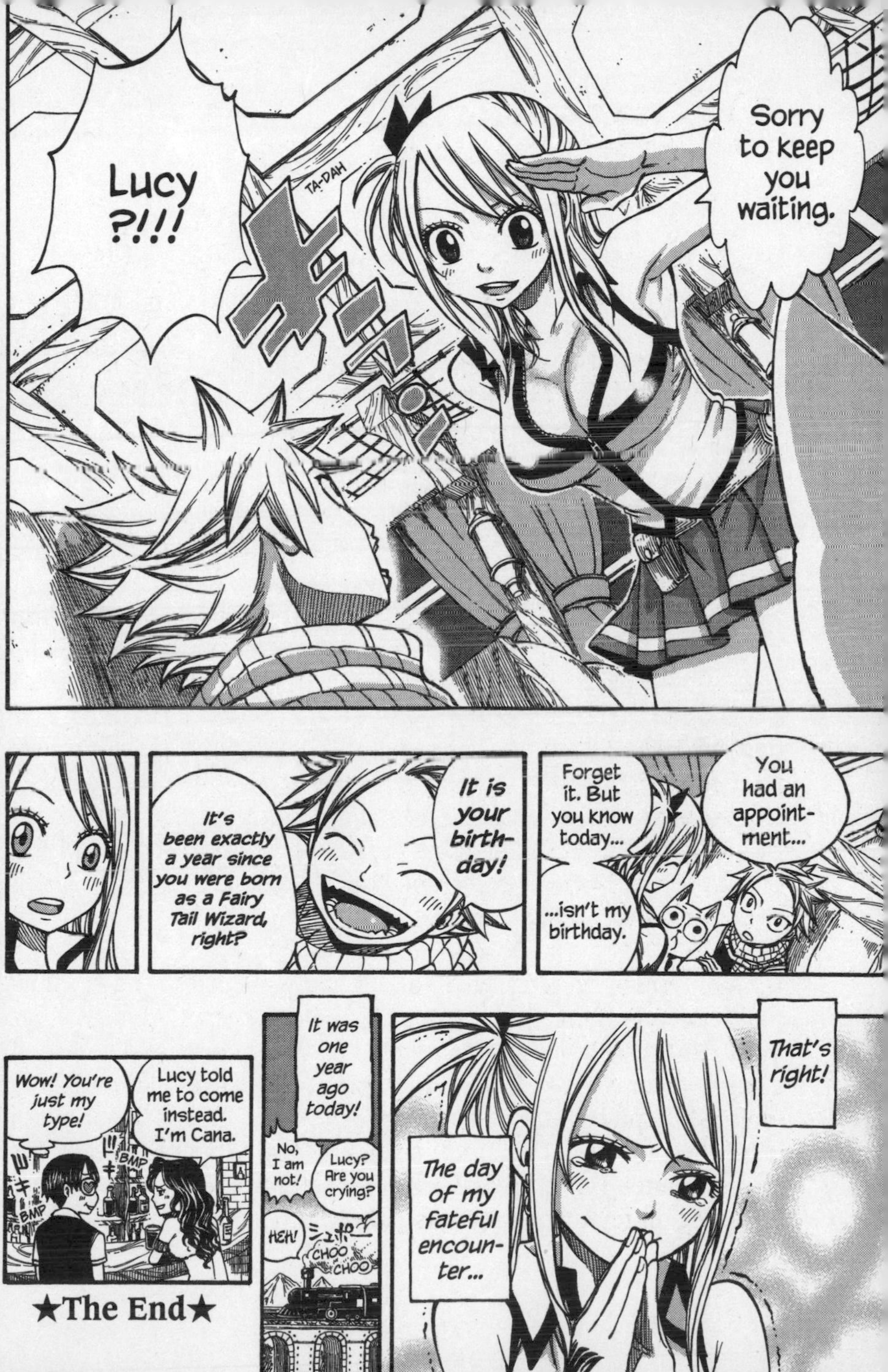

Sorry to keep you waiting.
TA-DAH
Lucy ?!!!
You had an appoint-ment...
Forget it. But you know today...
...isn't my birthday.
It is your birth-day!
It's been exactly a year since you were born as a Fairy Tail Wizard, right?
That's right!
The day of my fateful encoun-ter...
It was one year ago today!
Lucy? Are you crying?
No, I am not!
HEH!
シュポー
CHOO CHOO
Lucy told me to come instead. I'm Cana.
Wow! You're just my type!
BMP
BMP
★The End★

Afterword

あとがき

My room's a mess... I know it's been written about in places before, but there are really people out there who can't clean up. Um...me, for instance. Every two to three months, I get the entire staff to help out, and we do a grand cleaning of our workplace. And it's about then that I think, "This time, I'll make sure the place doesn't get cluttered up!!" But before I know it, there's stuff all over the place, and it looks like a wreck again. Of course I like it better when it's clean, but there are reference materials and drawing implements... I always want to put them someplace close where I can get my hands on them quickly, and before I know it, it's chaos around my desk... And it was in that awful state that I suddenly had a guest come by!! I was so embarrassed, and I felt bad for the guest, so I bowed and bowed, apologizing! Arrgh! Well next time, it won't get cluttered!!

On a different subject, a while ago, I wrote about how I got a new paint tool program for my computer, and I've been studying it ever since. But then I thought I'd try out a different one, and I decided to try to color it in Photoshop this time. Once I tried it, I have to say that PS is a pretty fantastic paint tool with a different flavor all its own! Of course I'm still studying the program I've been using for years, Painter. Hm... I wonder if somebody can teach these to me. Studying on my own is a pretty painful process...

Continued from the left-hand page.

Nirvana's leg-like things... Did they go from 8 legs to 6? (sweat)

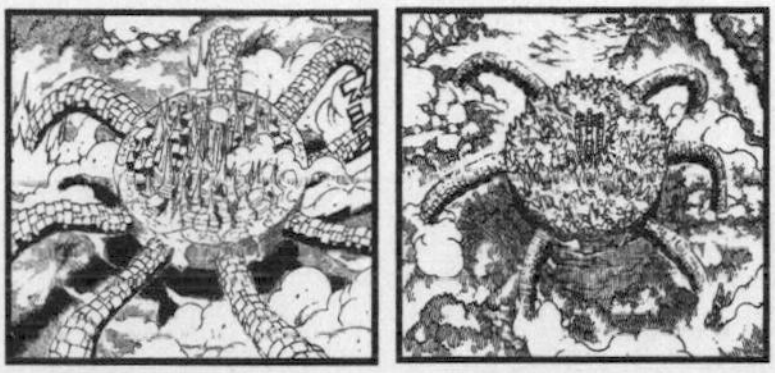

Mira: ....

Lucy: ....

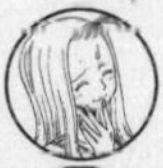
: Um... About that...

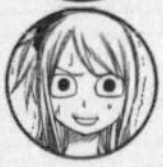
: I'm impressed, Mira-san! You're going to try to explain that one?

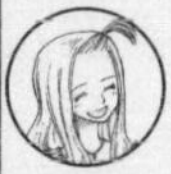
: While it was walking, two legs, like, fell off? Maybe?

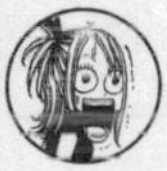
: Well, ***that*** wouldn't happen!!!!

Mira: Yes, that must be it! Let's just stick with that!

Lucy: Okay, how about this? It needed to get to Cait Shelter as quickly as possible, so it transformed its ***shape***, removing two legs!

Mira: On to the last question!

Lucy: Wait a second!!!!

It seems to me that there is absolutely no family resemblance between Brain and Midnight.

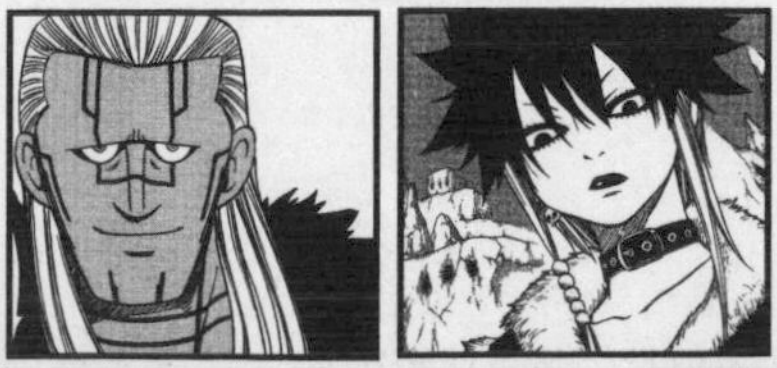

Mira: Oh, that...

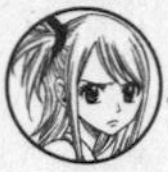
: What's the matter, Mira-san?

Mira: You see, there's a bit of conceptual stuff here that never made it into the actual story.

Lucy: Ehh?!!

Mira: A lot happened in between, and it got cut, but the Oración Seis were originally supposed to have been children that Brain led out of the Tower of Heaven.

Lucy: Ehh?!!

Mira: They were supposed to be five children of extraordinary magical talent that he banded together and raised.

Lucy: That's kind of sad!

Mira: So for all of them, Brain is something of a father figure.

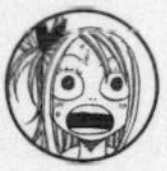
: So Brain and Midnight actually ***aren't*** father and son?

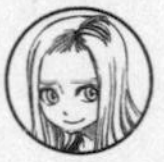
: That's right.

Lucy: Wow! So people who don't read this extra or the people who only read it in the magazine would always be under the impression that they're related!

Mira: Now don't you feel special for having this info?

Lucy: But now the info seems a bit iffy...

Mira: And in future editions, we'll give you even more background and conceptual information! How about that?!

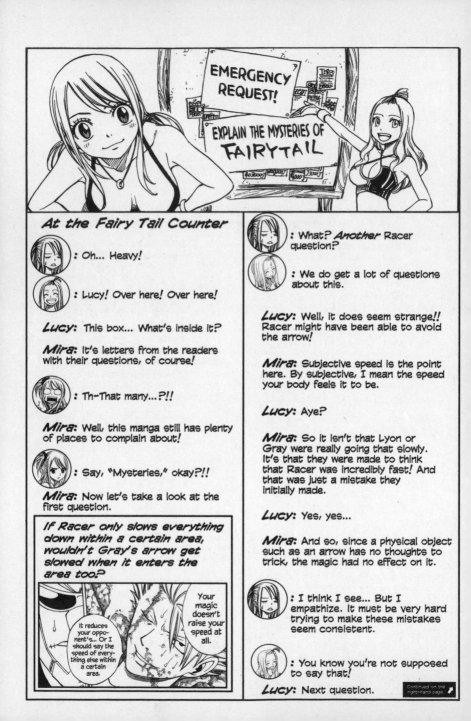

EMERGENCY REQUEST!
EXPLAIN THE MYSTERIES OF FAIRYTAIL

At the Fairy Tail Counter

 : Oh... Heavy!

 : Lucy! Over here! Over here!

Lucy: This box... What's inside it?

Mira: It's letters from the readers with their questions, of course!

 : Th-That many...?!!

Mira: Well, this manga still has plenty of places to complain about!

 : Say, "Mysteries," okay?!!

Mira: Now let's take a look at the first question.

If Racer only slows everything down within a certain area, wouldn't Gray's arrow get slowed when it enters the area too?

Your magic doesn't raise your speed at all.
It reduces your opponent's... Or I should say the speed of everything else within a certain area.

 : What? *Another* Racer question?

 : We do get a lot of questions about this.

Lucy: Well, it does seem strange!! Racer might have been able to avoid the arrow!

Mira: Subjective speed is the point here. By subjective, I mean the speed your body feels it to be.

Lucy: Aye?

Mira: So it isn't that Lyon or Gray were really going that slowly. It's that they were made to think that Racer was incredibly fast! And that was just a mistake they initially made.

Lucy: Yes, yes...

Mira: And so, since a physical object such as an arrow has no thoughts to trick, the magic had no effect on it.

 : I think I see... But I empathize. It must be very hard trying to make these mistakes seem consistent.

 : You know you're not supposed to say that!

Lucy: Next question.

Continued on the right-hand page.

TAIL d'ART

The Fairy Tail Guild d'Art is looking for illustrations! Please send in your art on a post card or at post-card size, and do it in black pen, okay? Those chosen to be published will get a signed mini poster! ♪ Make sure you write your real name and address on the back of your illustration!

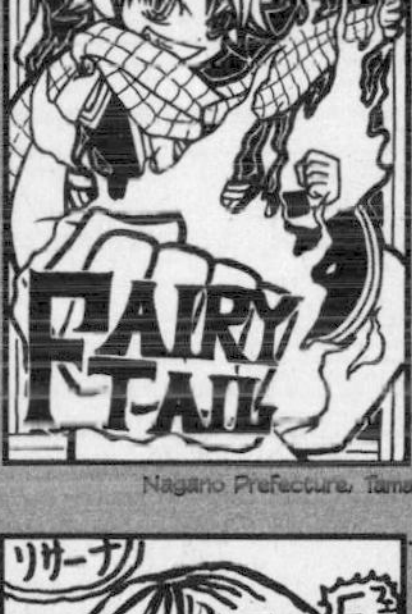
FAIRY TAIL

▼Whooooa!! This fires me up! This is how Natsu is supposed to be!

Nagano Prefecture, Tama

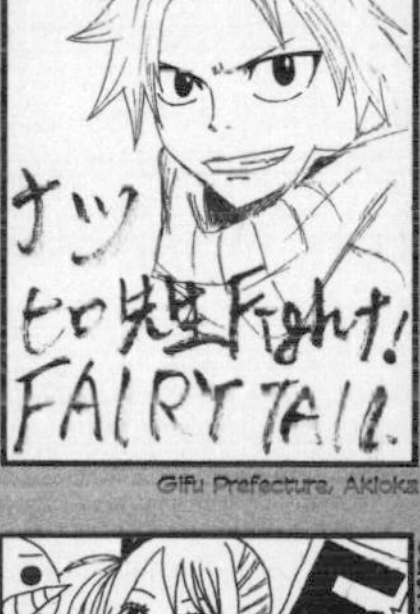
ナツ
ヒロ先生Fight!
FAIRY TAIL

▼ Ohh...! Is that a message for me?! Thanks! I'll do my best!

Gifu Prefecture, Akioka

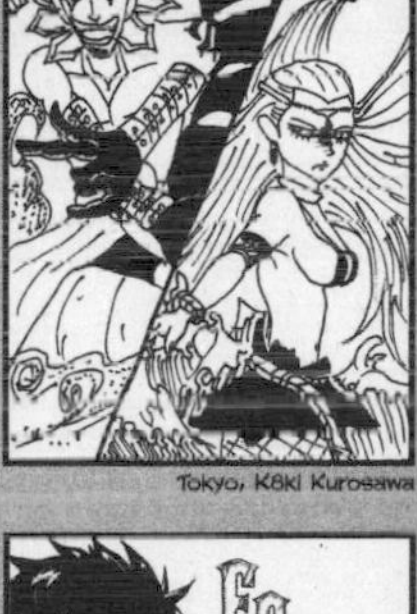

▼ Scorpio and Aquarius! What a great-looking couple...maybe?

Tokyo, K8ki Kurosawa

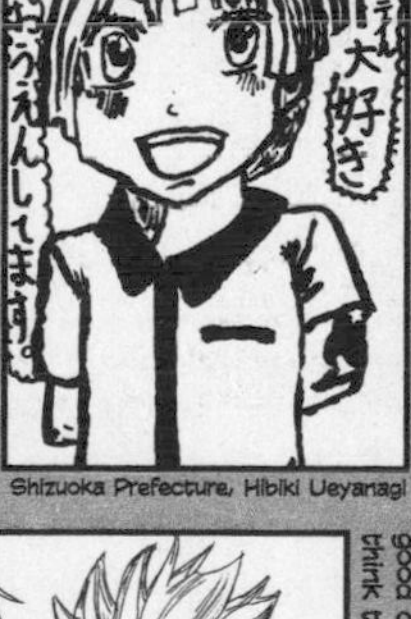
リサーナ
大好き
おうえんしてます。

▼ It's rare to see a drawing of Lisanna! I hear she has more of a part in the anime.

Shizuoka Prefecture, Hibiki Ueyanagi

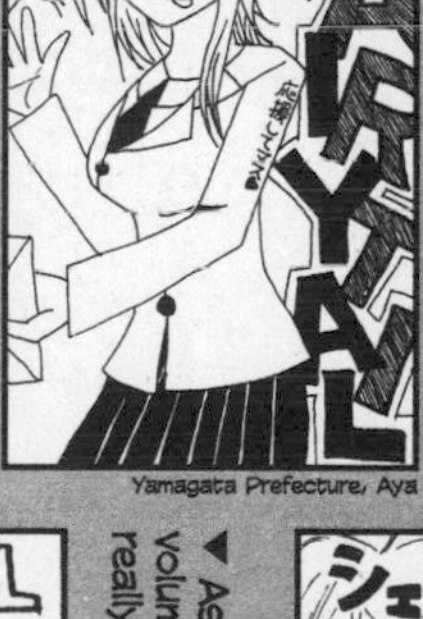
FAIRY TAIL

▼ For some reason, I get a lot of pictures with Lucy in school-girl outfits.

Yamagata Prefecture, Aya

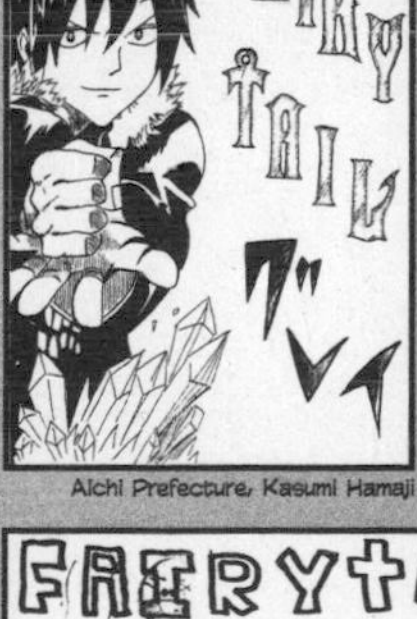
FAIRY TAIL

▼ Ice Make...er... What's he making?

Aichi Prefecture, Kasumi Hamaji

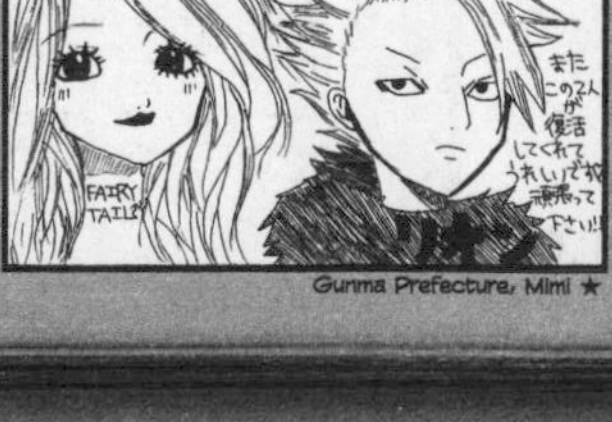
シェリー
FAIRY TAIL
またこの2人が復活してくれてうれしいです 頑張って下さい!!

▼ Lyon and Sherry make a good couple...but just as you think that...

Gunma Prefecture, Mimi ★

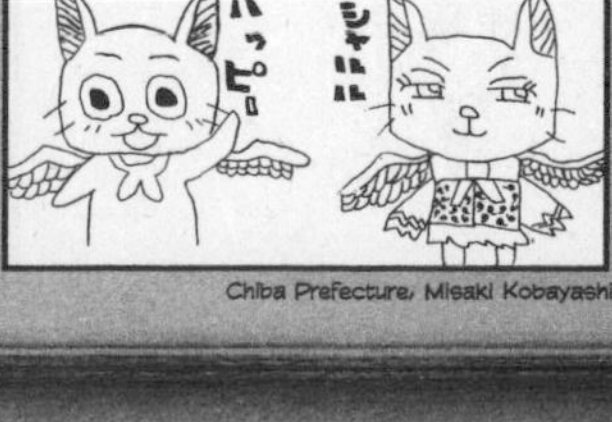
FAIRYTAIL
ハッピー

▼ As I drew this volume, I realized I really like these two!

Chiba Prefecture, Misaki Kobayashi

Send to Hiro Mashima, Kodansha Comics
451 Park Ave. South, 7th Floor New York, NY 10016

FAIRY GUILD

▼ Here's a strangely cute Erza!

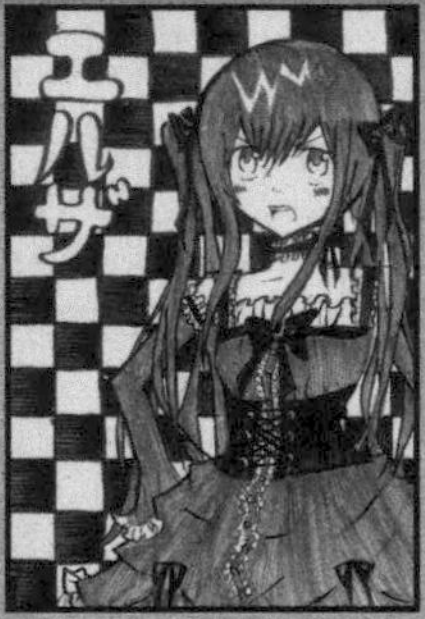

エルザ

Nagasaki Prefecture, Alice

▼ Hibiki who has quietly gained a lot of fans. But he's hard to draw.

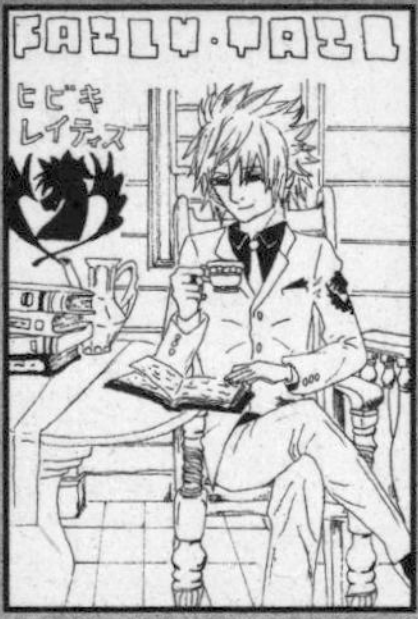

FAILY TAIL
ヒビキ
レイティス

Kanagawa Prefecture, Kenta Noro

▼ Dwaaa! It's got too much power!! It's huge!!

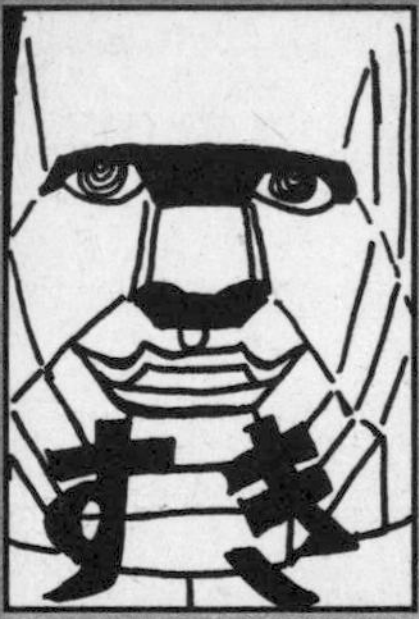

すき

Aomori Prefecture, French Bread

▼ Read the question corner that these two head up also, okay?

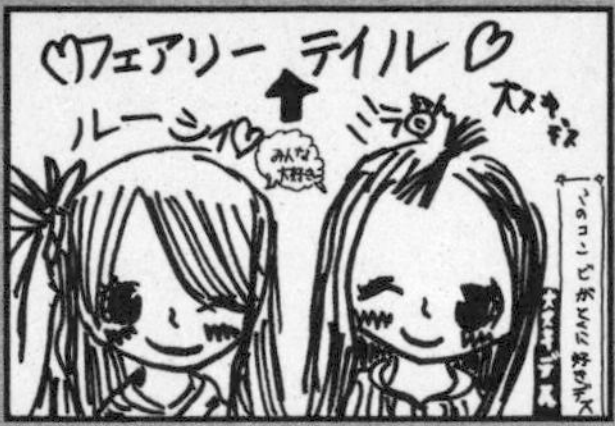

フェアリーテイル
ルーシィ
ミラ

Yamagata Prefecture, Rina

▼ Both Santa and the snowman are Plue!

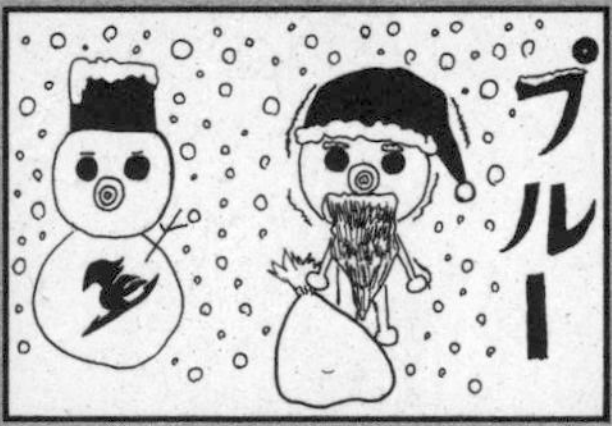

プルー

Hokkaido, Seiko Sato

REJECTION CORNER

This one just sort of struck me as funny... D-Dammit, he's so boxy... Heh heh!

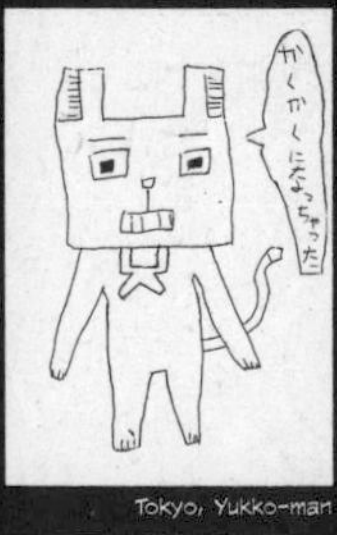

かくかくになっちゃった

Tokyo, Yukko-man

▼ Cute and really well done!

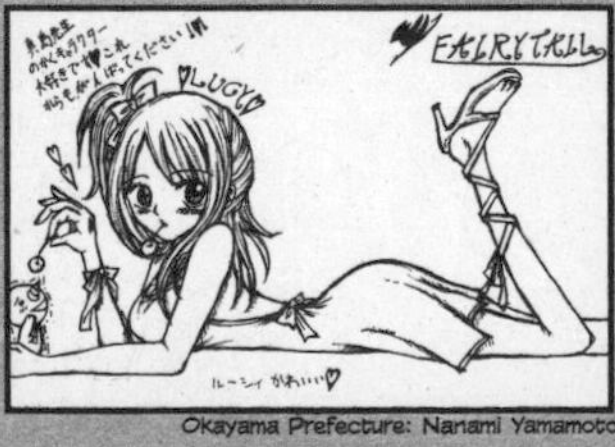

FAIRY TAIL
LUCY

Okayama Prefecture: Nanami Yamamoto

Any letters and post cards you send means that your personal information such as your name, address, postal code, and other information you include will be handed over, as is, to the author. When you send mail, please keep that in mind.

Translation Notes:

Japanese is a tricky language for most Westerners, and translation is often more art than science. For your edification and reading pleasure, here are notes on some of the places where we could have gone in a different direction with our translation of the work, or where a Japanese cultural reference is used.

Page 4, Nabura

Although in Japanese, there is a word, *nabura*, that's a technical word in the world of fishing, it seems to have nothing to do with the *nabura* that Master Robaul keeps repeating. This is called a *kuchiguse* ("mouth habit") or a word that the speaker is just in the habit of saying. As the other members of his guild note, it doesn't have any meaning that anyone can completely define. So if you don't understand the word *nabura*, you're not alone. Neither do the Japanese readers, nor do I.

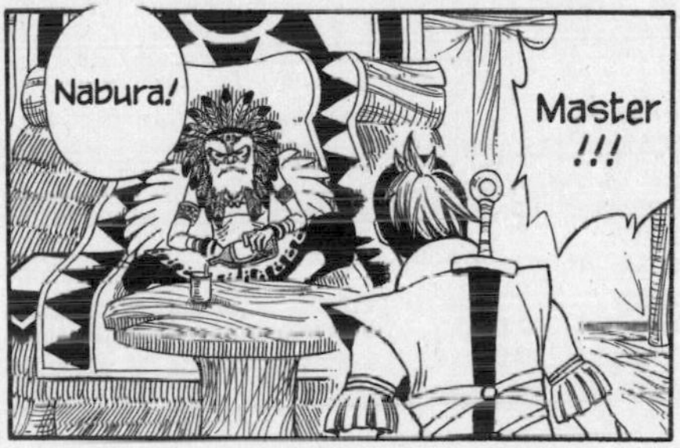

Master !!!
Nabura!

Page 11, Richard-dono

The honorific *-dono* is a somewhat archaic word that Jura (and some other manga/anime characters) uses. It means about the same thing as *-sama*. See more on this in the notes for Volume 18.

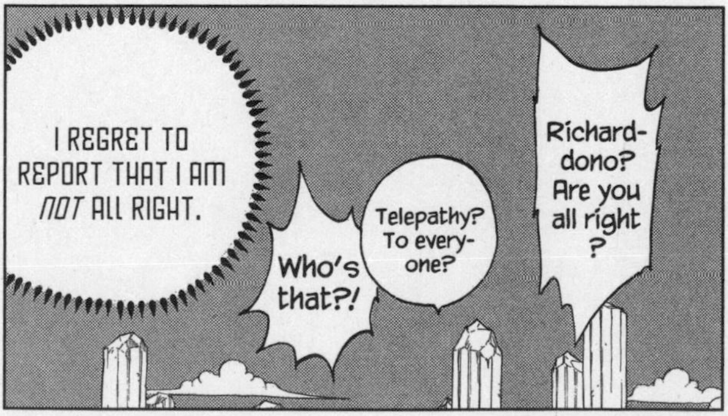

Richard-dono? Are you all right ?
Telepathy? To every-one?
Who's that?!
I REGRET TO REPORT THAT I AM NOT ALL RIGHT.

Page 178, Reaching for the same book

This trope (an often-used story-telling cliché) is used almost as often as the "transfer student" in Japanese story telling. It's especially overused in Japanese romantic comedies in live-action TV and films. The lure of the trope is obvious – not only do both parties share an interest in reading, but they are also interested in exactly the same book, showing a certain compatibility. Plus it allows the soon-to-be-romantic couple to touch for the first time. But as Lucy said, it's used so often that it's an old, worn-out cliché.

Like I'm going to pick a book...
And somebody will reach for the very same book...like that huh?
FATEFUL ENCOUNTER
ANIMAL
Like one of those old clichéd plot twists from a novel?
WHOOSH
!!!
ANIMAL

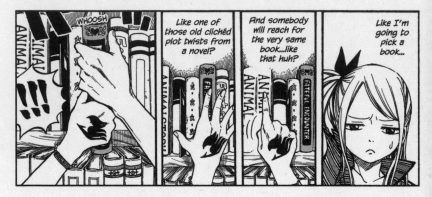

FROM HIRO MASHIMA

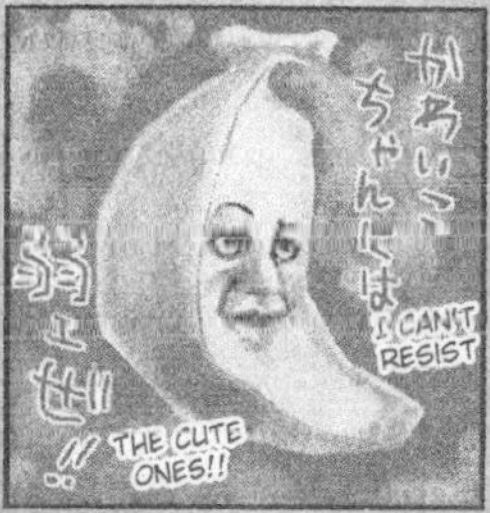
かわいこちゃんには
弱ェ!!
I CAN'T RESIST
THE CUTE ONES!!

After I realized that I hadn't eaten a banana in a very long time, I sort of got the urge and drew this picture. Even so, it isn't like I suddenly got the urge to eat bananas. But it isn't like I hate them or anything. Still, once I drew the picture, I felt completely satisfied. And the phrase, "I can't resist the cute ones!"... I wrote it, and no, I have no idea what it's supposed to mean.

Original Jacket Design: Hisao Ogawa

Preview of Fairy Tail, volume 20

We're pleased to present you a preview from Fairy Tail, volume 20, now available from Kodansha Comics. Check out our Web site (www.kodanshacomics.com) for details.

FAIRY TAIL

フェアリーテイル

20

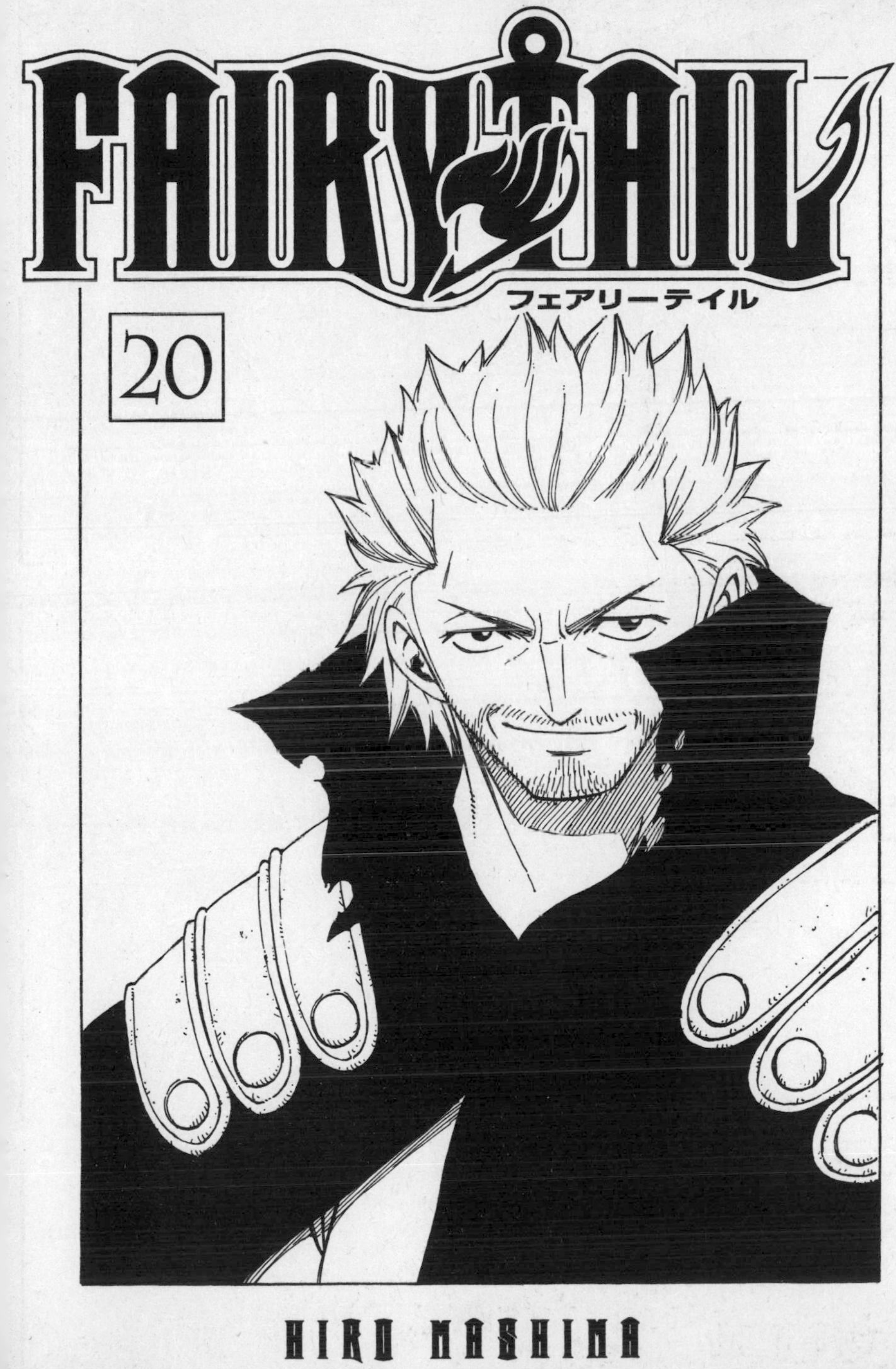

HIRO MASHIMA

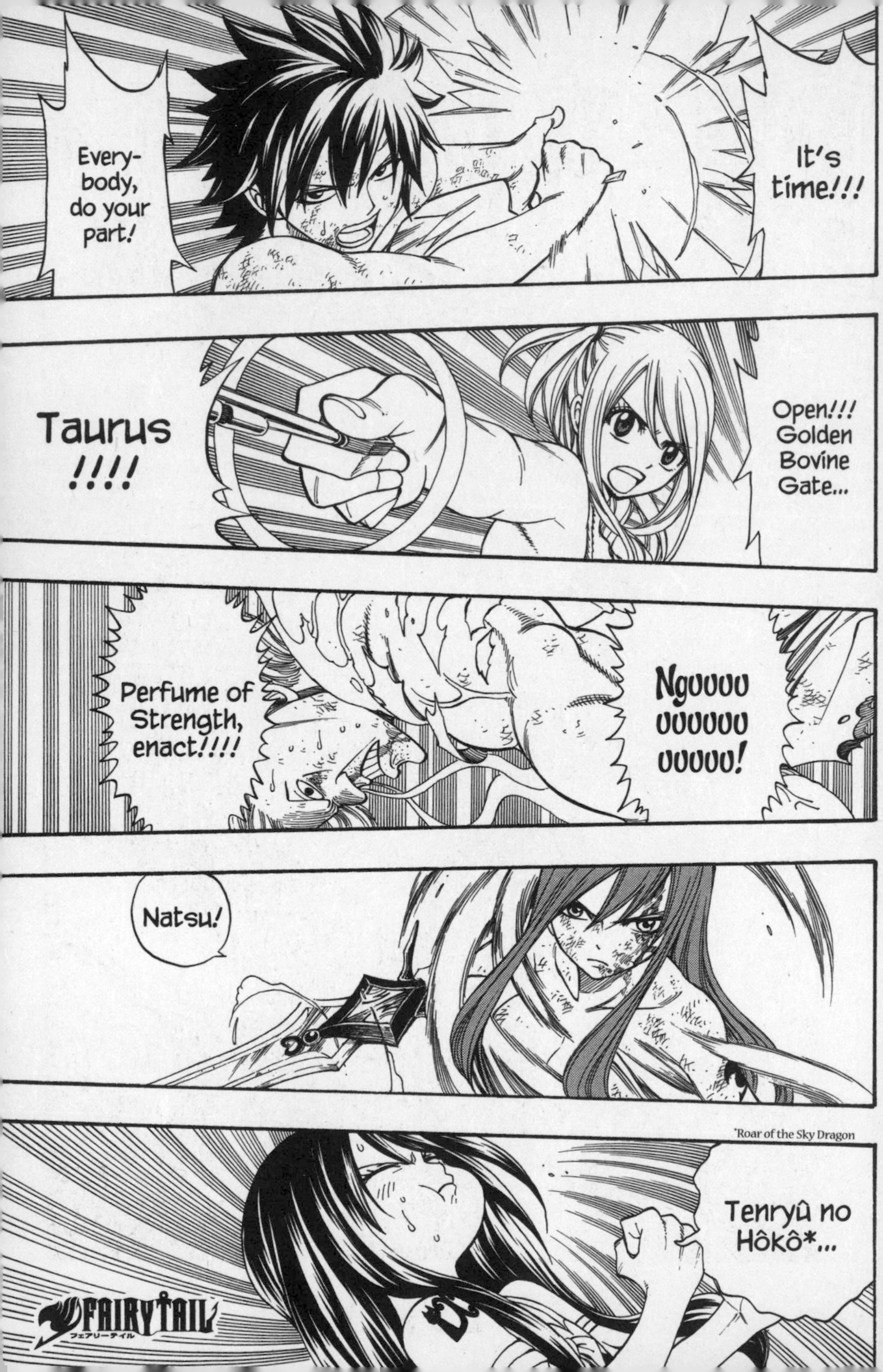
It's time!!!
Every-body, do your part!
Open!!! Golden Bovine Gate...
Taurus !!!!
Ngoooo oooooo ooooo!
Perfume of Strength, enact!!!!
Natsu!
Tenryû no Hôkô*...
FAIRY TAIL
フェアリーテイル

*Roar of the Sky Dragon

Chapter 161, Fight for Right

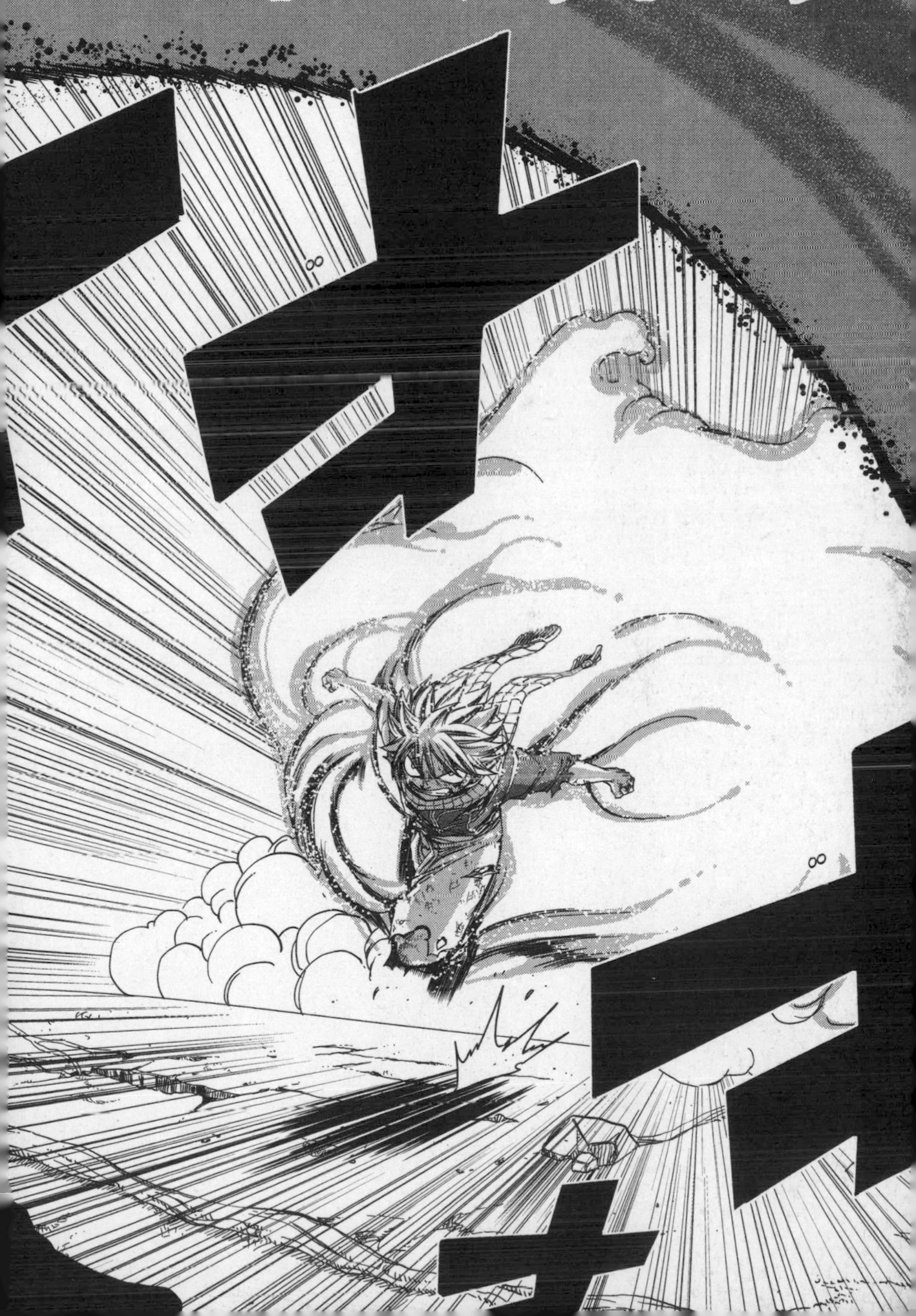

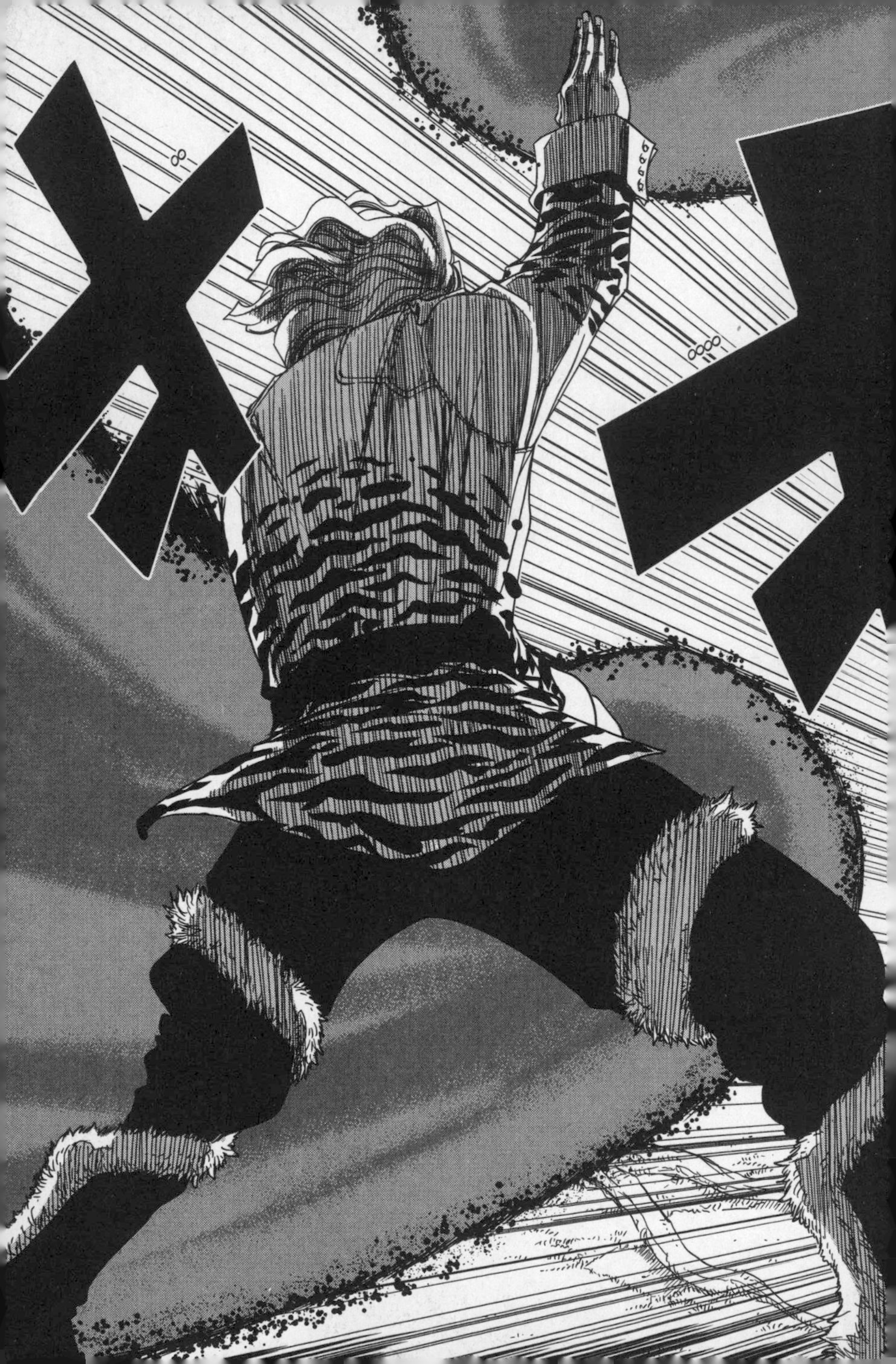

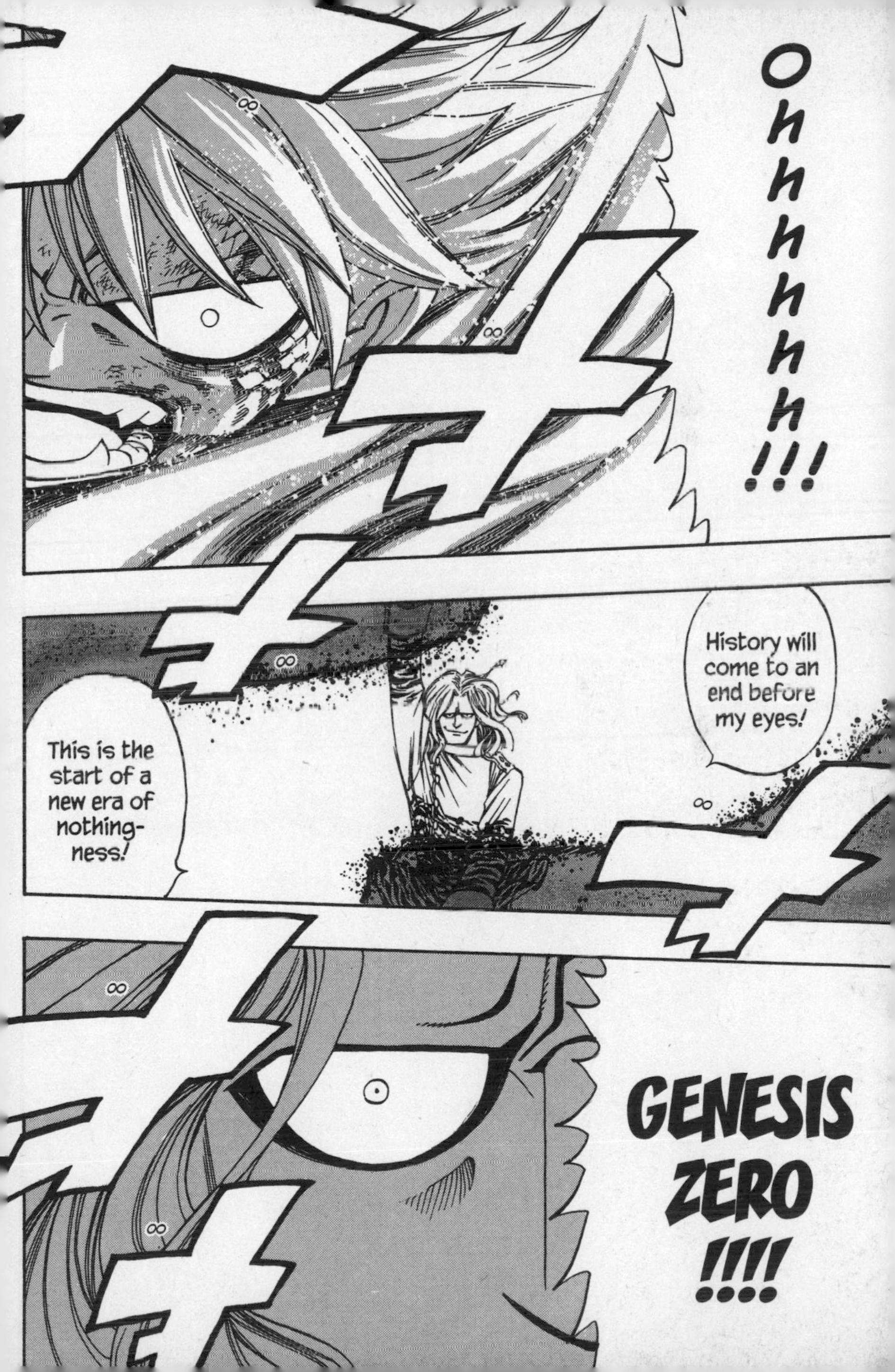
Ohhhhhh!!!
History will come to an end before my eyes!
This is the start of a new era of nothingness!
GENESIS ZERO!!!!

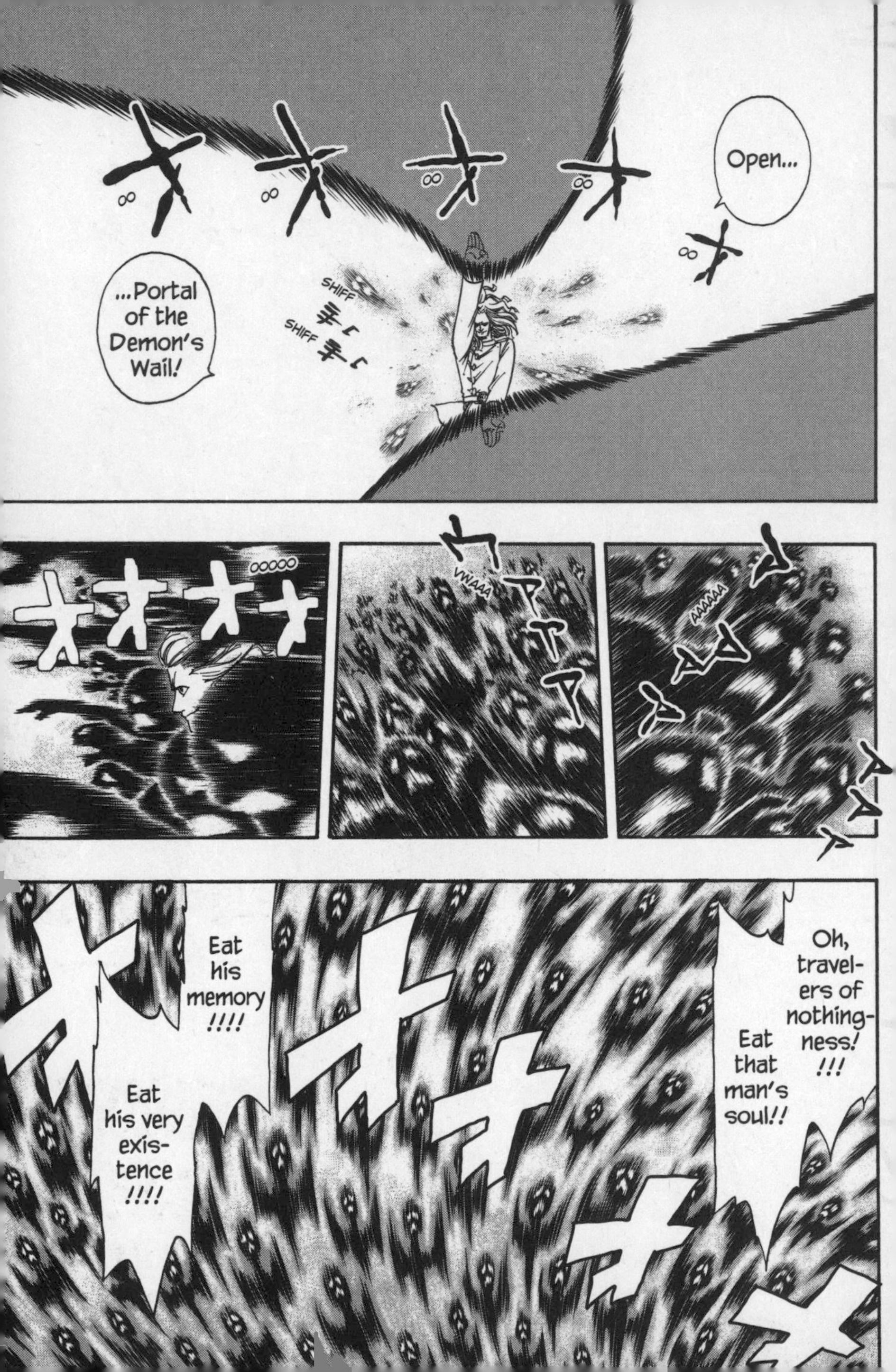

Open...
...Portal of the Demon's Wail!
SHIFF
SHIFF
AAAAAA
VWAAA
OOOOO
Oh, travel-ers of nothing-ness!!!!
Eat that man's soul!!
Eat his memory!!!!
Eat his very exis-tence!!!!

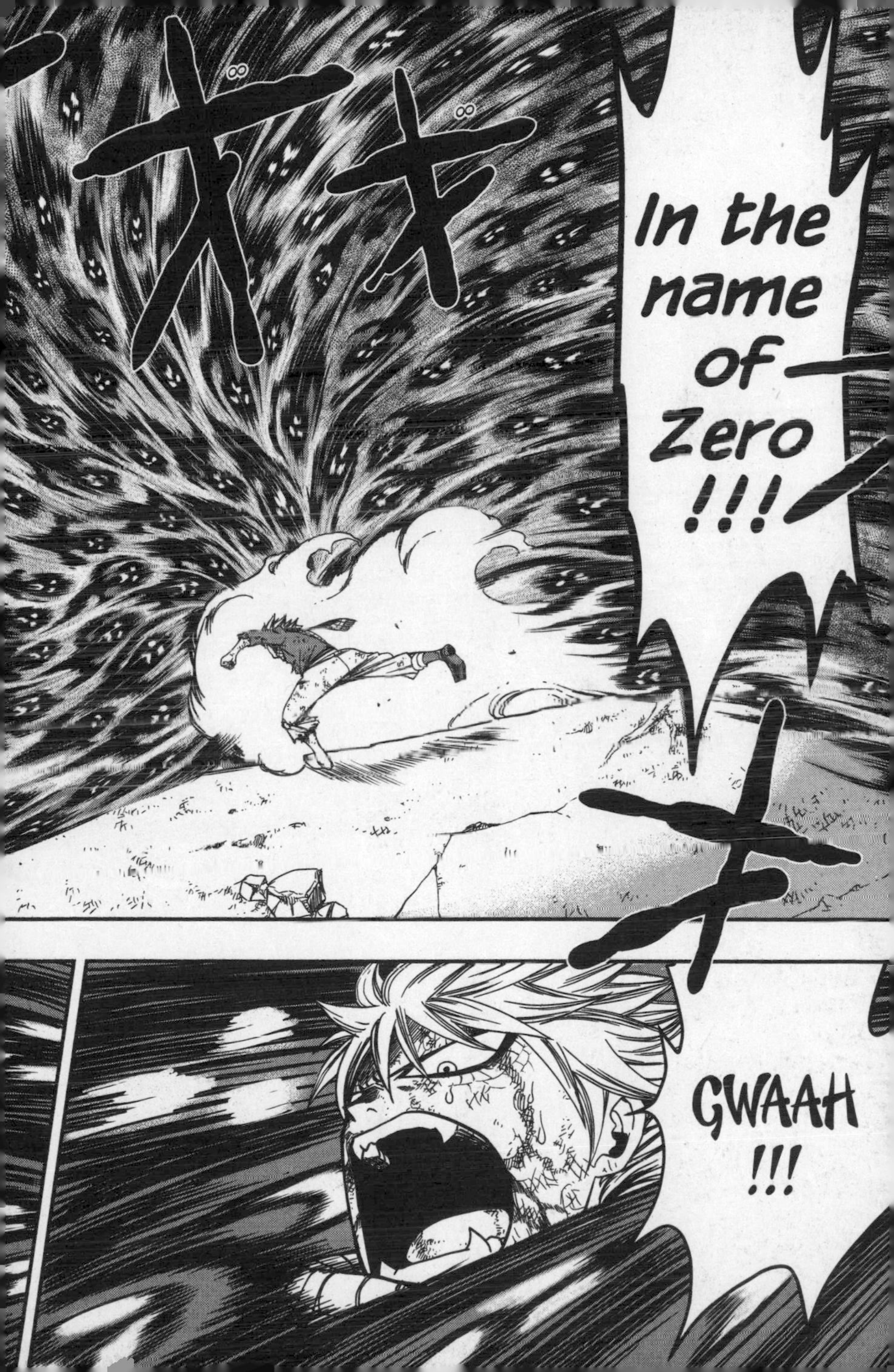
In the name of Zero—!!!
GWAAH!!!

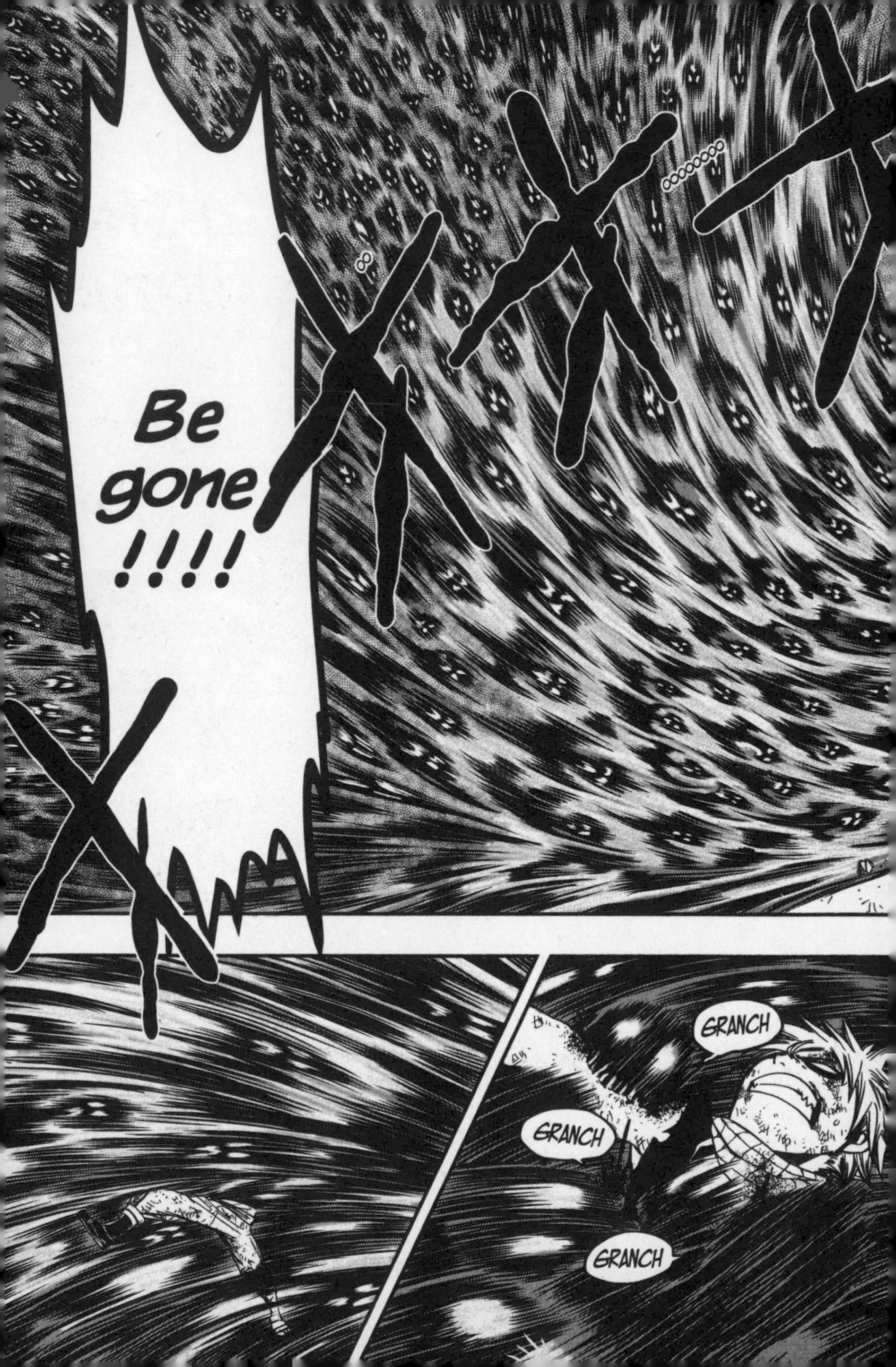
Be gone!!!!
GRANCH
GRANCH
GRANCH

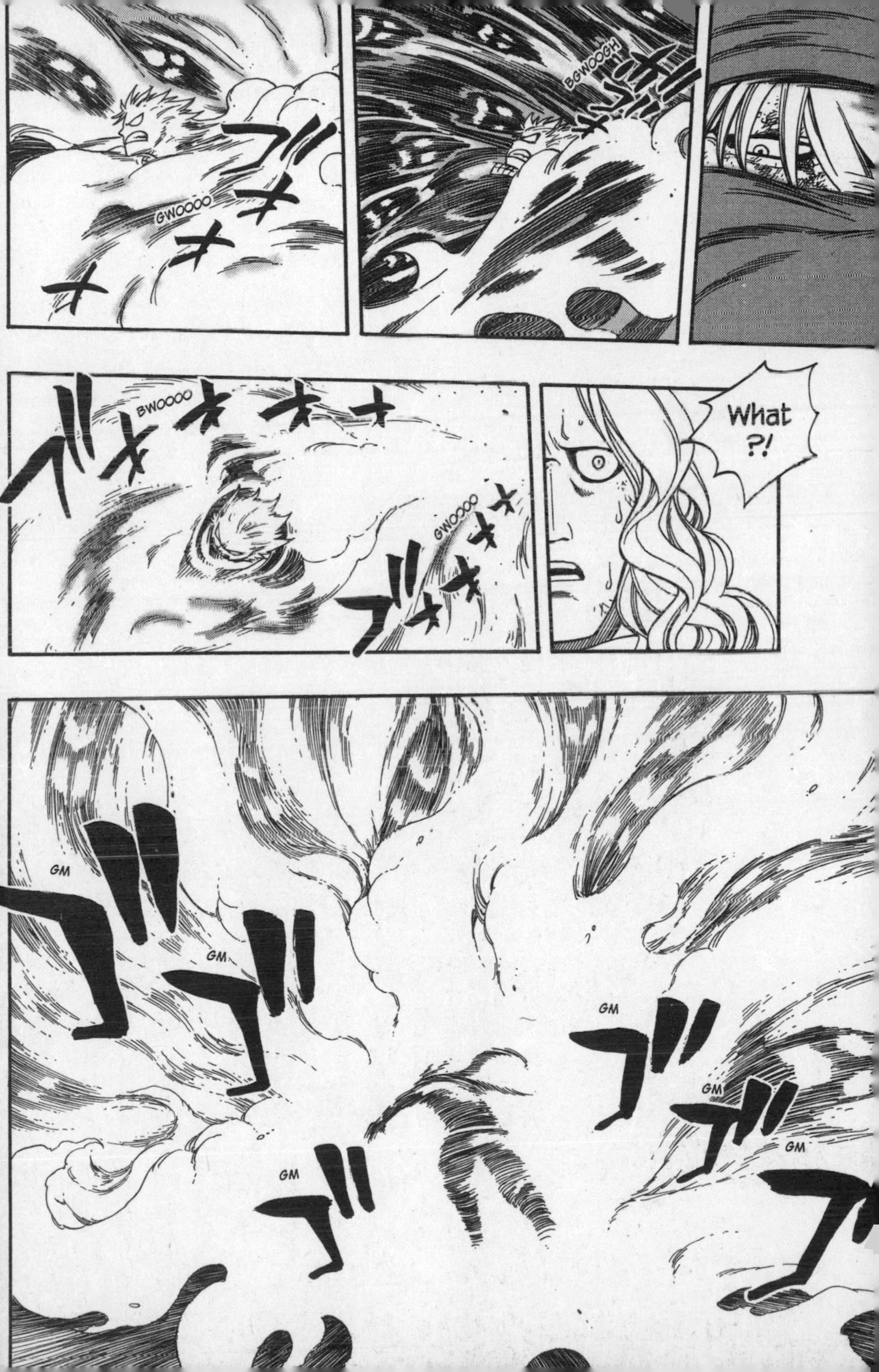
BGWOOGH
GWOOOO
What ?!
BWOOOO
GWOOOO
GM
GM
GM
GM
GM
GM

DON'T MISS THE MOST ACCLAIMED ACTION MANGA OF 2013!

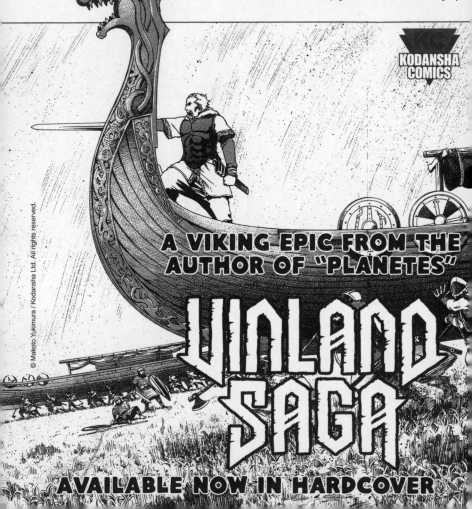

KODANSHA COMICS

A VIKING EPIC FROM THE AUTHOR OF "PLANETES"

VINLAND SAGA

AVAILABLE NOW IN HARDCOVER

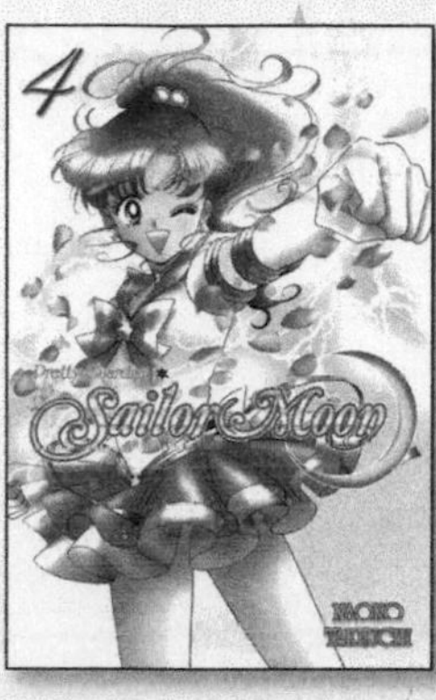
4
Pretty Guardian
Sailor Moon
NAOKO TAKEUCHI
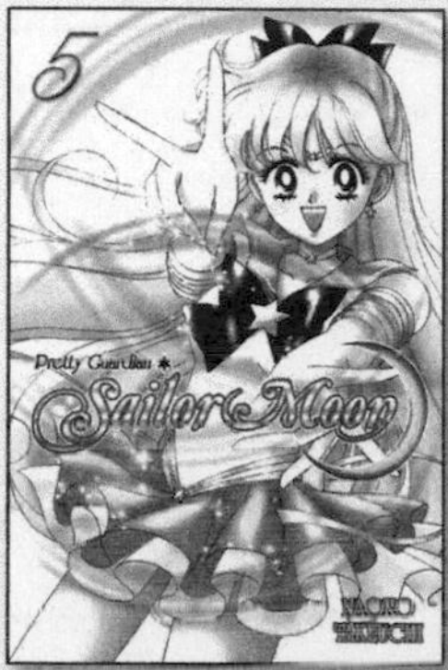
5
Pretty Guardian
Sailor Moon
NAOKO TAKEUCHI
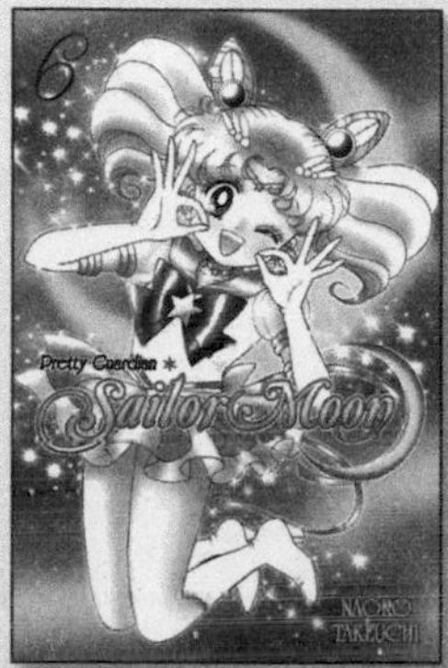
6
Pretty Guardian
Sailor Moon
NAOKO TAKEUCHI
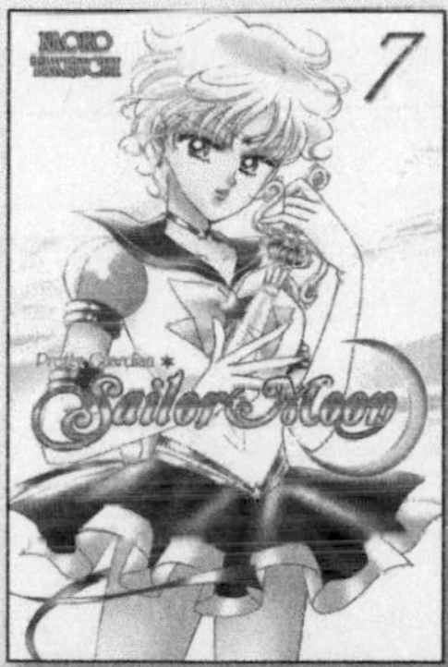
NAOKO TAKEUCHI
7
Pretty Guardian
Sailor Moon
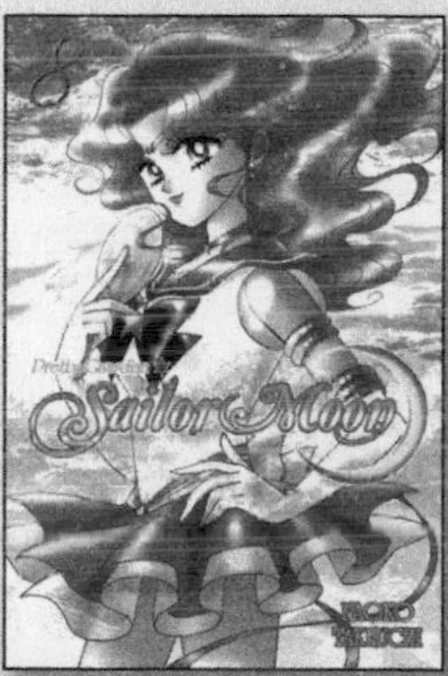
8
Pretty Guardian
Sailor Moon
NAOKO TAKEUCHI
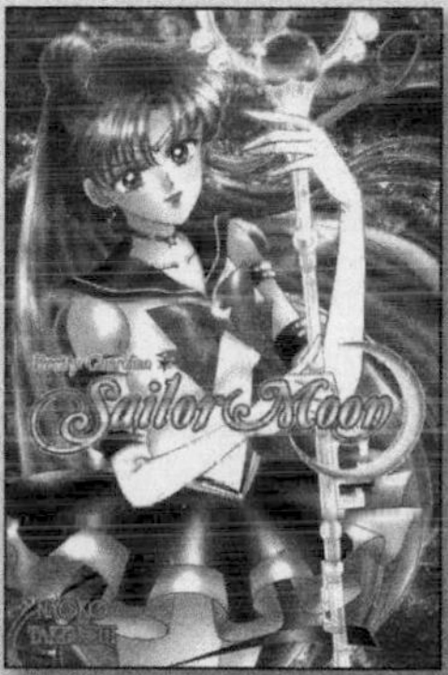
9
Pretty Guardian
Sailor Moon
NAOKO TAKEUCHI
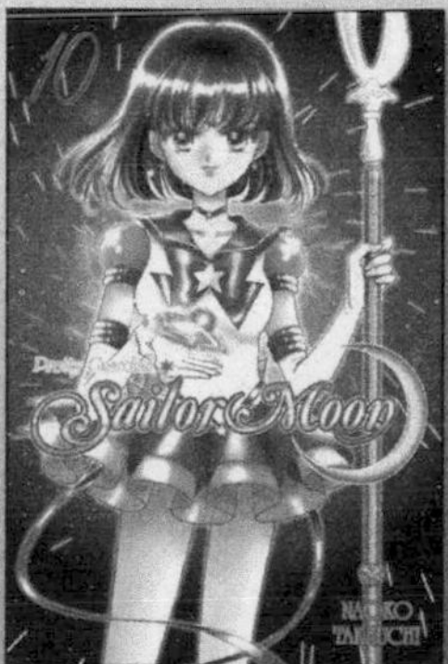
10
Pretty Guardian
Sailor Moon
NAOKO TAKEUCHI
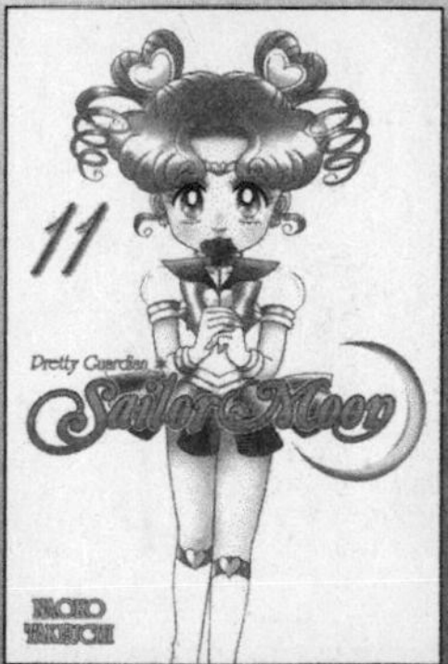
11
Pretty Guardian
Sailor Moon
NAOKO TAKEUCHI
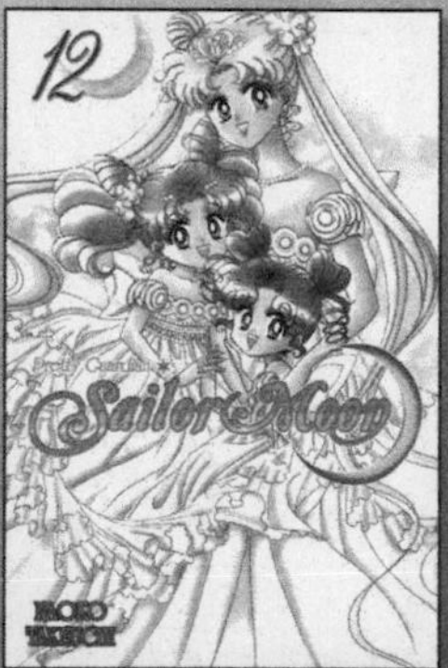
12
Pretty Guardian
Sailor Moon
NAOKO TAKEUCHI

The Pretty Guardians are back!

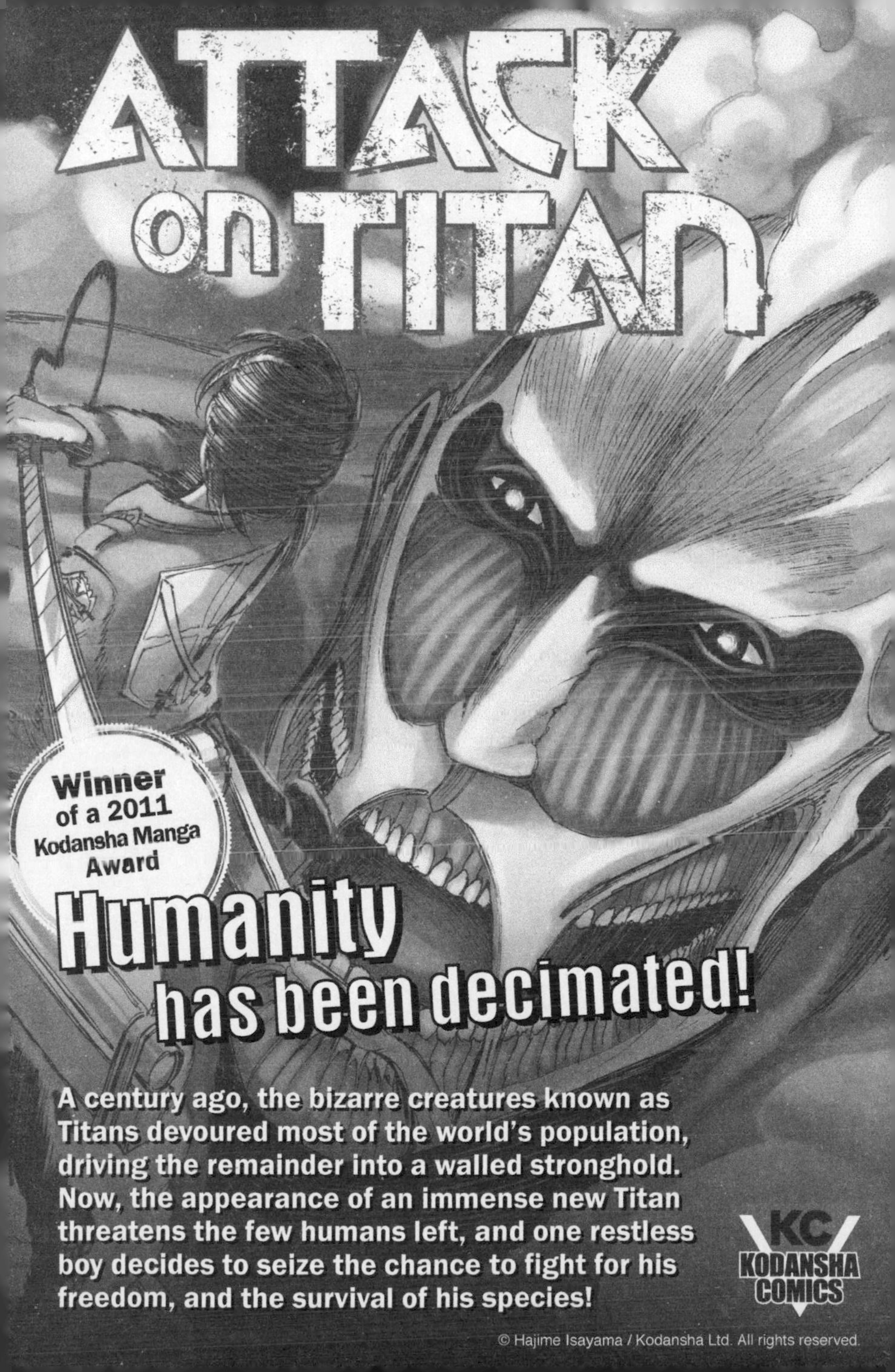
ATTACK ON TITAN
Winner of a 2011 Kodansha Manga Award
Humanity has been decimated!
A century ago, the bizarre creatures known as Titans devoured most of the world's population, driving the remainder into a walled stronghold. Now, the appearance of an immense new Titan threatens the few humans left, and one restless boy decides to seize the chance to fight for his freedom, and the survival of his species!
KC KODANSHA COMICS
© Hajime Isayama / Kodansha Ltd. All rights reserved.

Fairy Tail volume 19 is a work of fiction. Names, characters, places, and incidents are the products of the author's imagination or are used fictitiously. Any resemblance to actual events, locales, or persons, living or dead, is entirely coincidental.

A Kodansha Comics Trade Paperback Original

Published in the United States by Kodansha Comics, an imprint of Kodansha USA Publishing, LLC., New York.

Publication rights for this English edition arranged through Kodansha Ltd., Tokyo.

First published in Japan in 2010 by Kodansha Ltd., Tokyo.

ISBN 978-1-612-62056-5

Printed in the United States of America.

www.kodanshacomics.com

9 8 7 6 5 4

Translator/Adapter: William Flanagan
Lettering: AndWorld Design

TOMARE!

止まれ

[STOP!]

You're going the wrong way!

Manga is a completely different type of reading experience.

To start at the *beginning,* go to the *end!*

That's right! Authentic manga is read the traditional Japanese way—from right to left, exactly the *opposite* of how American books are read. It's easy to follow: Just go to the other end of the book and read each page—and each panel—from right side to left side, starting at the top right. Now you're experiencing manga as it was meant to be!